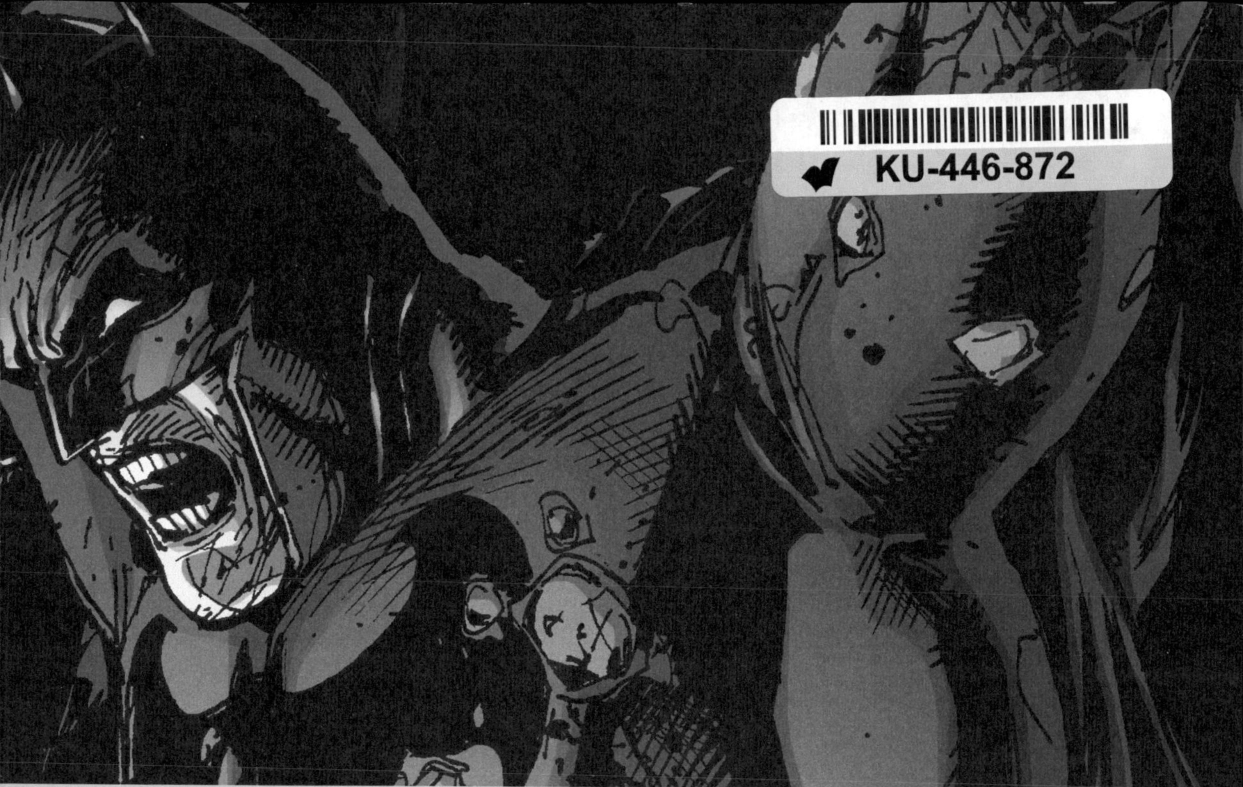

BATMAN
DETECTIVE COMICS

VOL. 2:
ARKHAM KNIGHT

PETER J. TOMASI
WRITER

BRAD WALKER
ANDREW HENNESSY
DOUG MAHNKE
TRAVIS MOORE
MAX RAYNOR
JAIME MENDOZA
ARTISTS

NATHAN FAIRBAIRN
DAVID BARON
TAMRA BONVILLAIN
NICK FILARDI
COLORISTS

ROB LEIGH
LETTERER

BRAD WALKER
ANDREW HENNESSY
and NATHAN FAIRBAIRN
COLLECTION COVER ARTISTS

BATMAN CREATED BY **BOB KANE** WITH **BILL FINGER**

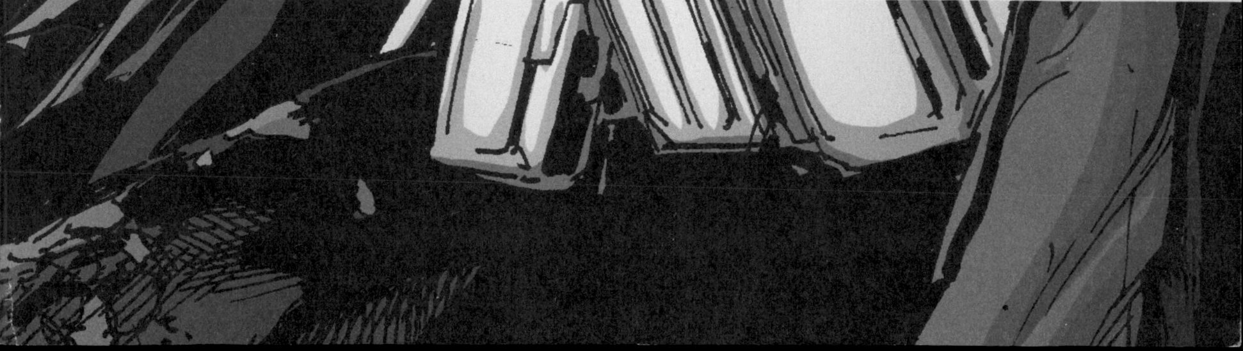

BATMAN: DETECTIVE COMICS VOL. 2: ARKHAM KNIGHT

Published by DC Comics. Compilation and all new material Copyright © 2020
DC Comics. All Rights Reserved. Originally published in single magazine form
in *Detective Comics* 1000-1005, *Detective Comics Annual* 2. Copyright © 2019
DC Comics. All Rights Reserved. All characters, their distinctive likenesses,
and related elements featured in this publication are trademarks of DC Comics.
The stories, characters, and incidents featured in this publication are entirely
fictional. DC Comics does not read or accept unsolicited submissions of ideas,
stories, or artwork. DC – a WarnerMedia Company.

DC Comics, 2900 West Alameda Ave., Burbank, CA 91505
Printed by LSC Communications, Owensville, MO, USA. 5/1/20. First Printing.
ISBN: 978-1-77950-251-3

Library of Congress Cataloging-in-Publication Data is available.

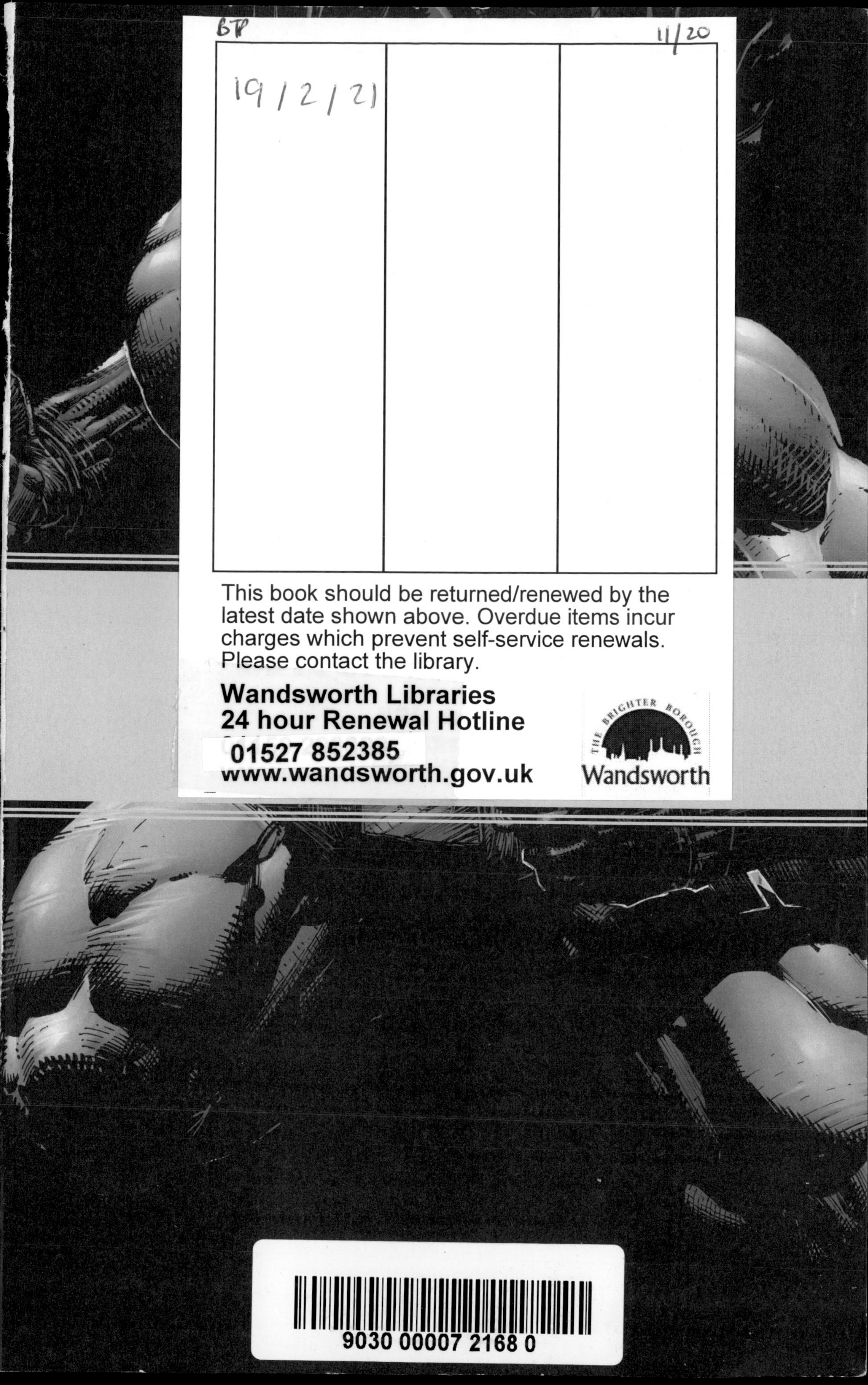

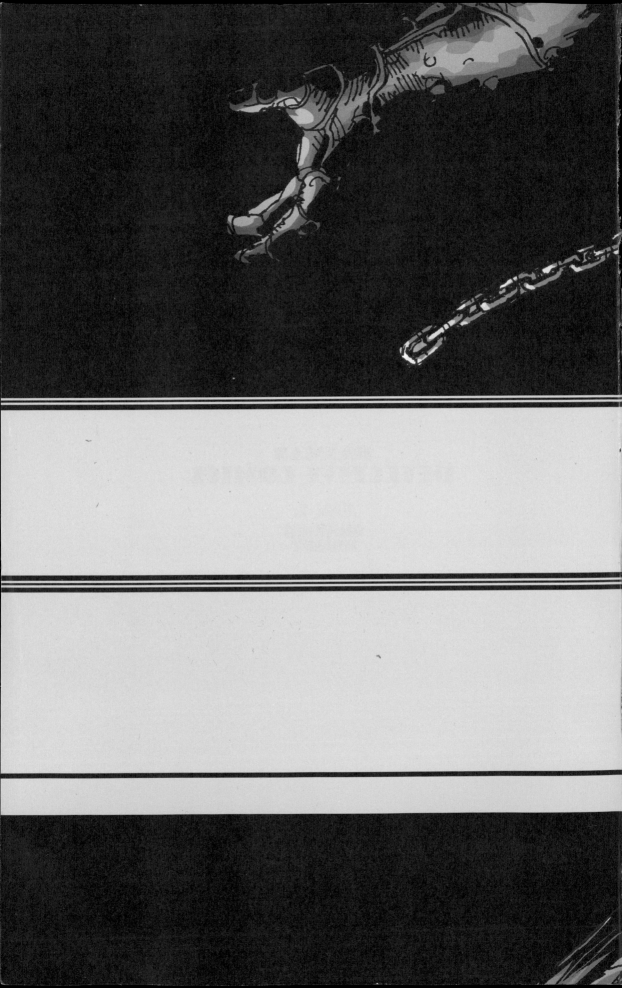

I HAVE SEEN HIM.
CLOSE.
AS CLOSE AS HOLDING YOUR OWN HAND TO YOUR FACE.
AND I HAVE SEEN HIM FROM AFAR.
THROUGH THE EYES OF OTHERS.
STORIES TOLD IN WHISPERS.
STORIES TOLD IN CONFIDENCE.
STORIES TOLD IN SECRET PLACES.
SHARED PERSPECTIVES WITH ONE PURE, COMMON BELIEF...

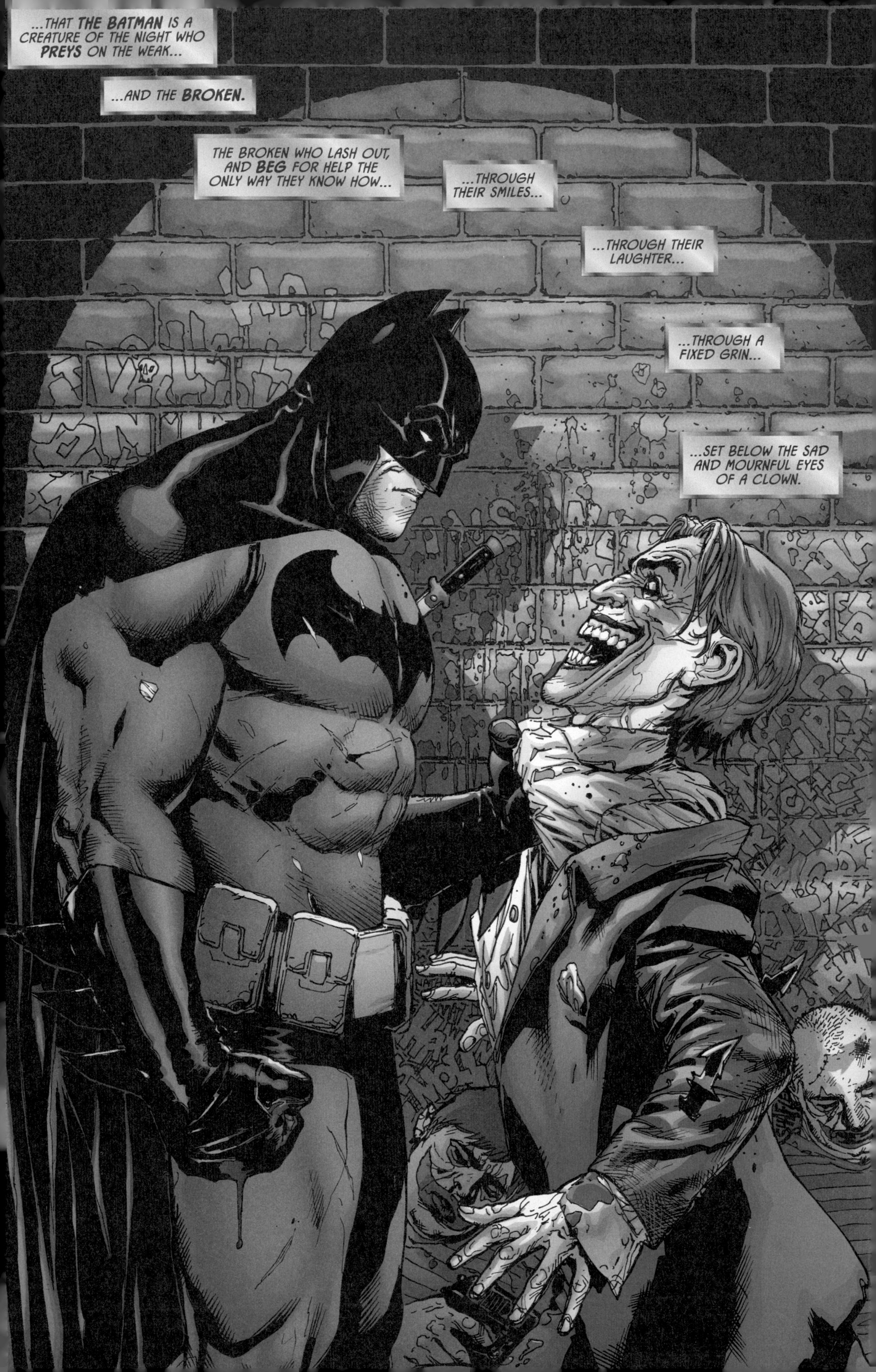
...THAT THE BATMAN IS A CREATURE OF THE NIGHT WHO PREYS ON THE WEAK...
...AND THE BROKEN.
THE BROKEN WHO LASH OUT, AND BEG FOR HELP THE ONLY WAY THEY KNOW HOW...
...THROUGH THEIR SMILES...
...THROUGH THEIR LAUGHTER...
...THROUGH A FIXED GRIN...
...SET BELOW THE SAD AND MOURNFUL EYES OF A CLOWN.

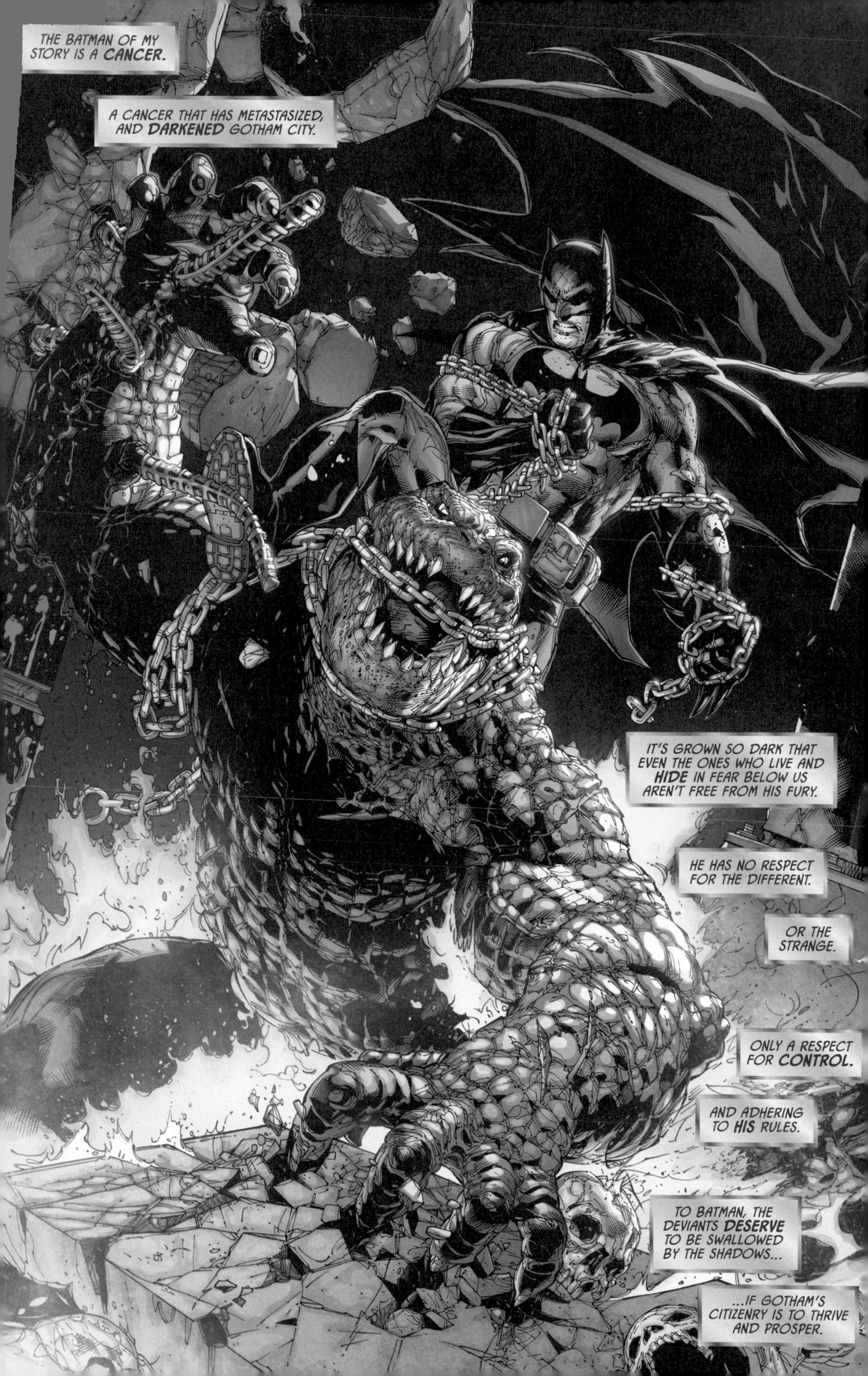
THE BATMAN OF MY STORY IS A CANCER.
A CANCER THAT HAS METASTASIZED, AND DARKENED GOTHAM CITY.
IT'S GROWN SO DARK THAT EVEN THE ONES WHO LIVE AND HIDE IN FEAR BELOW US AREN'T FREE FROM HIS FURY.
HE HAS NO RESPECT FOR THE DIFFERENT.
OR THE STRANGE.
ONLY A RESPECT FOR CONTROL.
AND ADHERING TO HIS RULES.
TO BATMAN, THE DEVIANTS DESERVE TO BE SWALLOWED BY THE SHADOWS...
...IF GOTHAM'S CITIZENRY IS TO THRIVE AND PROSPER.

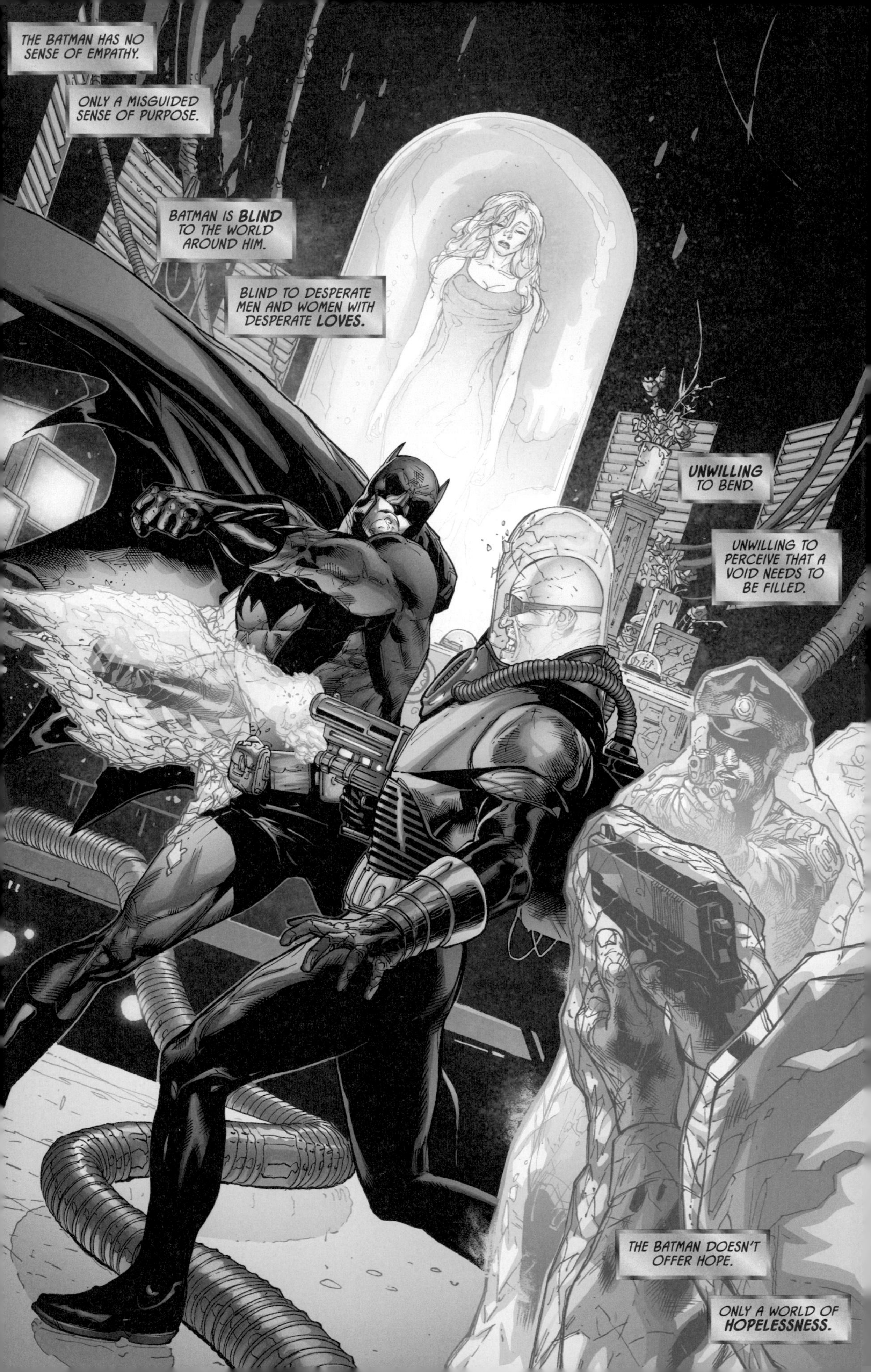
THE BATMAN HAS NO SENSE OF EMPATHY.
ONLY A MISGUIDED SENSE OF PURPOSE.
BATMAN IS **BLIND** TO THE WORLD AROUND HIM.
BLIND TO DESPERATE MEN AND WOMEN WITH DESPERATE **LOVES.**
UNWILLING TO BEND.
UNWILLING TO PERCEIVE THAT A VOID NEEDS TO BE FILLED.
THE BATMAN DOESN'T OFFER HOPE.
ONLY A WORLD OF **HOPELESSNESS.**

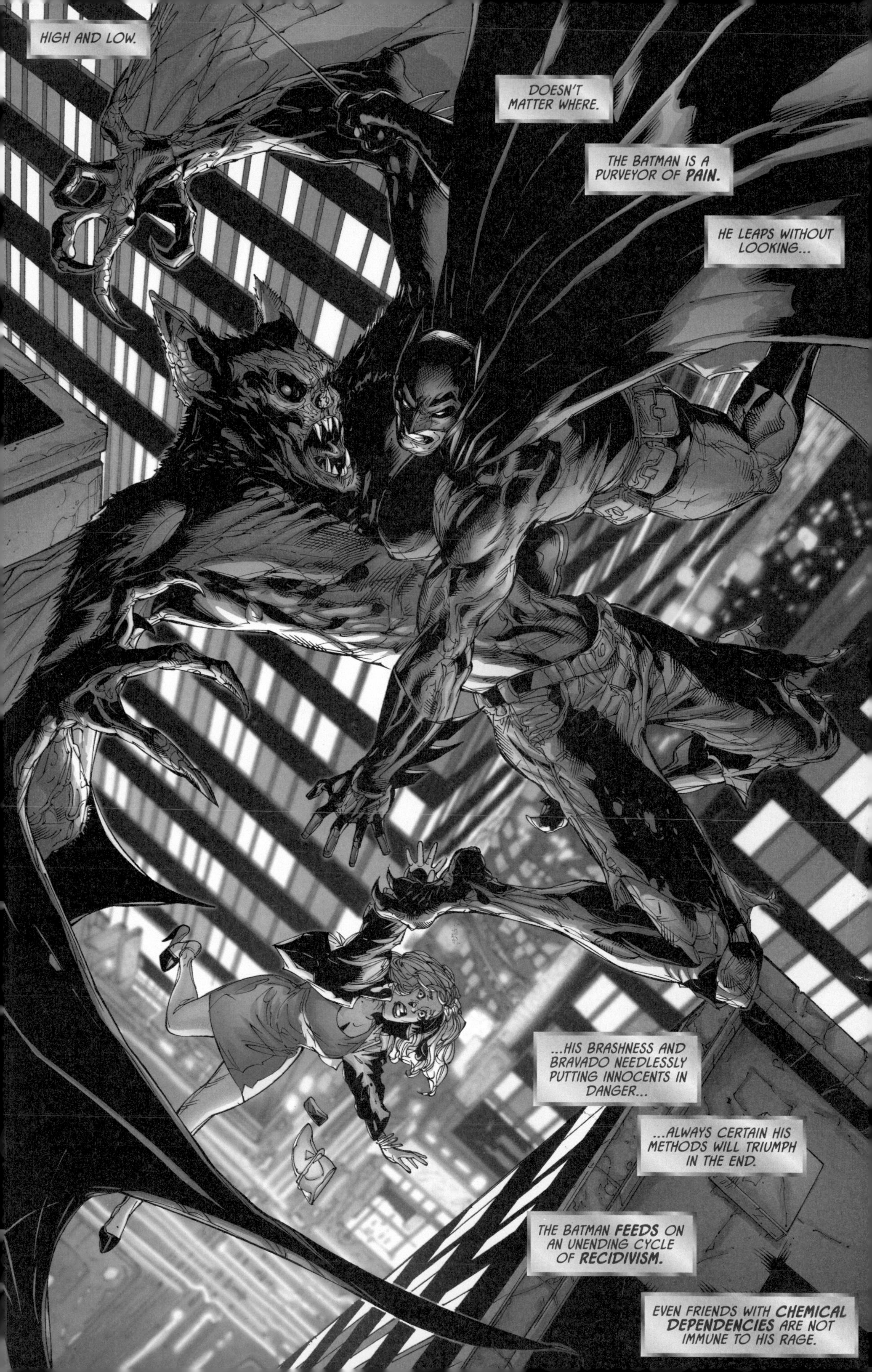
HIGH AND LOW.
DOESN'T MATTER WHERE.
THE BATMAN IS A PURVEYOR OF **PAIN.**
HE LEAPS WITHOUT LOOKING...
...HIS BRASHNESS AND BRAVADO NEEDLESSLY PUTTING INNOCENTS IN DANGER...
...ALWAYS CERTAIN HIS METHODS WILL TRIUMPH IN THE END.
THE BATMAN **FEEDS** ON AN UNENDING CYCLE OF **RECIDIVISM.**
EVEN FRIENDS WITH **CHEMICAL DEPENDENCIES** ARE NOT IMMUNE TO HIS RAGE.

THERE ARE MANY STORIES ABOUT THE BATMAN'S RAGE TRAVELING ACROSS THE WORLD.
WHISPERS ABOUT LONG-FORGOTTEN PITS HIDDEN IN WIND-SWEPT DESERTS AND ICE-COVERED MOUNTAINS.
MAGICAL PITS IMBUED WITH UNKNOWN ENERGY.
PITS OF LIQUID THAT GRANT ETERNAL LIFE.
ARE THE TALES TRUE THAT HE FOUGHT THE DEMON'S HEAD AND HIS DAUGHTER TO IMMERSE HIMSELF IN ONE OF THESE PITS?
IT WOULD EXPLAIN HIS BODY'S ABILITY TO WITHSTAND THE GRUELING PUNISHMENT HE'S EXPOSED IT TO OVER THE YEARS.
IS THE BATMAN IMMORTAL?
OR IS HE ONLY HUMAN?
I INTEND TO FIND OUT.

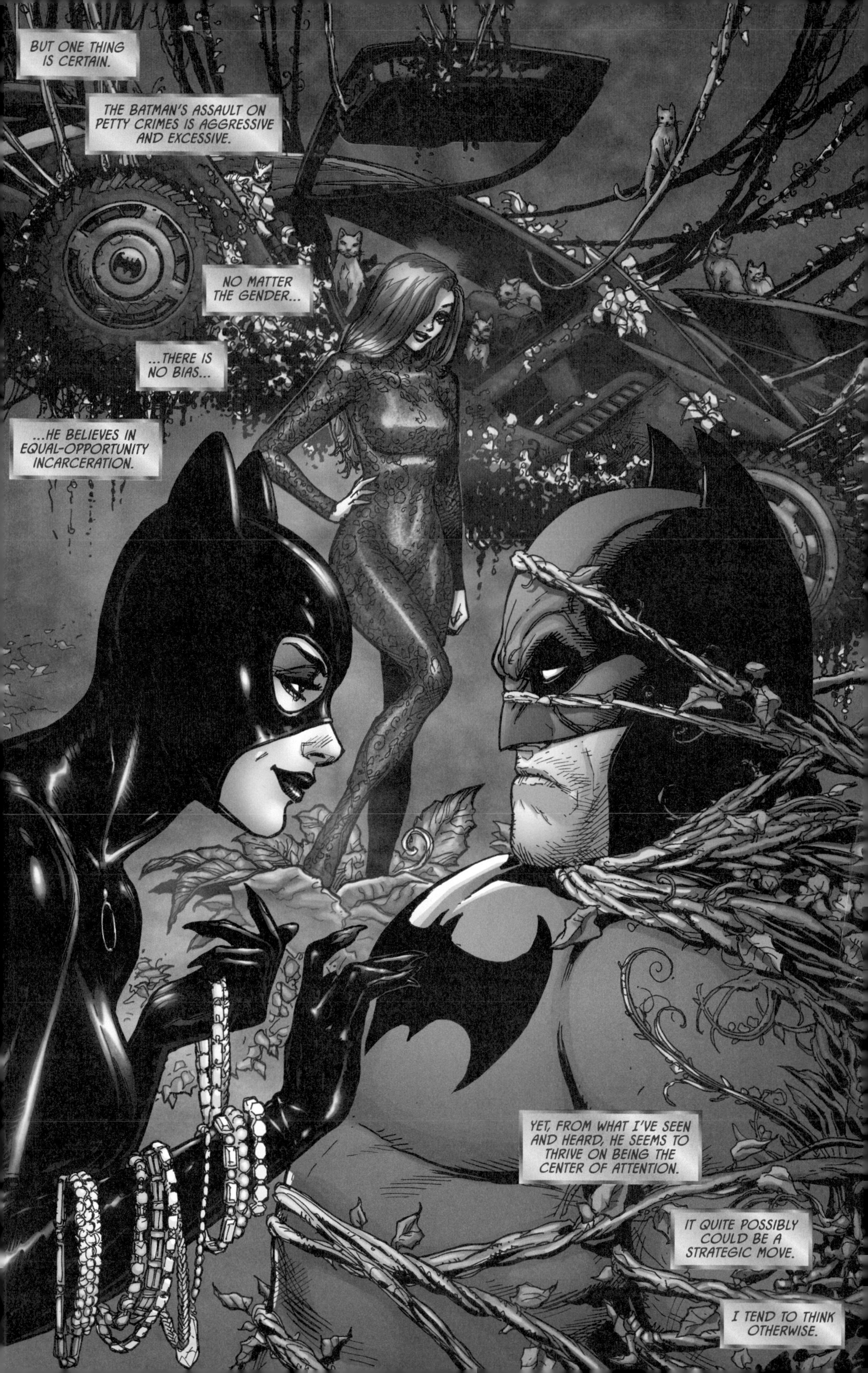

BUT ONE THING IS CERTAIN.
THE BATMAN'S ASSAULT ON PETTY CRIMES IS AGGRESSIVE AND EXCESSIVE.
NO MATTER THE GENDER...
...THERE IS NO BIAS...
...HE BELIEVES IN EQUAL-OPPORTUNITY INCARCERATION.
YET, FROM WHAT I'VE SEEN AND HEARD, HE SEEMS TO THRIVE ON BEING THE CENTER OF ATTENTION.
IT QUITE POSSIBLY COULD BE A STRATEGIC MOVE.
I TEND TO THINK OTHERWISE.

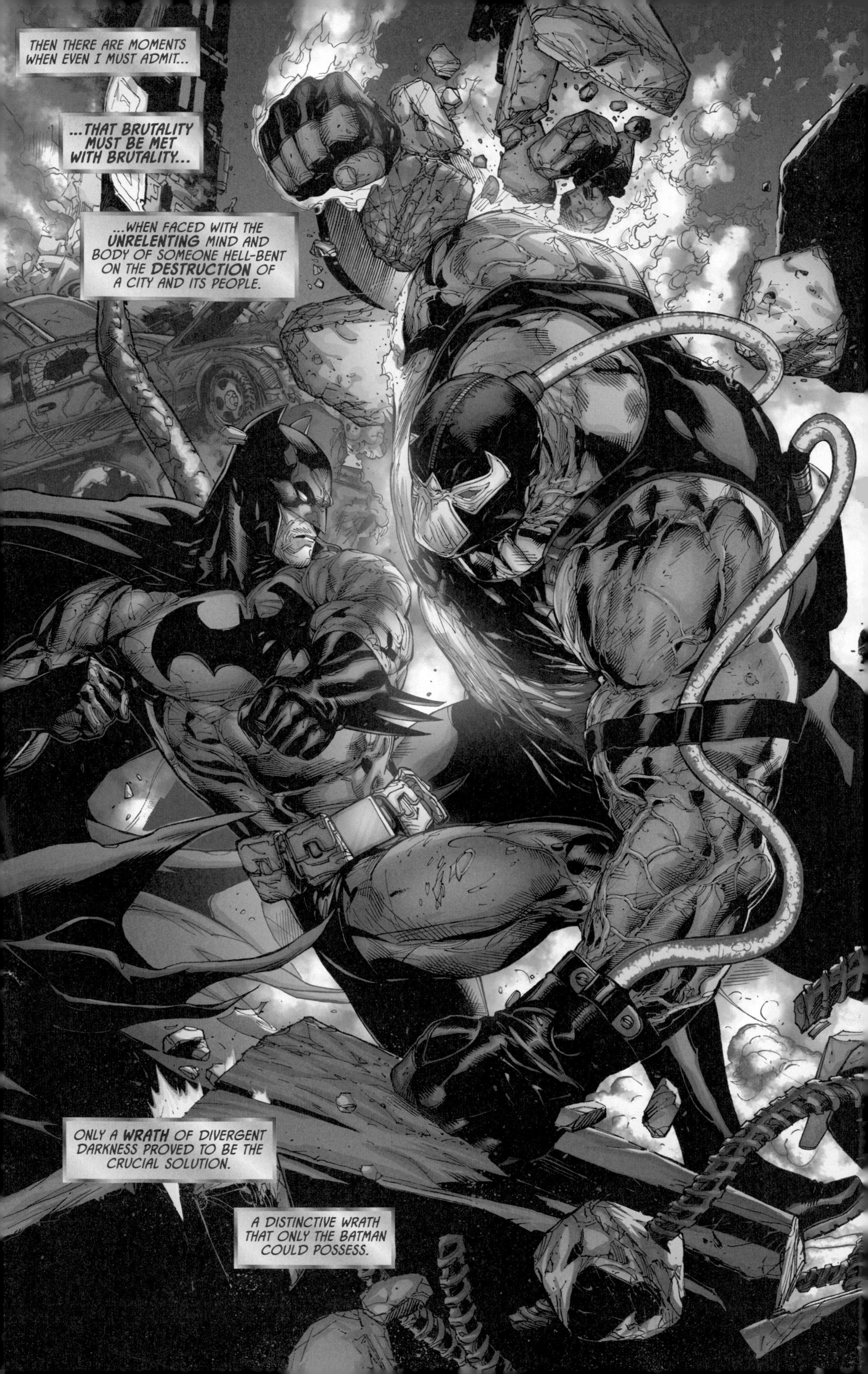
THEN THERE ARE MOMENTS WHEN EVEN I MUST ADMIT...
...THAT BRUTALITY MUST BE MET WITH BRUTALITY...
...WHEN FACED WITH THE UNRELENTING MIND AND BODY OF SOMEONE HELL-BENT ON THE DESTRUCTION OF A CITY AND ITS PEOPLE.
ONLY A WRATH OF DIVERGENT DARKNESS PROVED TO BE THE CRUCIAL SOLUTION.
A DISTINCTIVE WRATH THAT ONLY THE BATMAN COULD POSSESS.

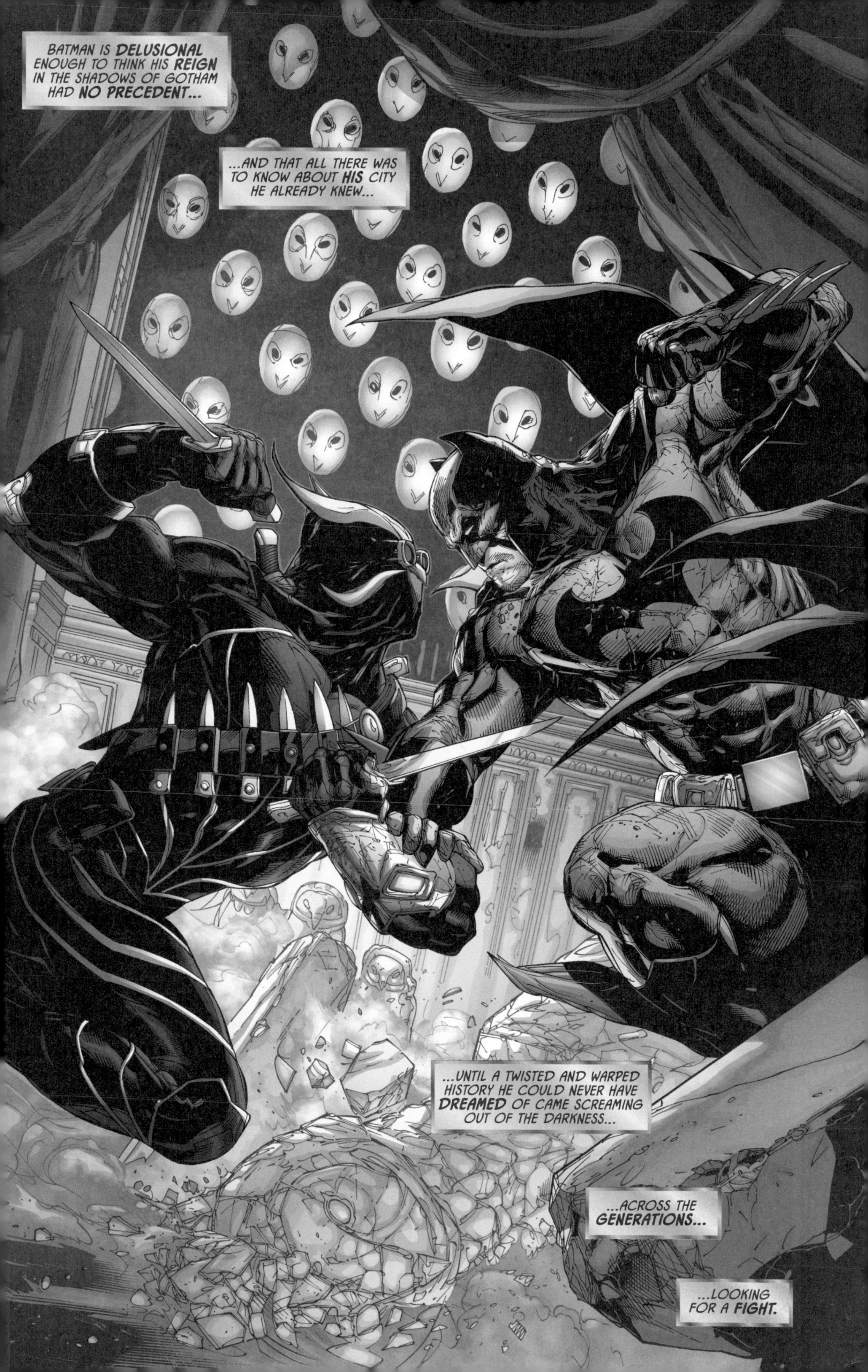
BATMAN IS DELUSIONAL ENOUGH TO THINK HIS REIGN IN THE SHADOWS OF GOTHAM HAD NO PRECEDENT...
...AND THAT ALL THERE WAS TO KNOW ABOUT HIS CITY HE ALREADY KNEW...
...UNTIL A TWISTED AND WARPED HISTORY HE COULD NEVER HAVE DREAMED OF CAME SCREAMING OUT OF THE DARKNESS...
...ACROSS THE GENERATIONS...
...LOOKING FOR A FIGHT.

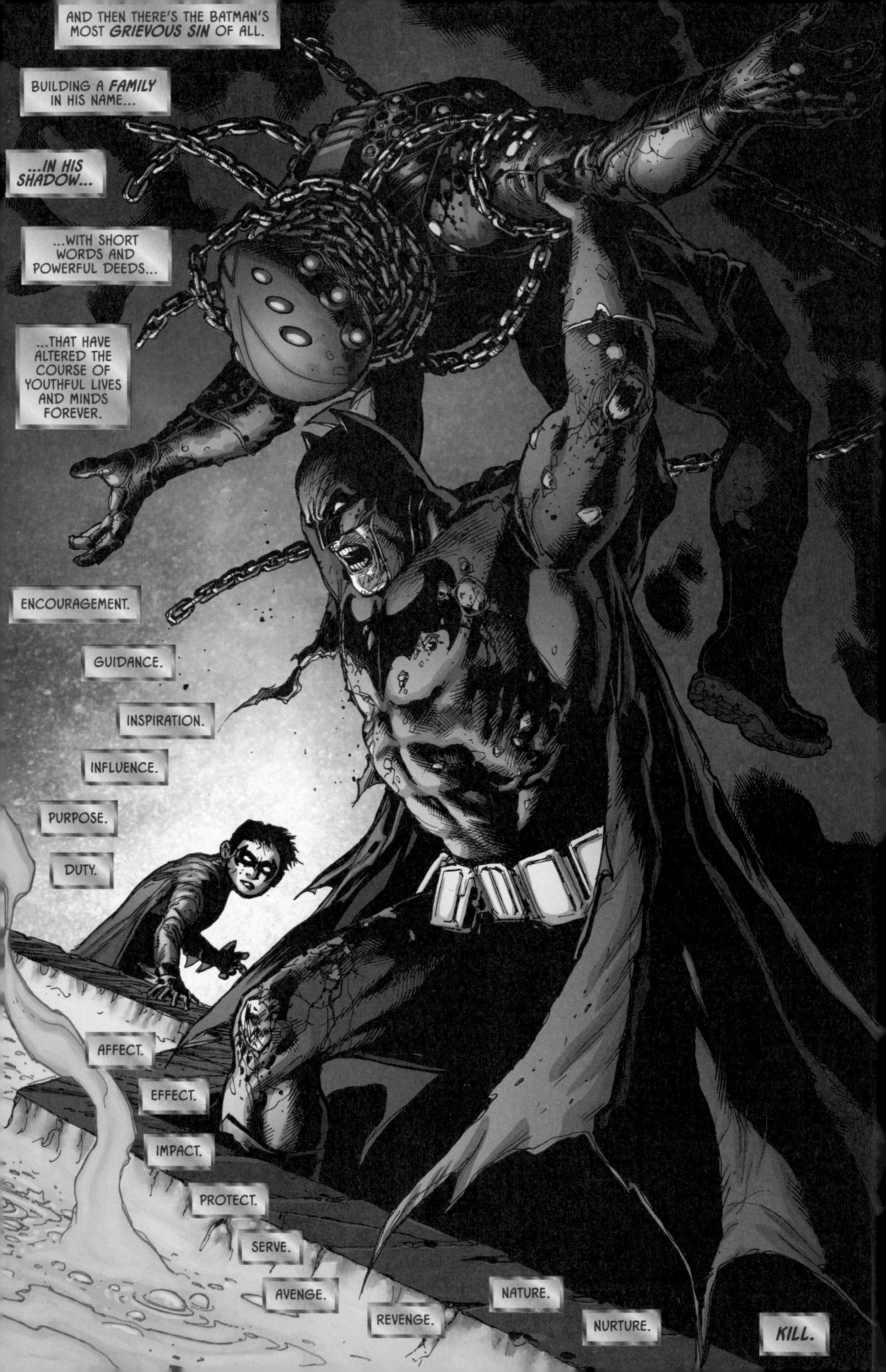
AND THEN THERE'S THE BATMAN'S MOST *GRIEVOUS SIN* OF ALL.
BUILDING A *FAMILY* IN HIS NAME...
...IN HIS SHADOW...
...WITH SHORT WORDS AND POWERFUL DEEDS...
...THAT HAVE ALTERED THE COURSE OF YOUTHFUL LIVES AND MINDS FOREVER.
ENCOURAGEMENT.
GUIDANCE.
INSPIRATION.
INFLUENCE.
PURPOSE.
DUTY.
AFFECT.
EFFECT.
IMPACT.
PROTECT.
SERVE.
AVENGE.
REVENGE.
NATURE.
NURTURE.
KILL.

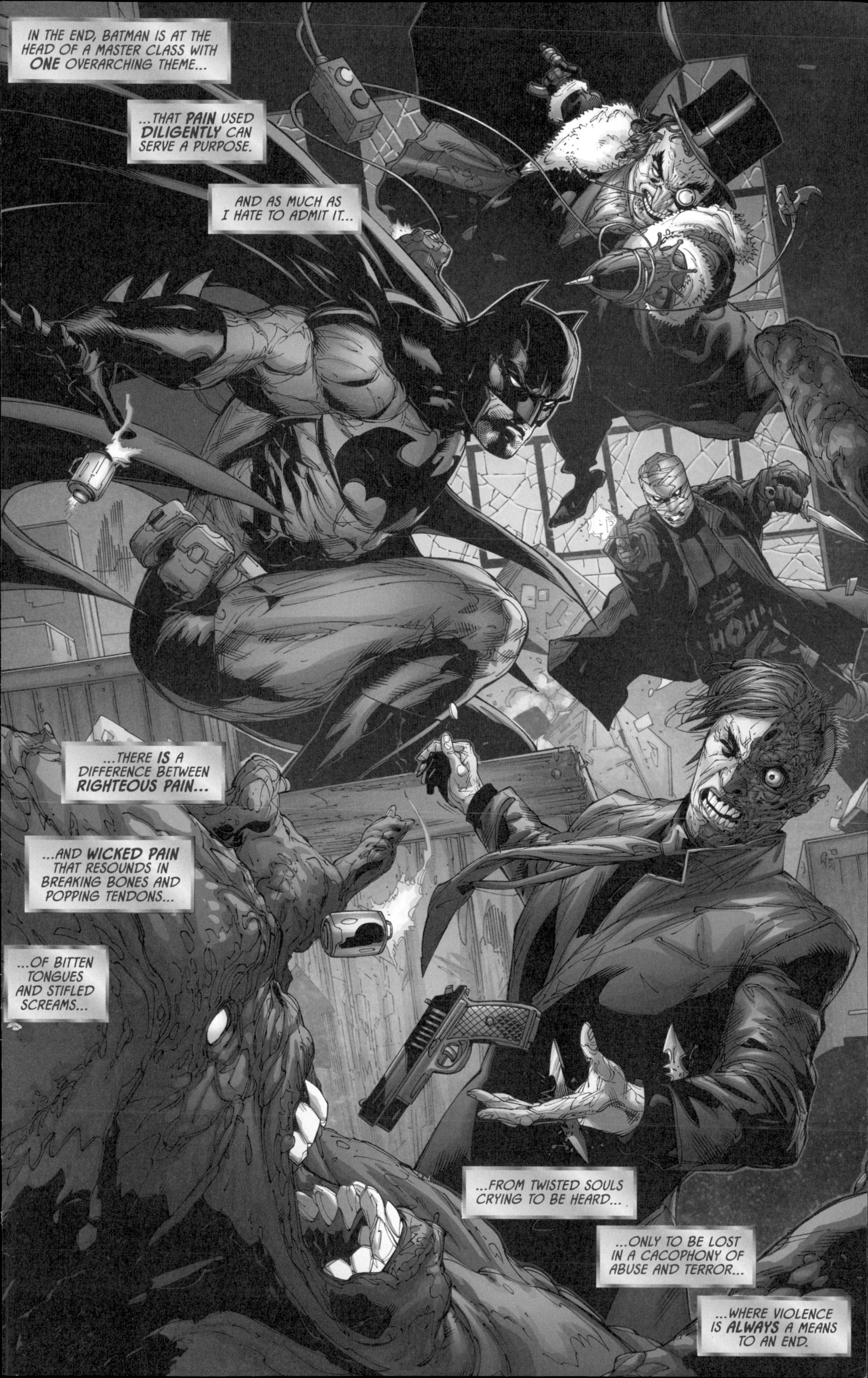
IN THE END, BATMAN IS AT THE HEAD OF A MASTER CLASS WITH ONE OVERARCHING THEME...
...THAT PAIN USED DILIGENTLY CAN SERVE A PURPOSE.
AND AS MUCH AS I HATE TO ADMIT IT...
...THERE IS A DIFFERENCE BETWEEN RIGHTEOUS PAIN...
...AND WICKED PAIN THAT RESOUNDS IN BREAKING BONES AND POPPING TENDONS...
...OF BITTEN TONGUES AND STIFLED SCREAMS...
...FROM TWISTED SOULS CRYING TO BE HEARD...
...ONLY TO BE LOST IN A CACOPHONY OF ABUSE AND TERROR...
...WHERE VIOLENCE IS ALWAYS A MEANS TO AN END.

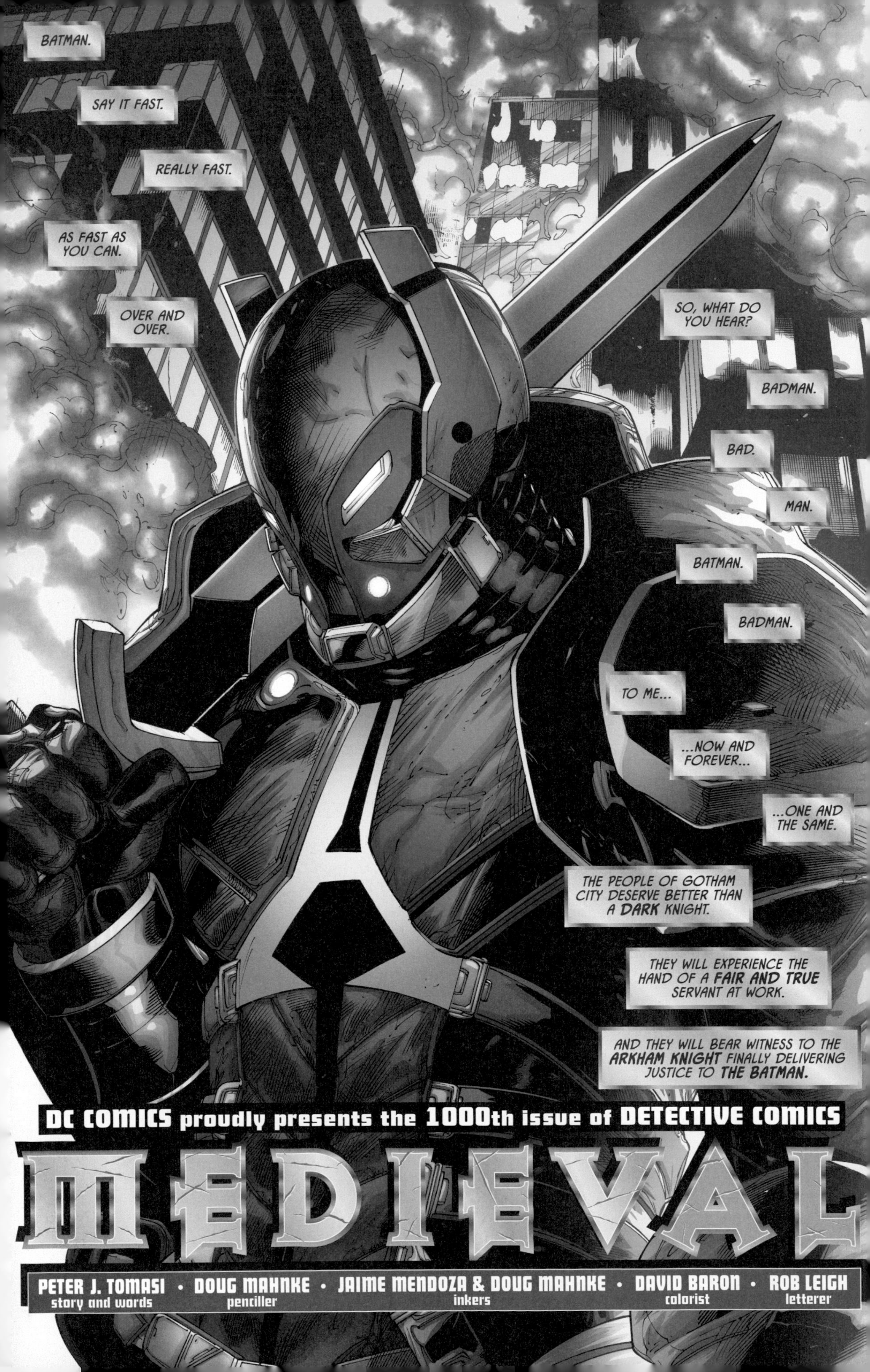
BATMAN.
SAY IT FAST.
REALLY FAST.
AS FAST AS YOU CAN.
OVER AND OVER.
SO, WHAT DO YOU HEAR?
BADMAN.
BAD.
MAN.
BATMAN.
BADMAN.
TO ME...
...NOW AND FOREVER...
...ONE AND THE SAME.
THE PEOPLE OF GOTHAM CITY DESERVE BETTER THAN A DARK KNIGHT.
THEY WILL EXPERIENCE THE HAND OF A FAIR AND TRUE SERVANT AT WORK.
AND THEY WILL BEAR WITNESS TO THE ARKHAM KNIGHT FINALLY DELIVERING JUSTICE TO THE BATMAN.
DC COMICS proudly presents the 1000th issue of DETECTIVE COMICS
MEDIEVAL
PETER J. TOMASI story and words • DOUG MAHNKE penciller • JAIME MENDOZA & DOUG MAHNKE inkers • DAVID BARON colorist • ROB LEIGH letterer

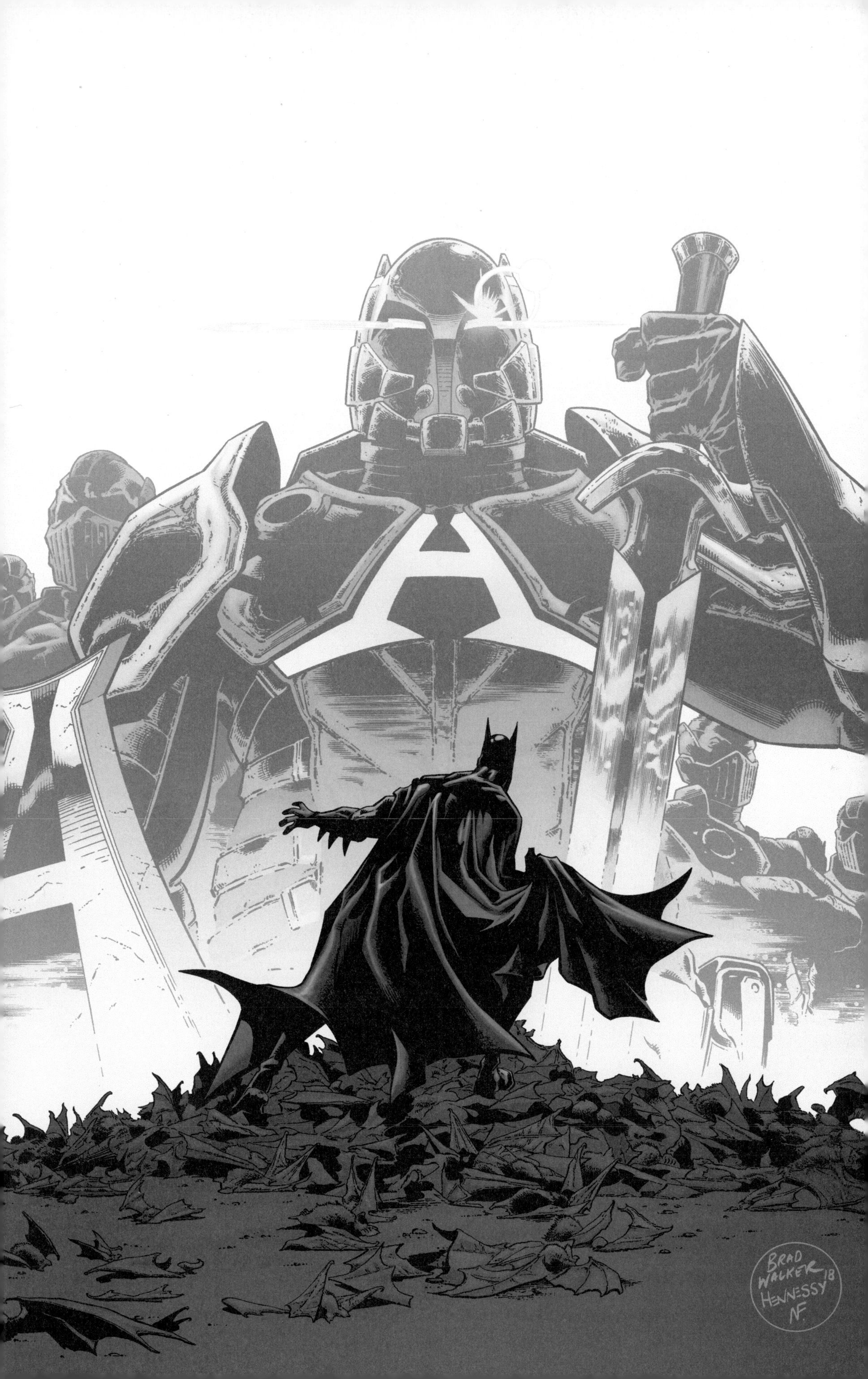
BRAD WALKER 18 HENNESSY NF.

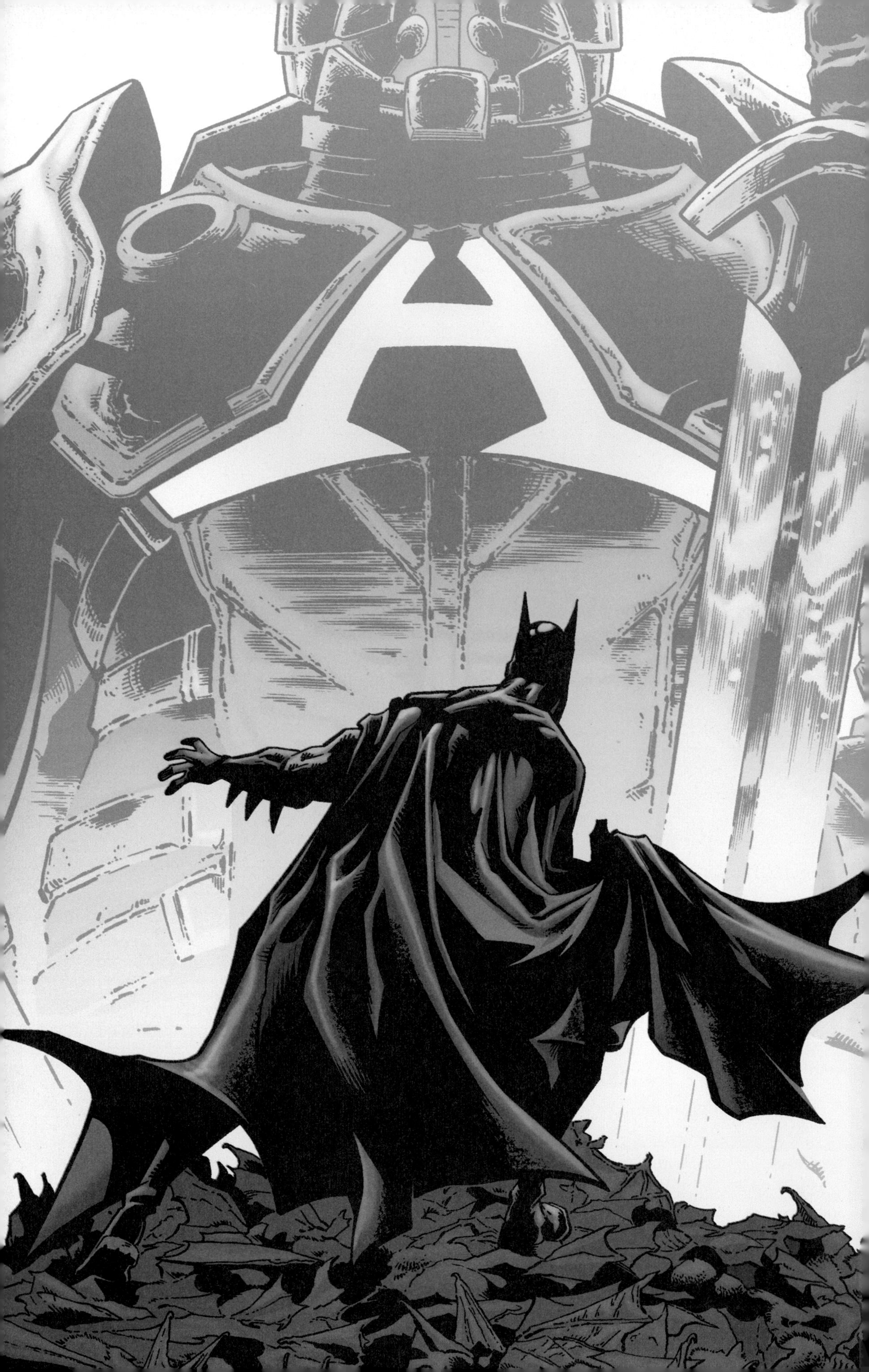

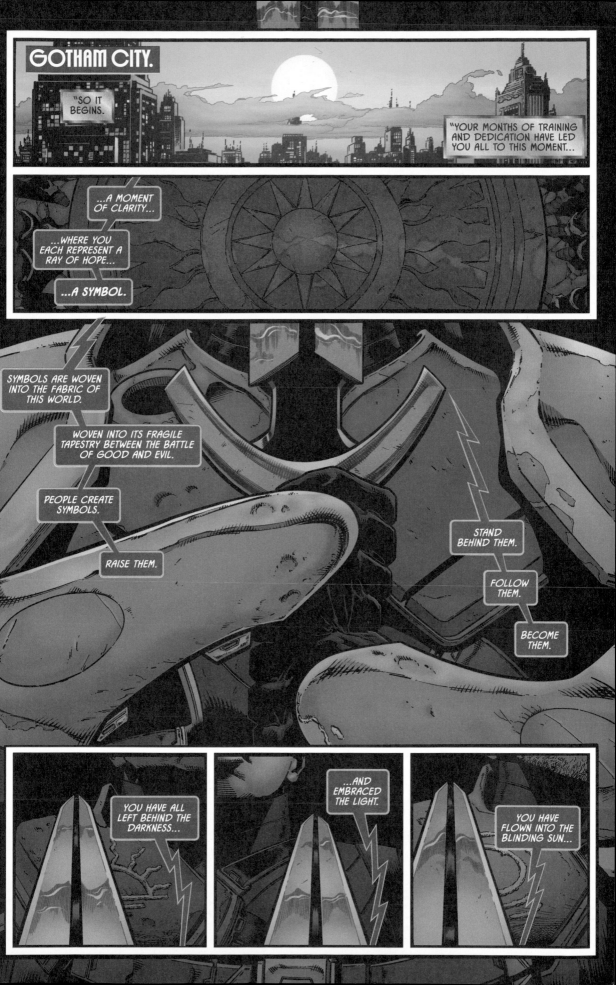

GOTHAM CITY.

"SO IT BEGINS.

"YOUR MONTHS OF TRAINING AND DEDICATION HAVE LED YOU ALL TO THIS MOMENT...

...A MOMENT OF CLARITY...

...WHERE YOU EACH REPRESENT A RAY OF HOPE...

...A SYMBOL.

SYMBOLS ARE WOVEN INTO THE FABRIC OF THIS WORLD.

WOVEN INTO ITS FRAGILE TAPESTRY BETWEEN THE BATTLE OF GOOD AND EVIL.

PEOPLE CREATE SYMBOLS.

RAISE THEM.

STAND BEHIND THEM.

FOLLOW THEM.

BECOME THEM.

YOU HAVE ALL LEFT BEHIND THE DARKNESS...

...AND EMBRACED THE LIGHT.

YOU HAVE FLOWN INTO THE BLINDING SUN...

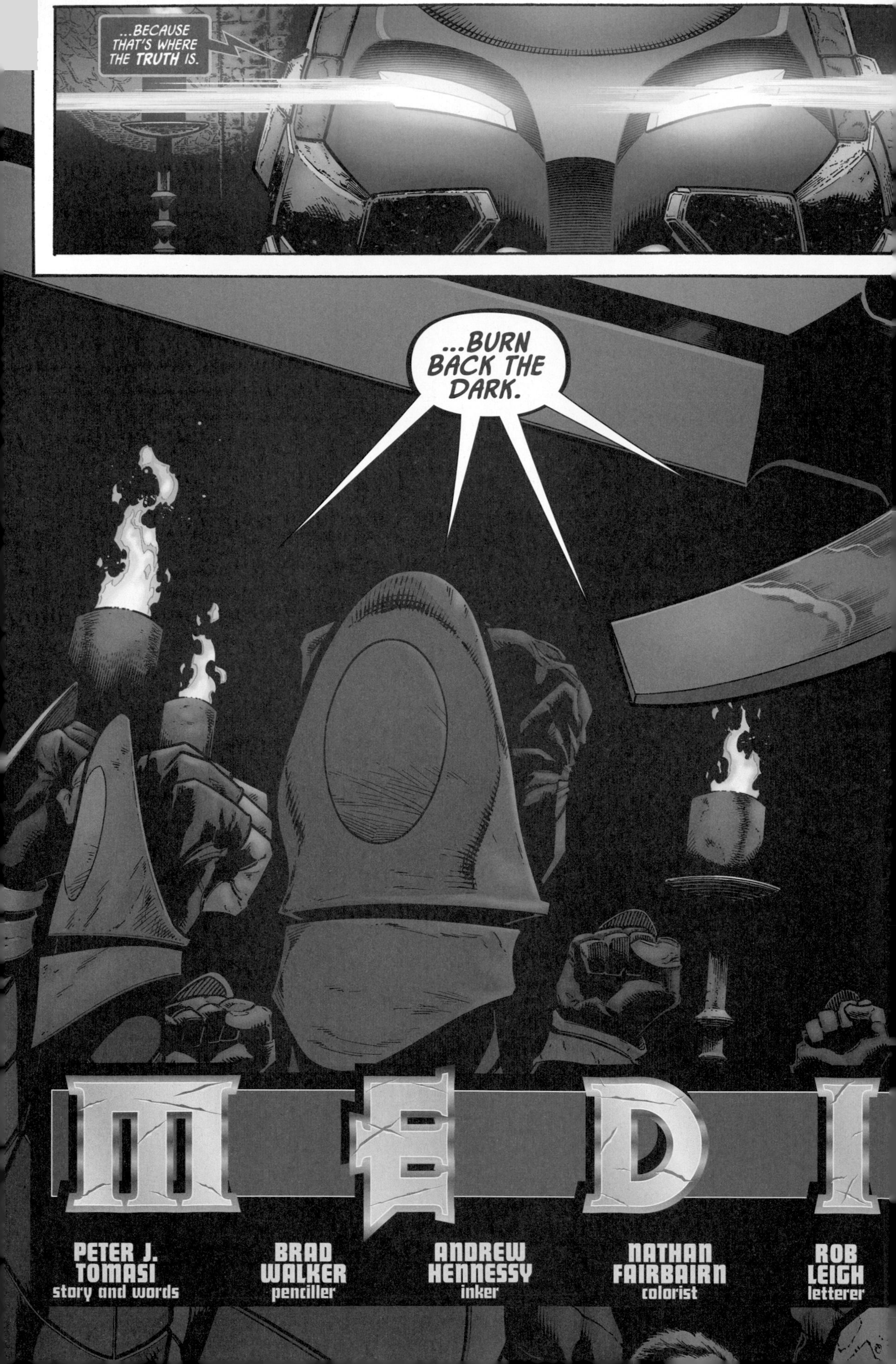

...BECAUSE THAT'S WHERE THE TRUTH IS.
...BURN BACK THE DARK.
M E D I
PETER J. TOMASI story and words
BRAD WALKER penciller
ANDREW HENNESSY inker
NATHAN FAIRBAIRN colorist
ROB LEIGH letterer

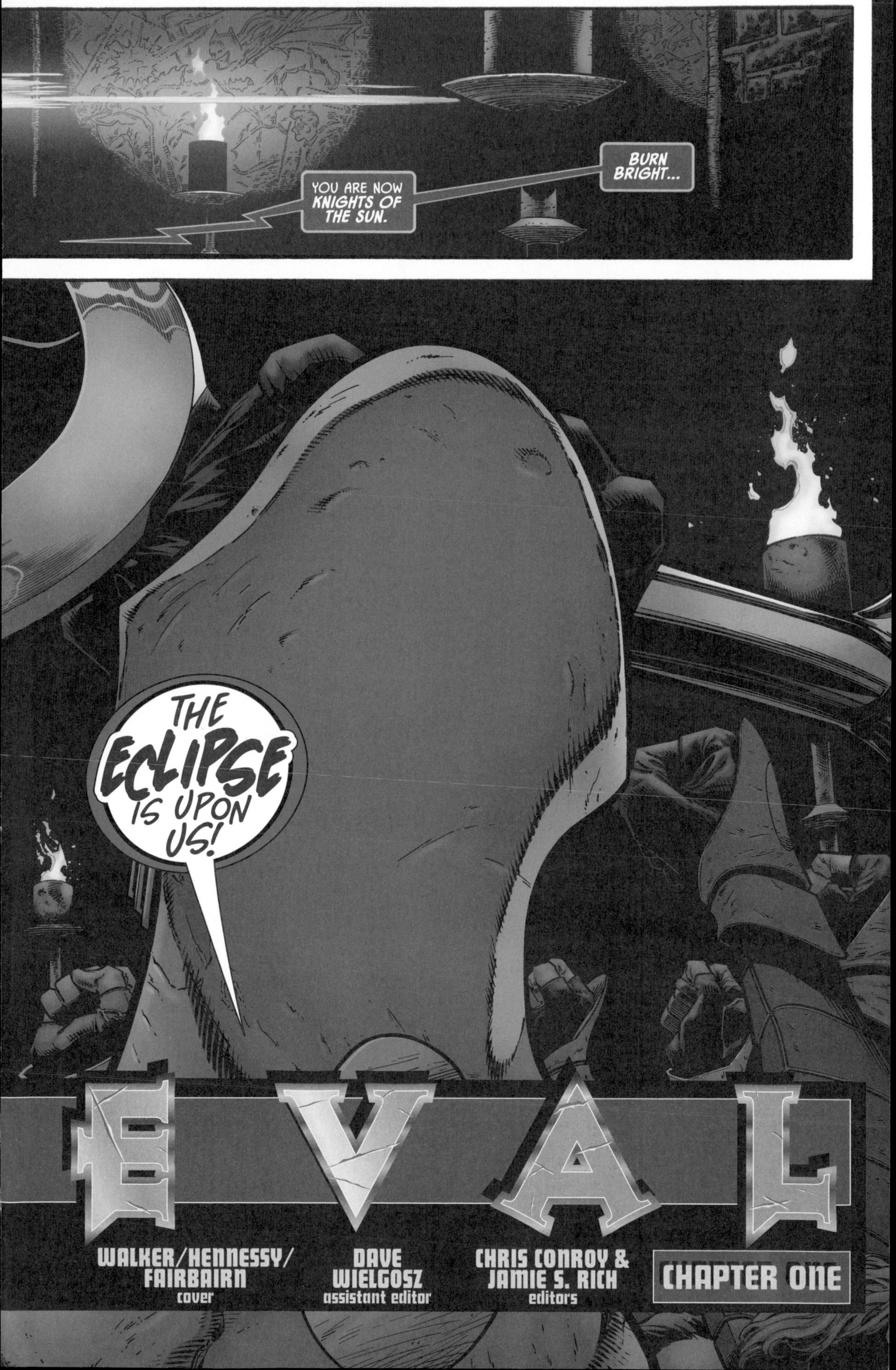

YOU ARE NOW KNIGHTS OF THE SUN.
BURN BRIGHT...
THE ECLIPSE IS UPON US!
EVAL
WALKER/HENNESSY/ FAIRBAIRN cover
DAVE WIELGOSZ assistant editor
CHRIS CONROY & JAMIE S. RICH editors
CHAPTER ONE

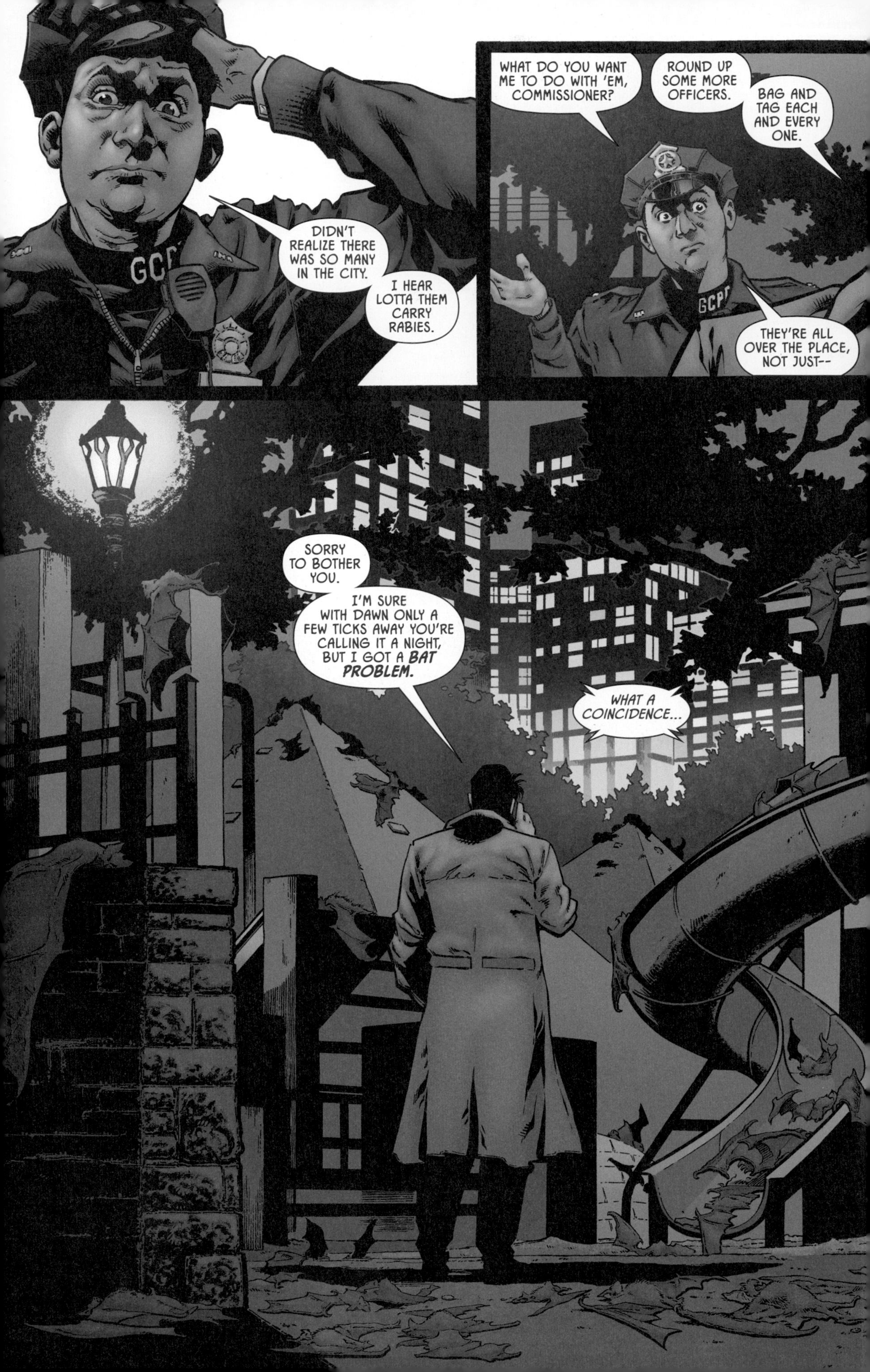
DIDN'T REALIZE THERE WAS SO MANY IN THE CITY.
I HEAR LOTTA THEM CARRY RABIES.
WHAT DO YOU WANT ME TO DO WITH 'EM, COMMISSIONER?
ROUND UP SOME MORE OFFICERS.
BAG AND TAG EACH AND EVERY ONE.
THEY'RE ALL OVER THE PLACE, NOT JUST--
SORRY TO BOTHER YOU.
I'M SURE WITH DAWN ONLY A FEW TICKS AWAY YOU'RE CALLING IT A NIGHT, BUT I GOT A BAT PROBLEM.
WHAT A COINCIDENCE...

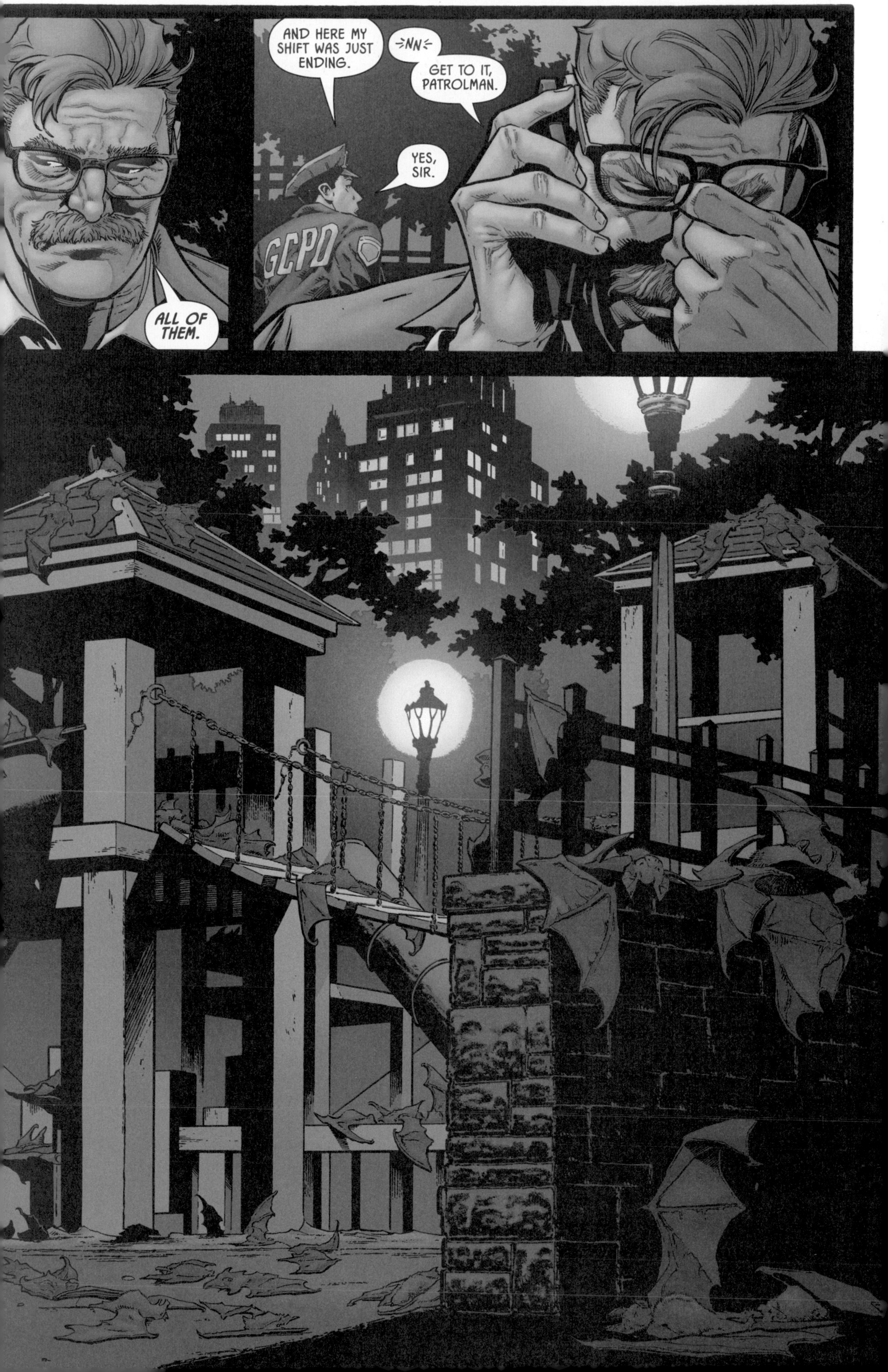
ALL OF THEM.
AND HERE MY SHIFT WAS JUST ENDING.
NN
GET TO IT, PATROLMAN.
YES, SIR.

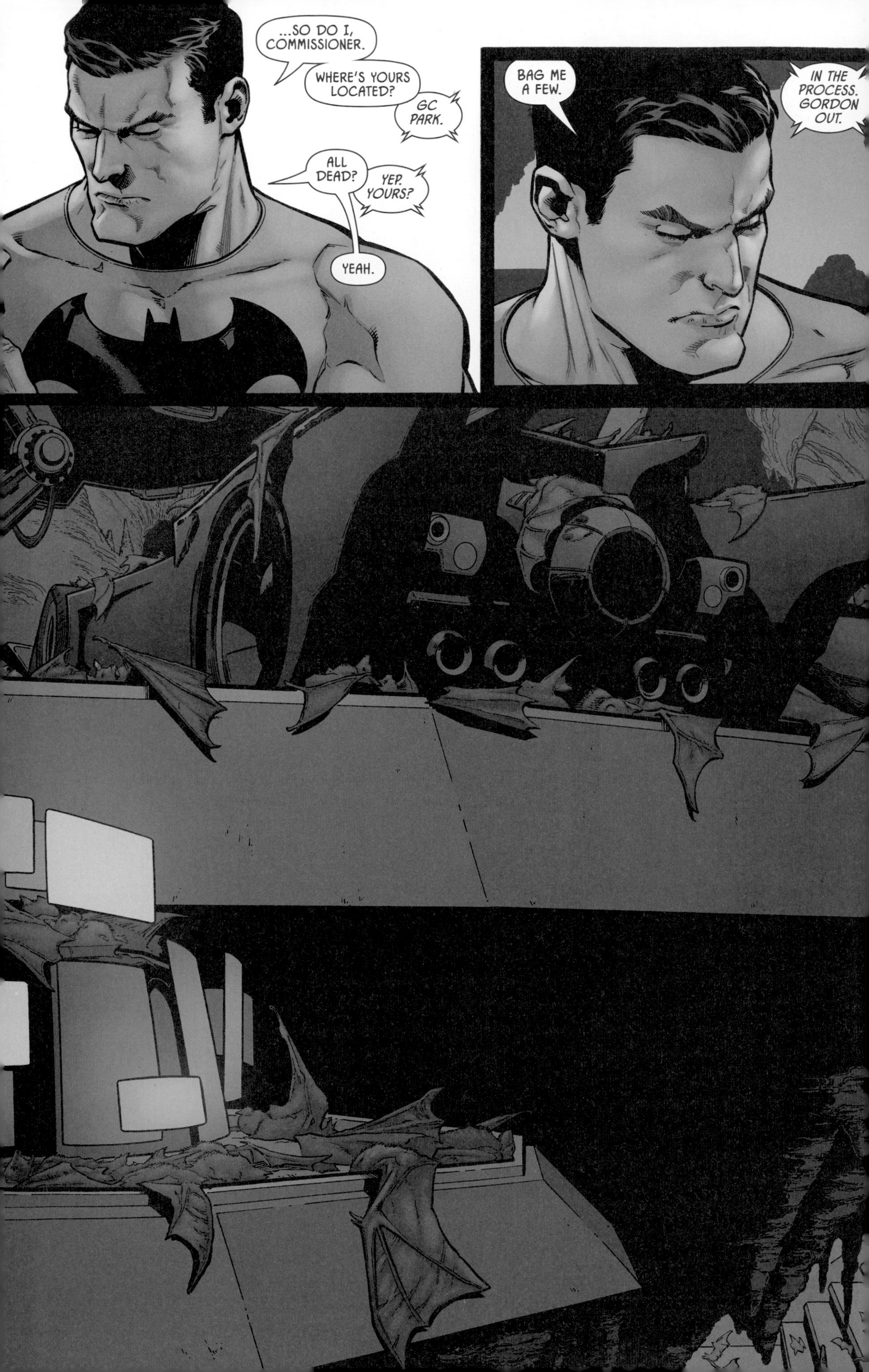
...SO DO I, COMMISSIONER.
WHERE'S YOURS LOCATED?
GC PARK.
ALL DEAD?
YEP. YOURS?
YEAH.
BAG ME A FEW.
IN THE PROCESS. GORDON OUT.

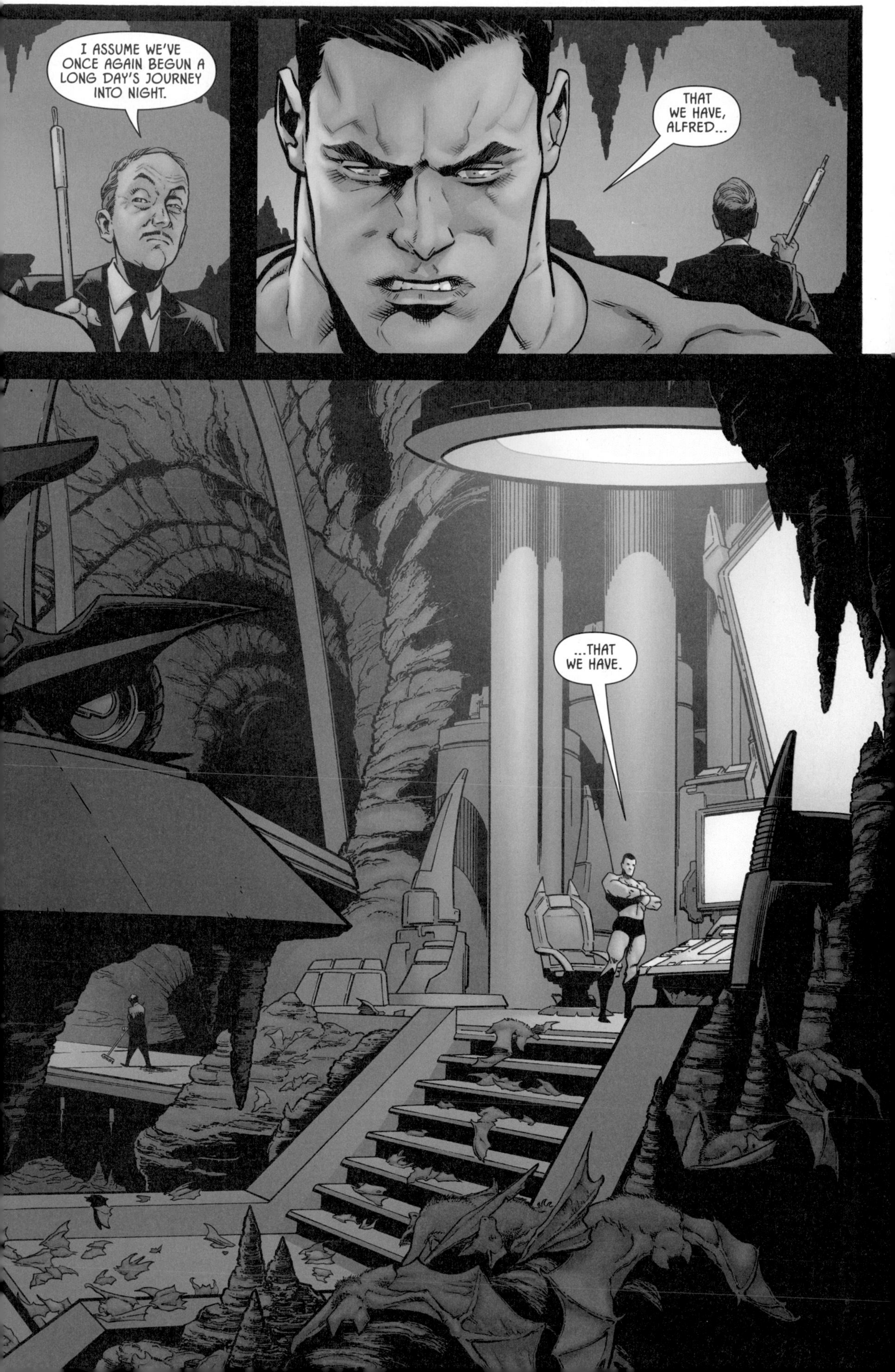
I ASSUME WE'VE ONCE AGAIN BEGUN A LONG DAY'S JOURNEY INTO NIGHT.
THAT WE HAVE, ALFRED...
...THAT WE HAVE.

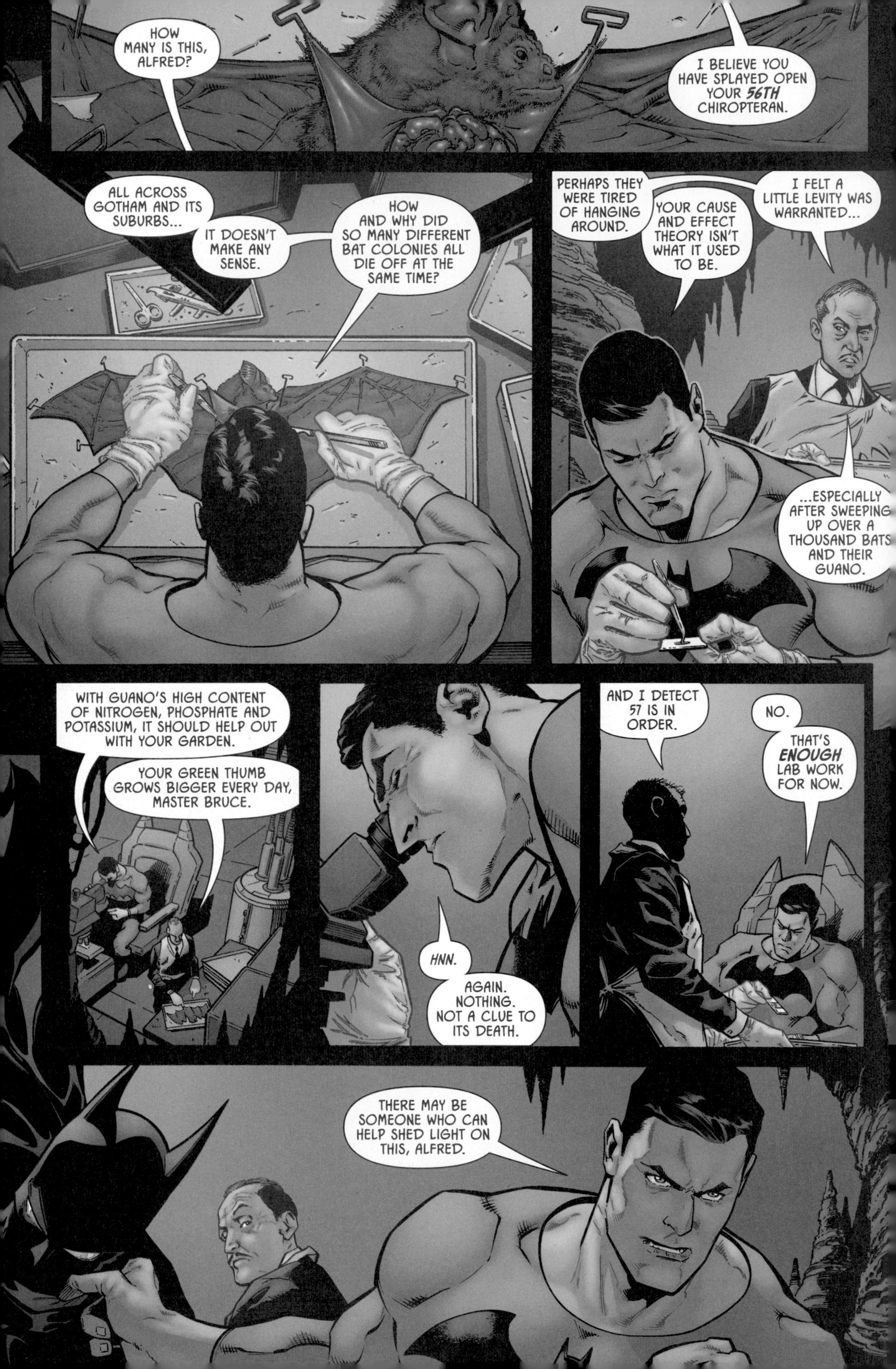
HOW MANY IS THIS, ALFRED?
I BELIEVE YOU HAVE SPLAYED OPEN YOUR *56TH* CHIROPTERAN.
ALL ACROSS GOTHAM AND ITS SUBURBS...
IT DOESN'T MAKE ANY SENSE.
HOW AND WHY DID SO MANY DIFFERENT BAT COLONIES ALL DIE OFF AT THE SAME TIME?
PERHAPS THEY WERE TIRED OF HANGING AROUND.
YOUR CAUSE AND EFFECT THEORY ISN'T WHAT IT USED TO BE.
I FELT A LITTLE LEVITY WAS WARRANTED...
...ESPECIALLY AFTER SWEEPING UP OVER A THOUSAND BATS AND THEIR GUANO.
WITH GUANO'S HIGH CONTENT OF NITROGEN, PHOSPHATE AND POTASSIUM, IT SHOULD HELP OUT WITH YOUR GARDEN.
YOUR GREEN THUMB GROWS BIGGER EVERY DAY, MASTER BRUCE.
HNN.
AGAIN. NOTHING. NOT A CLUE TO ITS DEATH.
AND I DETECT 57 IS IN ORDER.
NO.
THAT'S ***ENOUGH*** LAB WORK FOR NOW.
THERE MAY BE SOMEONE WHO CAN HELP SHED LIGHT ON THIS, ALFRED.

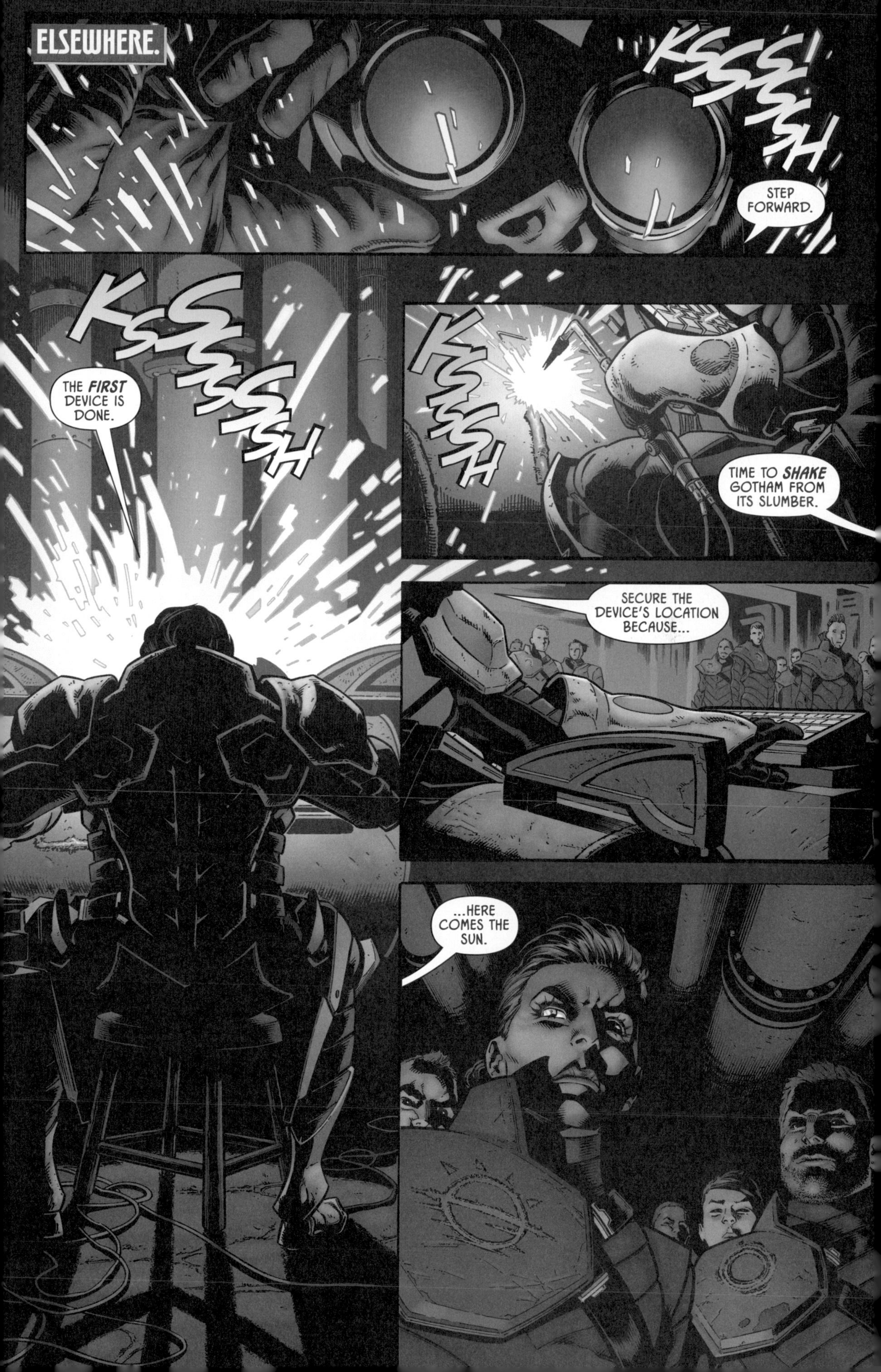
ELSEWHERE.
KSSSSSSH
STEP FORWARD.
KSSSSSSSH
THE FIRST DEVICE IS DONE.
KSSSSH
TIME TO SHAKE GOTHAM FROM ITS SLUMBER.
SECURE THE DEVICE'S LOCATION BECAUSE...
...HERE COMES THE SUN.

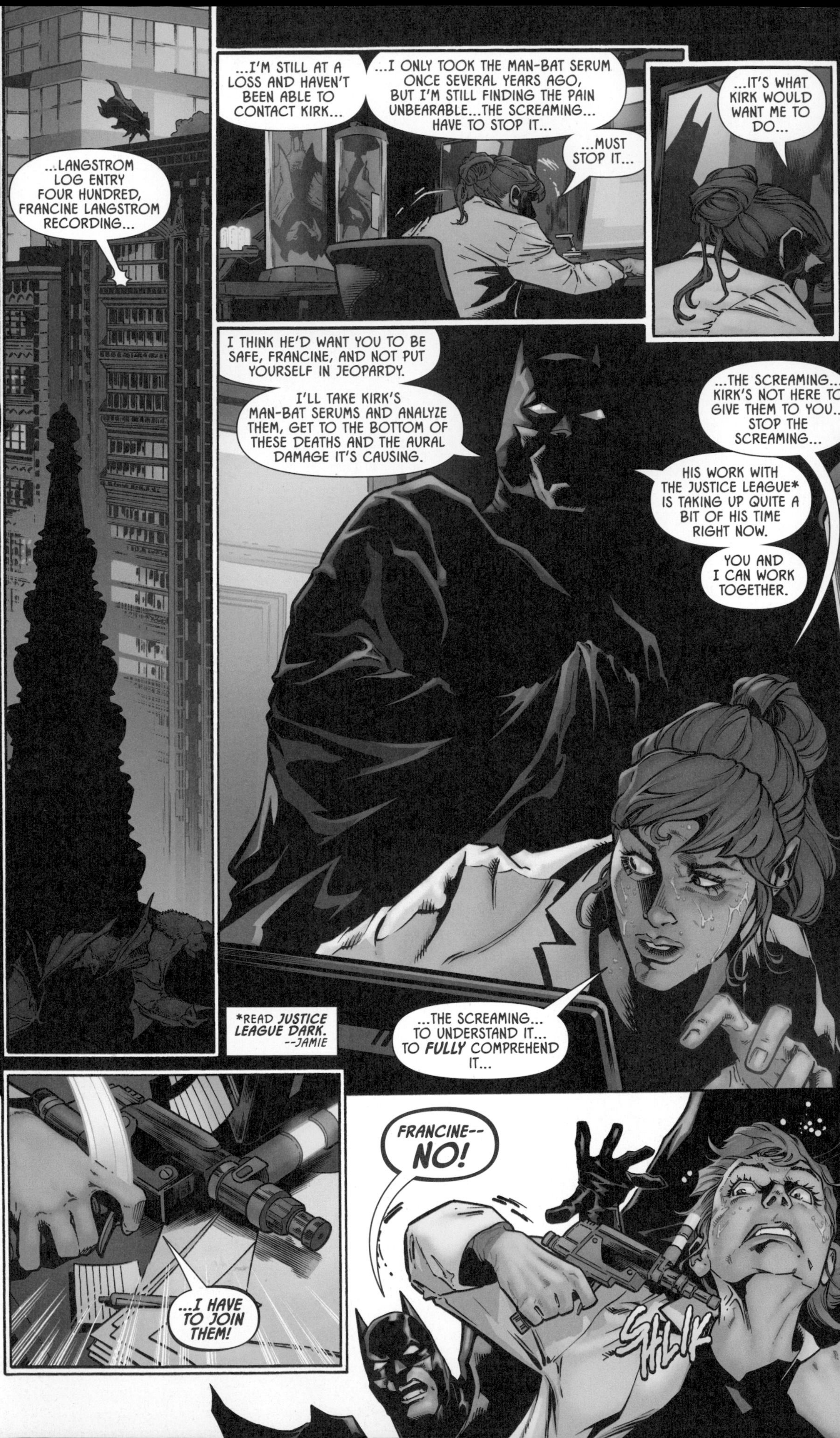
...LANGSTROM LOG ENTRY FOUR HUNDRED, FRANCINE LANGSTROM RECORDING...
...I'M STILL AT A LOSS AND HAVEN'T BEEN ABLE TO CONTACT KIRK...
...I ONLY TOOK THE MAN-BAT SERUM ONCE SEVERAL YEARS AGO, BUT I'M STILL FINDING THE PAIN UNBEARABLE...THE SCREAMING... HAVE TO STOP IT...
...MUST STOP IT...
...IT'S WHAT KIRK WOULD WANT ME TO DO...
I THINK HE'D WANT YOU TO BE SAFE, FRANCINE, AND NOT PUT YOURSELF IN JEOPARDY.
I'LL TAKE KIRK'S MAN-BAT SERUMS AND ANALYZE THEM, GET TO THE BOTTOM OF THESE DEATHS AND THE AURAL DAMAGE IT'S CAUSING.
...THE SCREAMING... KIRK'S NOT HERE TO GIVE THEM TO YOU... STOP THE SCREAMING...
HIS WORK WITH THE JUSTICE LEAGUE* IS TAKING UP QUITE A BIT OF HIS TIME RIGHT NOW.
YOU AND I CAN WORK TOGETHER.
...THE SCREAMING... TO UNDERSTAND IT... TO FULLY COMPREHEND IT...
*READ JUSTICE LEAGUE DARK. --JAMIE
...I HAVE TO JOIN THEM!
FRANCINE-- NO!
SHLIK

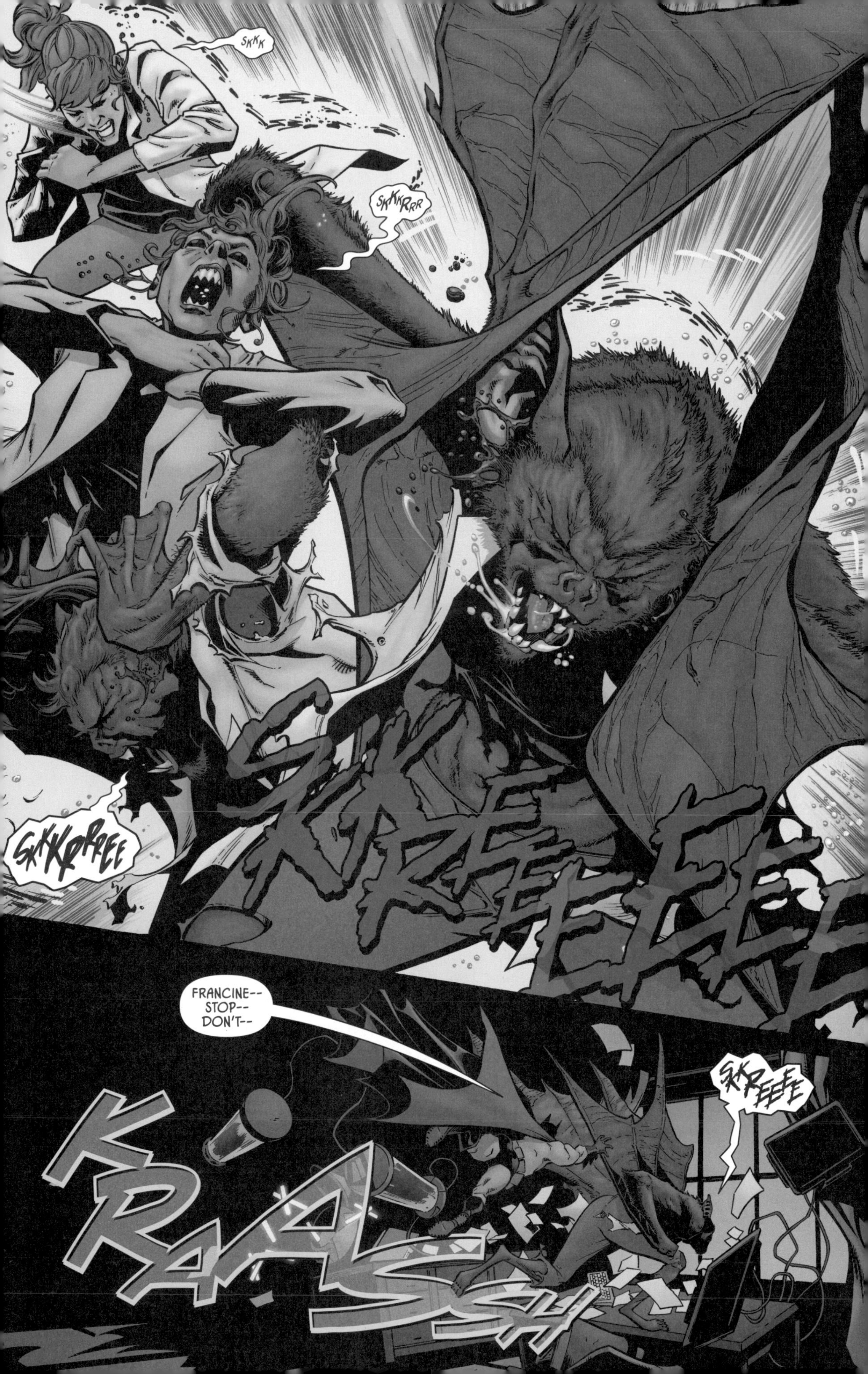
SKKK
SKKKRRR
SKKKRRREE
SKREEEEEEE
FRANCINE--
STOP--
DON'T--
SKKREEEE
KRAASH

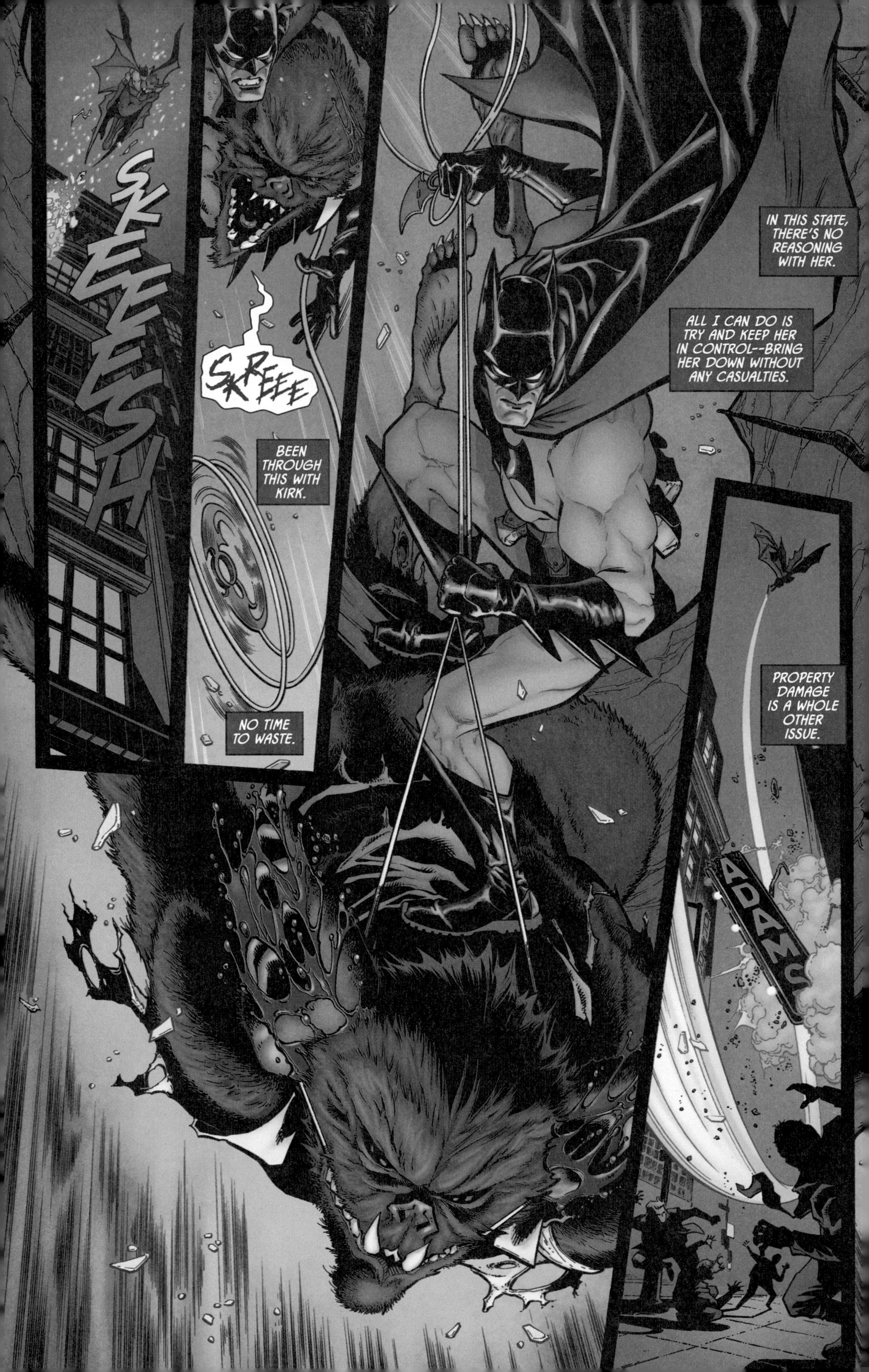
SKREEESH
SKREEE
BEEN THROUGH THIS WITH KIRK.
NO TIME TO WASTE.
IN THIS STATE, THERE'S NO REASONING WITH HER.
ALL I CAN DO IS TRY AND KEEP HER IN CONTROL--BRING HER DOWN WITHOUT ANY CASUALTIES.
PROPERTY DAMAGE IS A WHOLE OTHER ISSUE.
ADAMS

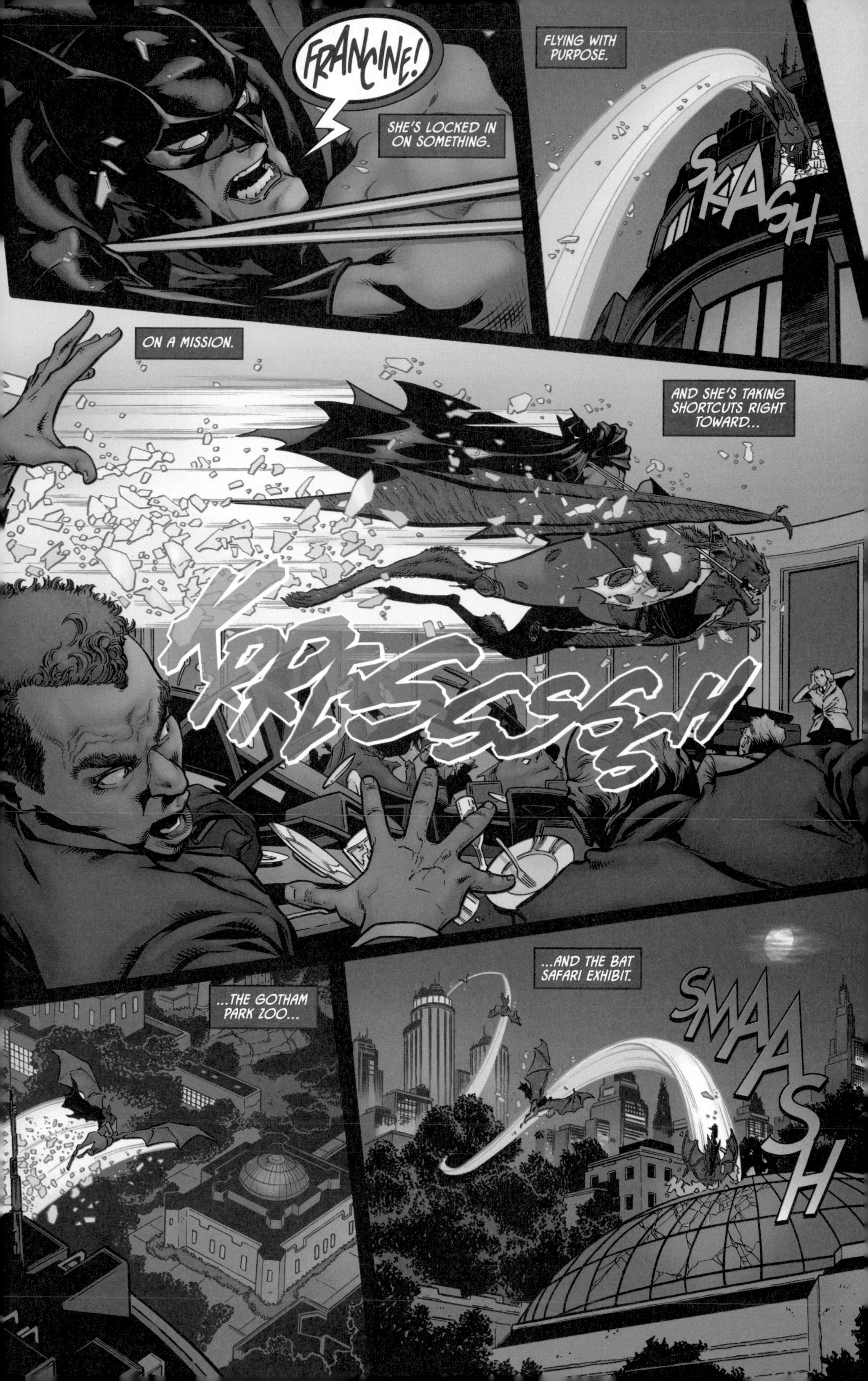

FRANCINE!
SHE'S LOCKED IN ON SOMETHING.
FLYING WITH PURPOSE.
SKRASH
ON A MISSION.
AND SHE'S TAKING SHORTCUTS RIGHT TOWARD...
KRRSSSSSH
...THE GOTHAM PARK ZOO...
...AND THE BAT SAFARI EXHIBIT.
SMAASH

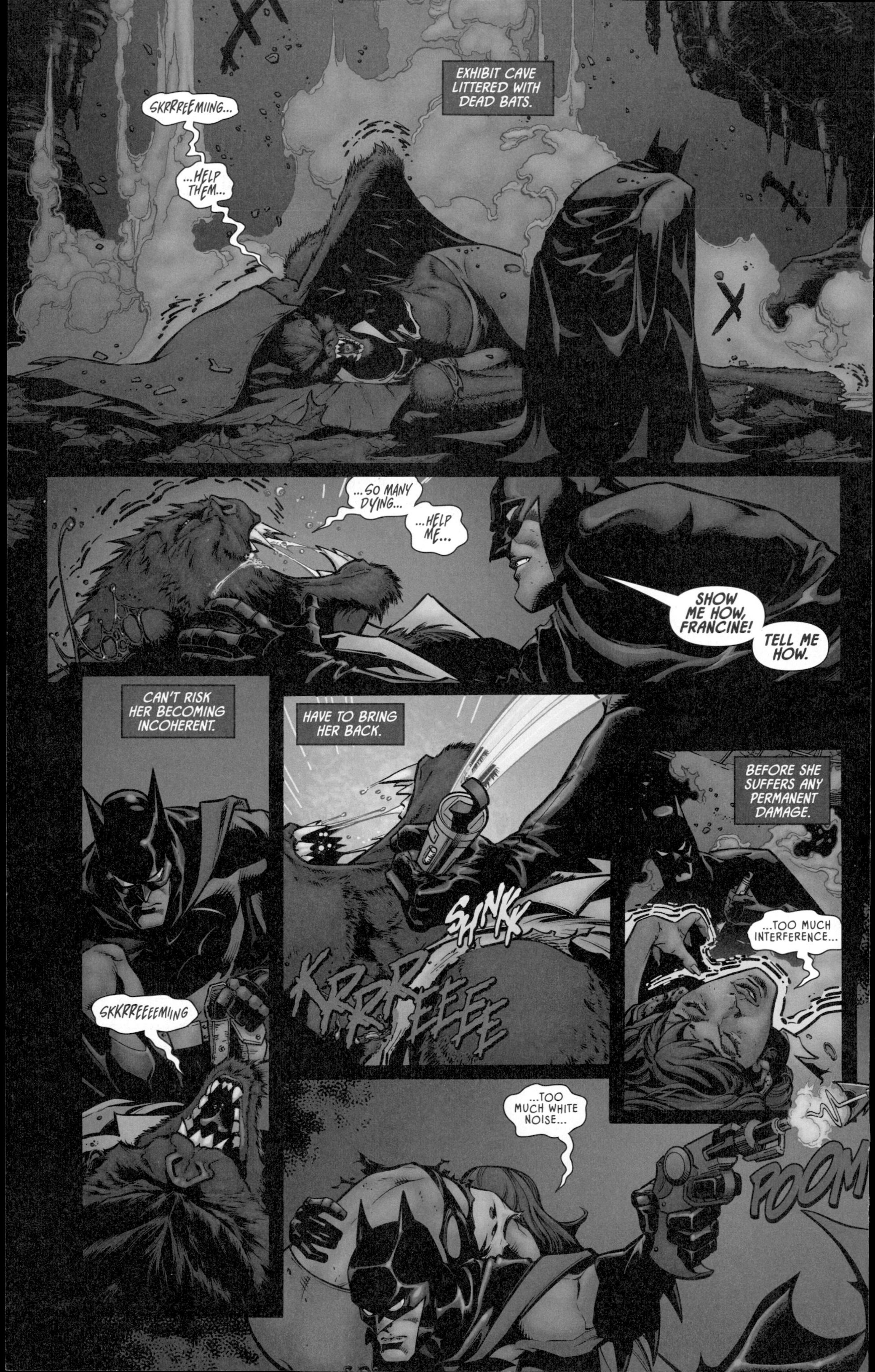
EXHIBIT CAVE LITTERED WITH DEAD BATS.
SKRRREEEMIING...
...HELP THEM...
...SO MANY DYING...
...HELP ME...
SHOW ME HOW, FRANCINE!
TELL ME HOW.
CAN'T RISK HER BECOMING INCOHERENT.
SKKRREEEEEMIING
HAVE TO BRING HER BACK.
SHNKK
KRRREEEEE
BEFORE SHE SUFFERS ANY PERMANENT DAMAGE.
...TOO MUCH INTERFERENCE...
...TOO MUCH WHITE NOISE...
POOM

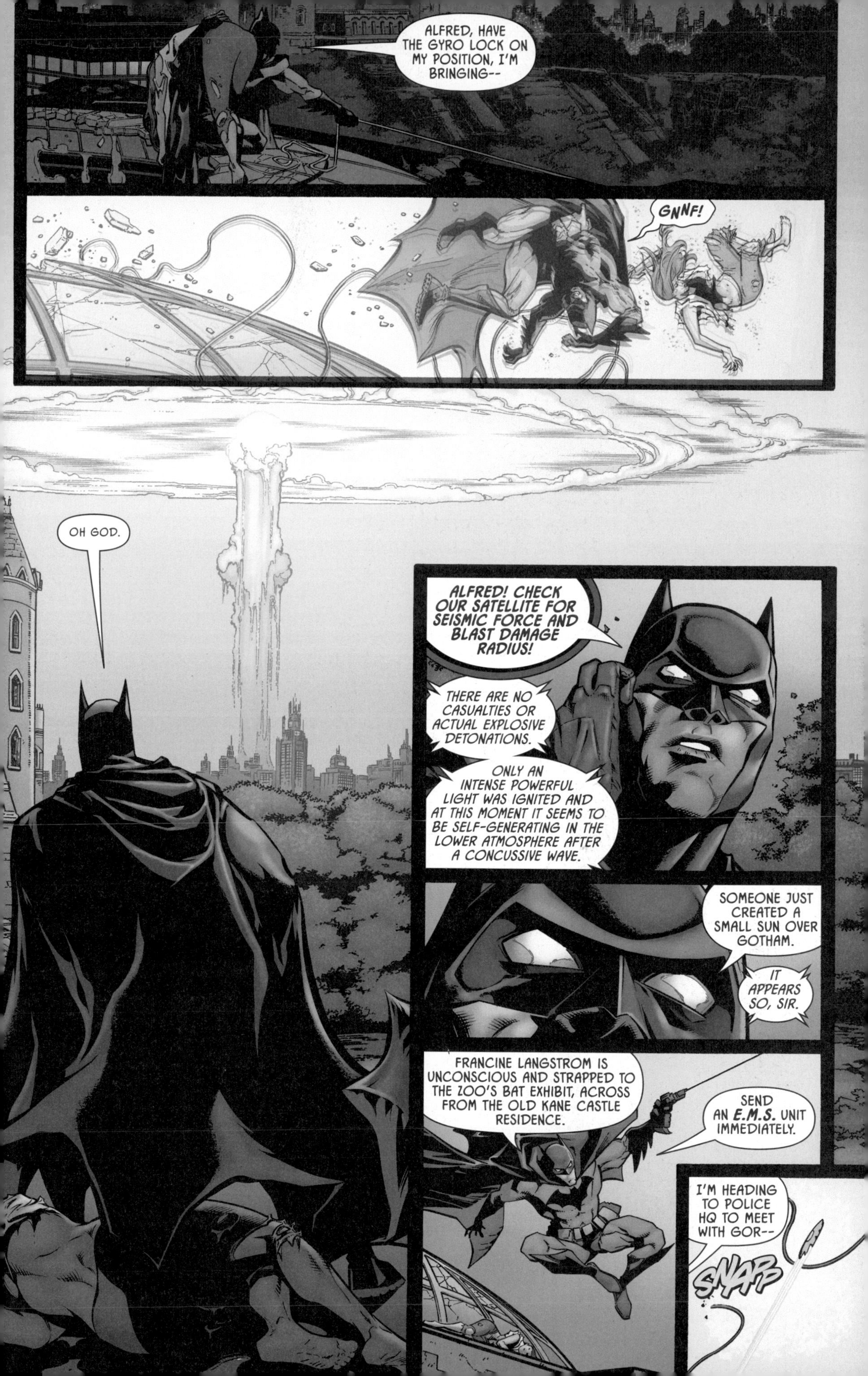
ALFRED, HAVE THE GYRO LOCK ON MY POSITION, I'M BRINGING--
GNNF!
OH GOD.
ALFRED! CHECK OUR SATELLITE FOR SEISMIC FORCE AND BLAST DAMAGE RADIUS!
THERE ARE NO CASUALTIES OR ACTUAL EXPLOSIVE DETONATIONS.
ONLY AN INTENSE POWERFUL LIGHT WAS IGNITED AND AT THIS MOMENT IT SEEMS TO BE SELF-GENERATING IN THE LOWER ATMOSPHERE AFTER A CONCUSSIVE WAVE.
SOMEONE JUST CREATED A SMALL SUN OVER GOTHAM.
IT APPEARS SO, SIR.
FRANCINE LANGSTROM IS UNCONSCIOUS AND STRAPPED TO THE ZOO'S BAT EXHIBIT, ACROSS FROM THE OLD KANE CASTLE RESIDENCE.
SEND AN E.M.S. UNIT IMMEDIATELY.
I'M HEADING TO POLICE HQ TO MEET WITH GOR--
SNAP

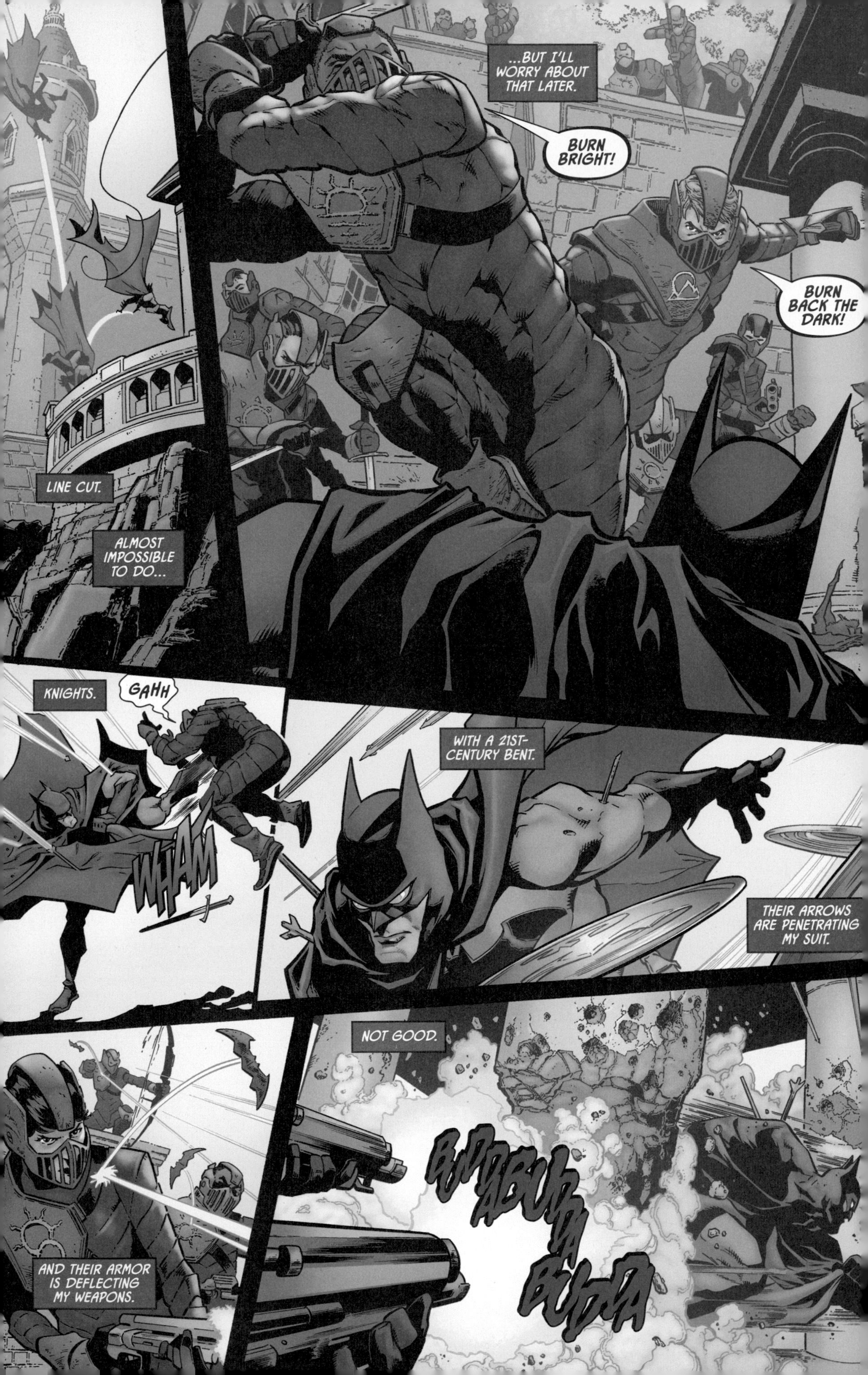
LINE CUT.
ALMOST IMPOSSIBLE TO DO...
...BUT I'LL WORRY ABOUT THAT LATER.
BURN BRIGHT!
BURN BACK THE DARK!
KNIGHTS.
GAHH
WHAM
WITH A 21ST-CENTURY BENT.
THEIR ARROWS ARE PENETRATING MY SUIT.
AND THEIR ARMOR IS DEFLECTING MY WEAPONS.
NOT GOOD.

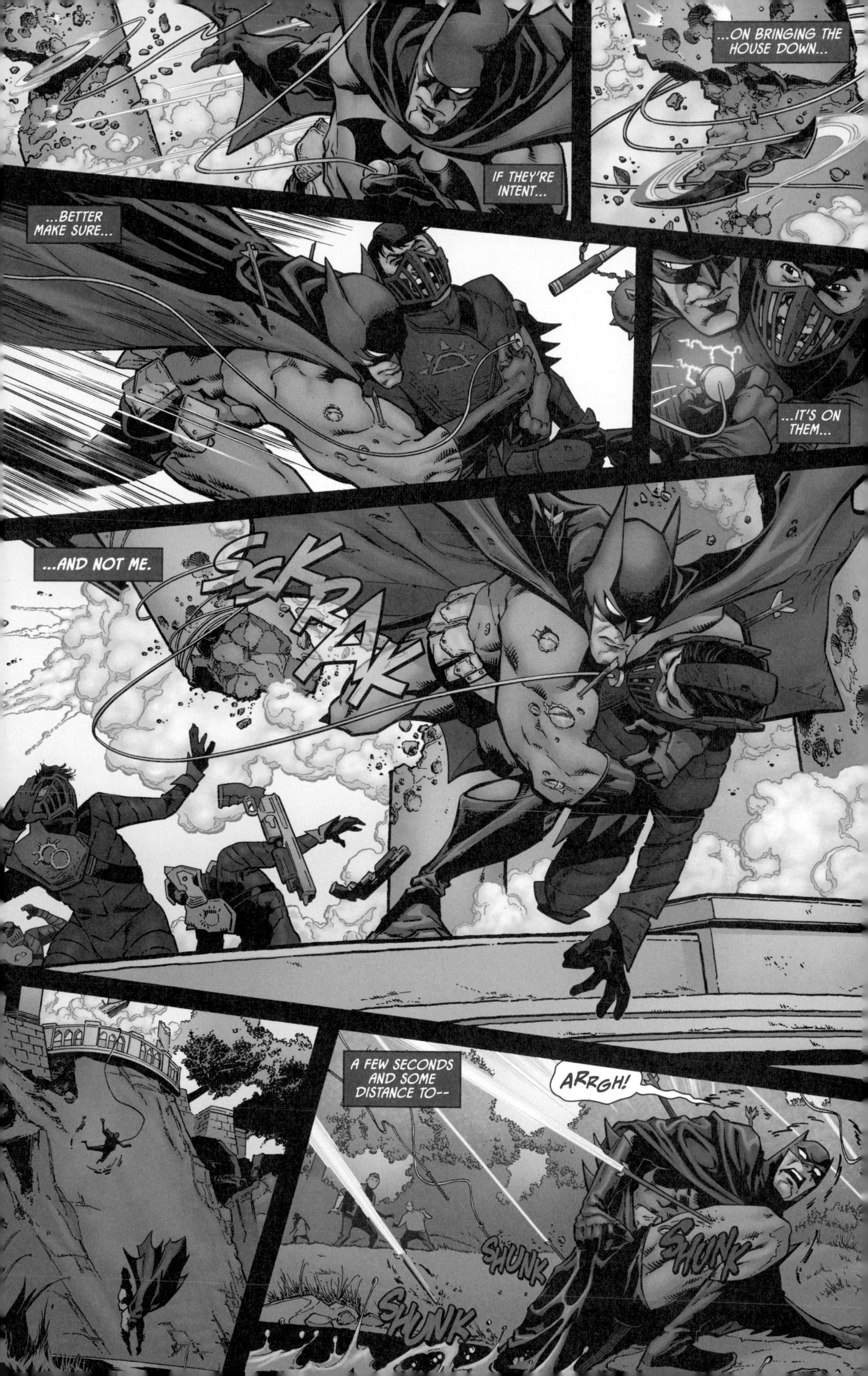
...ON BRINGING THE HOUSE DOWN...
IF THEY'RE INTENT...
...BETTER MAKE SURE...
...IT'S ON THEM...
...AND NOT ME.
SKRAK
A FEW SECONDS AND SOME DISTANCE TO--
ARRGH!
SHUNK
SHUNK
SHUNK

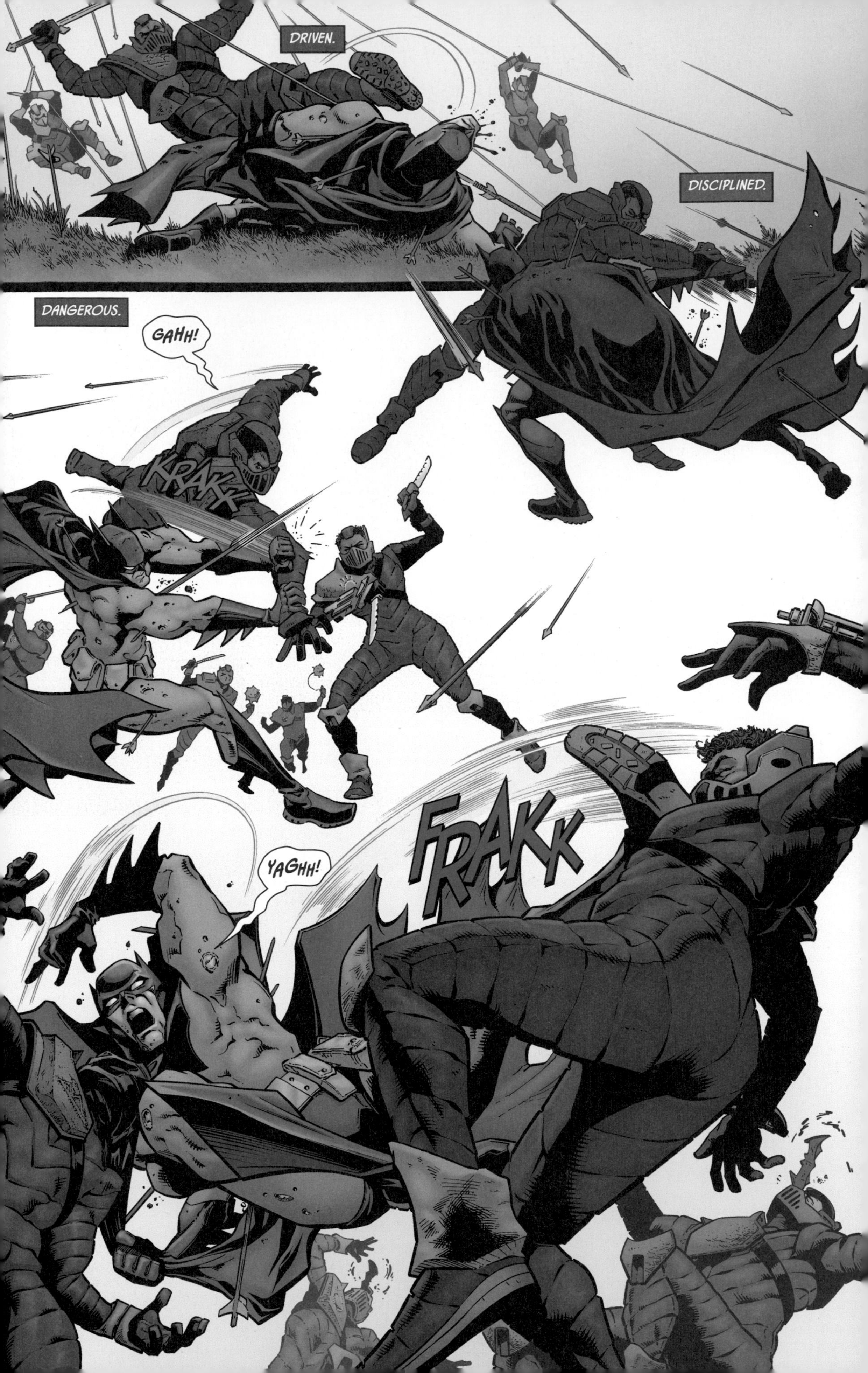
DRIVEN.
DISCIPLINED.
DANGEROUS.
GAHH!
KRAKK
YAGHH!
FRAKK

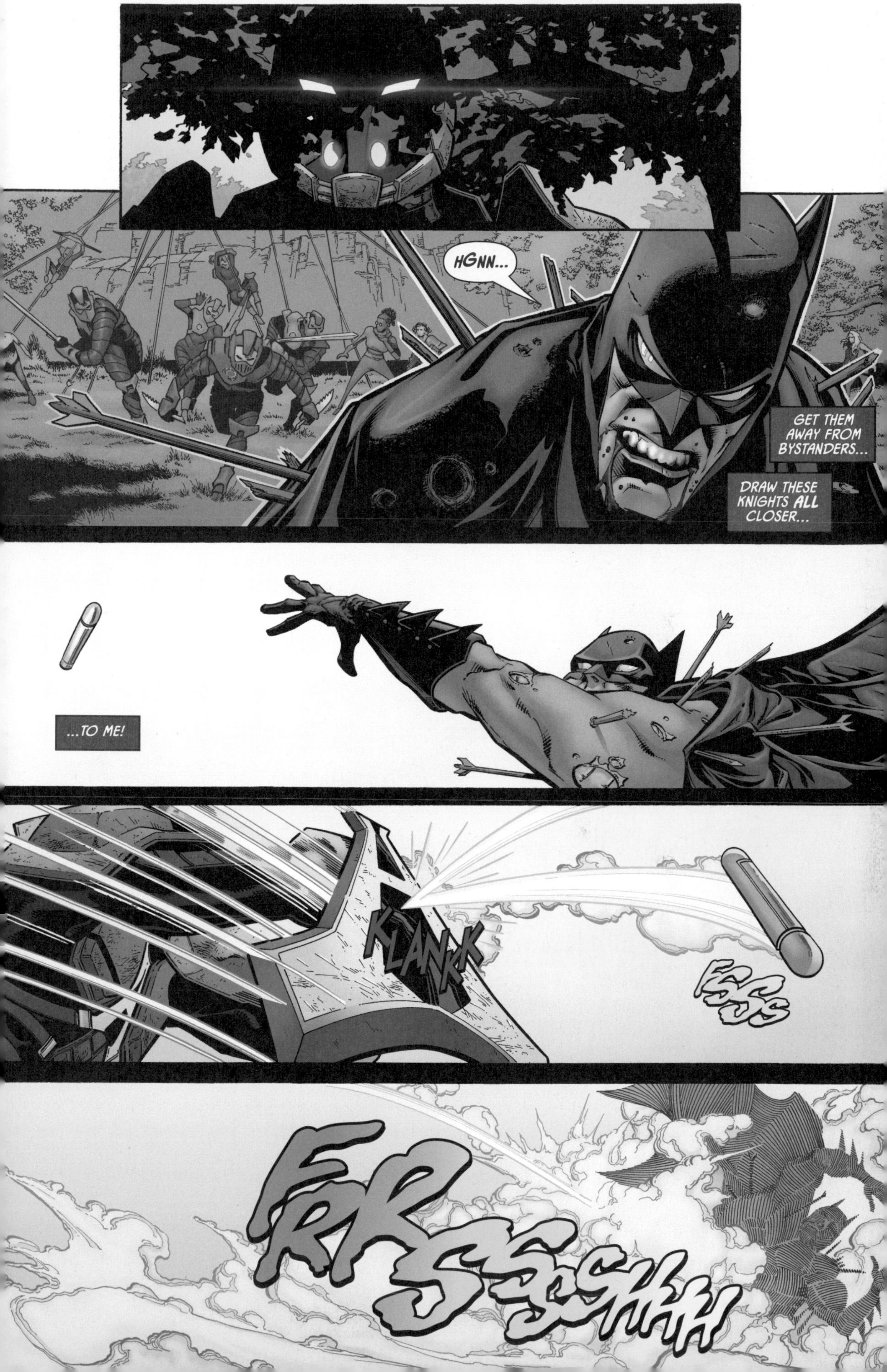
HGNN...
GET THEM AWAY FROM BYSTANDERS...
DRAW THESE KNIGHTS ALL CLOSER...
...TO ME!
KLANKK
FSSS
FRRSSSSHHH

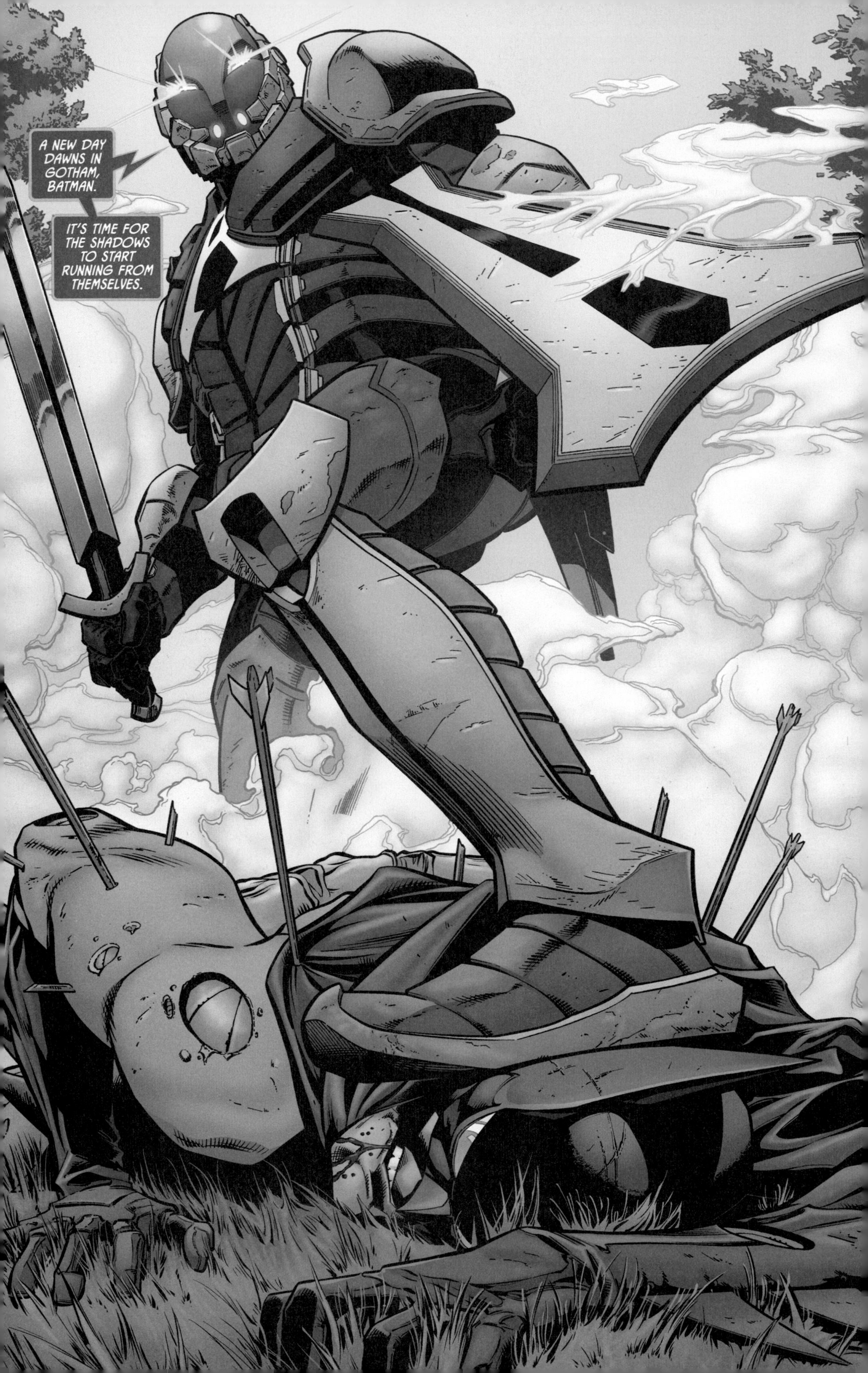
A NEW DAY DAWNS IN GOTHAM, BATMAN.
IT'S TIME FOR THE SHADOWS TO START RUNNING FROM THEMSELVES.

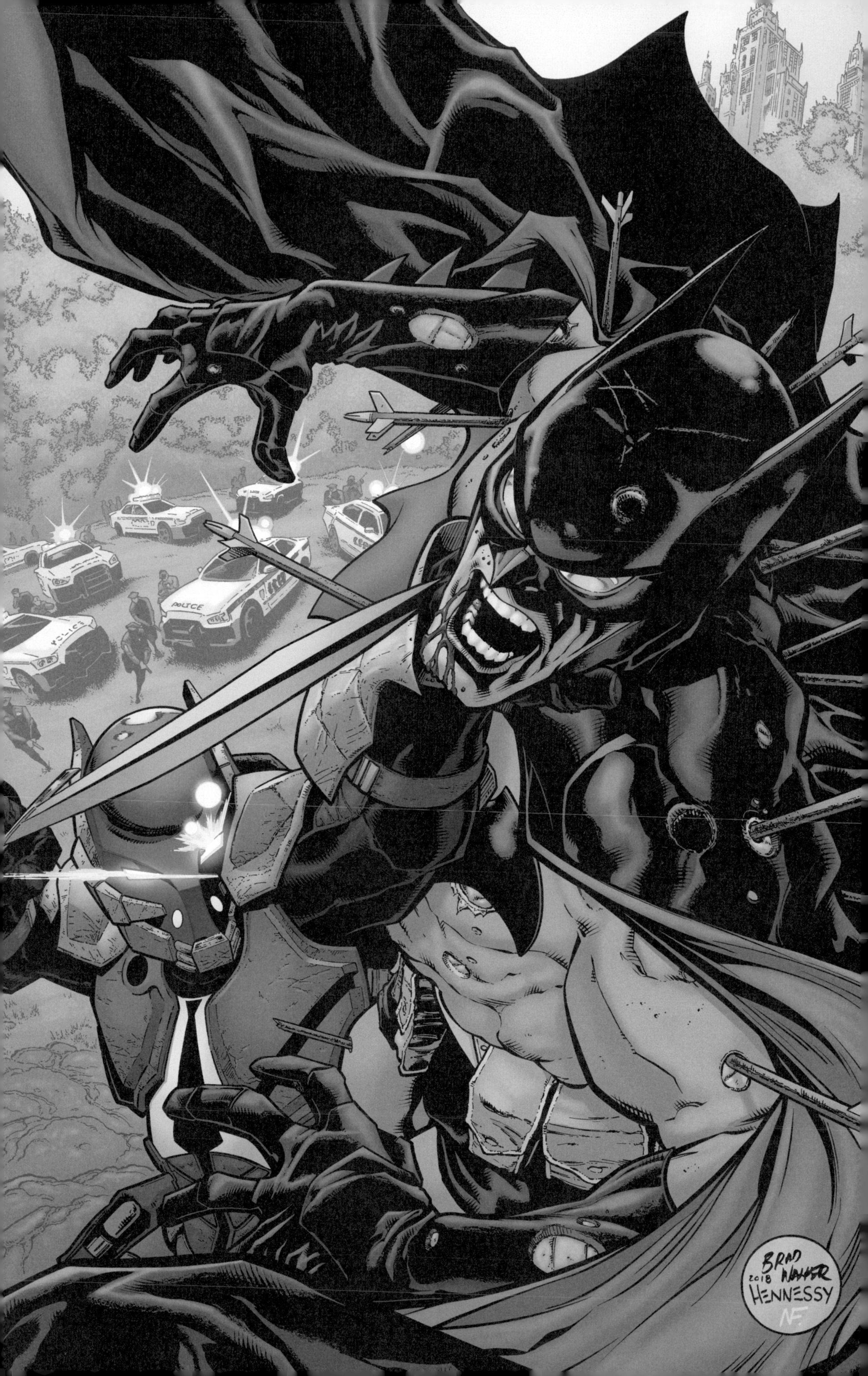
POLICE
BRAD WALKER
2018
HENNESSY
NF.

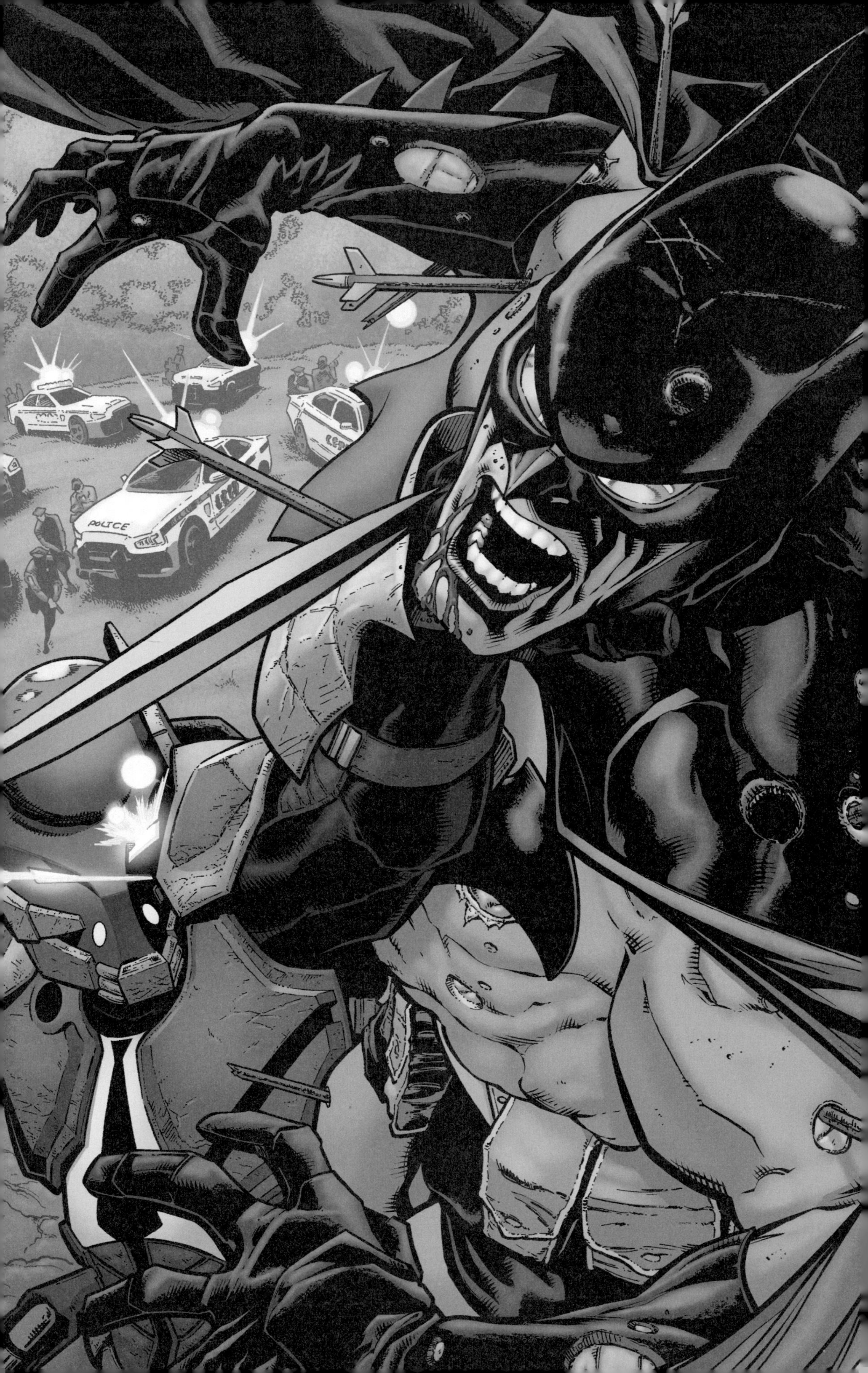
POLICE

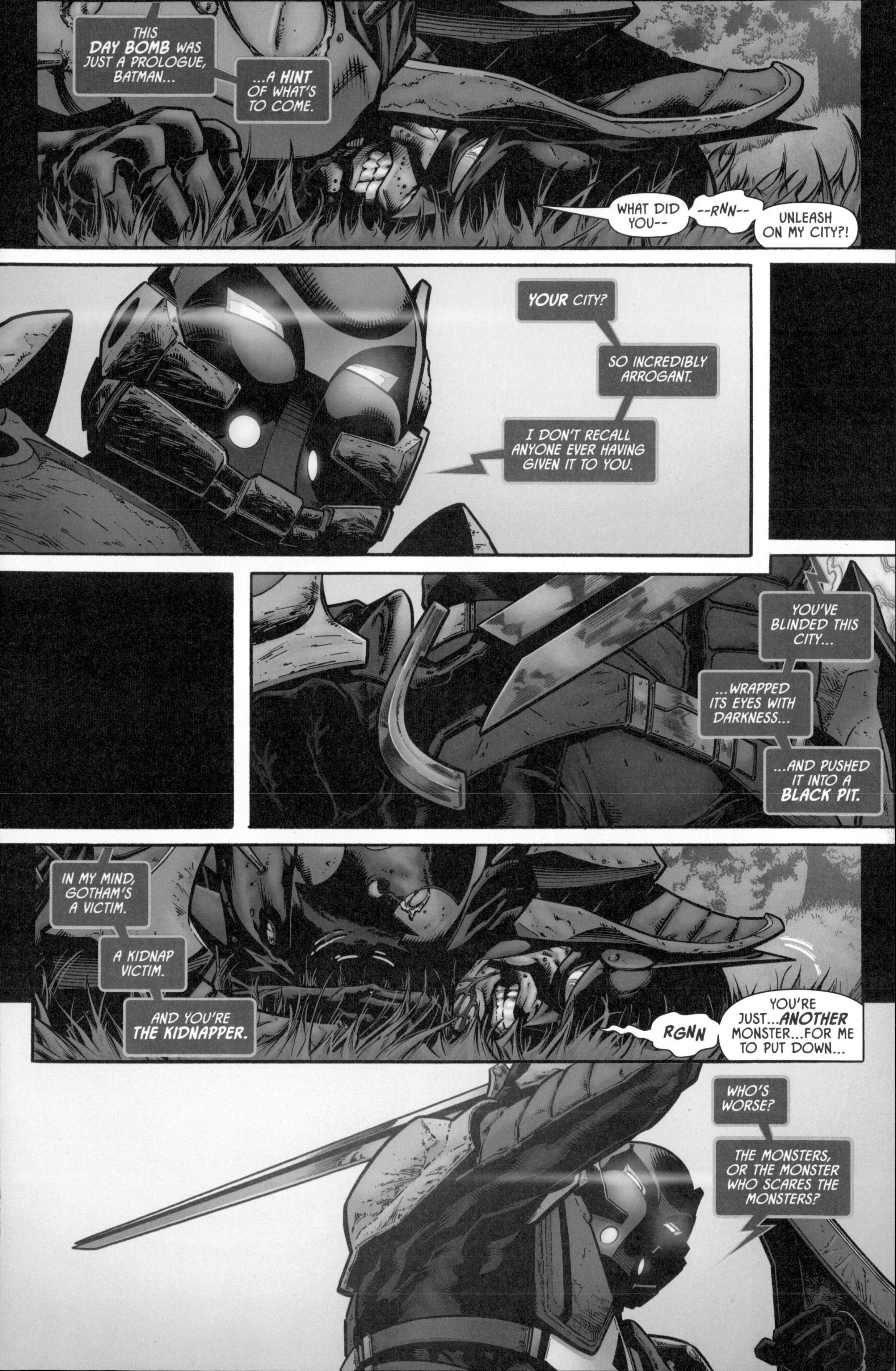
THIS DAY BOMB WAS JUST A PROLOGUE, BATMAN...
...A HINT OF WHAT'S TO COME.
WHAT DID YOU--
--RNN--
UNLEASH ON MY CITY?!
YOUR CITY?
SO INCREDIBLY ARROGANT.
I DON'T RECALL ANYONE EVER HAVING GIVEN IT TO YOU.
YOU'VE BLINDED THIS CITY...
...WRAPPED ITS EYES WITH DARKNESS...
...AND PUSHED IT INTO A BLACK PIT.
IN MY MIND, GOTHAM'S A VICTIM.
A KIDNAP VICTIM.
AND YOU'RE THE KIDNAPPER.
RGNN
YOU'RE JUST...ANOTHER MONSTER...FOR ME TO PUT DOWN...
WHO'S WORSE?
THE MONSTERS, OR THE MONSTER WHO SCARES THE MONSTERS?

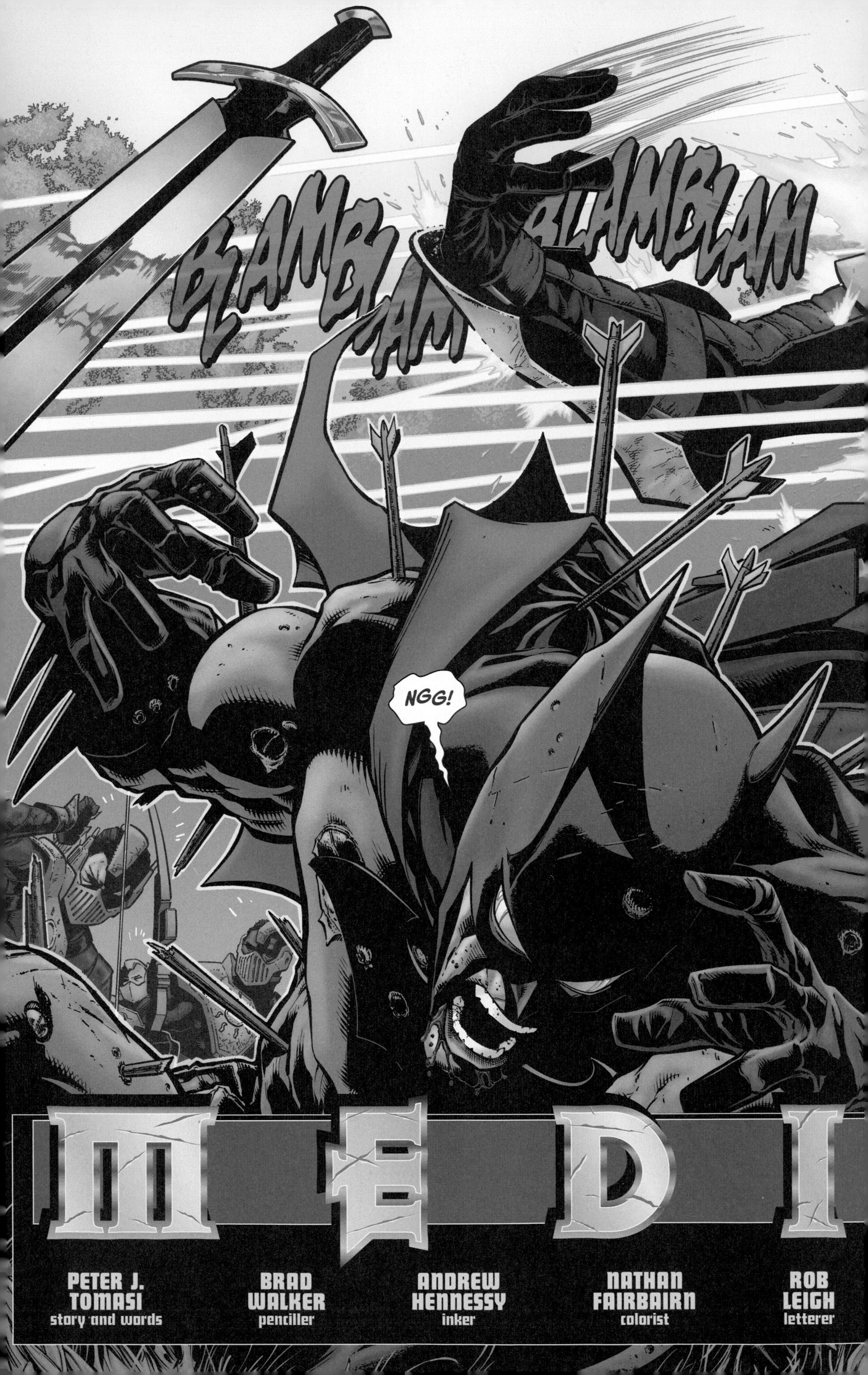

BLAMBLAM
BLAMBLAMBLAM
NGG!
MEDI
PETER J. TOMASI story and words
BRAD WALKER penciller
ANDREW HENNESSY inker
NATHAN FAIRBAIRN colorist
ROB LEIGH letterer

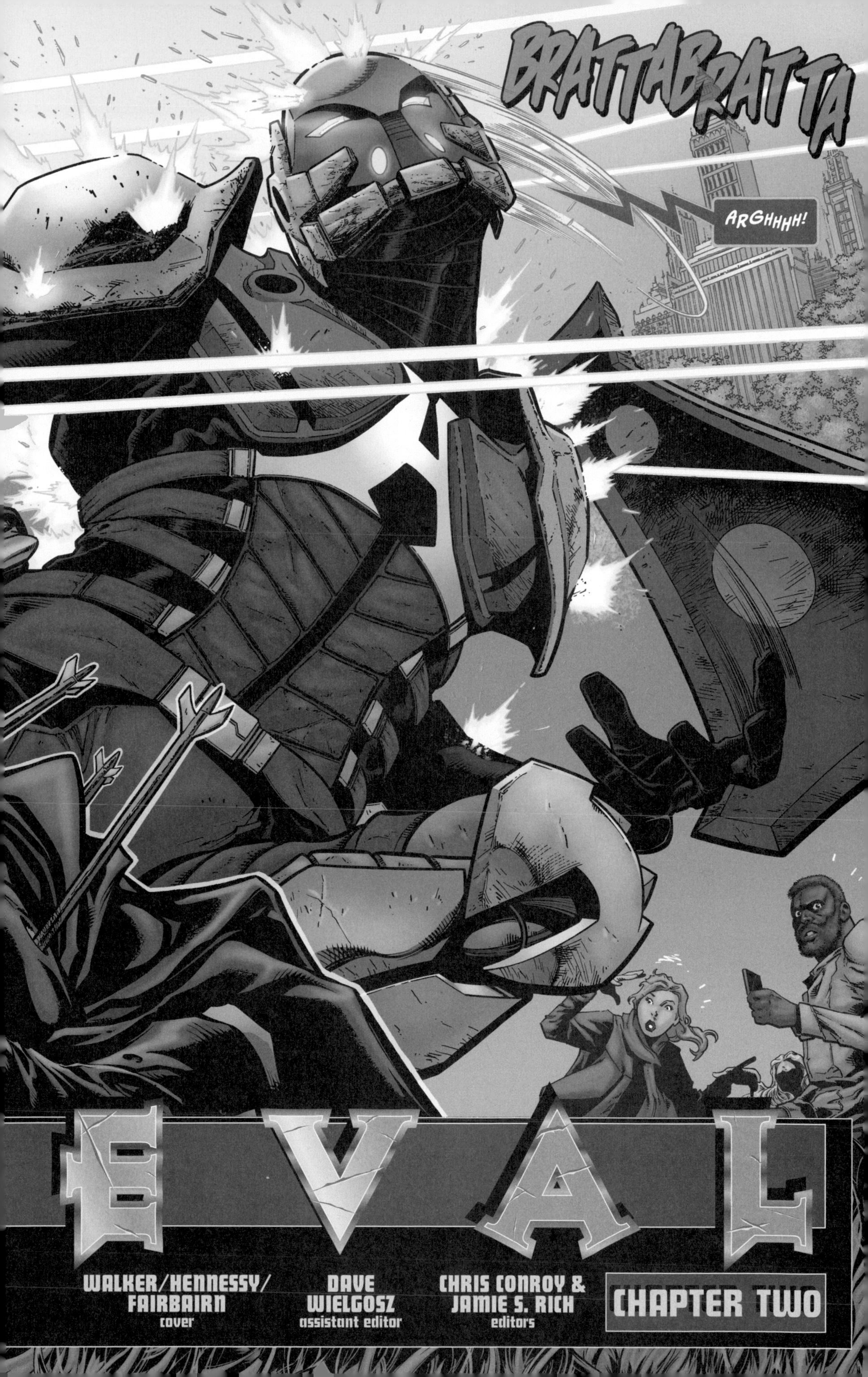
BRATTABRATTA
ARGHHHH!
E V A L
WALKER/HENNESSY/ FAIRBAIRN cover
DAVE WIELGOSZ assistant editor
CHRIS CONROY & JAMIE S. RICH editors
CHAPTER TWO

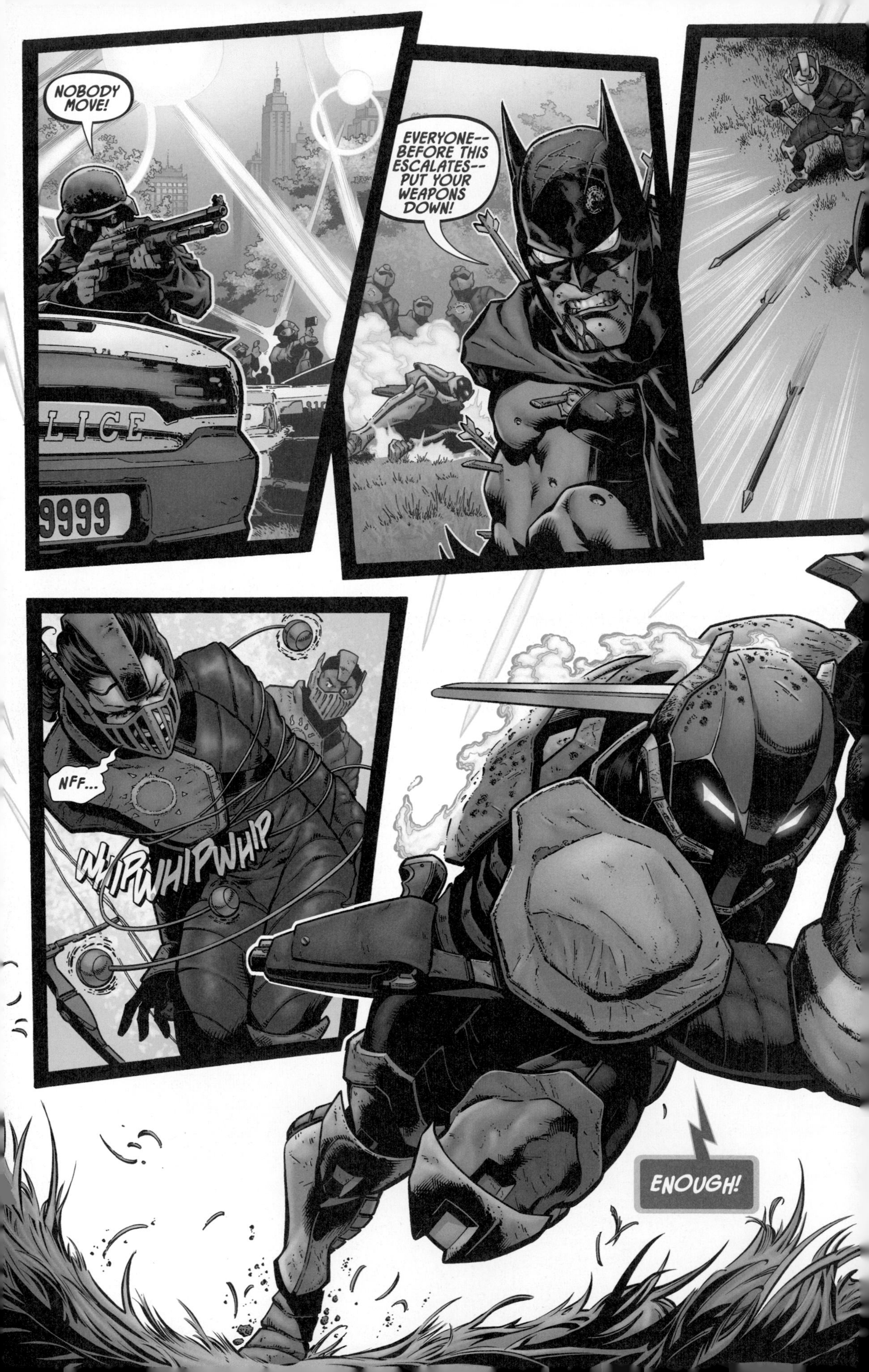
NOBODY MOVE!
LICE
9999
EVERYONE-- BEFORE THIS ESCALATES-- PUT YOUR WEAPONS DOWN!
NFF...
WHIPWHIPWHIP
ENOUGH!

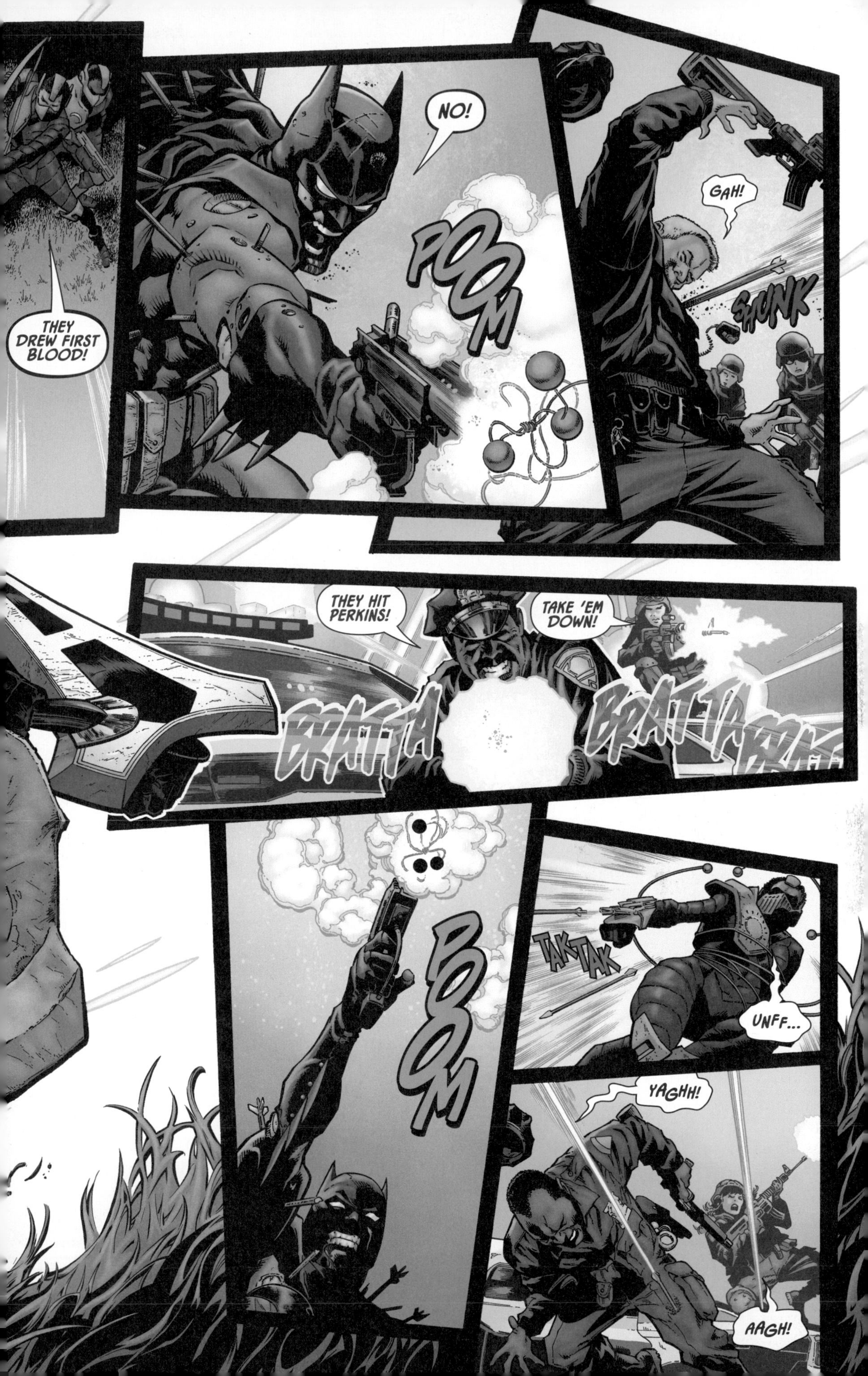
THEY DREW FIRST BLOOD!
NO!
POOOM
GAH!
SHUNK
THEY HIT PERKINS!
TAKE 'EM DOWN!
BRAT-TA
BRAT-TA
BOOOM
TAKTAK
UNFF...
YAGHH!
AAGH!

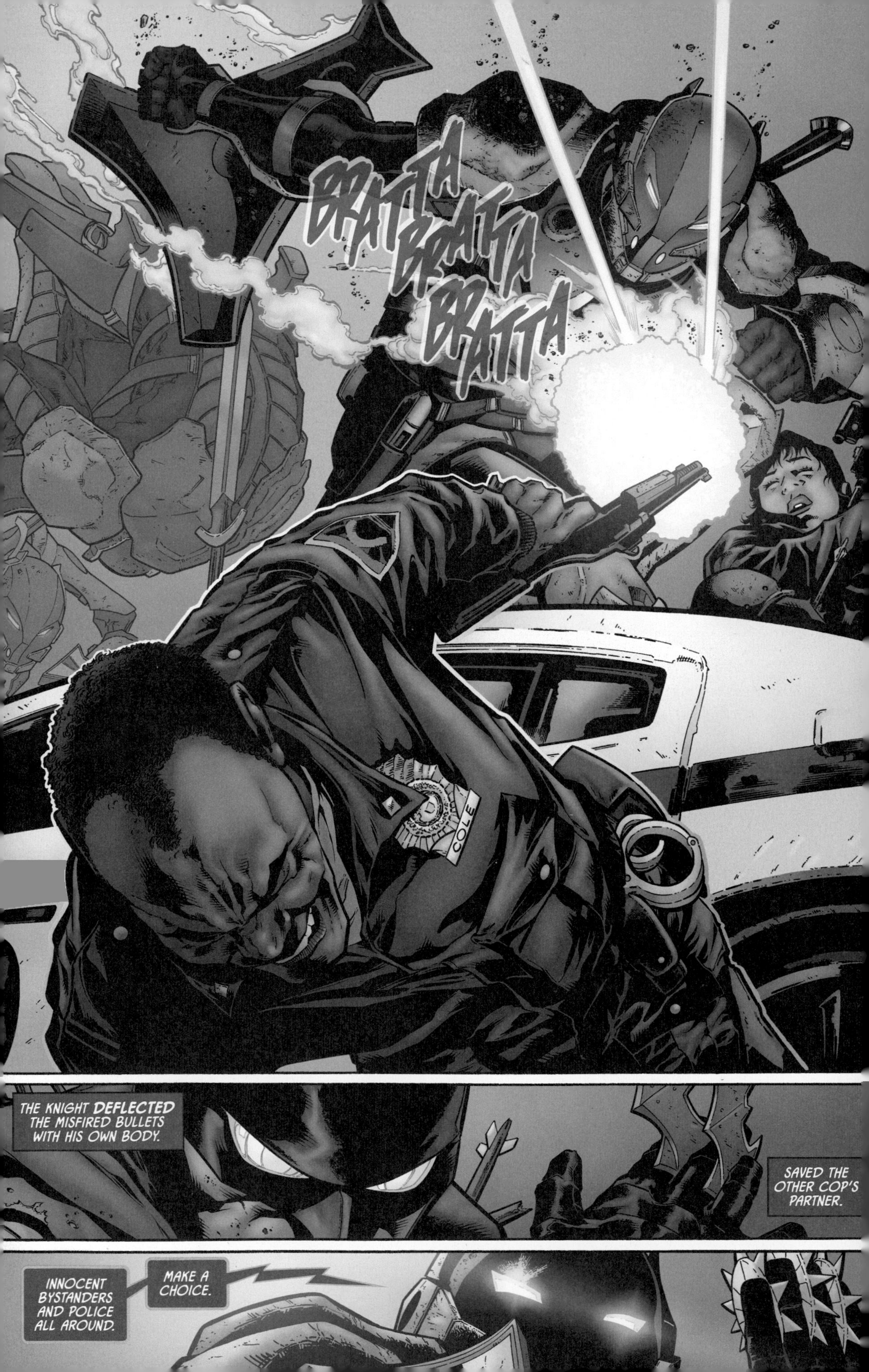
BRATTA
BRATTA
BRATTA
COLE
THE KNIGHT DEFLECTED THE MISFIRED BULLETS WITH HIS OWN BODY.
SAVED THE OTHER COP'S PARTNER.
INNOCENT BYSTANDERS AND POLICE ALL AROUND.
MAKE A CHOICE.

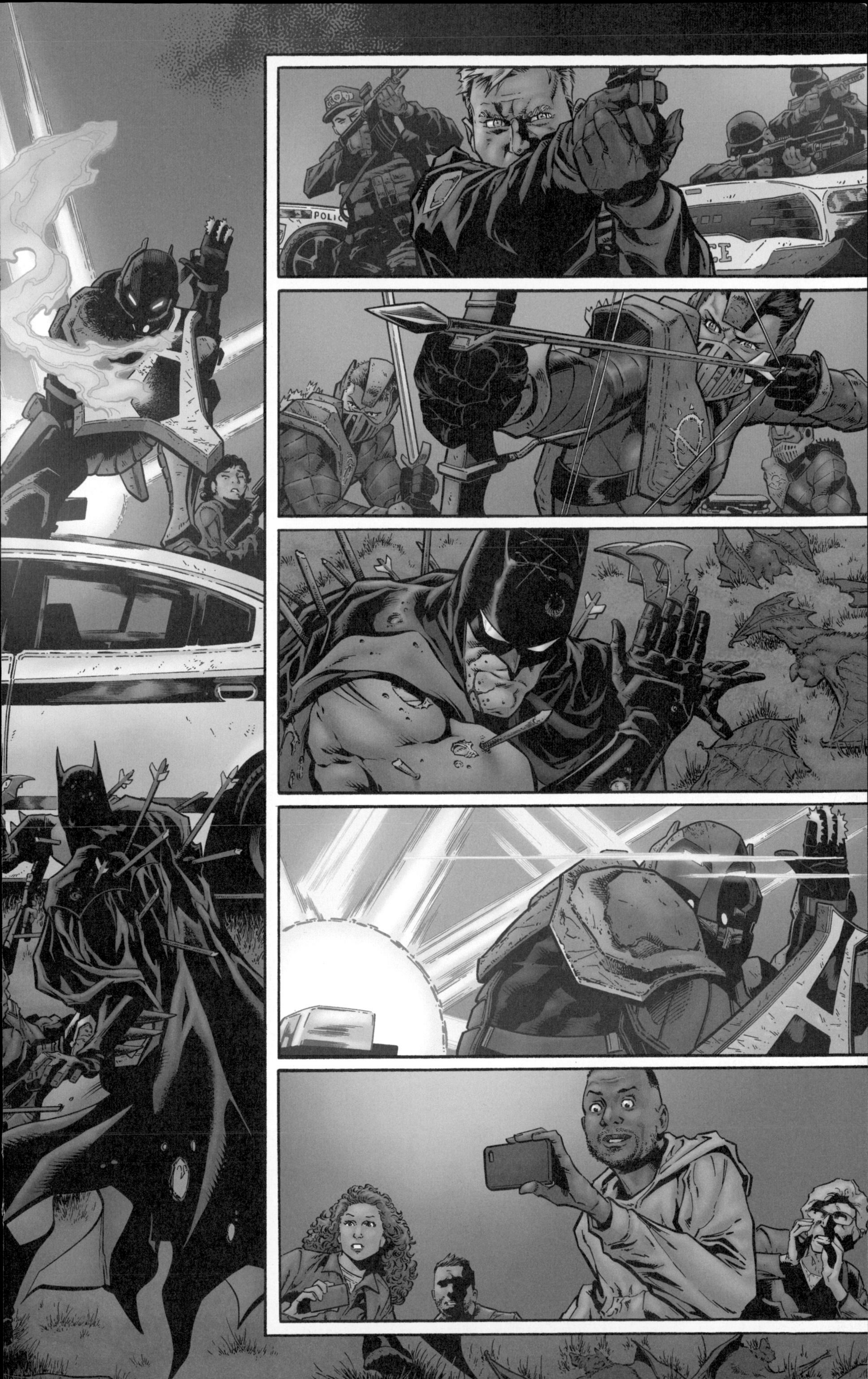

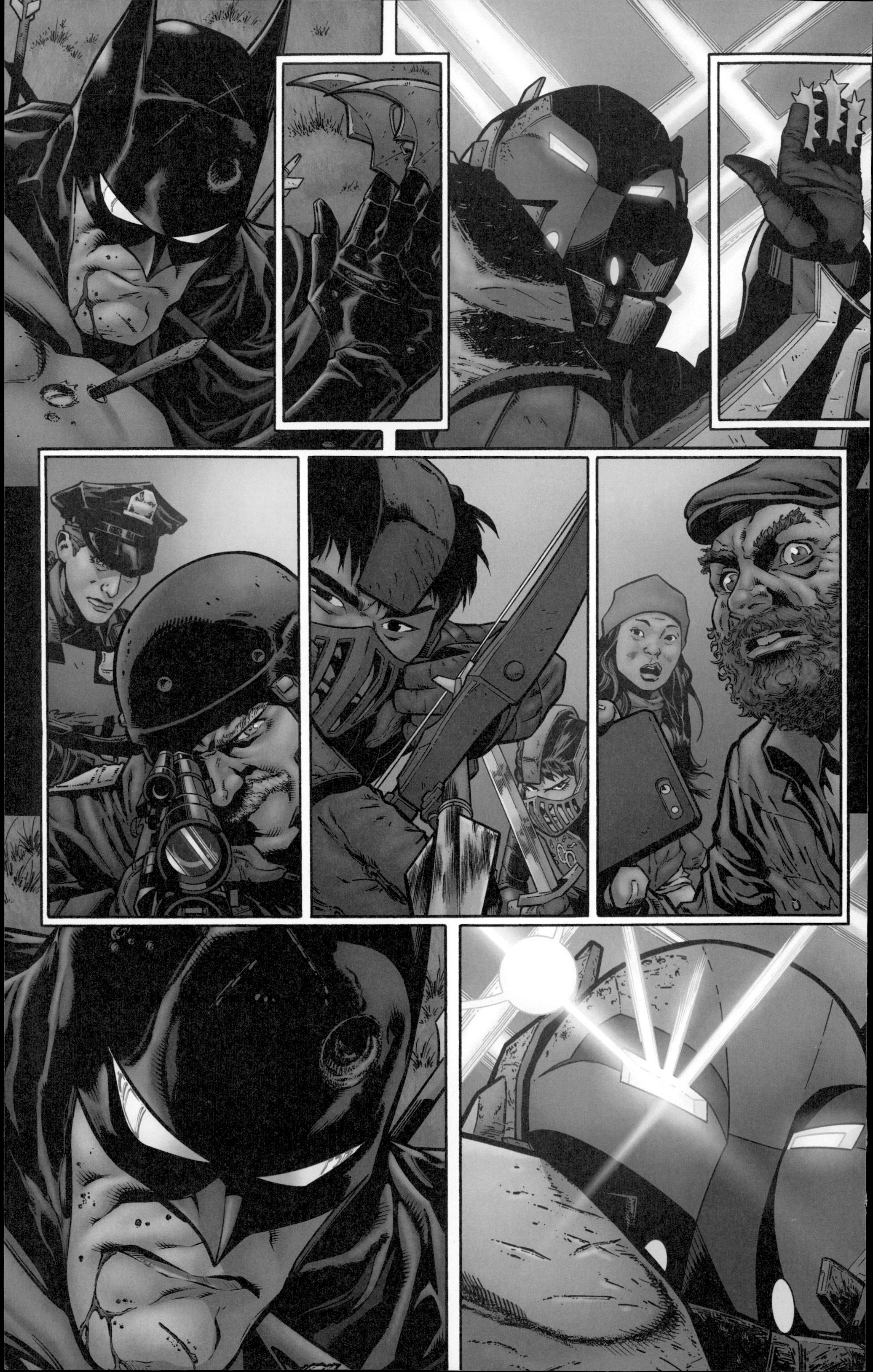

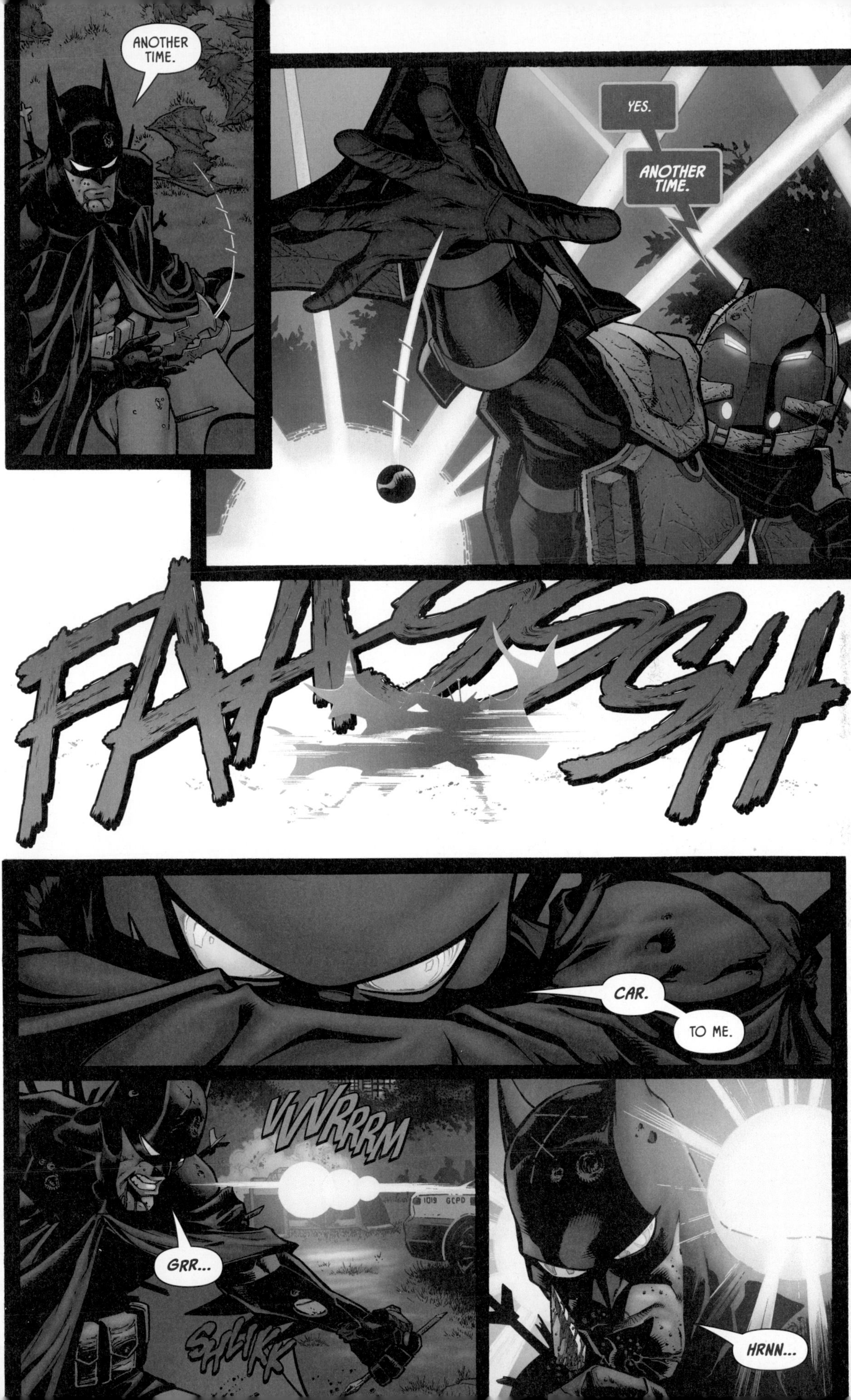

ANOTHER TIME.
YES.
ANOTHER TIME.
FAASSGH
CAR.
TO ME.
VVVRRRM
GRR...
SHLIKK
HRNN...

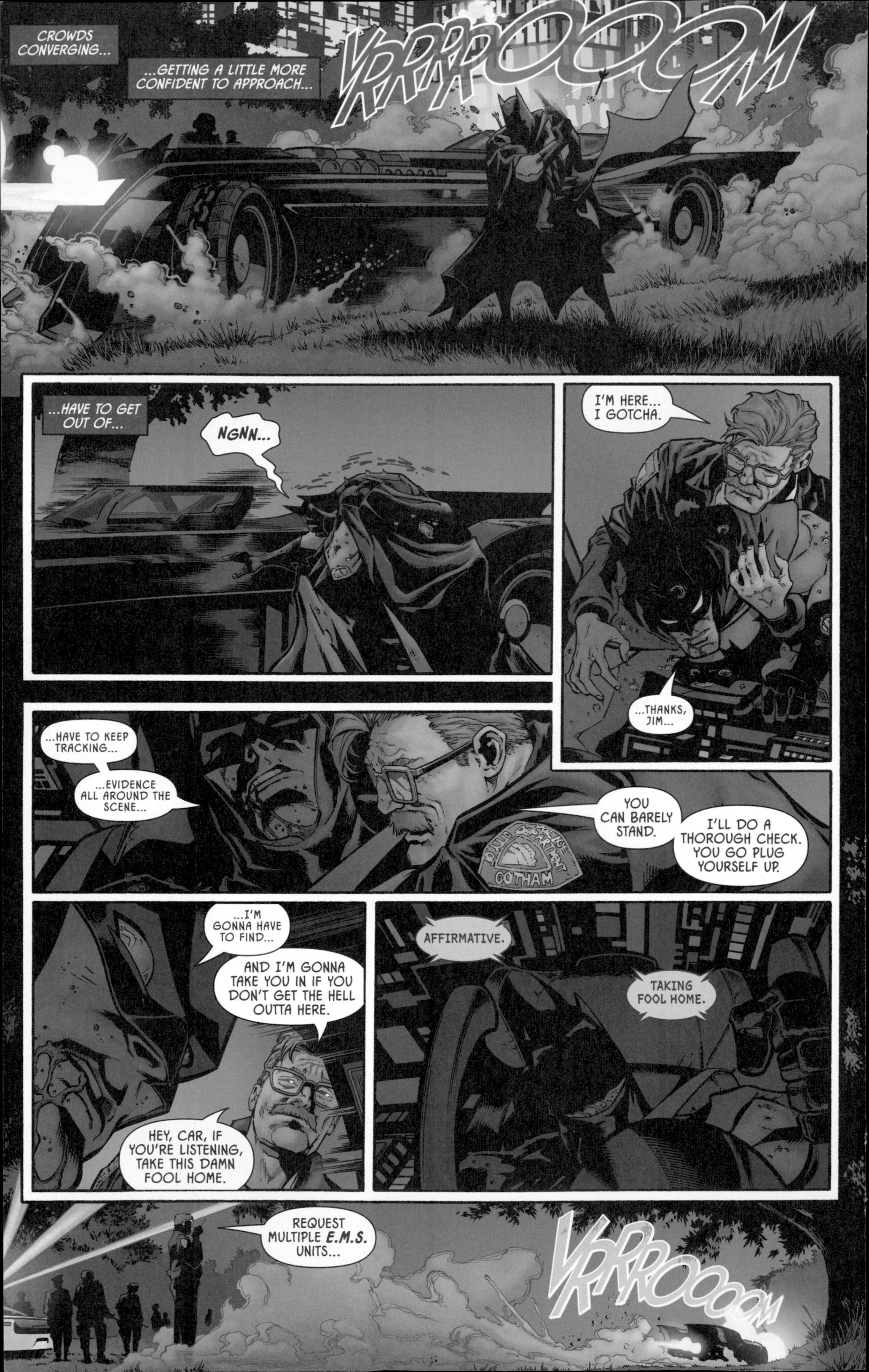
CROWDS CONVERGING...
...GETTING A LITTLE MORE CONFIDENT TO APPROACH...
VRRRROOOOM
...HAVE TO GET OUT OF...
NGNN...
I'M HERE... I GOTCHA.
...THANKS, JIM...
...HAVE TO KEEP TRACKING...
...EVIDENCE ALL AROUND THE SCENE...
YOU CAN BARELY STAND.
I'LL DO A THOROUGH CHECK. YOU GO PLUG YOURSELF UP.
GOTHAM
...I'M GONNA HAVE TO FIND...
AND I'M GONNA TAKE YOU IN IF YOU DON'T GET THE HELL OUTTA HERE.
HEY, CAR, IF YOU'RE LISTENING, TAKE THIS DAMN FOOL HOME.
AFFIRMATIVE.
TAKING FOOL HOME.
REQUEST MULTIPLE E.M.S. UNITS...
VRRROOOOOM

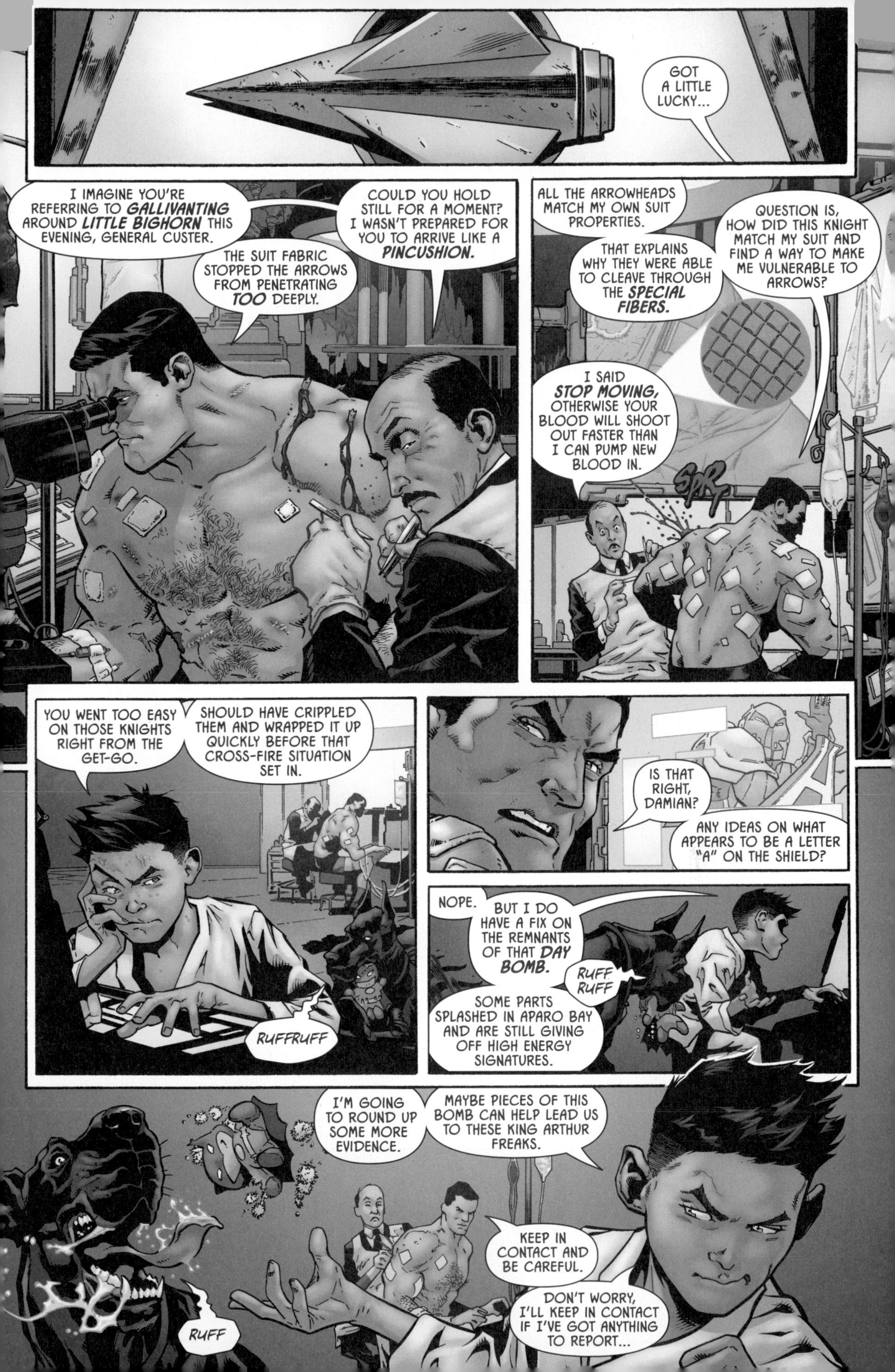
GOT A LITTLE LUCKY...
I IMAGINE YOU'RE REFERRING TO GALLIVANTING AROUND LITTLE BIGHORN THIS EVENING, GENERAL CUSTER.
COULD YOU HOLD STILL FOR A MOMENT? I WASN'T PREPARED FOR YOU TO ARRIVE LIKE A PINCUSHION.
THE SUIT FABRIC STOPPED THE ARROWS FROM PENETRATING TOO DEEPLY.
ALL THE ARROWHEADS MATCH MY OWN SUIT PROPERTIES.
THAT EXPLAINS WHY THEY WERE ABLE TO CLEAVE THROUGH THE SPECIAL FIBERS.
QUESTION IS, HOW DID THIS KNIGHT MATCH MY SUIT AND FIND A WAY TO MAKE ME VULNERABLE TO ARROWS?
I SAID STOP MOVING, OTHERWISE YOUR BLOOD WILL SHOOT OUT FASTER THAN I CAN PUMP NEW BLOOD IN.
SPRT
YOU WENT TOO EASY ON THOSE KNIGHTS RIGHT FROM THE GET-GO.
SHOULD HAVE CRIPPLED THEM AND WRAPPED IT UP QUICKLY BEFORE THAT CROSS-FIRE SITUATION SET IN.
RUFFRUFF
IS THAT RIGHT, DAMIAN?
ANY IDEAS ON WHAT APPEARS TO BE A LETTER "A" ON THE SHIELD?
NOPE.
BUT I DO HAVE A FIX ON THE REMNANTS OF THAT DAY BOMB.
RUFF RUFF
SOME PARTS SPLASHED IN APARO BAY AND ARE STILL GIVING OFF HIGH ENERGY SIGNATURES.
I'M GOING TO ROUND UP SOME MORE EVIDENCE.
MAYBE PIECES OF THIS BOMB CAN HELP LEAD US TO THESE KING ARTHUR FREAKS.
KEEP IN CONTACT AND BE CAREFUL.
DON'T WORRY, I'LL KEEP IN CONTACT IF I'VE GOT ANYTHING TO REPORT...
RUFF

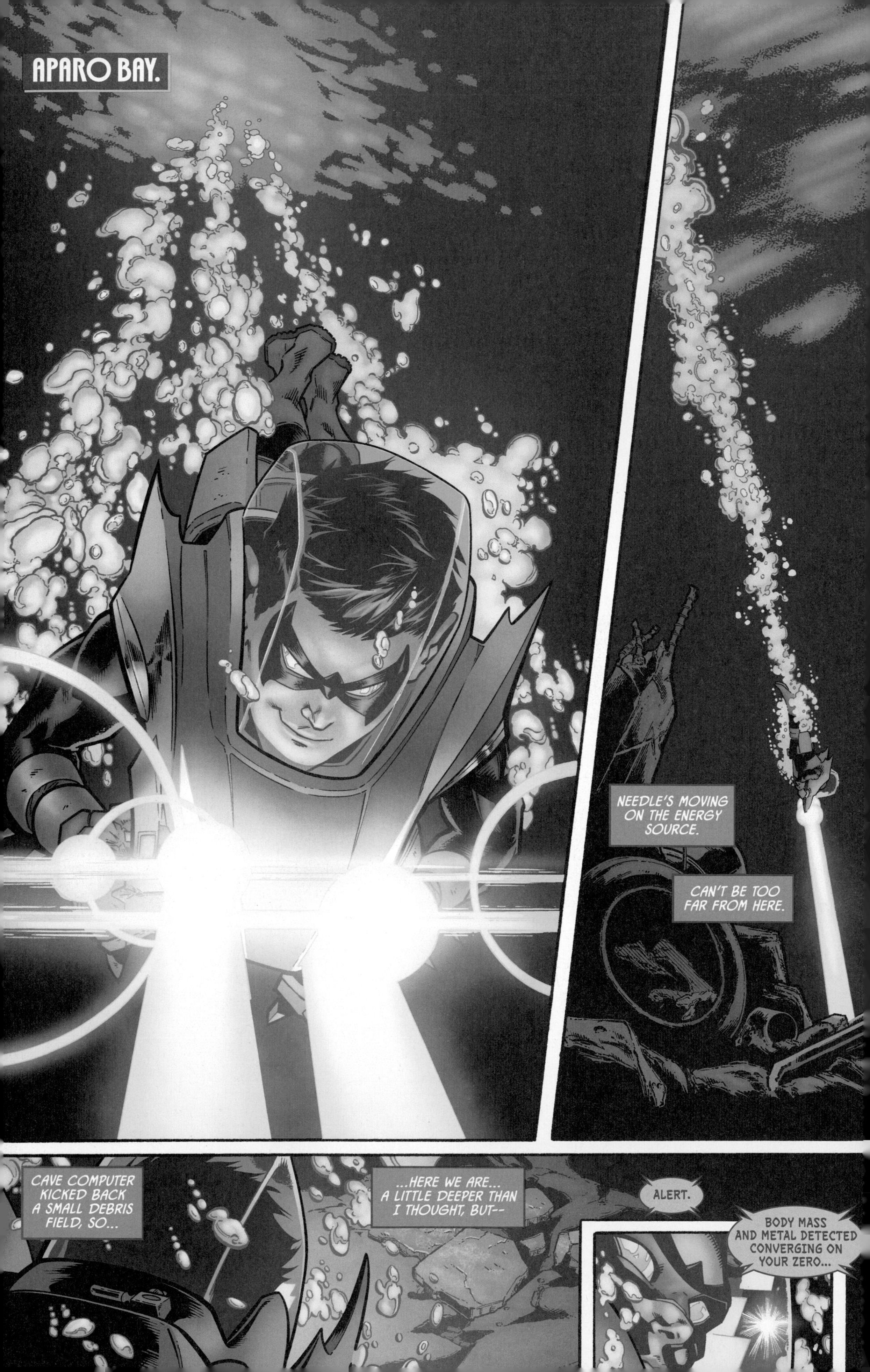
APARO BAY.
NEEDLE'S MOVING ON THE ENERGY SOURCE.
CAN'T BE TOO FAR FROM HERE.
CAVE COMPUTER KICKED BACK A SMALL DEBRIS FIELD, SO...
...HERE WE ARE... A LITTLE DEEPER THAN I THOUGHT, BUT--
ALERT.
BODY MASS AND METAL DETECTED CONVERGING ON YOUR ZERO...

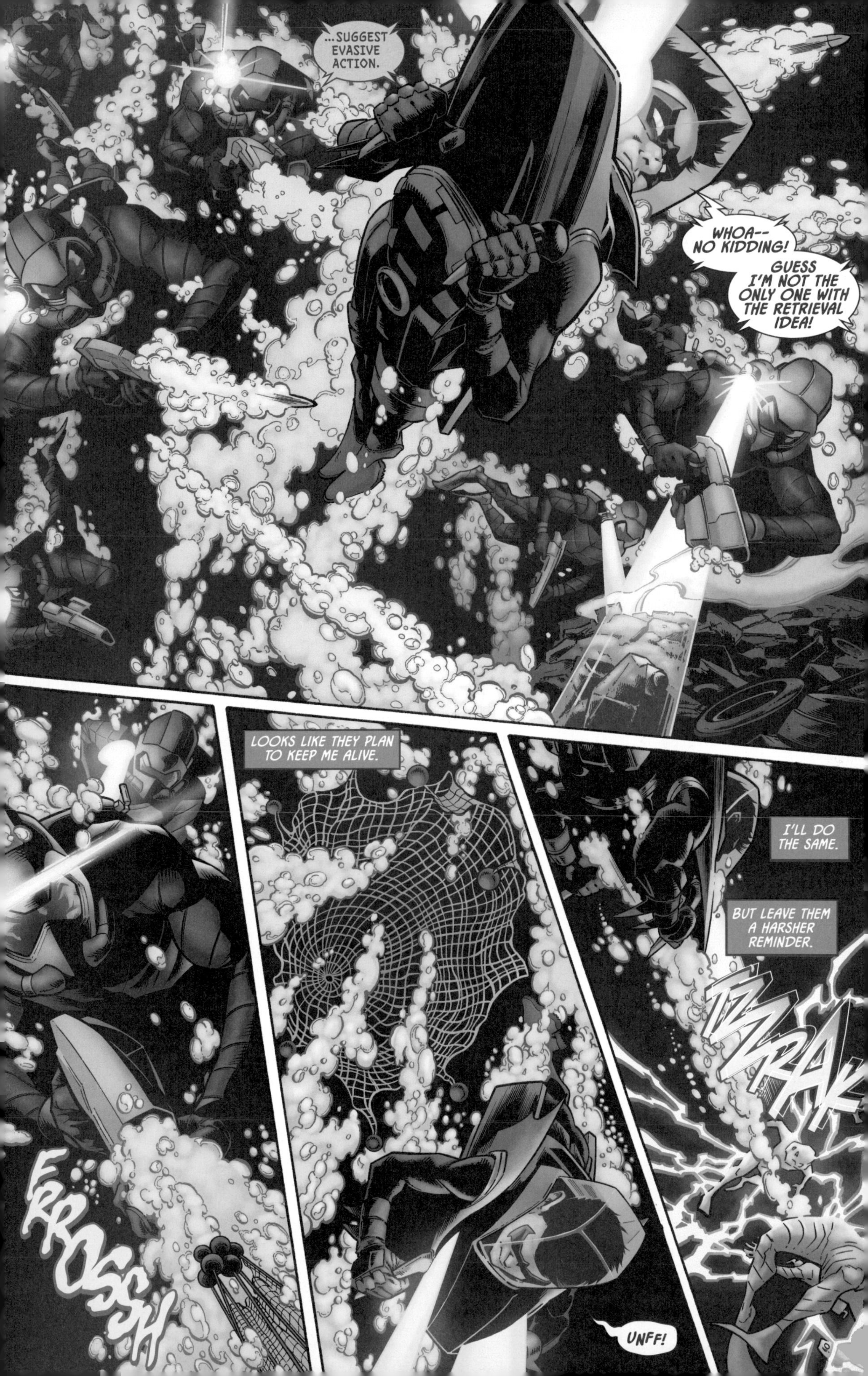
...SUGGEST EVASIVE ACTION.
WHOA-- NO KIDDING!
GUESS I'M NOT THE ONLY ONE WITH THE RETRIEVAL IDEA!
FRROSSH
LOOKS LIKE THEY PLAN TO KEEP ME ALIVE.
UNFF!
I'LL DO THE SAME.
BUT LEAVE THEM A HARSHER REMINDER.
TZZZRAK

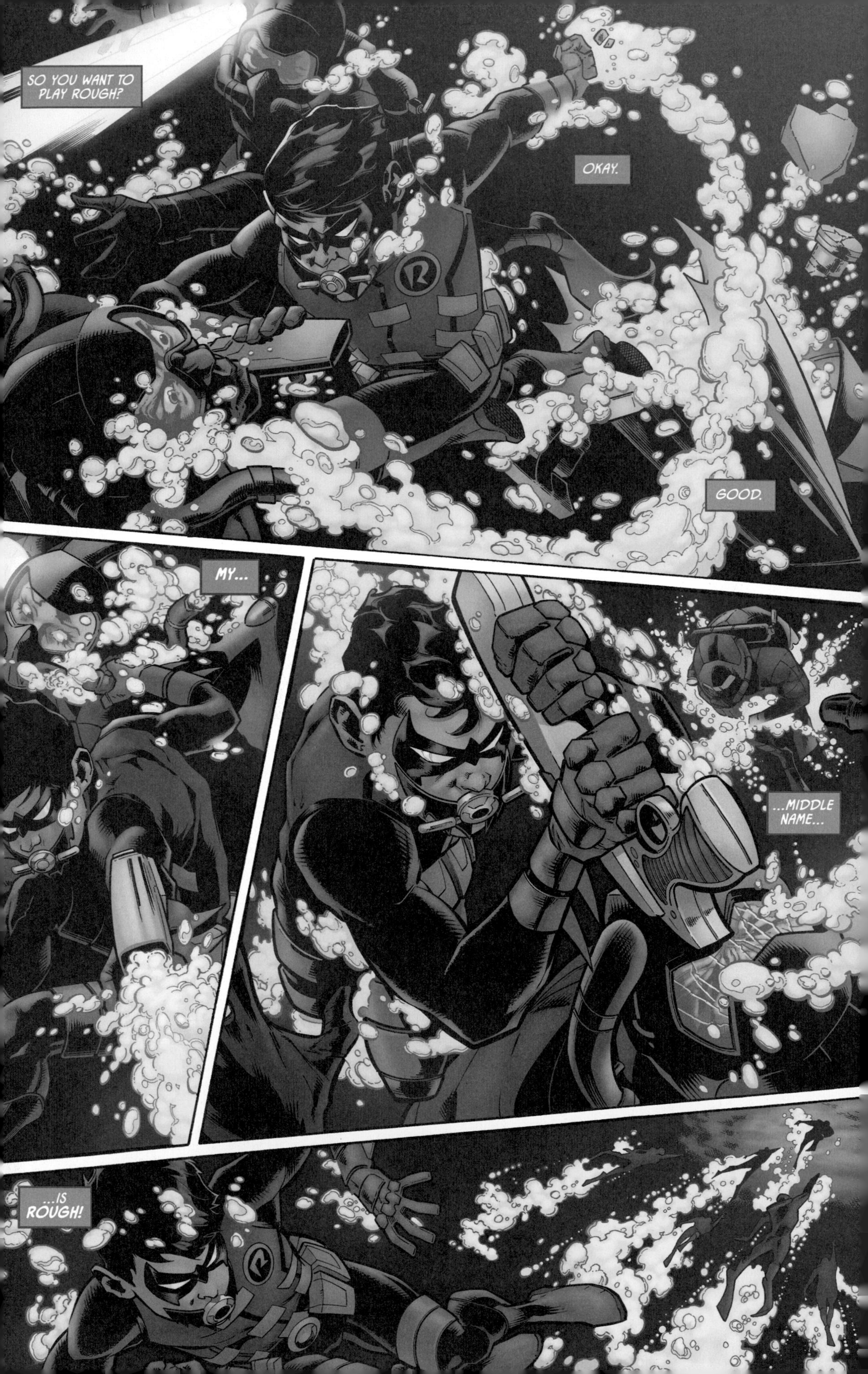
SO YOU WANT TO PLAY ROUGH?
OKAY.
GOOD.
MY...
...MIDDLE NAME...
...IS ROUGH!

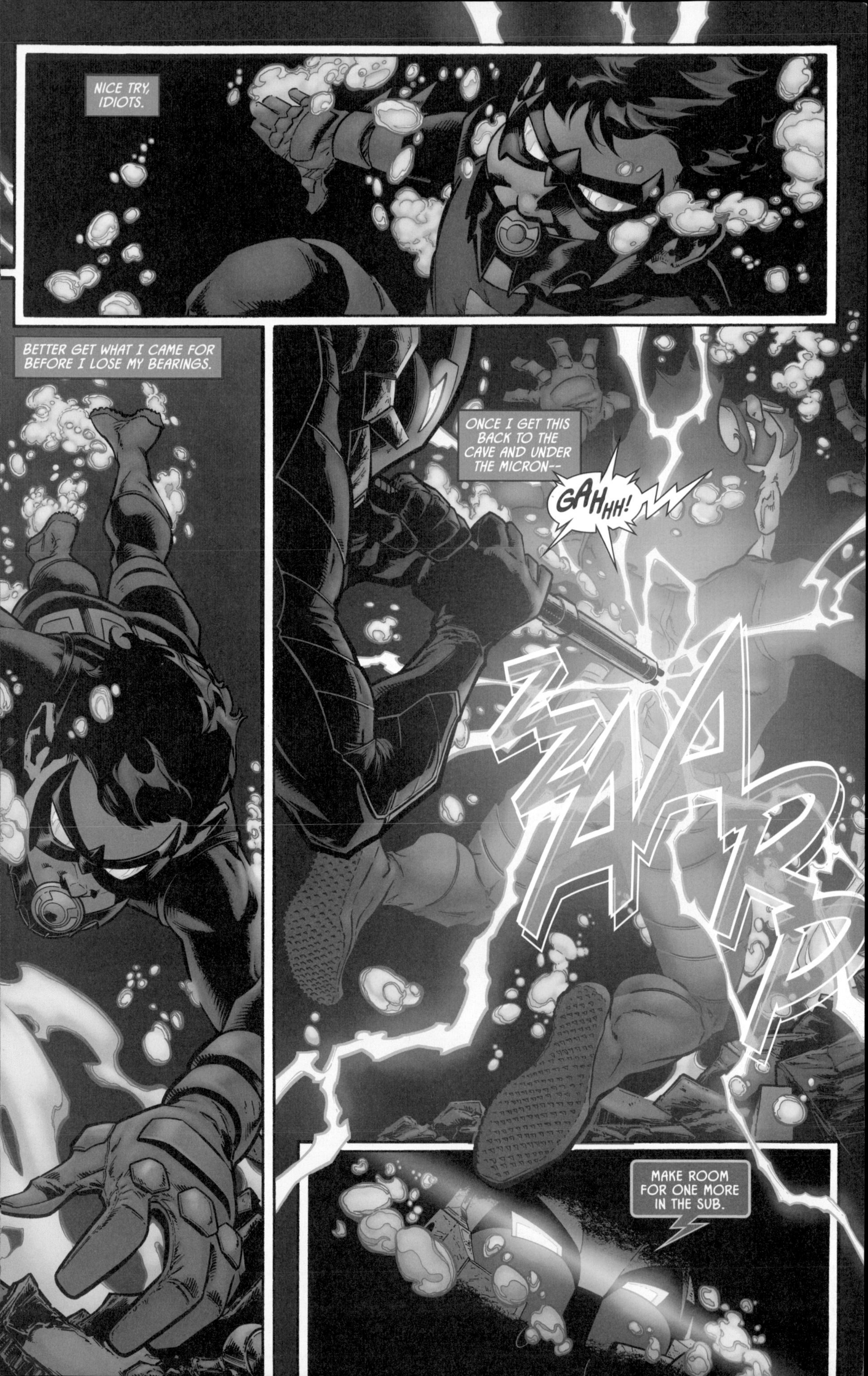
NICE TRY, IDIOTS.
BETTER GET WHAT I CAME FOR BEFORE I LOSE MY BEARINGS.
ONCE I GET THIS BACK TO THE CAVE AND UNDER THE MICRON--
GAHHH!
ZZAP
MAKE ROOM FOR ONE MORE IN THE SUB.

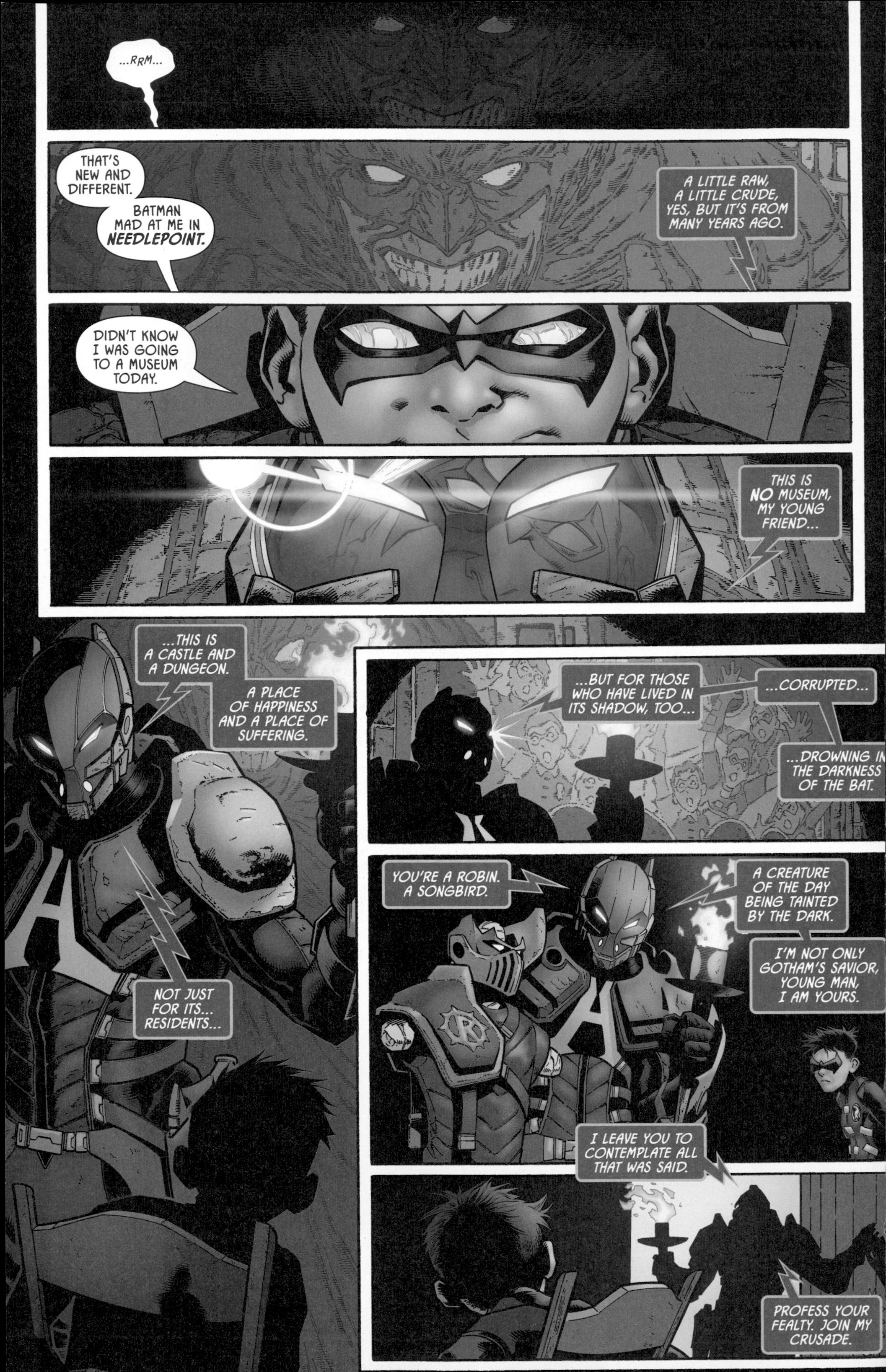
...RRM...
THAT'S NEW AND DIFFERENT.
BATMAN MAD AT ME IN NEEDLEPOINT.
A LITTLE RAW, A LITTLE CRUDE, YES, BUT IT'S FROM MANY YEARS AGO.
DIDN'T KNOW I WAS GOING TO A MUSEUM TODAY.
THIS IS NO MUSEUM, MY YOUNG FRIEND...
...THIS IS A CASTLE AND A DUNGEON.
A PLACE OF HAPPINESS AND A PLACE OF SUFFERING.
NOT JUST FOR ITS... RESIDENTS...
...BUT FOR THOSE WHO HAVE LIVED IN ITS SHADOW, TOO...
...CORRUPTED...
...DROWNING IN THE DARKNESS OF THE BAT.
YOU'RE A ROBIN. A SONGBIRD.
A CREATURE OF THE DAY BEING TAINTED BY THE DARK.
I'M NOT ONLY GOTHAM'S SAVIOR, YOUNG MAN, I AM YOURS.
I LEAVE YOU TO CONTEMPLATE ALL THAT WAS SAID.
PROFESS YOUR FEALTY. JOIN MY CRUSADE.

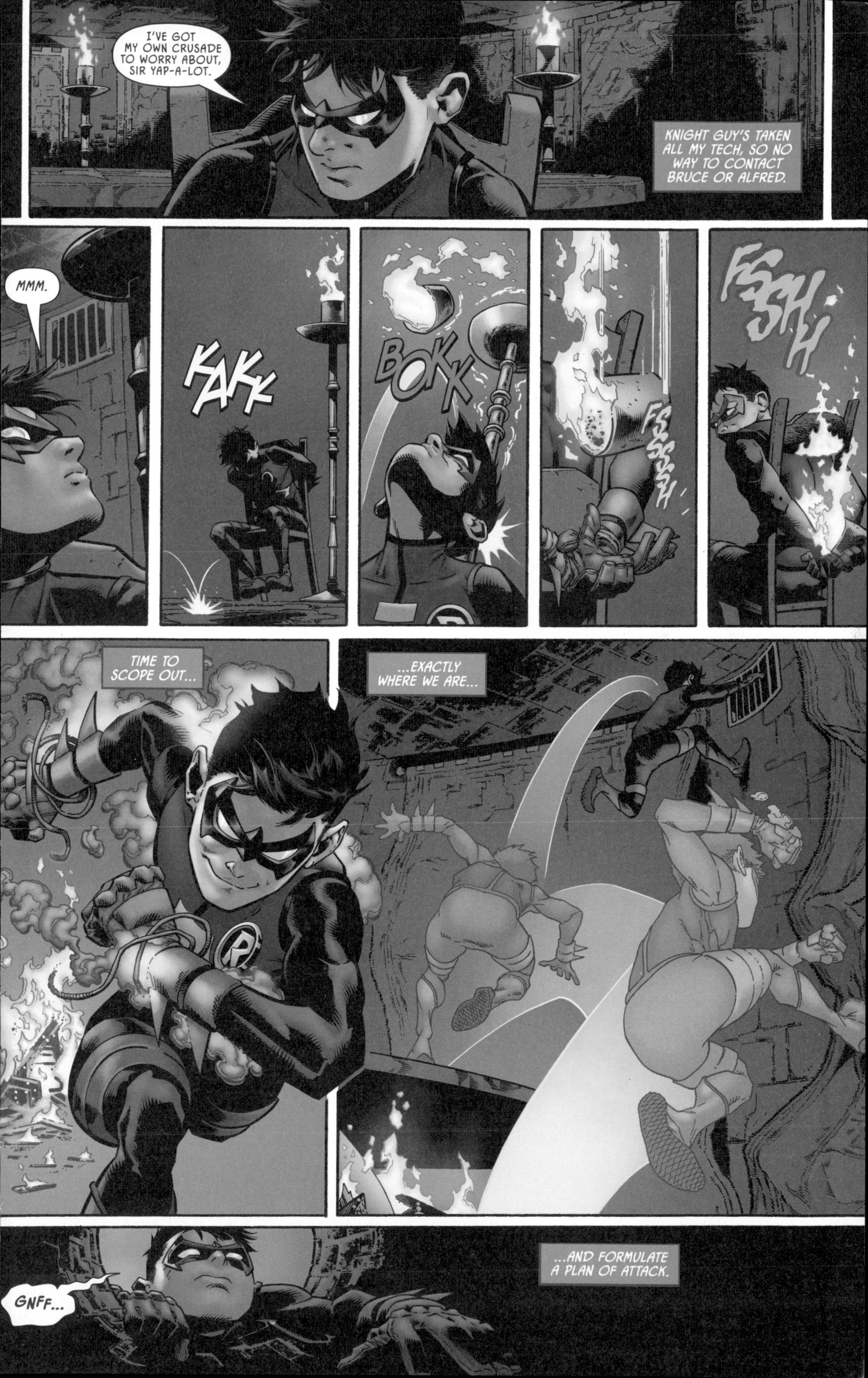

I'VE GOT MY OWN CRUSADE TO WORRY ABOUT, SIR YAP-A-LOT.
KNIGHT GUY'S TAKEN ALL MY TECH, SO NO WAY TO CONTACT BRUCE OR ALFRED.
MMM.
KAKK
BOKK
FSSSSH
FSSHH
TIME TO SCOPE OUT...
...EXACTLY WHERE WE ARE...
...AND FORMULATE A PLAN OF ATTACK.
GNFF...

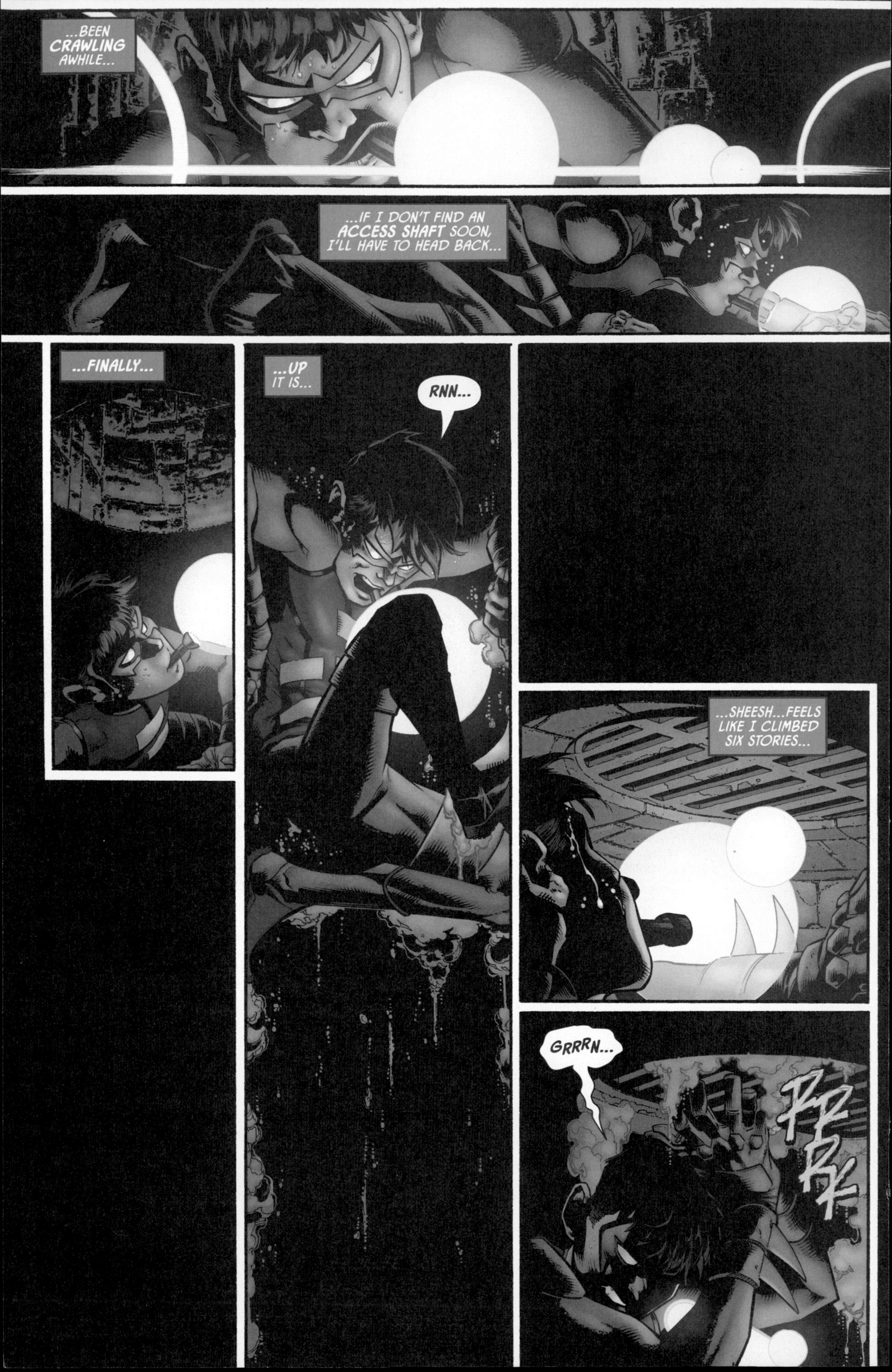
...BEEN CRAWLING AWHILE...
...IF I DON'T FIND AN ACCESS SHAFT SOON, I'LL HAVE TO HEAD BACK...
...FINALLY...
...UP IT IS...
RNN...
...SHEESH...FEELS LIKE I CLIMBED SIX STORIES...
GRRRN...
PRRRK

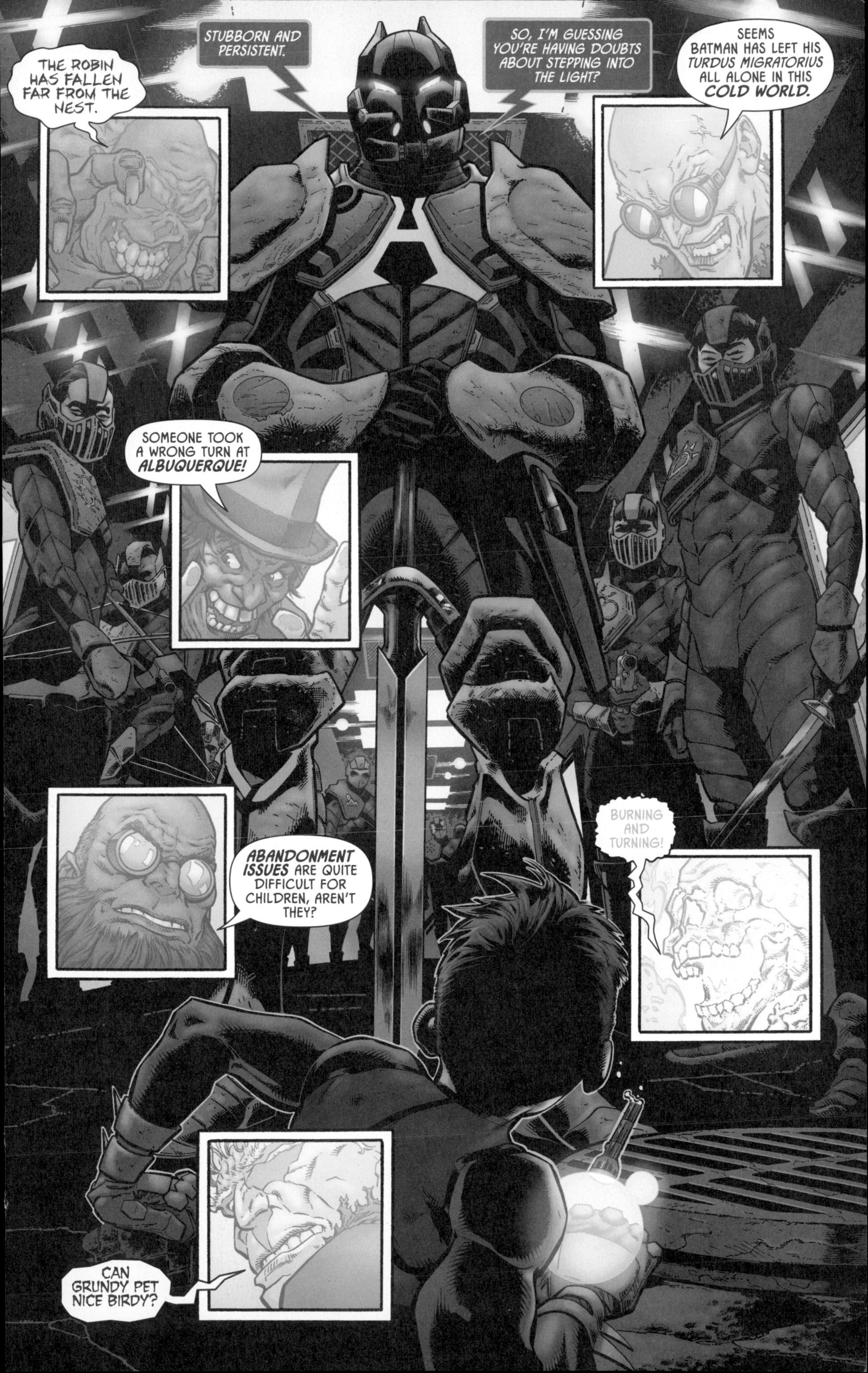
THE ROBIN HAS FALLEN FAR FROM THE NEST.
STUBBORN AND PERSISTENT.
SO, I'M GUESSING YOU'RE HAVING DOUBTS ABOUT STEPPING INTO THE LIGHT?
SEEMS BATMAN HAS LEFT HIS TURDUS MIGRATORIUS ALL ALONE IN THIS COLD WORLD.
SOMEONE TOOK A WRONG TURN AT ALBUQUERQUE!
BURNING AND TURNING!
ABANDONMENT ISSUES ARE QUITE DIFFICULT FOR CHILDREN, AREN'T THEY?
CAN GRUNDY PET NICE BIRDY?

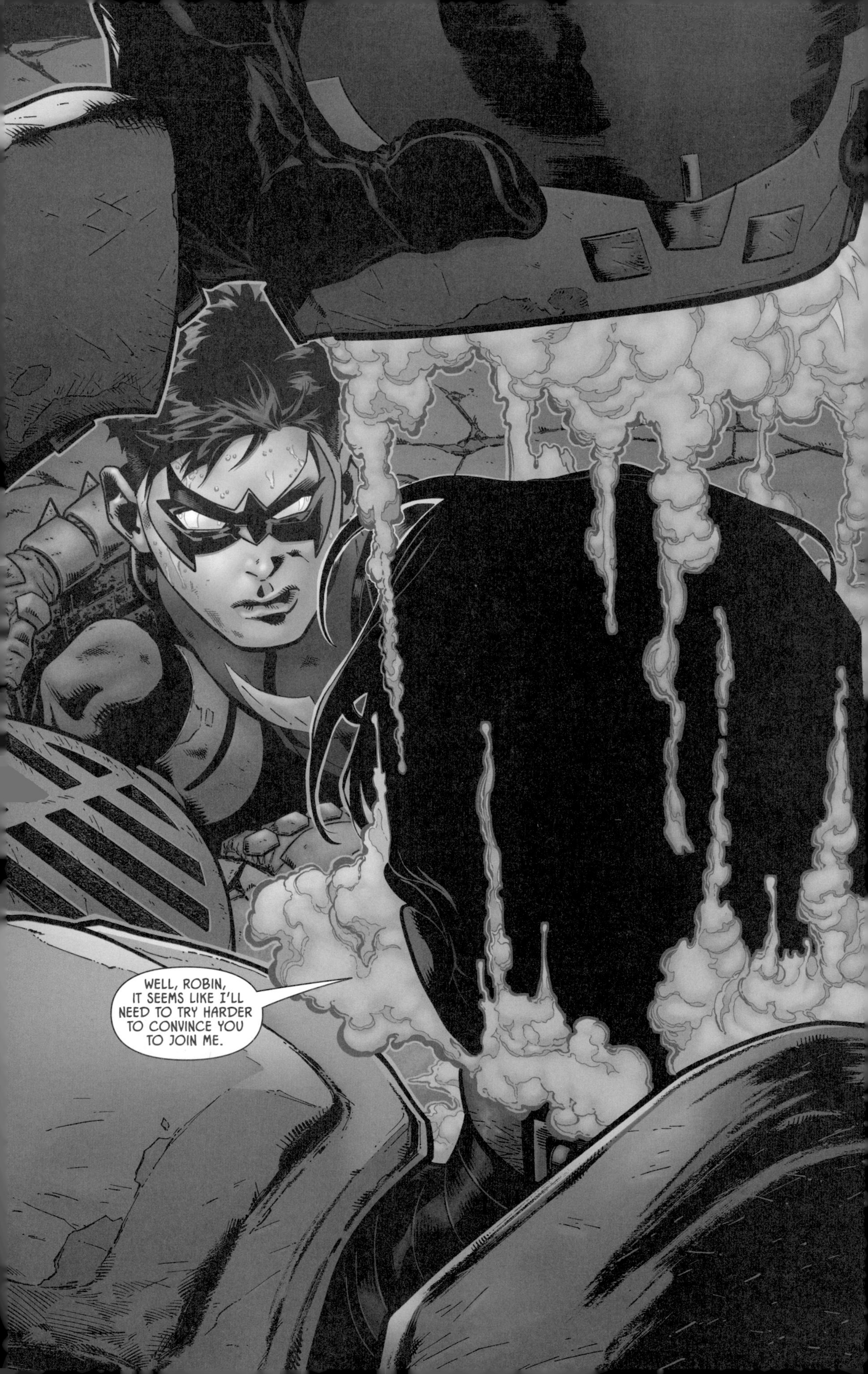
WELL, ROBIN, IT SEEMS LIKE I'LL NEED TO TRY HARDER TO CONVINCE YOU TO JOIN ME.

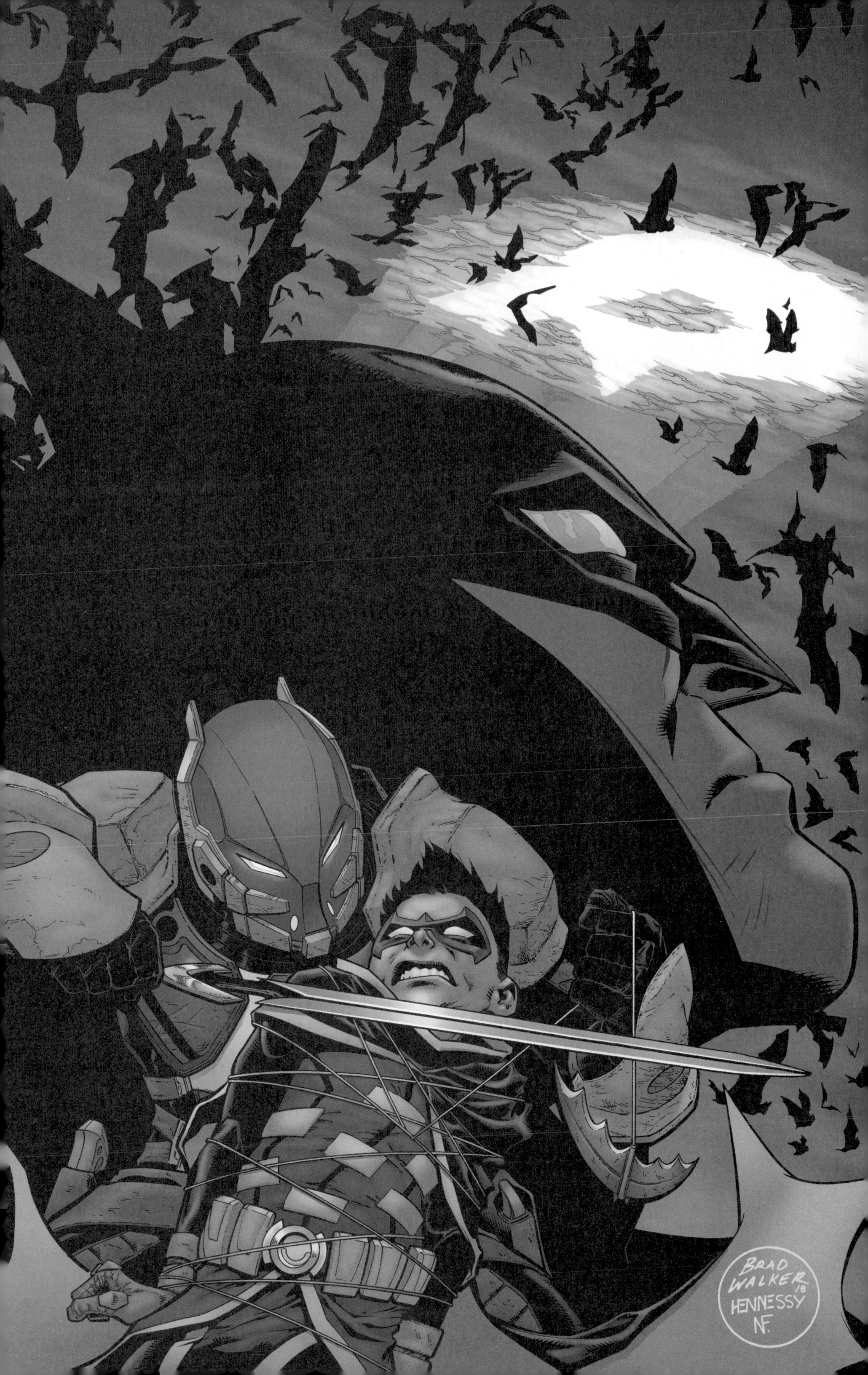
BRAD WALKER '18
HENNESSY
NF.

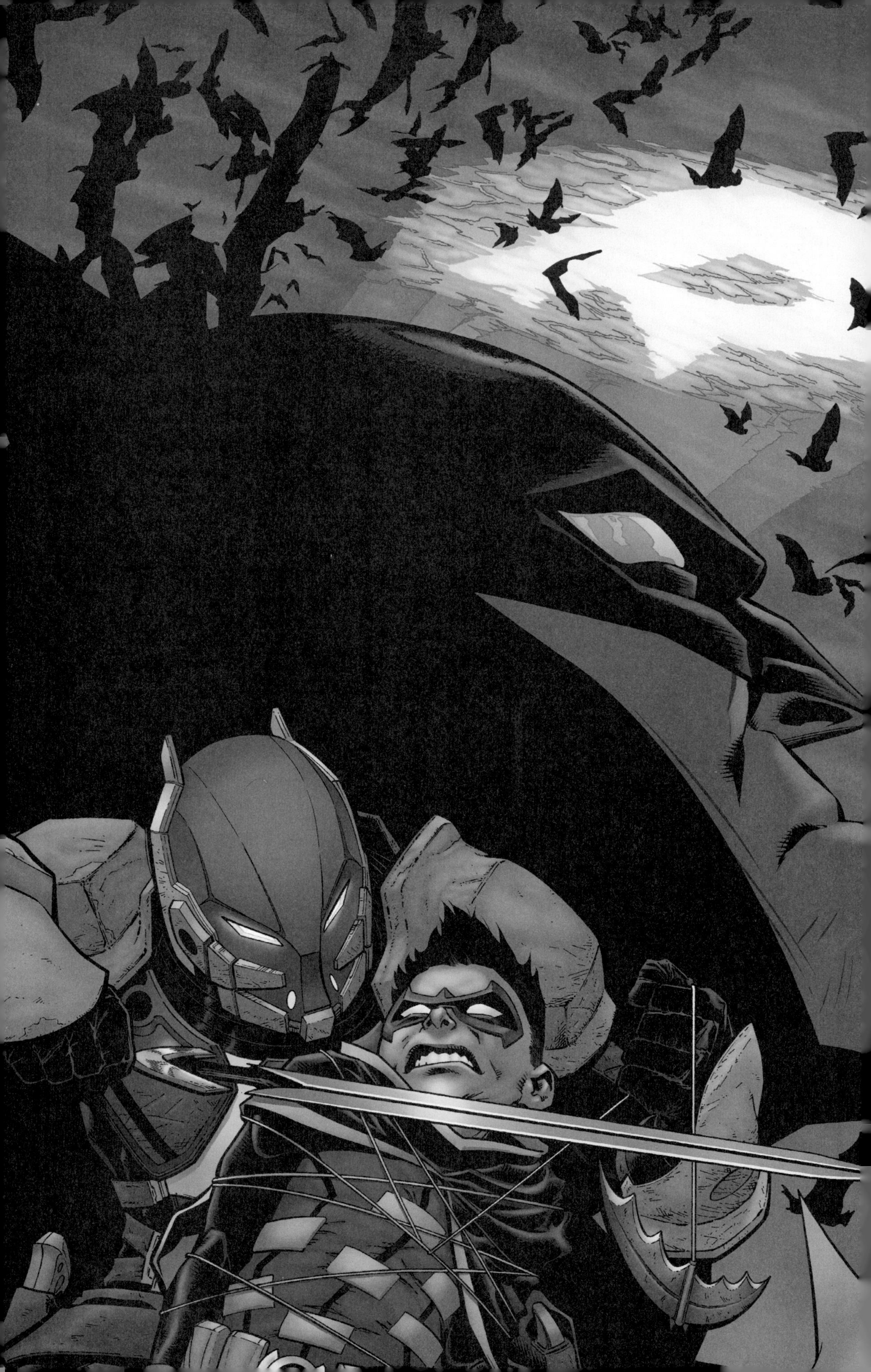

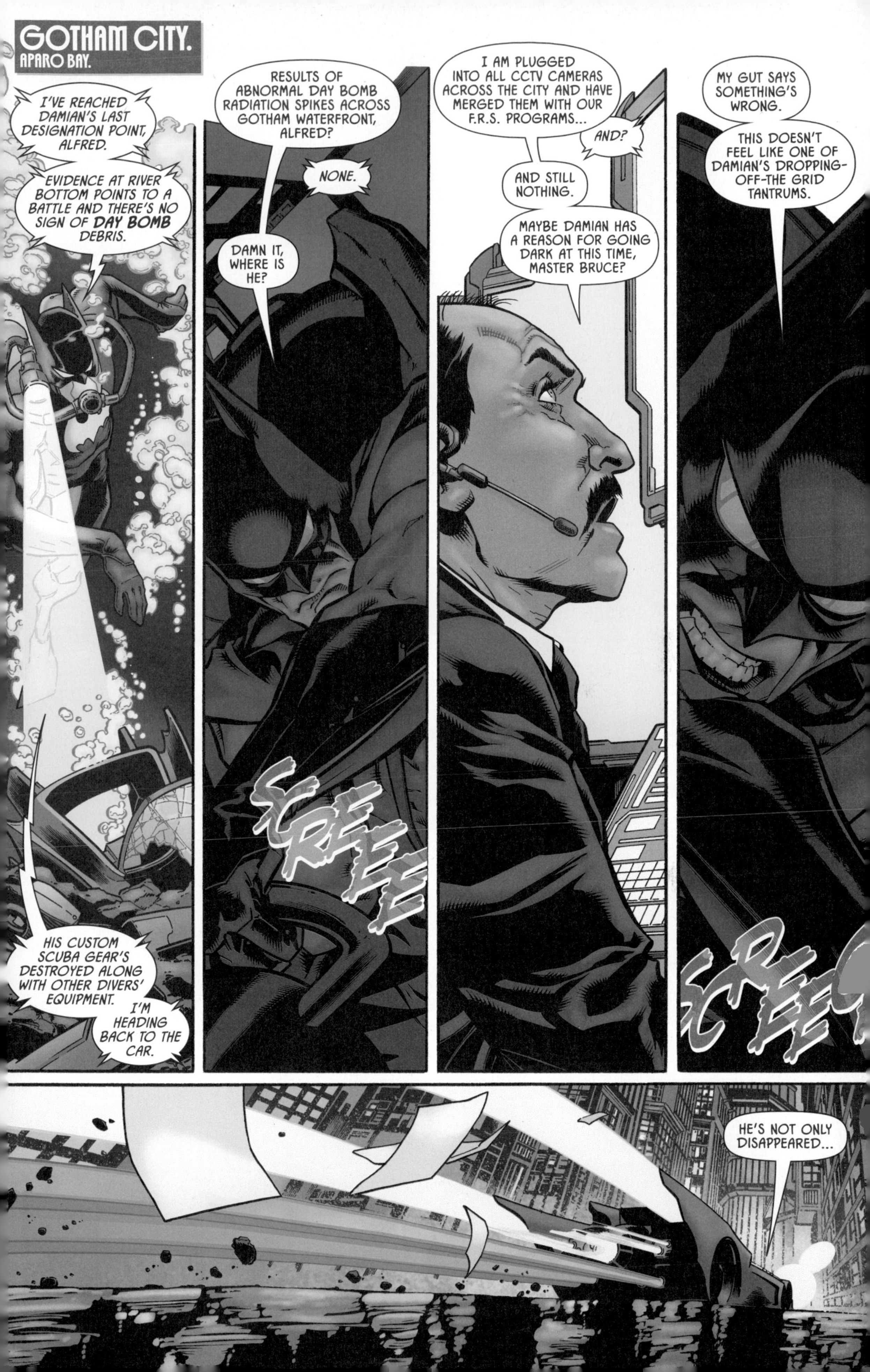

GOTHAM CITY.
APARO BAY.
I'VE REACHED DAMIAN'S LAST DESIGNATION POINT, ALFRED.
EVIDENCE AT RIVER BOTTOM POINTS TO A BATTLE AND THERE'S NO SIGN OF DAY BOMB DEBRIS.
HIS CUSTOM SCUBA GEAR'S DESTROYED ALONG WITH OTHER DIVERS' EQUIPMENT.
I'M HEADING BACK TO THE CAR.
RESULTS OF ABNORMAL DAY BOMB RADIATION SPIKES ACROSS GOTHAM WATERFRONT, ALFRED?
NONE.
DAMN IT, WHERE IS HE?
SCREEE
I AM PLUGGED INTO ALL CCTV CAMERAS ACROSS THE CITY AND HAVE MERGED THEM WITH OUR F.R.S. PROGRAMS...
AND?
AND STILL NOTHING.
MAYBE DAMIAN HAS A REASON FOR GOING DARK AT THIS TIME, MASTER BRUCE?
MY GUT SAYS SOMETHING'S WRONG.
THIS DOESN'T FEEL LIKE ONE OF DAMIAN'S DROPPING-OFF-THE GRID TANTRUMS.
SCREEE
HE'S NOT ONLY DISAPPEARED...

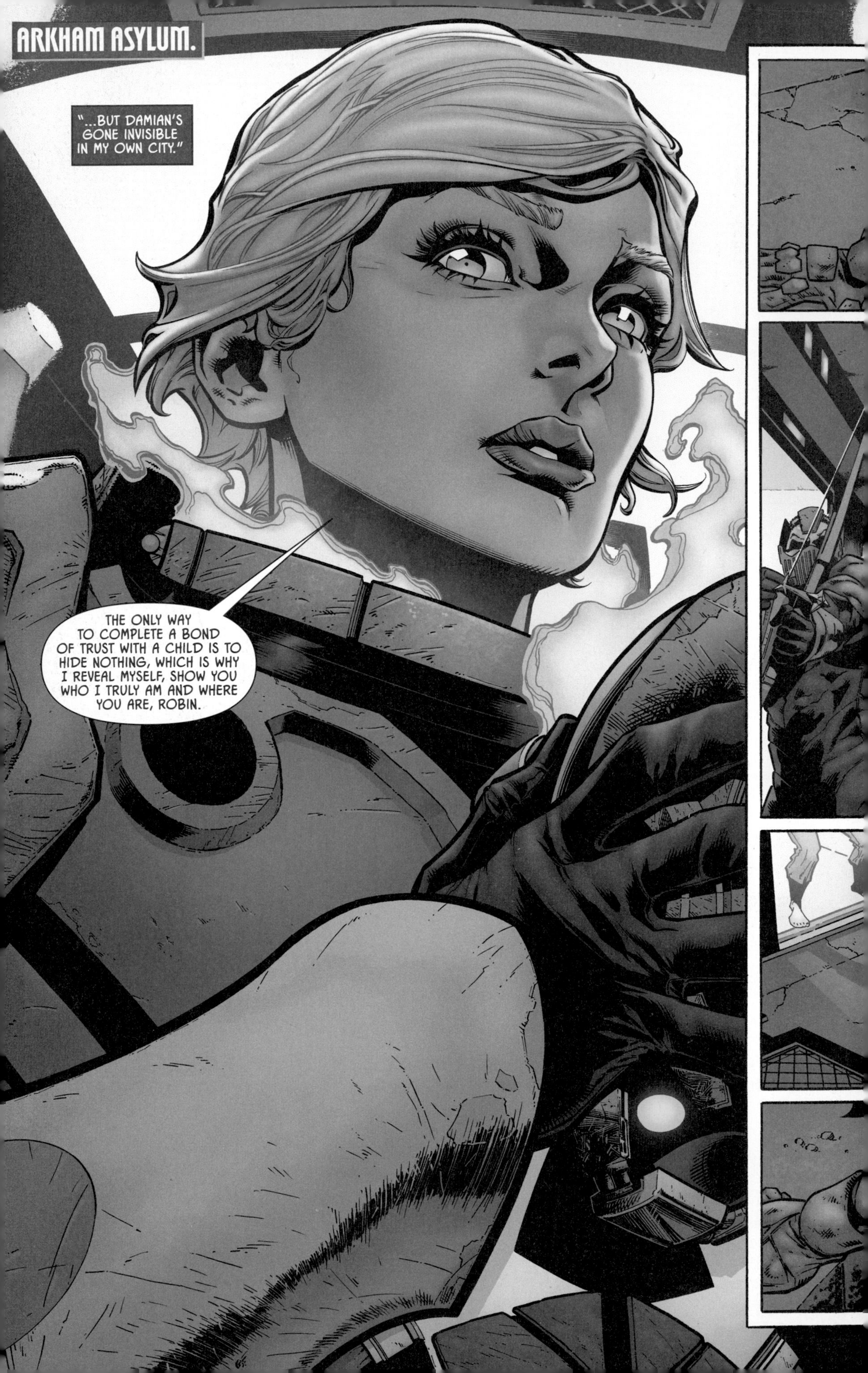
ARKHAM ASYLUM.
"...BUT DAMIAN'S GONE INVISIBLE IN MY OWN CITY."
THE ONLY WAY TO COMPLETE A BOND OF TRUST WITH A CHILD IS TO HIDE NOTHING, WHICH IS WHY I REVEAL MYSELF, SHOW YOU WHO I TRULY AM AND WHERE YOU ARE, ROBIN.

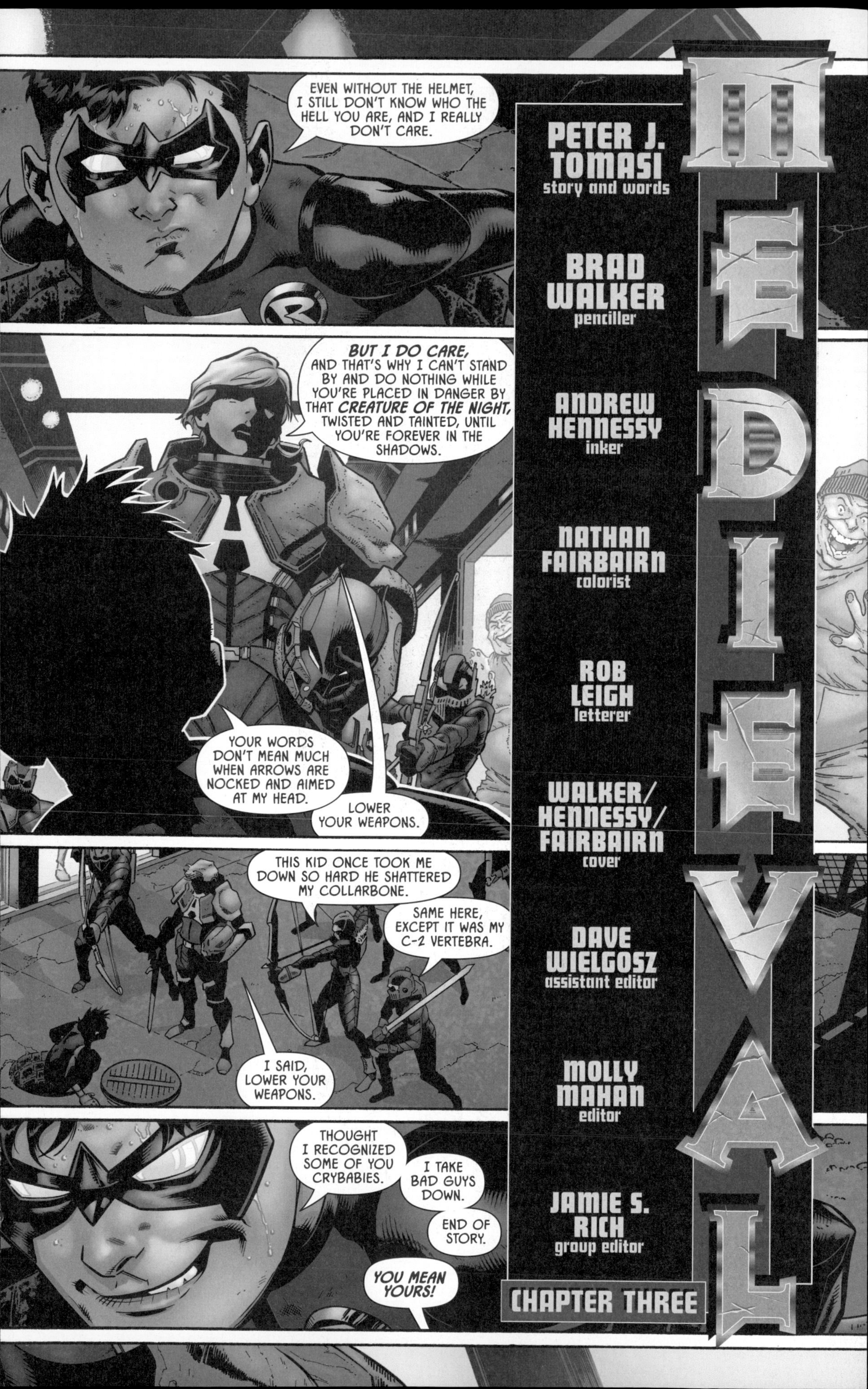
EVEN WITHOUT THE HELMET, I STILL DON'T KNOW WHO THE HELL YOU ARE, AND I REALLY DON'T CARE.
PETER J. TOMASI story and words
BRAD WALKER penciller
ANDREW HENNESSY inker
NATHAN FAIRBAIRN colorist
ROB LEIGH letterer
WALKER/ HENNESSY/ FAIRBAIRN cover
DAVE WIELGOSZ assistant editor
MOLLY MAHAN editor
JAMIE S. RICH group editor
MEDIEVAL
CHAPTER THREE
BUT I DO CARE, AND THAT'S WHY I CAN'T STAND BY AND DO NOTHING WHILE YOU'RE PLACED IN DANGER BY THAT CREATURE OF THE NIGHT, TWISTED AND TAINTED, UNTIL YOU'RE FOREVER IN THE SHADOWS.
YOUR WORDS DON'T MEAN MUCH WHEN ARROWS ARE NOCKED AND AIMED AT MY HEAD.
LOWER YOUR WEAPONS.
THIS KID ONCE TOOK ME DOWN SO HARD HE SHATTERED MY COLLARBONE.
SAME HERE, EXCEPT IT WAS MY C-2 VERTEBRA.
I SAID, LOWER YOUR WEAPONS.
THOUGHT I RECOGNIZED SOME OF YOU CRYBABIES.
I TAKE BAD GUYS DOWN.
END OF STORY.
YOU MEAN YOURS!

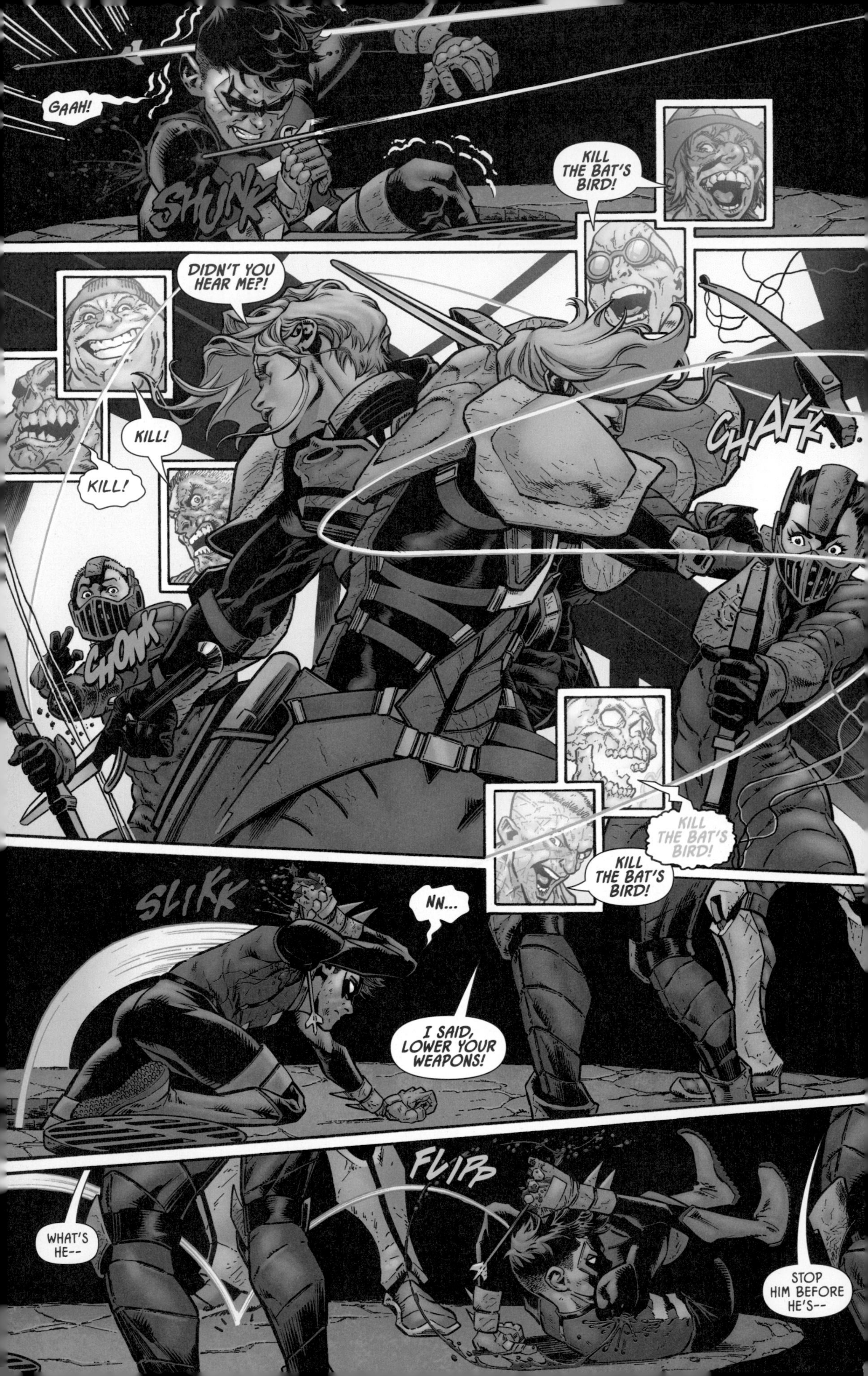
GAAH!
SHUNK
KILL THE BAT'S BIRD!
DIDN'T YOU HEAR ME?!
KILL!
KILL!
CHAKK
CHONK
KILL THE BAT'S BIRD!
KILL THE BAT'S BIRD!
SLIKK
NN...
I SAID, LOWER YOUR WEAPONS!
FLIPP
WHAT'S HE--
STOP HIM BEFORE HE'S--

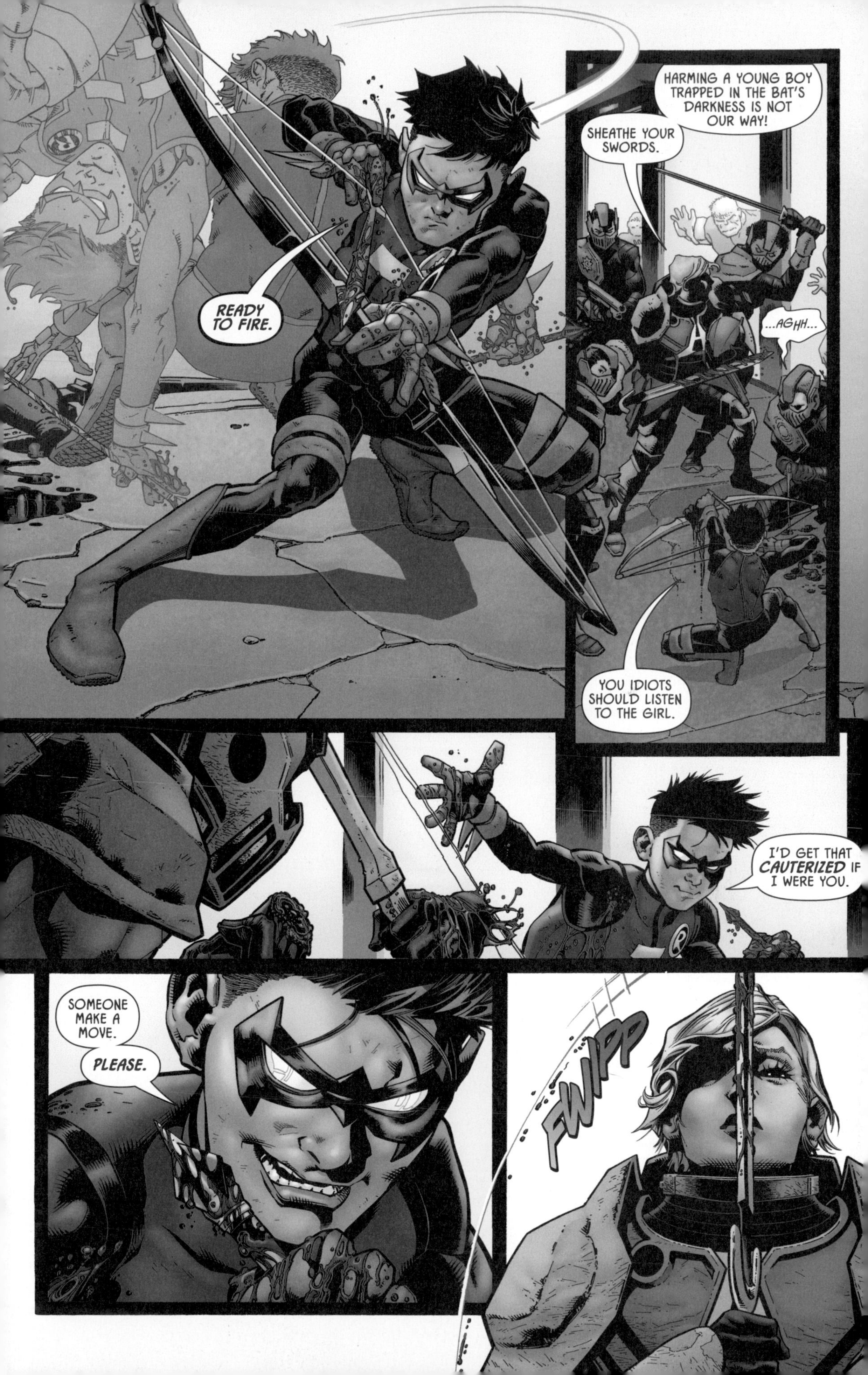
READY TO FIRE.
HARMING A YOUNG BOY TRAPPED IN THE BAT'S DARKNESS IS NOT OUR WAY!
SHEATHE YOUR SWORDS.
...AGHH...
YOU IDIOTS SHOULD LISTEN TO THE GIRL.
I'D GET THAT CAUTERIZED IF I WERE YOU.
SOMEONE MAKE A MOVE.
PLEASE.
FWIPP

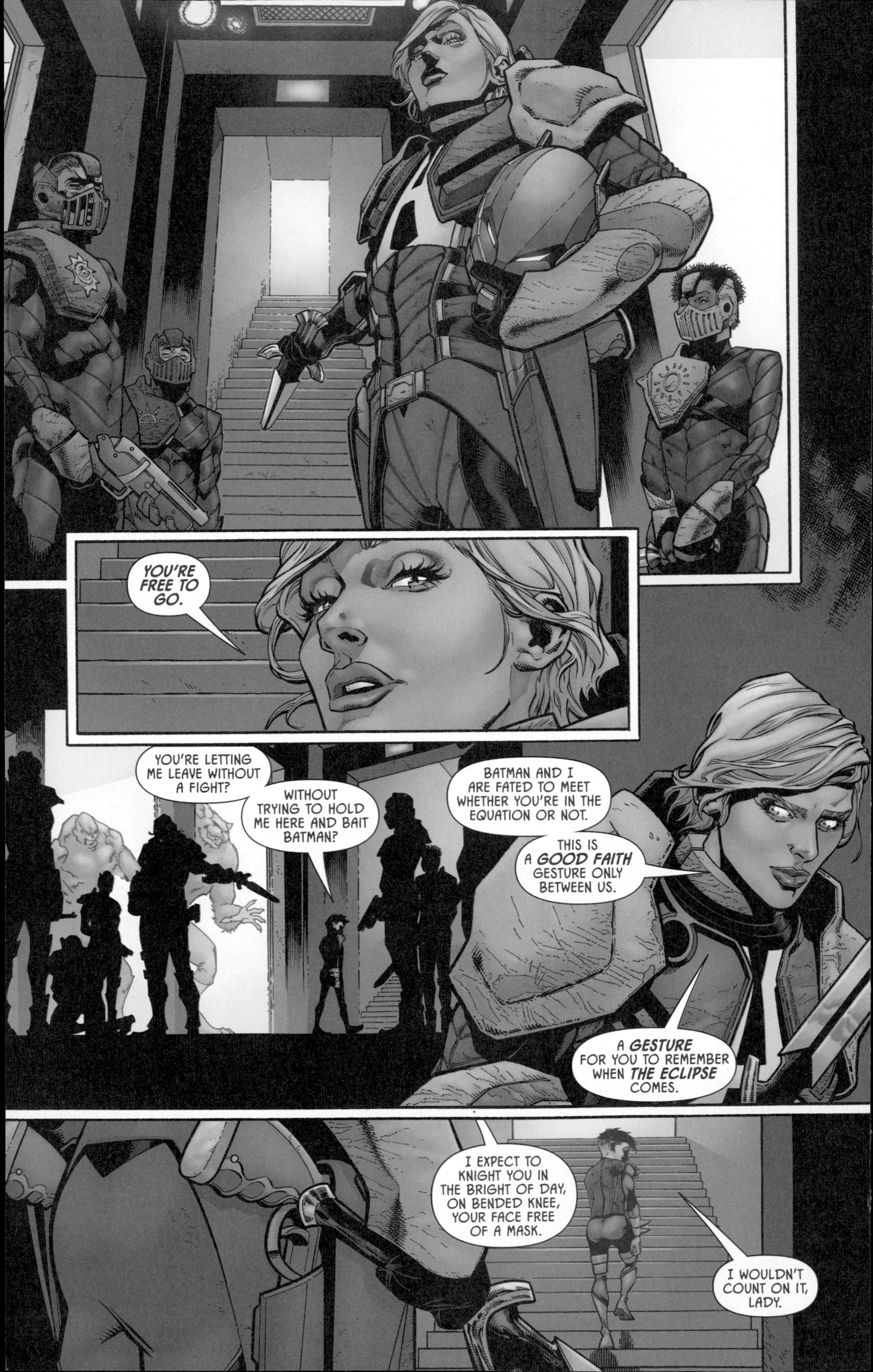
YOU'RE FREE TO GO.
YOU'RE LETTING ME LEAVE WITHOUT A FIGHT?
WITHOUT TRYING TO HOLD ME HERE AND BAIT BATMAN?
BATMAN AND I ARE FATED TO MEET WHETHER YOU'RE IN THE EQUATION OR NOT.
THIS IS A GOOD FAITH GESTURE ONLY BETWEEN US.
A GESTURE FOR YOU TO REMEMBER WHEN THE ECLIPSE COMES.
I EXPECT TO KNIGHT YOU IN THE BRIGHT OF DAY, ON BENDED KNEE, YOUR FACE FREE OF A MASK.
I WOULDN'T COUNT ON IT, LADY.

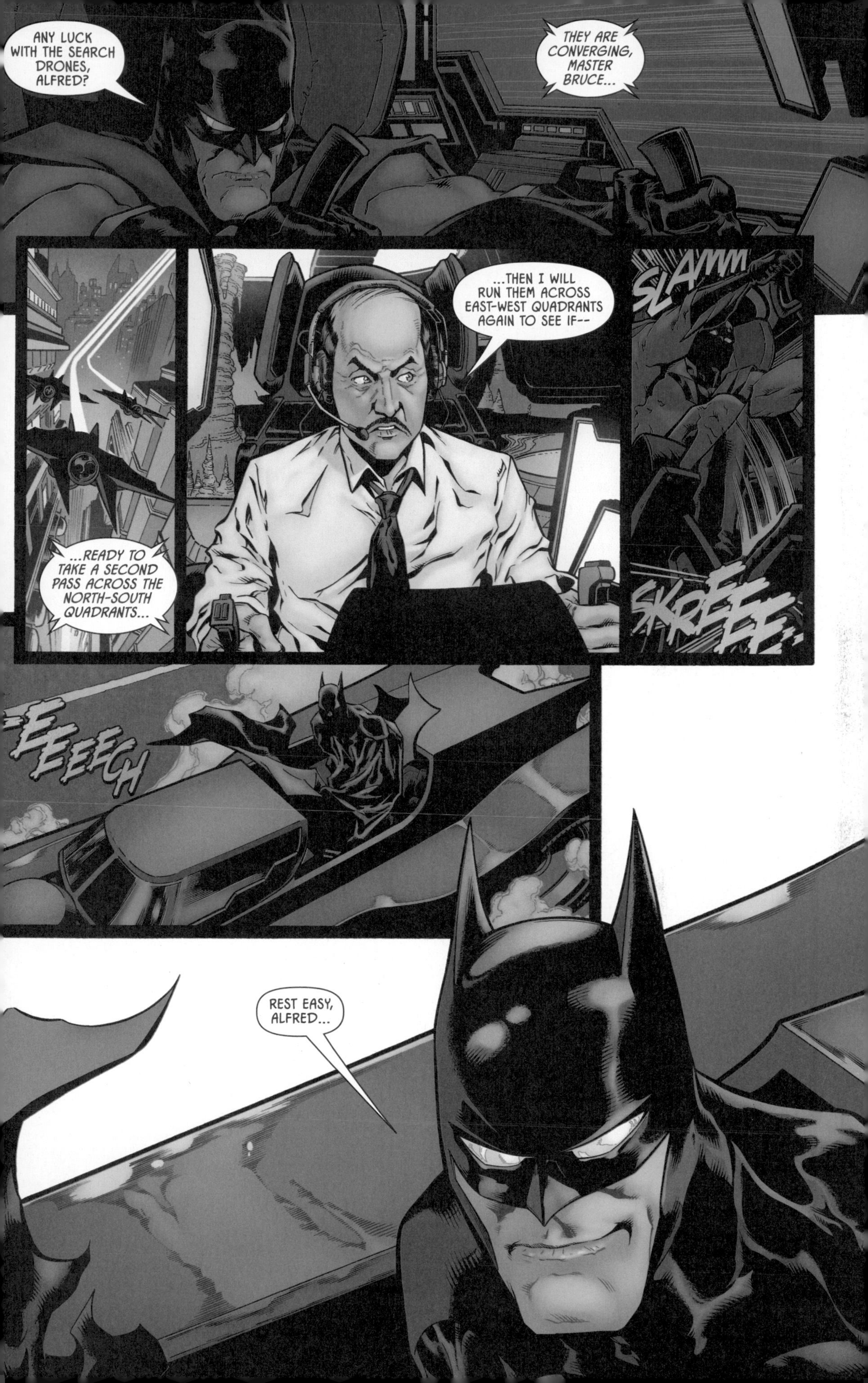
ANY LUCK WITH THE SEARCH DRONES, ALFRED?
THEY ARE CONVERGING, MASTER BRUCE...
...READY TO TAKE A SECOND PASS ACROSS THE NORTH-SOUTH QUADRANTS...
...THEN I WILL RUN THEM ACROSS EAST-WEST QUADRANTS AGAIN TO SEE IF--
SLAMM
SKREEEE
EEEECH
REST EASY, ALFRED...

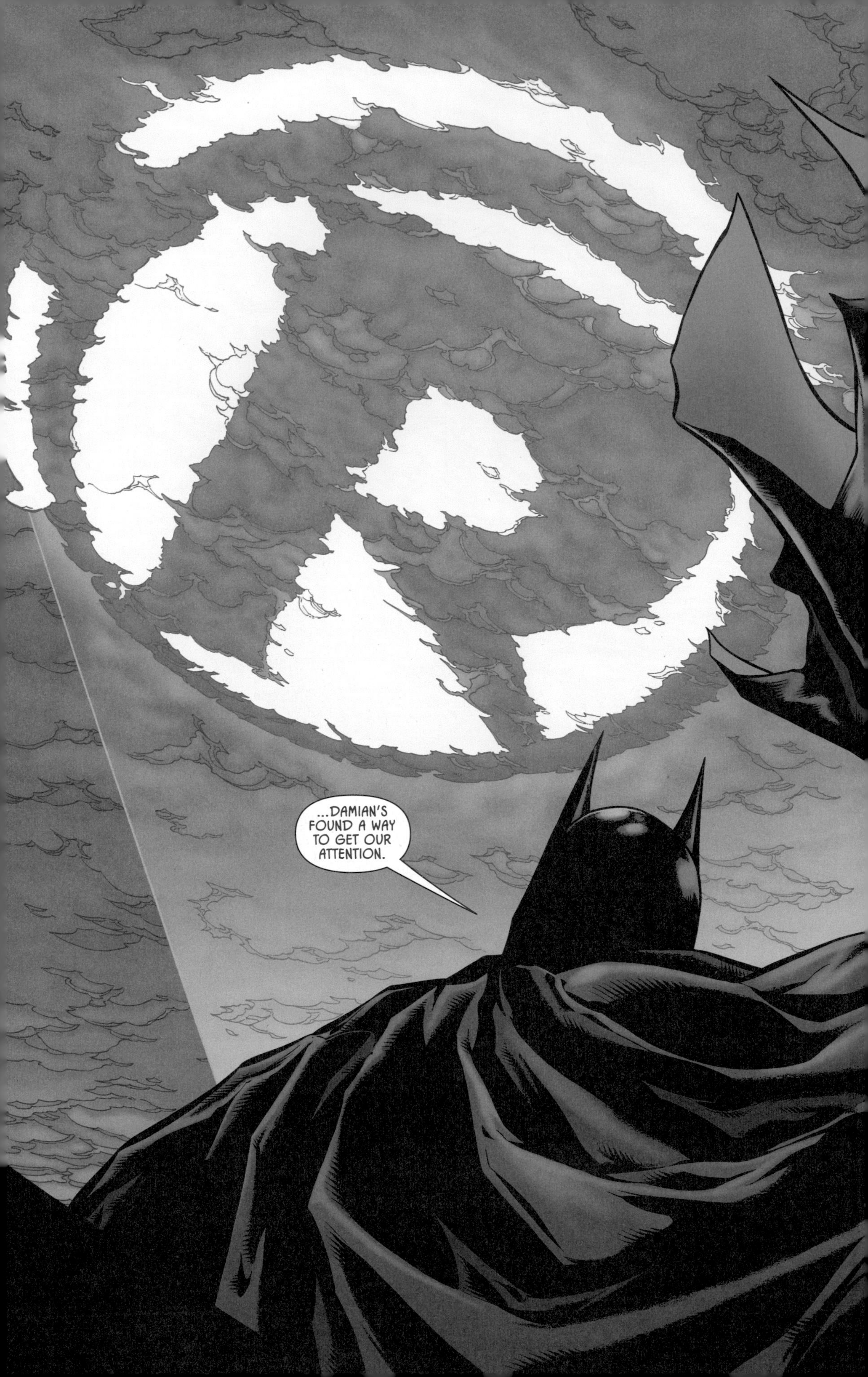
...DAMIAN'S FOUND A WAY TO GET OUR ATTENTION.

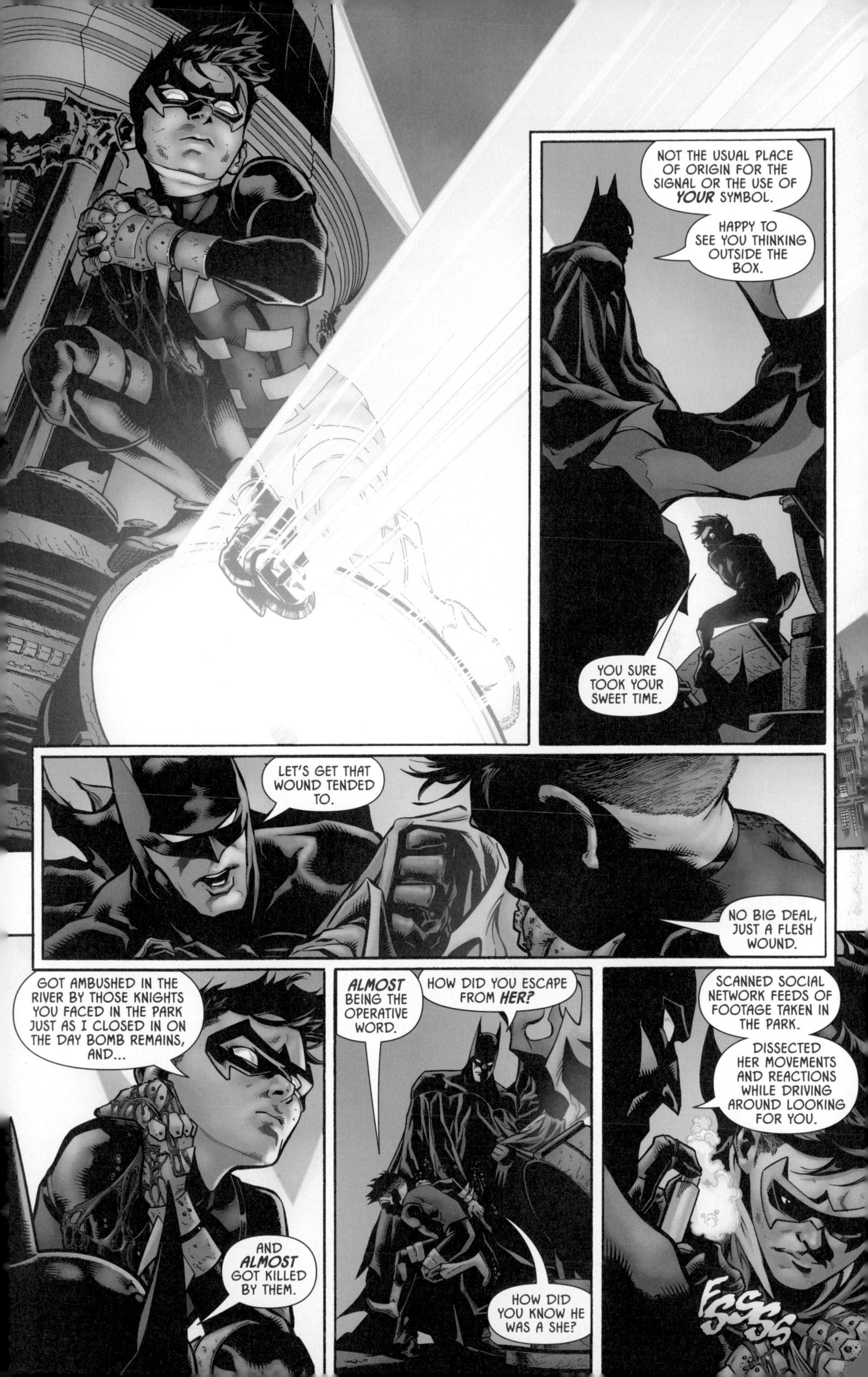
NOT THE USUAL PLACE OF ORIGIN FOR THE SIGNAL OR THE USE OF YOUR SYMBOL.
HAPPY TO SEE YOU THINKING OUTSIDE THE BOX.
YOU SURE TOOK YOUR SWEET TIME.
LET'S GET THAT WOUND TENDED TO.
NO BIG DEAL, JUST A FLESH WOUND.
GOT AMBUSHED IN THE RIVER BY THOSE KNIGHTS YOU FACED IN THE PARK JUST AS I CLOSED IN ON THE DAY BOMB REMAINS, AND...
AND ALMOST GOT KILLED BY THEM.
ALMOST BEING THE OPERATIVE WORD.
HOW DID YOU ESCAPE FROM HER?
HOW DID YOU KNOW HE WAS A SHE?
SCANNED SOCIAL NETWORK FEEDS OF FOOTAGE TAKEN IN THE PARK.
DISSECTED HER MOVEMENTS AND REACTIONS WHILE DRIVING AROUND LOOKING FOR YOU.
FSSSS

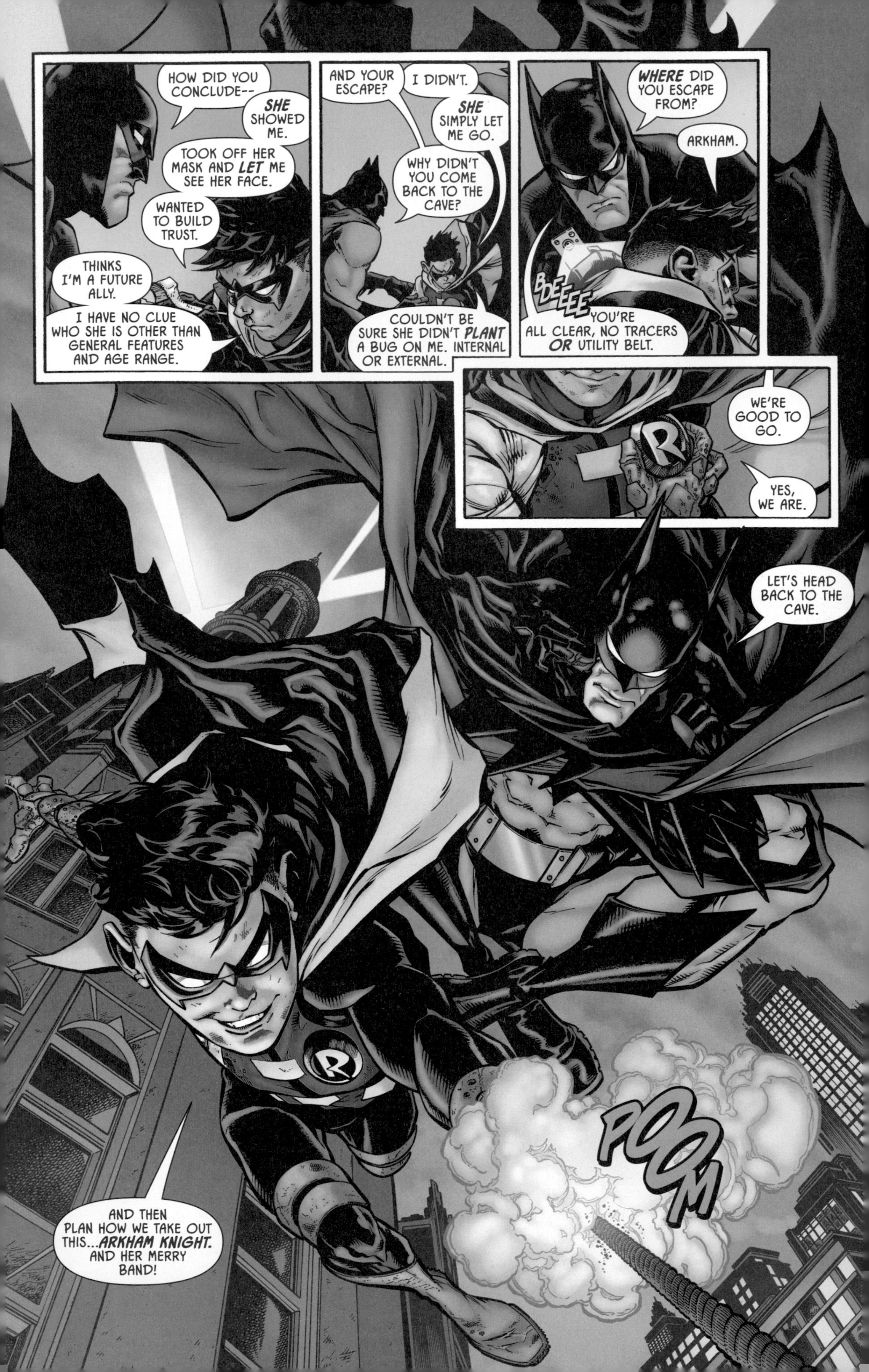

HOW DID YOU CONCLUDE--
SHE SHOWED ME.
TOOK OFF HER MASK AND LET ME SEE HER FACE.
WANTED TO BUILD TRUST.
THINKS I'M A FUTURE ALLY.
I HAVE NO CLUE WHO SHE IS OTHER THAN GENERAL FEATURES AND AGE RANGE.
AND YOUR ESCAPE?
I DIDN'T.
SHE SIMPLY LET ME GO.
WHY DIDN'T YOU COME BACK TO THE CAVE?
COULDN'T BE SURE SHE DIDN'T PLANT A BUG ON ME. INTERNAL OR EXTERNAL.
WHERE DID YOU ESCAPE FROM?
ARKHAM.
BDEEEE
YOU'RE ALL CLEAR, NO TRACERS OR UTILITY BELT.
WE'RE GOOD TO GO.
YES, WE ARE.
LET'S HEAD BACK TO THE CAVE.
AND THEN PLAN HOW WE TAKE OUT THIS...ARKHAM KNIGHT. AND HER MERRY BAND!
POOOM

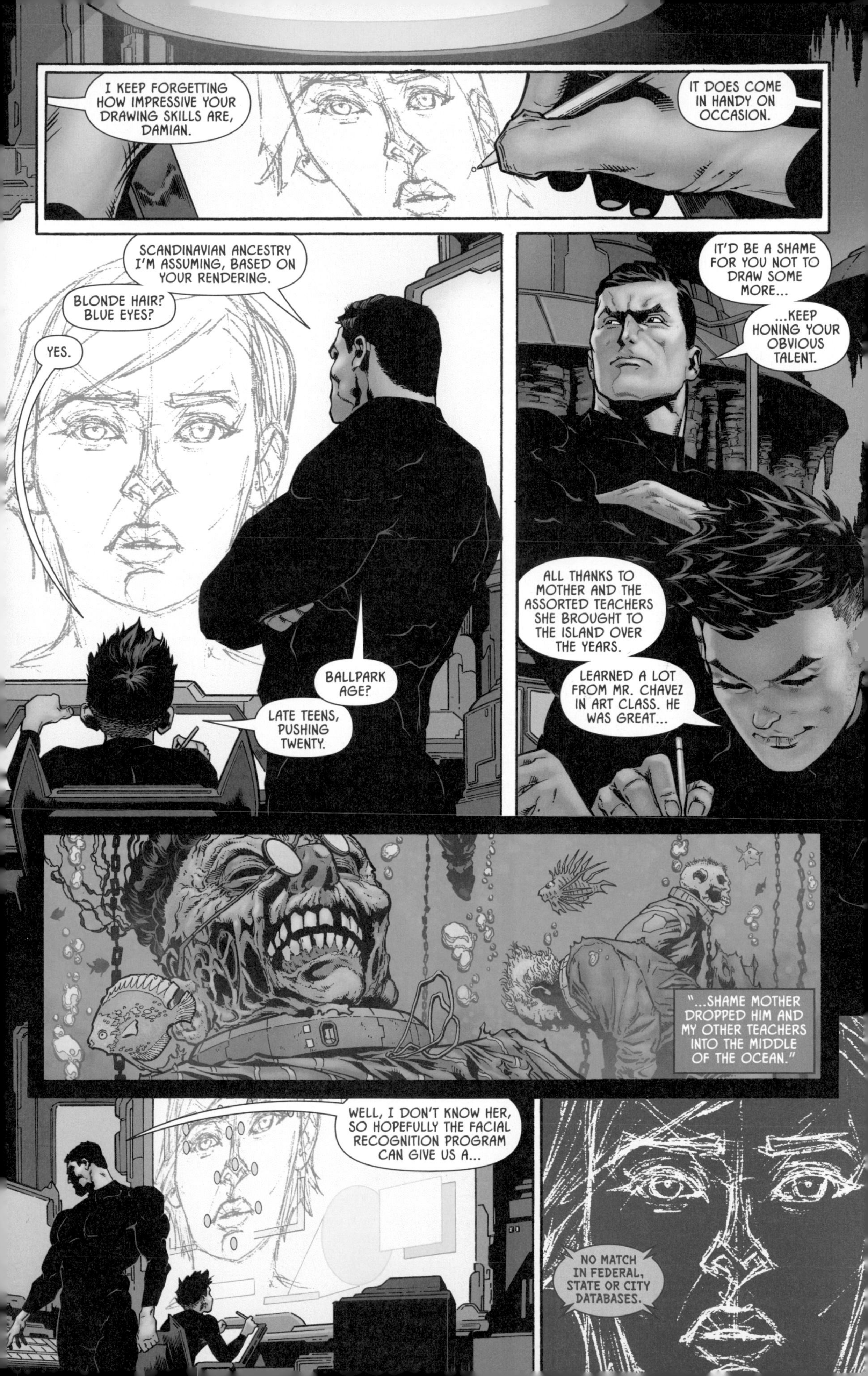
I KEEP FORGETTING HOW IMPRESSIVE YOUR DRAWING SKILLS ARE, DAMIAN.
IT DOES COME IN HANDY ON OCCASION.
SCANDINAVIAN ANCESTRY I'M ASSUMING, BASED ON YOUR RENDERING.
BLONDE HAIR? BLUE EYES?
YES.
BALLPARK AGE?
LATE TEENS, PUSHING TWENTY.
IT'D BE A SHAME FOR YOU NOT TO DRAW SOME MORE...
...KEEP HONING YOUR OBVIOUS TALENT.
ALL THANKS TO MOTHER AND THE ASSORTED TEACHERS SHE BROUGHT TO THE ISLAND OVER THE YEARS.
LEARNED A LOT FROM MR. CHAVEZ IN ART CLASS. HE WAS GREAT...
"...SHAME MOTHER DROPPED HIM AND MY OTHER TEACHERS INTO THE MIDDLE OF THE OCEAN."
WELL, I DON'T KNOW HER, SO HOPEFULLY THE FACIAL RECOGNITION PROGRAM CAN GIVE US A...
NO MATCH IN FEDERAL, STATE OR CITY DATABASES.

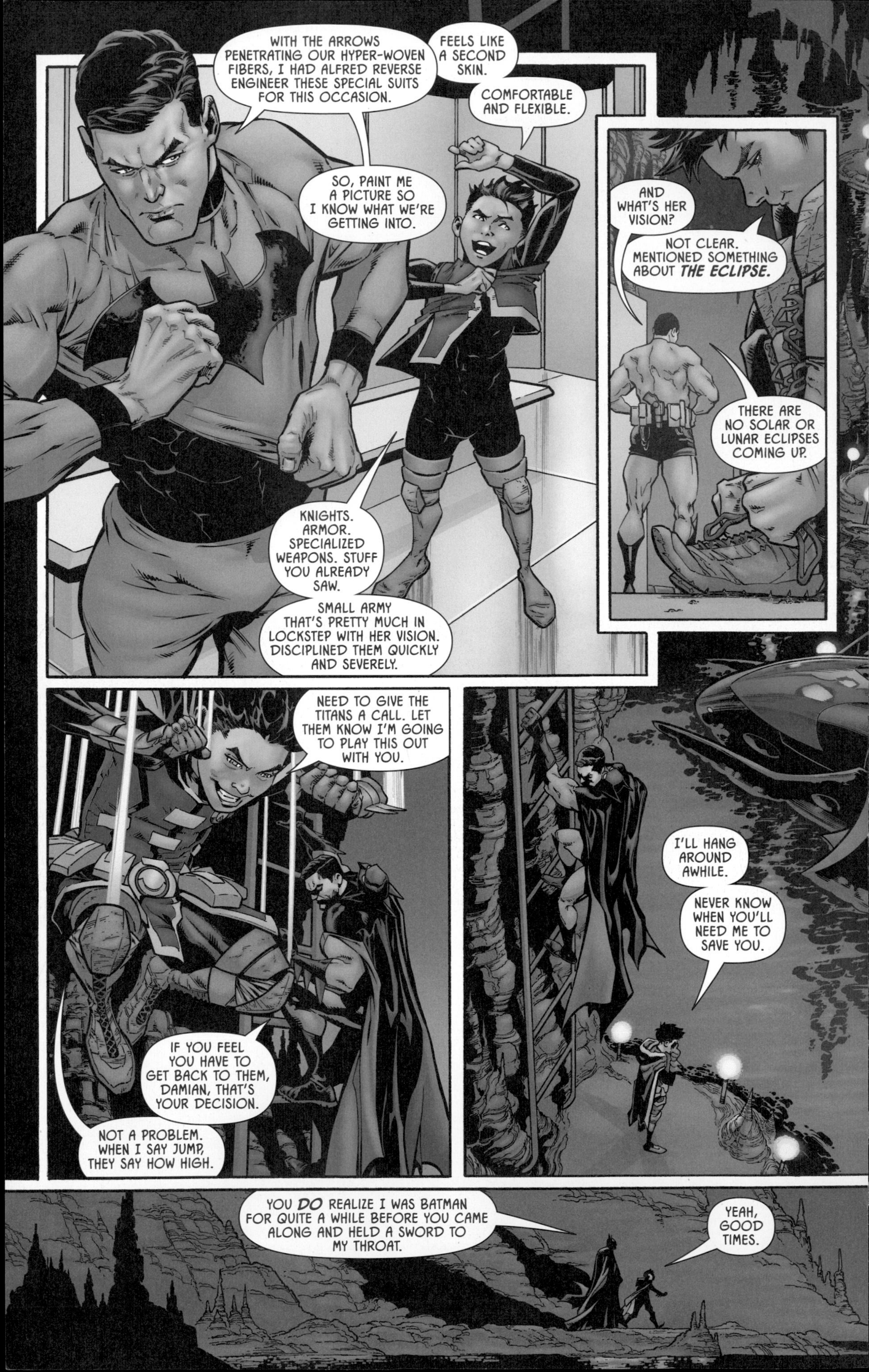
WITH THE ARROWS PENETRATING OUR HYPER-WOVEN FIBERS, I HAD ALFRED REVERSE ENGINEER THESE SPECIAL SUITS FOR THIS OCCASION.
FEELS LIKE A SECOND SKIN.
COMFORTABLE AND FLEXIBLE.
SO, PAINT ME A PICTURE SO I KNOW WHAT WE'RE GETTING INTO.
KNIGHTS. ARMOR. SPECIALIZED WEAPONS. STUFF YOU ALREADY SAW.
SMALL ARMY THAT'S PRETTY MUCH IN LOCKSTEP WITH HER VISION. DISCIPLINED THEM QUICKLY AND SEVERELY.
AND WHAT'S HER VISION?
NOT CLEAR. MENTIONED SOMETHING ABOUT THE ECLIPSE.
THERE ARE NO SOLAR OR LUNAR ECLIPSES COMING UP.
NEED TO GIVE THE TITANS A CALL. LET THEM KNOW I'M GOING TO PLAY THIS OUT WITH YOU.
IF YOU FEEL YOU HAVE TO GET BACK TO THEM, DAMIAN, THAT'S YOUR DECISION.
NOT A PROBLEM. WHEN I SAY JUMP, THEY SAY HOW HIGH.
I'LL HANG AROUND AWHILE.
NEVER KNOW WHEN YOU'LL NEED ME TO SAVE YOU.
YOU DO REALIZE I WAS BATMAN FOR QUITE A WHILE BEFORE YOU CAME ALONG AND HELD A SWORD TO MY THROAT.
YEAH, GOOD TIMES.

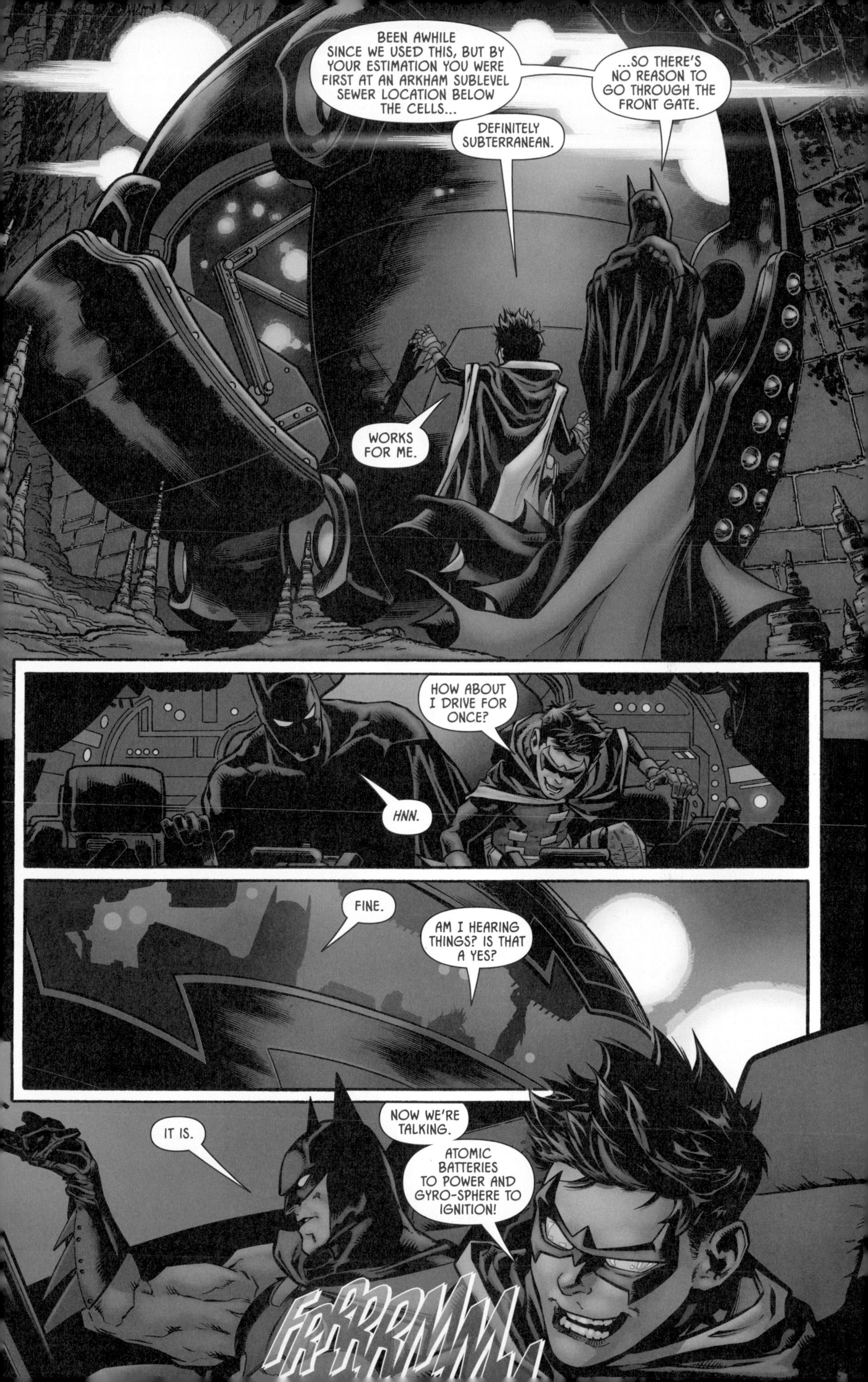
BEEN AWHILE SINCE WE USED THIS, BUT BY YOUR ESTIMATION YOU WERE FIRST AT AN ARKHAM SUBLEVEL SEWER LOCATION BELOW THE CELLS...
...SO THERE'S NO REASON TO GO THROUGH THE FRONT GATE.
DEFINITELY SUBTERRANEAN.
WORKS FOR ME.
HOW ABOUT I DRIVE FOR ONCE?
HNN.
FINE.
AM I HEARING THINGS? IS THAT A YES?
IT IS.
NOW WE'RE TALKING.
ATOMIC BATTERIES TO POWER AND GYRO-SPHERE TO IGNITION!
FRRRMMM

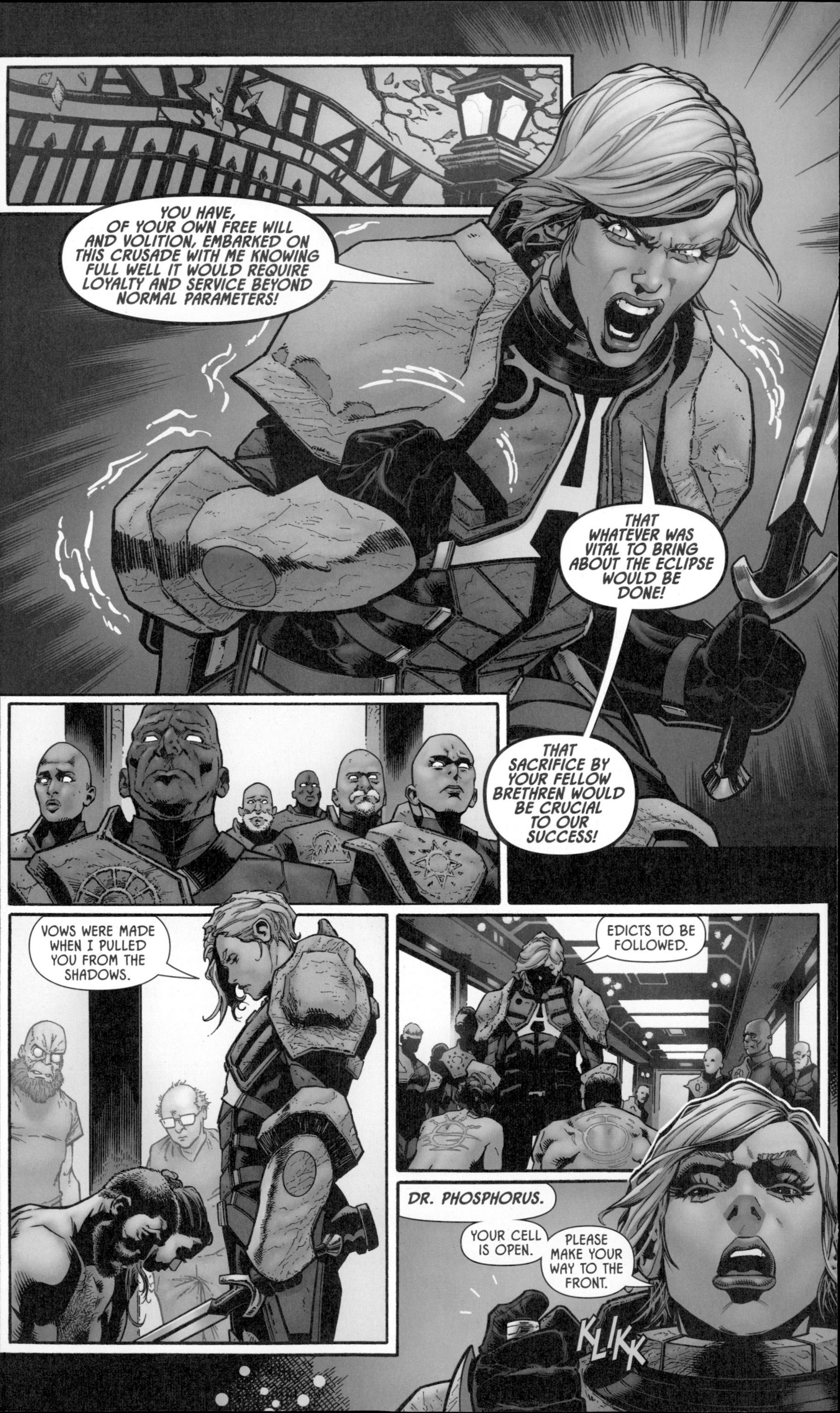
ARKHAM
YOU HAVE, OF YOUR OWN FREE WILL AND VOLITION, EMBARKED ON THIS CRUSADE WITH ME KNOWING FULL WELL IT WOULD REQUIRE LOYALTY AND SERVICE BEYOND NORMAL PARAMETERS!
THAT WHATEVER WAS VITAL TO BRING ABOUT THE ECLIPSE WOULD BE DONE!
THAT SACRIFICE BY YOUR FELLOW BRETHREN WOULD BE CRUCIAL TO OUR SUCCESS!
VOWS WERE MADE WHEN I PULLED YOU FROM THE SHADOWS.
EDICTS TO BE FOLLOWED.
DR. PHOSPHORUS.
YOUR CELL IS OPEN.
PLEASE MAKE YOUR WAY TO THE FRONT.
KLIKK

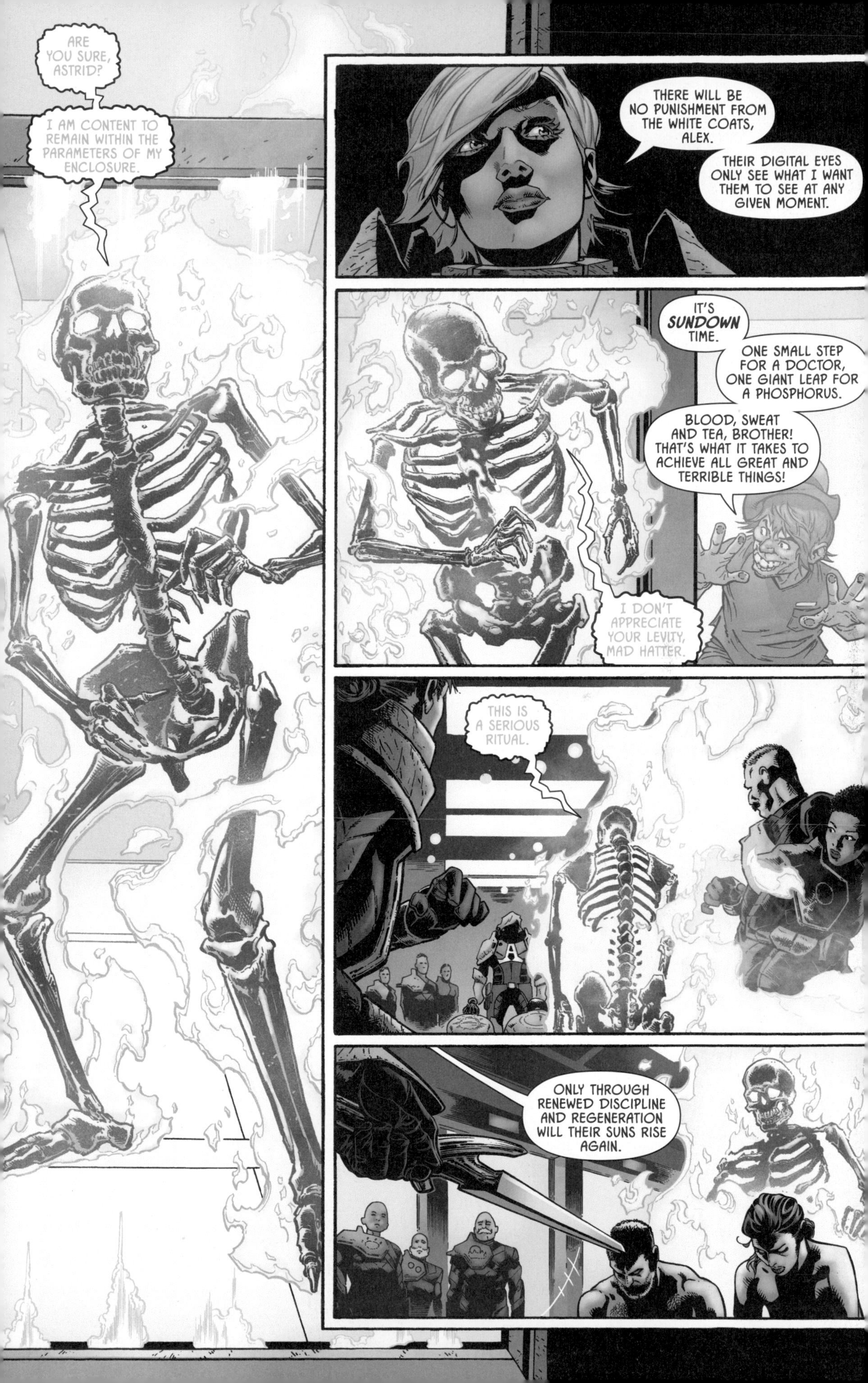
ARE YOU SURE, ASTRID?
I AM CONTENT TO REMAIN WITHIN THE PARAMETERS OF MY ENCLOSURE.
THERE WILL BE NO PUNISHMENT FROM THE WHITE COATS, ALEX.
THEIR DIGITAL EYES ONLY SEE WHAT I WANT THEM TO SEE AT ANY GIVEN MOMENT.
IT'S SUNDOWN TIME.
ONE SMALL STEP FOR A DOCTOR, ONE GIANT LEAP FOR A PHOSPHORUS.
BLOOD, SWEAT AND TEA, BROTHER! THAT'S WHAT IT TAKES TO ACHIEVE ALL GREAT AND TERRIBLE THINGS!
I DON'T APPRECIATE YOUR LEVITY, MAD HATTER.
THIS IS A SERIOUS RITUAL.
ONLY THROUGH RENEWED DISCIPLINE AND REGENERATION WILL THEIR SUNS RISE AGAIN.

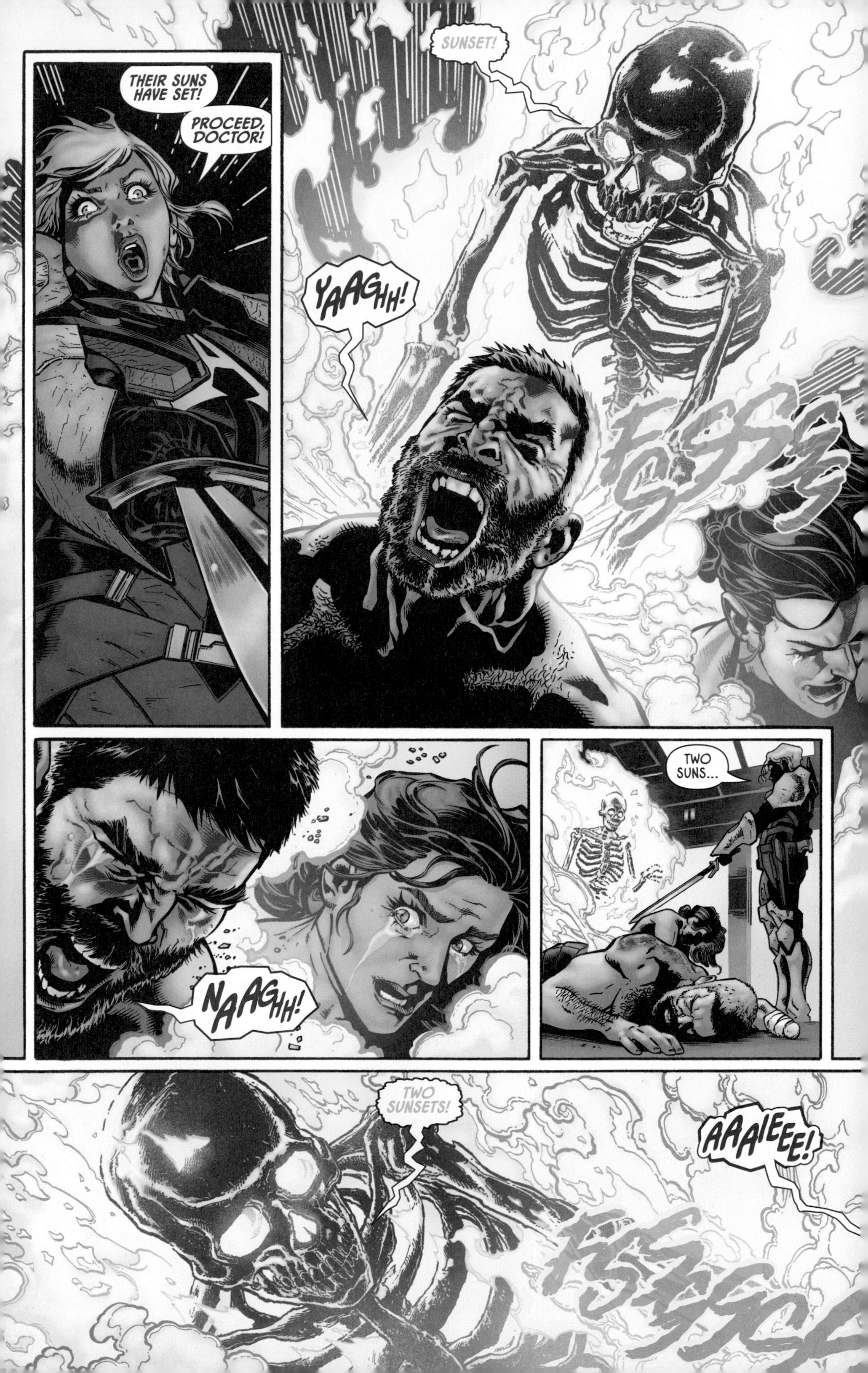
THEIR SUNS HAVE SET!
PROCEED, DOCTOR!
SUNSET!
YAAGHH!
FSSSS
NAAGHH!
TWO SUNS...
TWO SUNSETS!
AAAIEEE!

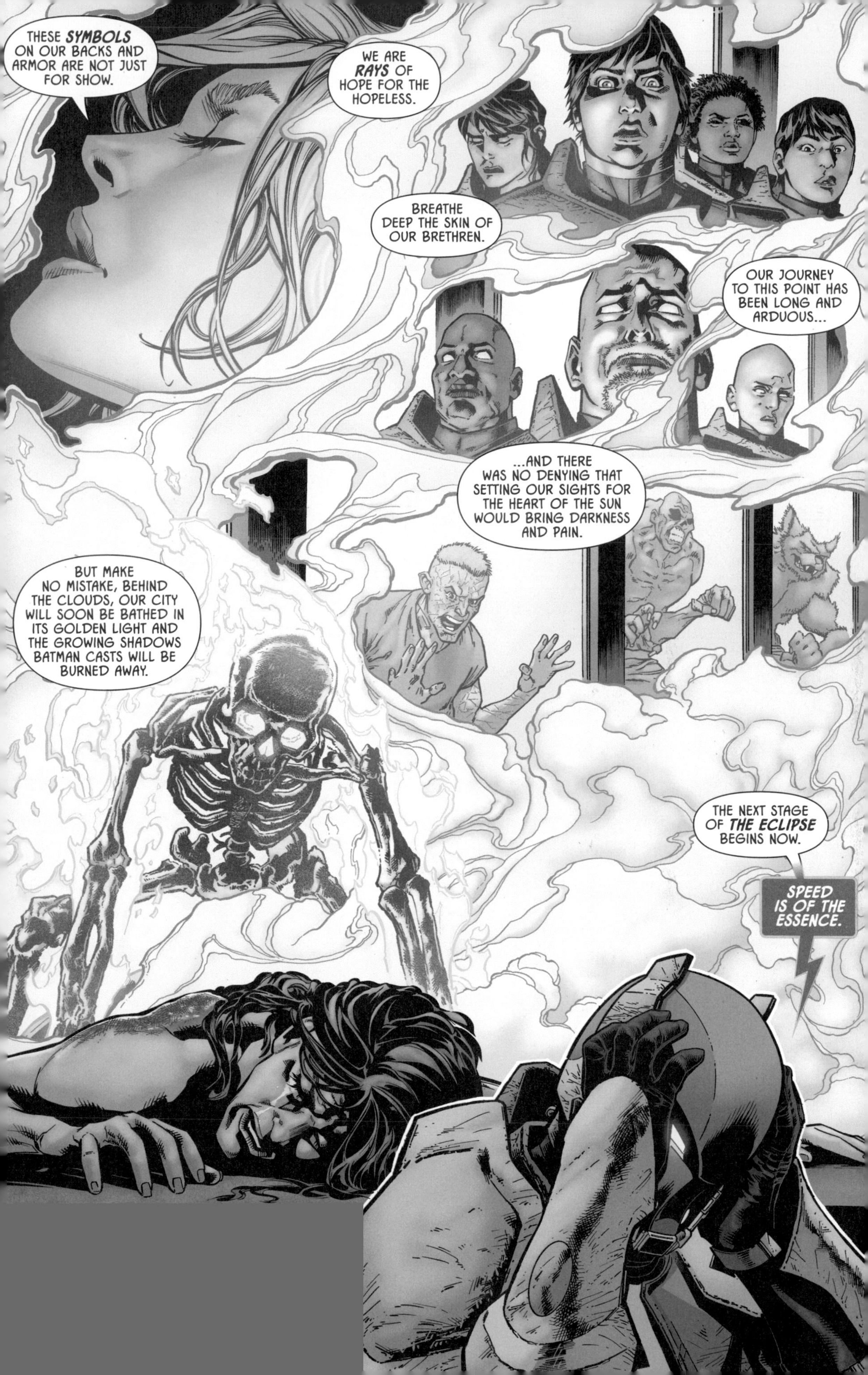
THESE SYMBOLS ON OUR BACKS AND ARMOR ARE NOT JUST FOR SHOW.
WE ARE RAYS OF HOPE FOR THE HOPELESS.
BREATHE DEEP THE SKIN OF OUR BRETHREN.
OUR JOURNEY TO THIS POINT HAS BEEN LONG AND ARDUOUS...
...AND THERE WAS NO DENYING THAT SETTING OUR SIGHTS FOR THE HEART OF THE SUN WOULD BRING DARKNESS AND PAIN.
BUT MAKE NO MISTAKE, BEHIND THE CLOUDS, OUR CITY WILL SOON BE BATHED IN ITS GOLDEN LIGHT AND THE GROWING SHADOWS BATMAN CASTS WILL BE BURNED AWAY.
THE NEXT STAGE OF THE ECLIPSE BEGINS NOW.
SPEED IS OF THE ESSENCE.

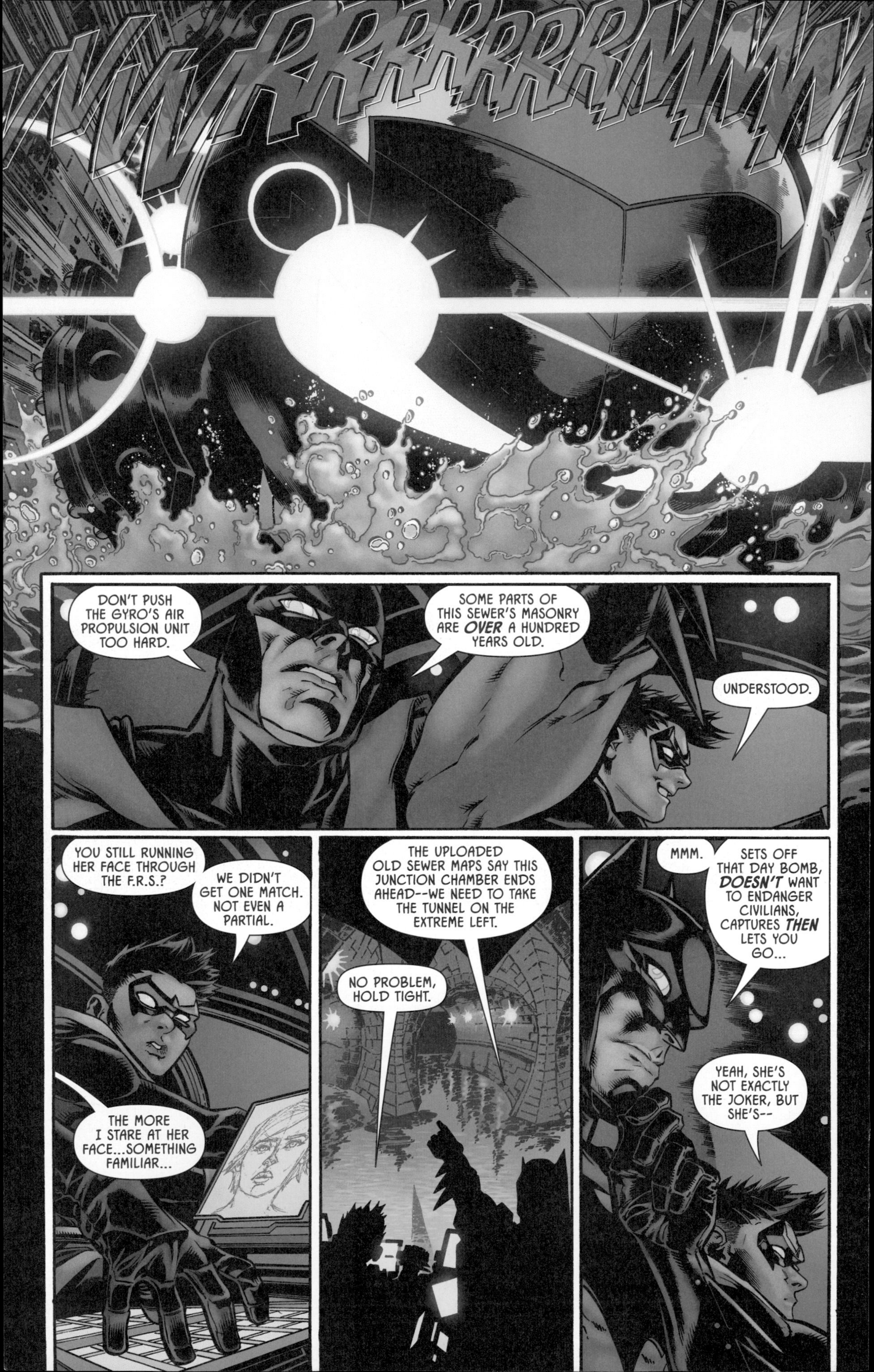
WHRRRRRRRMMMM
DON'T PUSH THE GYRO'S AIR PROPULSION UNIT TOO HARD.
SOME PARTS OF THIS SEWER'S MASONRY ARE *OVER* A HUNDRED YEARS OLD.
UNDERSTOOD.
YOU STILL RUNNING HER FACE THROUGH THE F.R.S.?
WE DIDN'T GET ONE MATCH. NOT EVEN A PARTIAL.
THE MORE I STARE AT HER FACE...SOMETHING FAMILIAR...
THE UPLOADED OLD SEWER MAPS SAY THIS JUNCTION CHAMBER ENDS AHEAD--WE NEED TO TAKE THE TUNNEL ON THE EXTREME LEFT.
NO PROBLEM, HOLD TIGHT.
MMM.
SETS OFF THAT DAY BOMB, *DOESN'T* WANT TO ENDANGER CIVILIANS, CAPTURES *THEN* LETS YOU GO...
YEAH, SHE'S NOT EXACTLY THE JOKER, BUT SHE'S--

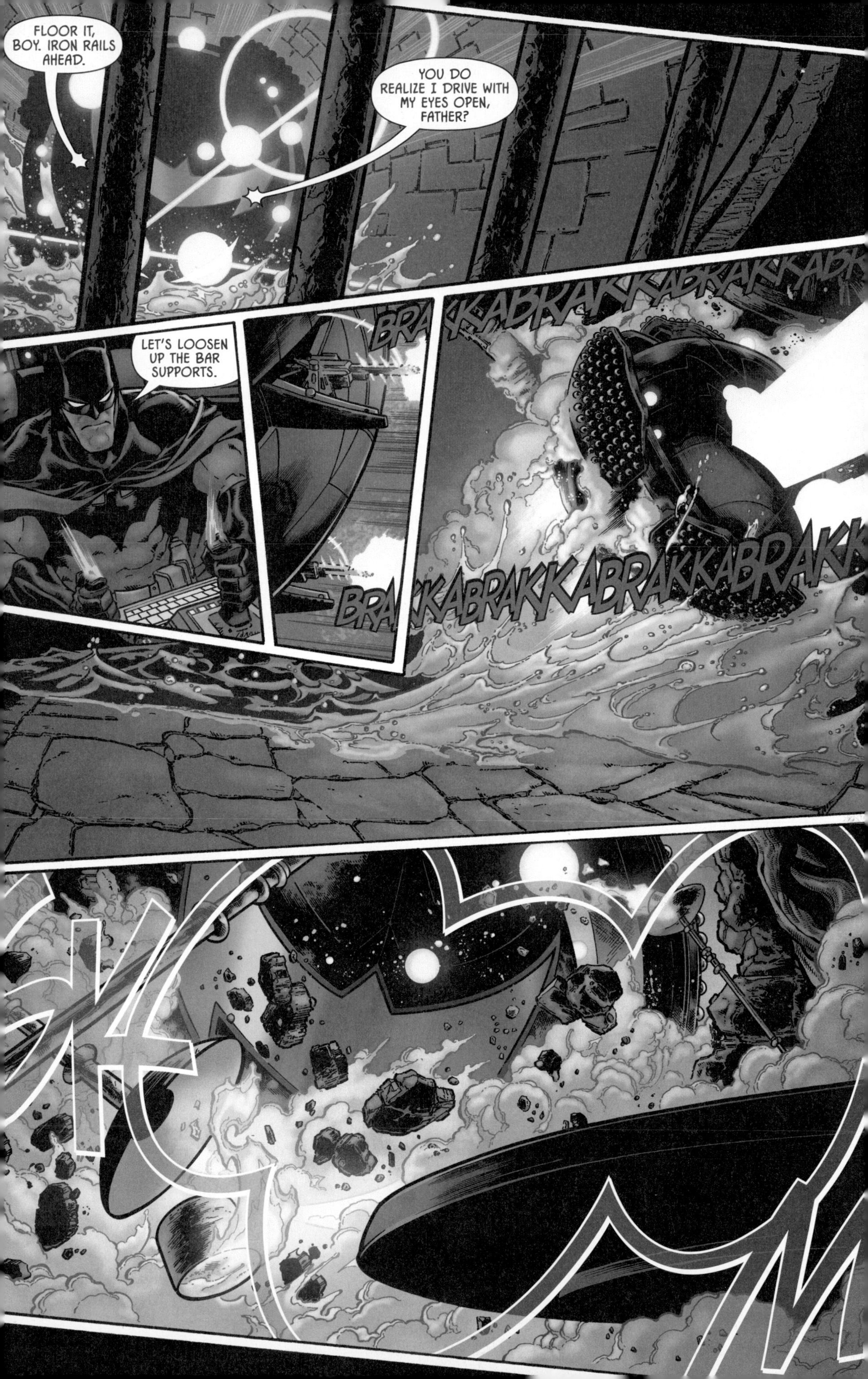
FLOOR IT, BOY. IRON RAILS AHEAD.
YOU DO REALIZE I DRIVE WITH MY EYES OPEN, FATHER?
BRAKKABRAKKABRAKKABRAKKABR
LET'S LOOSEN UP THE BAR SUPPORTS.
BRAKKABRAKKABRAKK

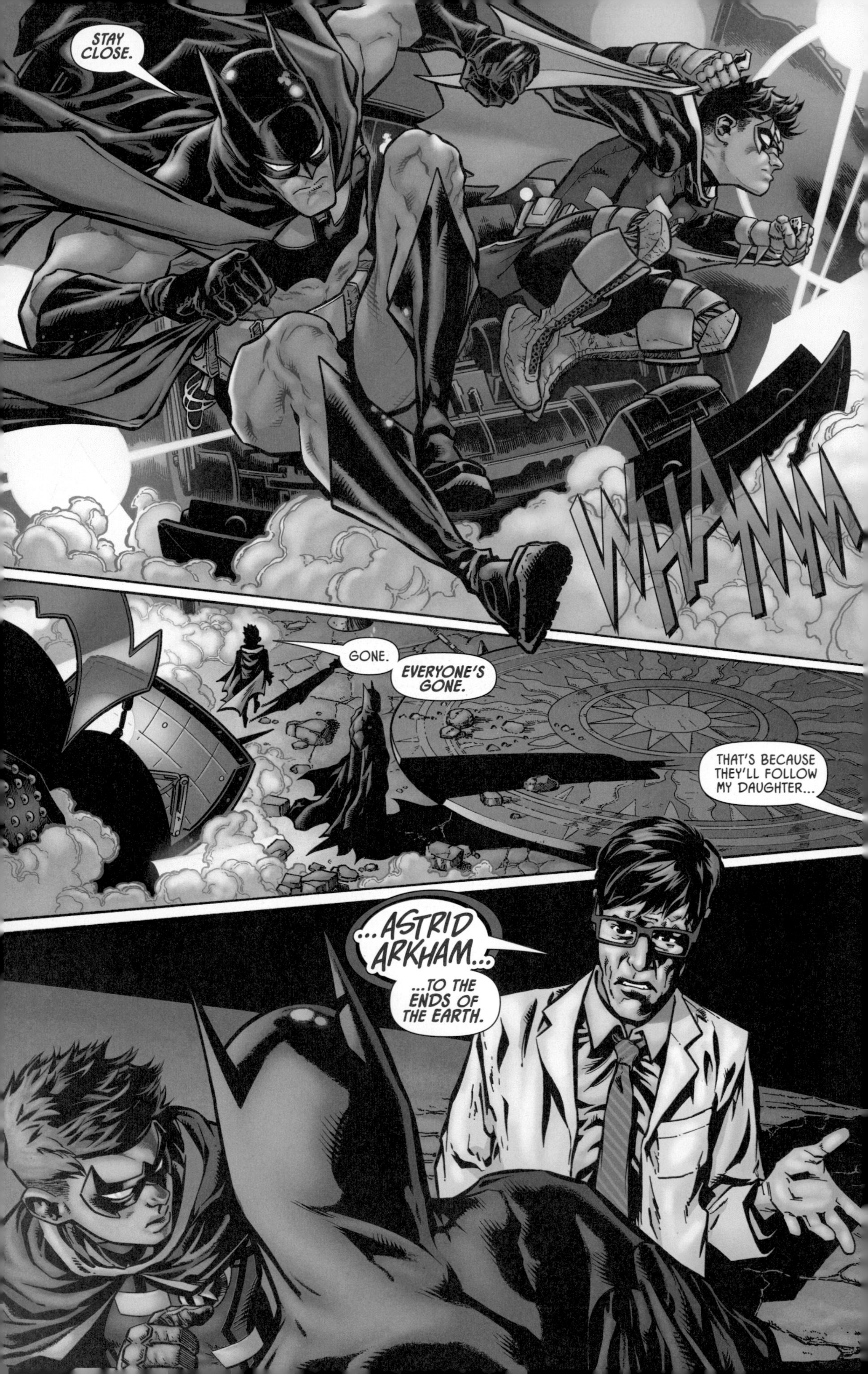
STAY CLOSE.
WHAMM
GONE.
EVERYONE'S GONE.
THAT'S BECAUSE THEY'LL FOLLOW MY DAUGHTER...
...ASTRID ARKHAM...
...TO THE ENDS OF THE EARTH.

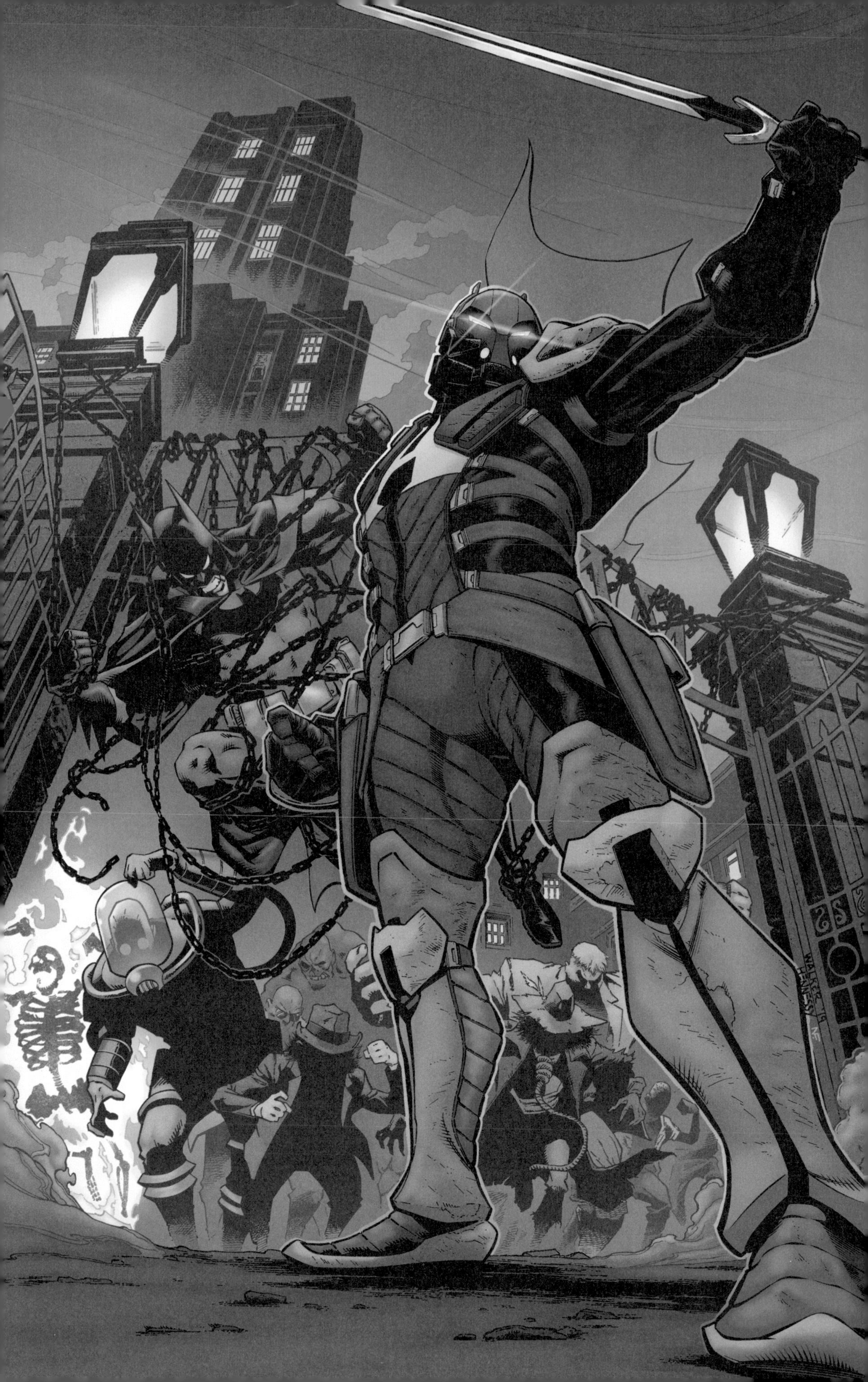
WALKER '19
HENNESSY
MF

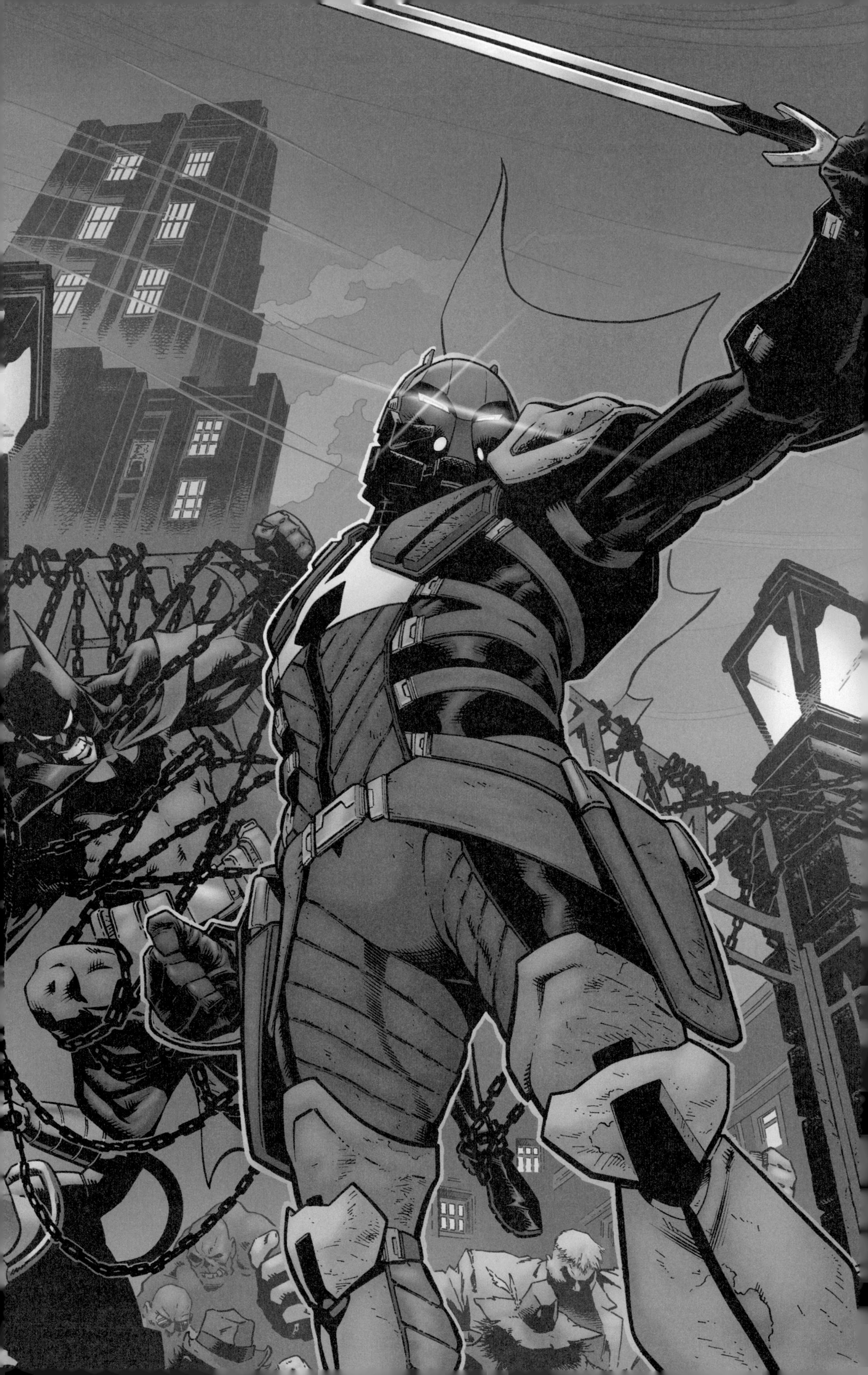

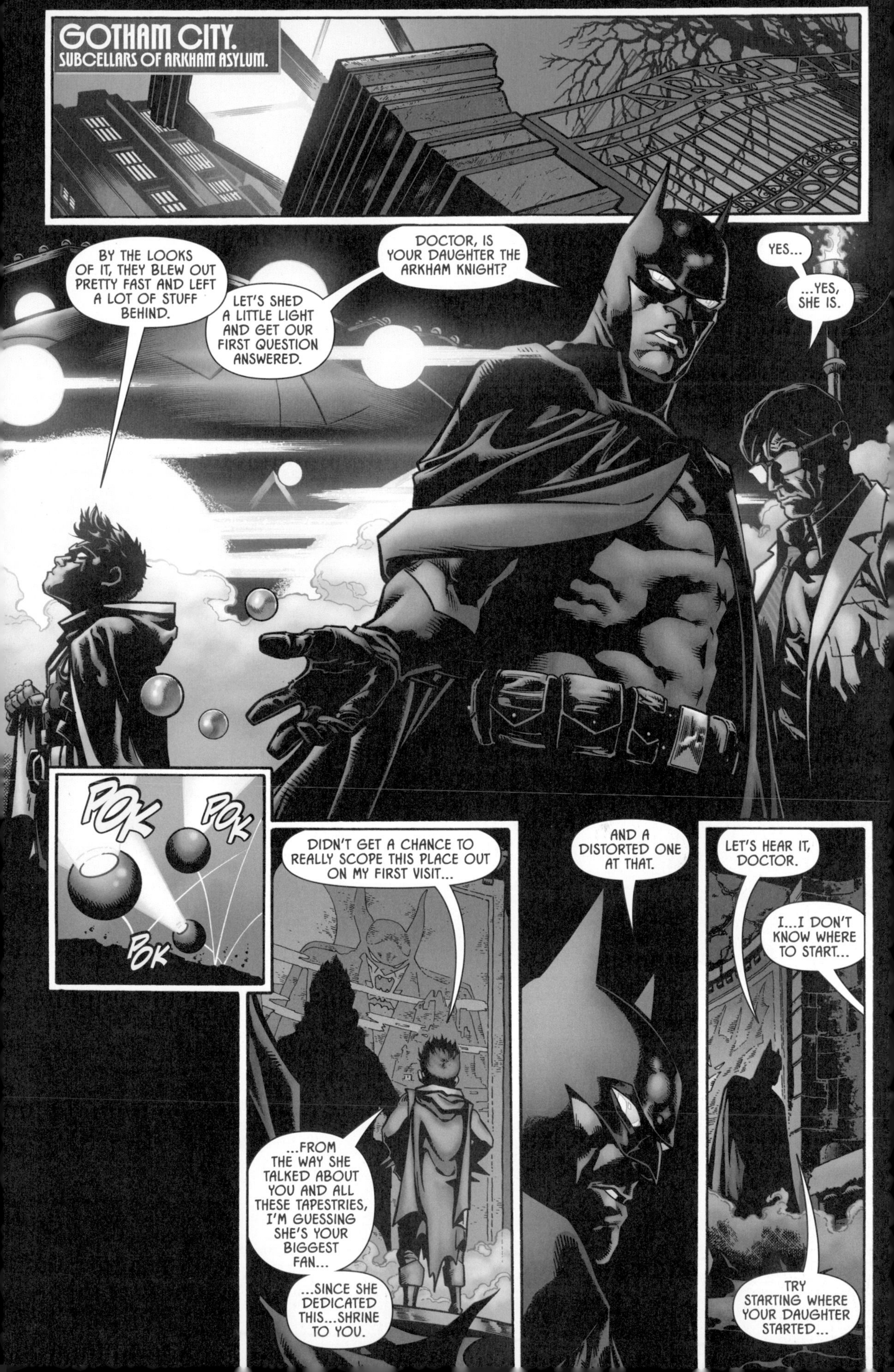
GOTHAM CITY.
SUBCELLARS OF ARKHAM ASYLUM.
BY THE LOOKS OF IT, THEY BLEW OUT PRETTY FAST AND LEFT A LOT OF STUFF BEHIND.
LET'S SHED A LITTLE LIGHT AND GET OUR FIRST QUESTION ANSWERED.
DOCTOR, IS YOUR DAUGHTER THE ARKHAM KNIGHT?
YES...
...YES, SHE IS.
POK
POK
POK
DIDN'T GET A CHANCE TO REALLY SCOPE THIS PLACE OUT ON MY FIRST VISIT...
...FROM THE WAY SHE TALKED ABOUT YOU AND ALL THESE TAPESTRIES, I'M GUESSING SHE'S YOUR BIGGEST FAN...
...SINCE SHE DEDICATED THIS...SHRINE TO YOU.
AND A DISTORTED ONE AT THAT.
LET'S HEAR IT, DOCTOR.
I...I DON'T KNOW WHERE TO START...
TRY STARTING WHERE YOUR DAUGHTER STARTED...

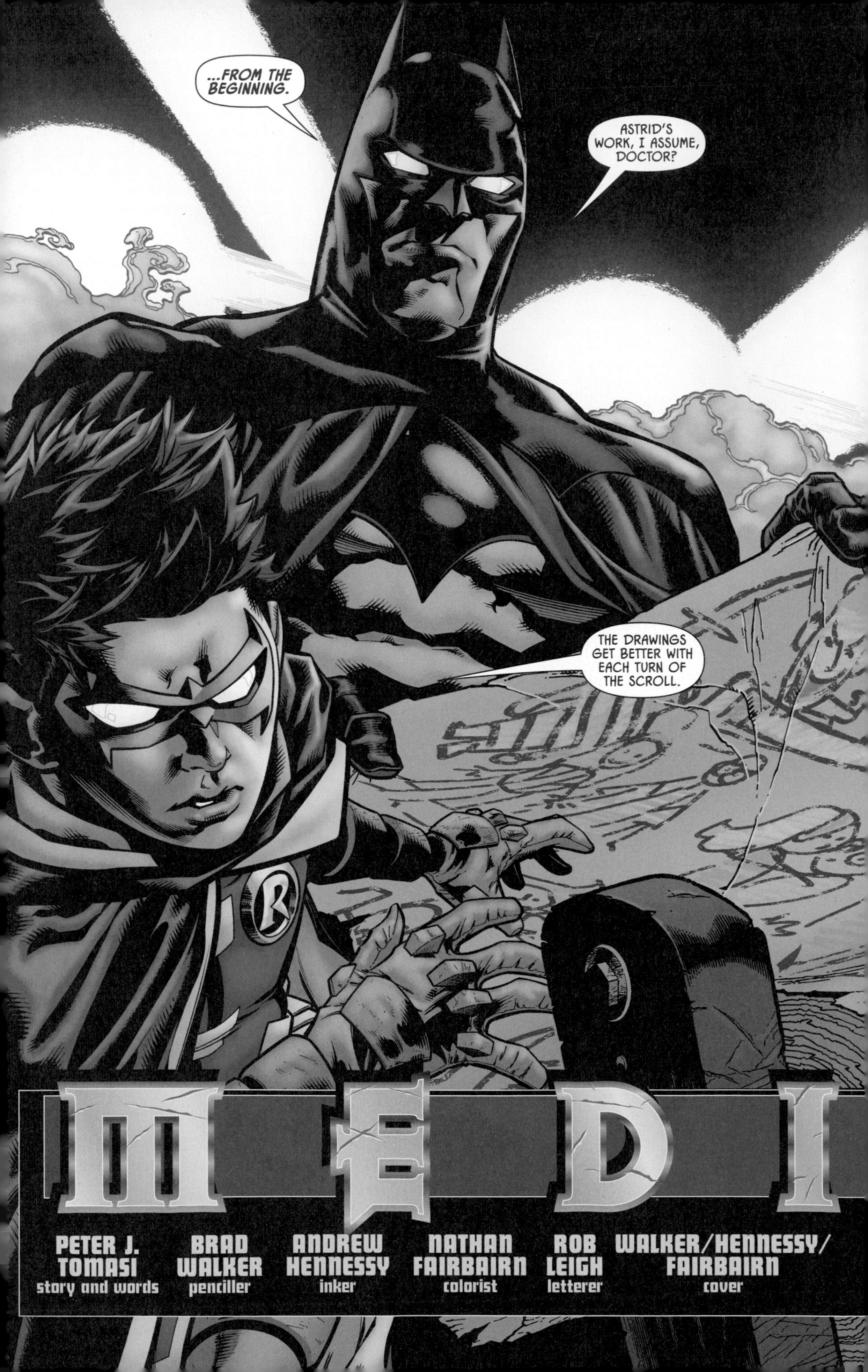

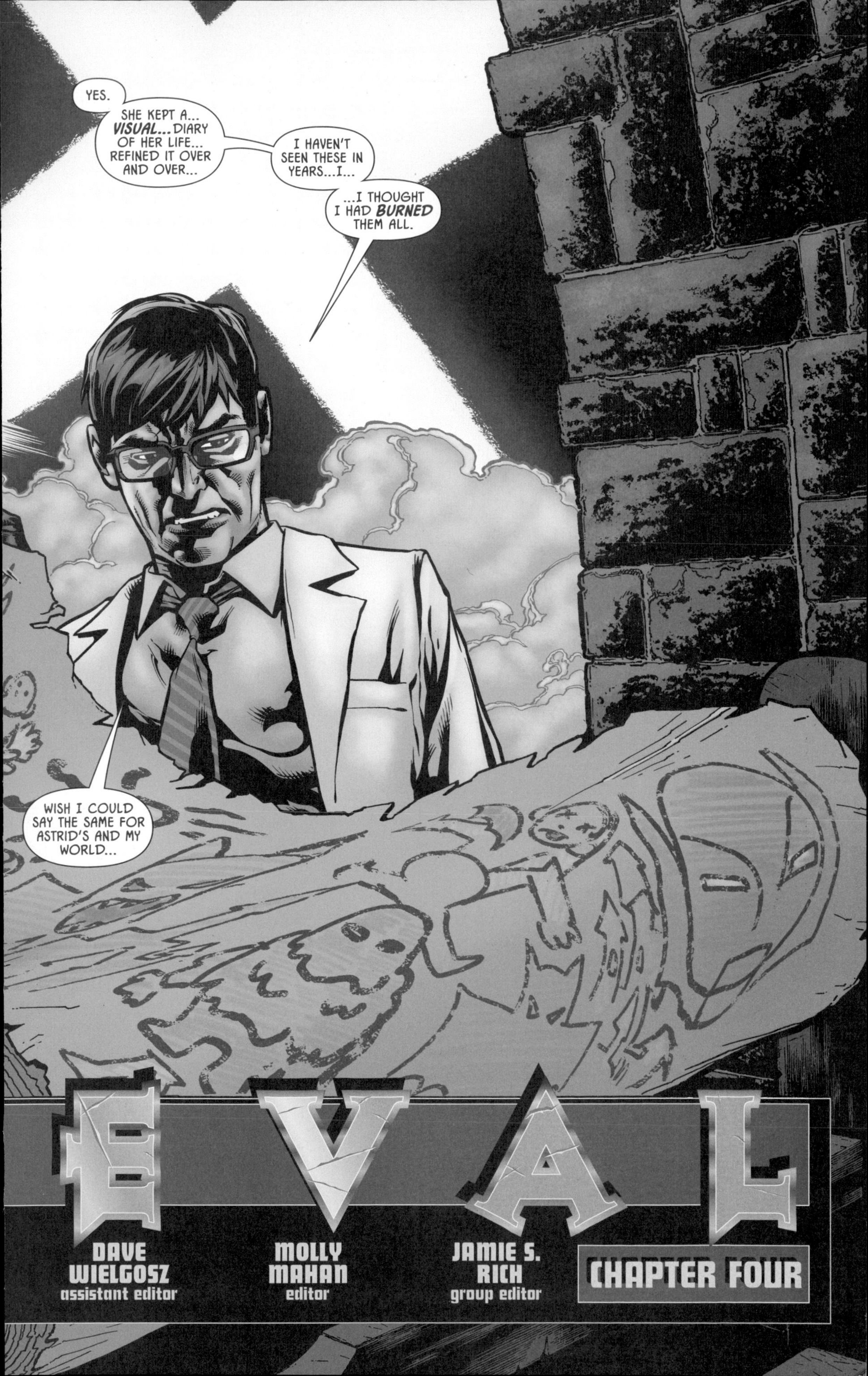
YES.
SHE KEPT A... VISUAL... DIARY OF HER LIFE... REFINED IT OVER AND OVER...
I HAVEN'T SEEN THESE IN YEARS...I...
...I THOUGHT I HAD BURNED THEM ALL.
WISH I COULD SAY THE SAME FOR ASTRID'S AND MY WORLD...
EVAL
DAVE WIELGOSZ assistant editor
MOLLY MAHAN editor
JAMIE S. RICH group editor
CHAPTER FOUR

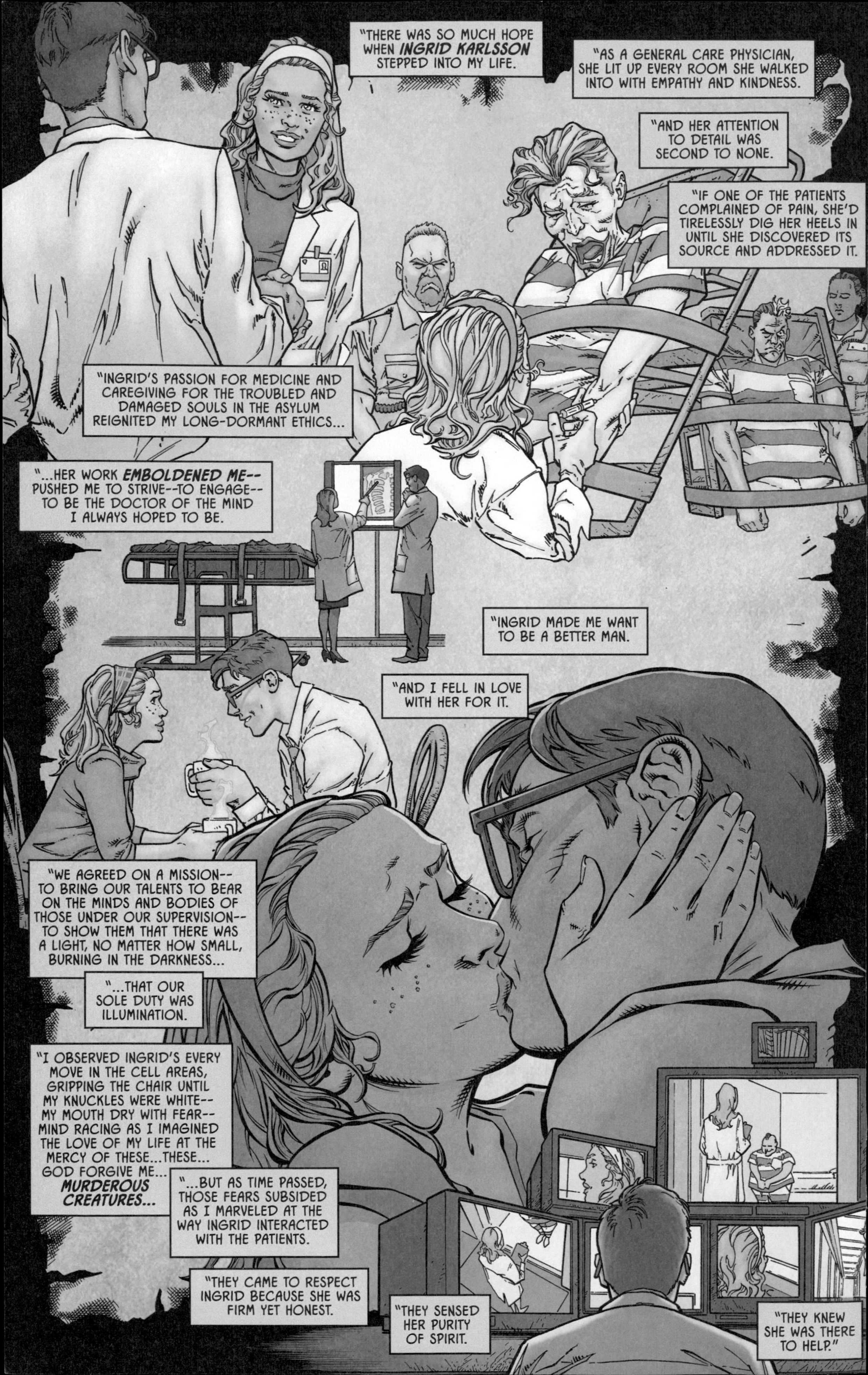
"THERE WAS SO MUCH HOPE WHEN INGRID KARLSSON STEPPED INTO MY LIFE.
"AS A GENERAL CARE PHYSICIAN, SHE LIT UP EVERY ROOM SHE WALKED INTO WITH EMPATHY AND KINDNESS.
"AND HER ATTENTION TO DETAIL WAS SECOND TO NONE.
"IF ONE OF THE PATIENTS COMPLAINED OF PAIN, SHE'D TIRELESSLY DIG HER HEELS IN UNTIL SHE DISCOVERED ITS SOURCE AND ADDRESSED IT.
"INGRID'S PASSION FOR MEDICINE AND CAREGIVING FOR THE TROUBLED AND DAMAGED SOULS IN THE ASYLUM REIGNITED MY LONG-DORMANT ETHICS...
"...HER WORK EMBOLDENED ME--PUSHED ME TO STRIVE--TO ENGAGE--TO BE THE DOCTOR OF THE MIND I ALWAYS HOPED TO BE.
"INGRID MADE ME WANT TO BE A BETTER MAN.
"AND I FELL IN LOVE WITH HER FOR IT.
"WE AGREED ON A MISSION--TO BRING OUR TALENTS TO BEAR ON THE MINDS AND BODIES OF THOSE UNDER OUR SUPERVISION--TO SHOW THEM THAT THERE WAS A LIGHT, NO MATTER HOW SMALL, BURNING IN THE DARKNESS...
"...THAT OUR SOLE DUTY WAS ILLUMINATION.
"I OBSERVED INGRID'S EVERY MOVE IN THE CELL AREAS, GRIPPING THE CHAIR UNTIL MY KNUCKLES WERE WHITE--MY MOUTH DRY WITH FEAR--MIND RACING AS I IMAGINED THE LOVE OF MY LIFE AT THE MERCY OF THESE...THESE... GOD FORGIVE ME... MURDEROUS CREATURES...
"...BUT AS TIME PASSED, THOSE FEARS SUBSIDED AS I MARVELED AT THE WAY INGRID INTERACTED WITH THE PATIENTS.
"THEY CAME TO RESPECT INGRID BECAUSE SHE WAS FIRM YET HONEST.
"THEY SENSED HER PURITY OF SPIRIT.
"THEY KNEW SHE WAS THERE TO HELP."

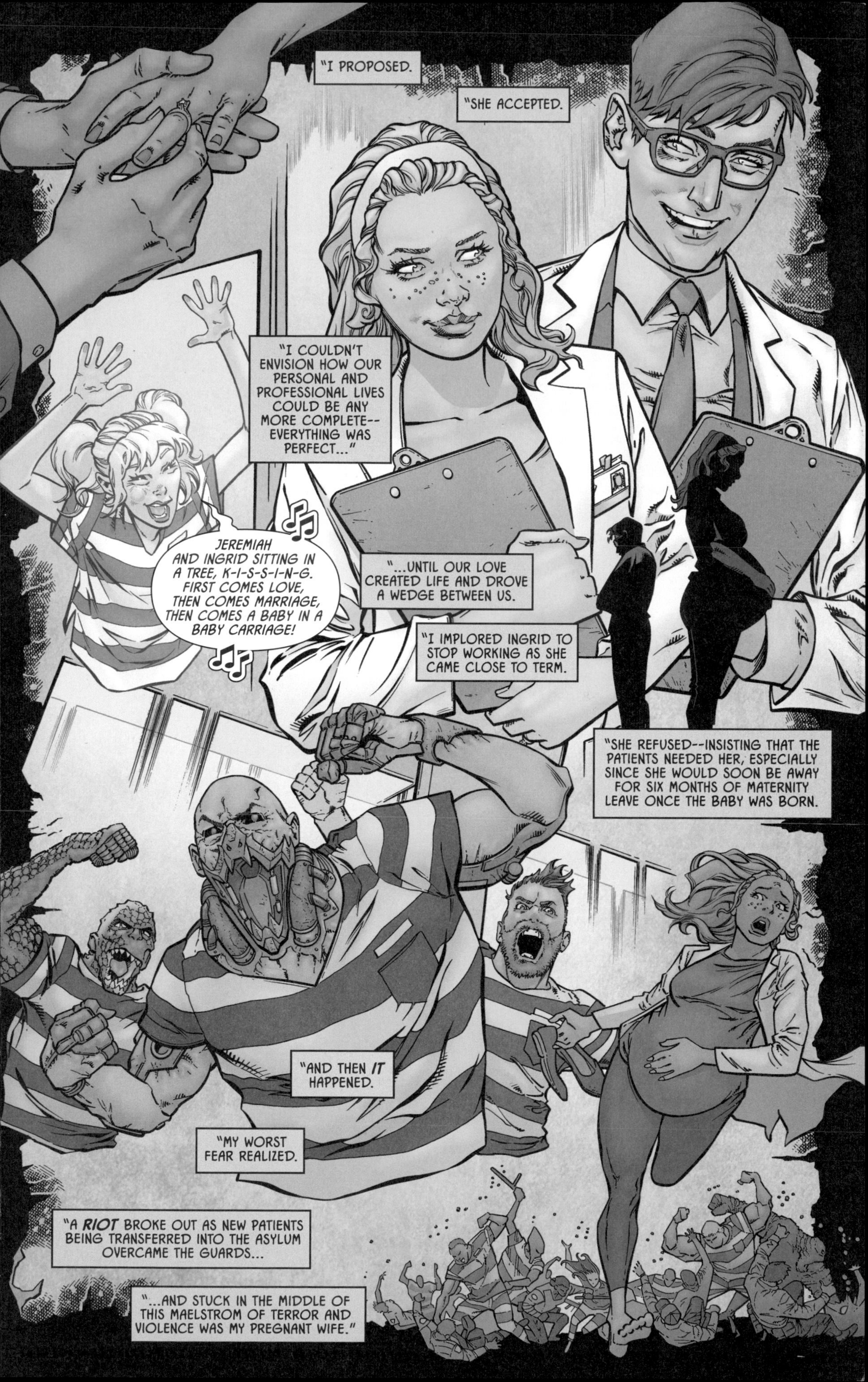
"I PROPOSED.
"SHE ACCEPTED.
"I COULDN'T ENVISION HOW OUR PERSONAL AND PROFESSIONAL LIVES COULD BE ANY MORE COMPLETE--EVERYTHING WAS PERFECT..."
JEREMIAH AND INGRID SITTING IN A TREE, K-I-S-S-I-N-G. FIRST COMES LOVE, THEN COMES MARRIAGE, THEN COMES A BABY IN A BABY CARRIAGE!
"...UNTIL OUR LOVE CREATED LIFE AND DROVE A WEDGE BETWEEN US.
"I IMPLORED INGRID TO STOP WORKING AS SHE CAME CLOSE TO TERM.
"SHE REFUSED--INSISTING THAT THE PATIENTS NEEDED HER, ESPECIALLY SINCE SHE WOULD SOON BE AWAY FOR SIX MONTHS OF MATERNITY LEAVE ONCE THE BABY WAS BORN.
"AND THEN *IT* HAPPENED.
"MY WORST FEAR REALIZED.
"A ***RIOT*** BROKE OUT AS NEW PATIENTS BEING TRANSFERRED INTO THE ASYLUM OVERCAME THE GUARDS...
"...AND STUCK IN THE MIDDLE OF THIS MAELSTROM OF TERROR AND VIOLENCE WAS MY PREGNANT WIFE."

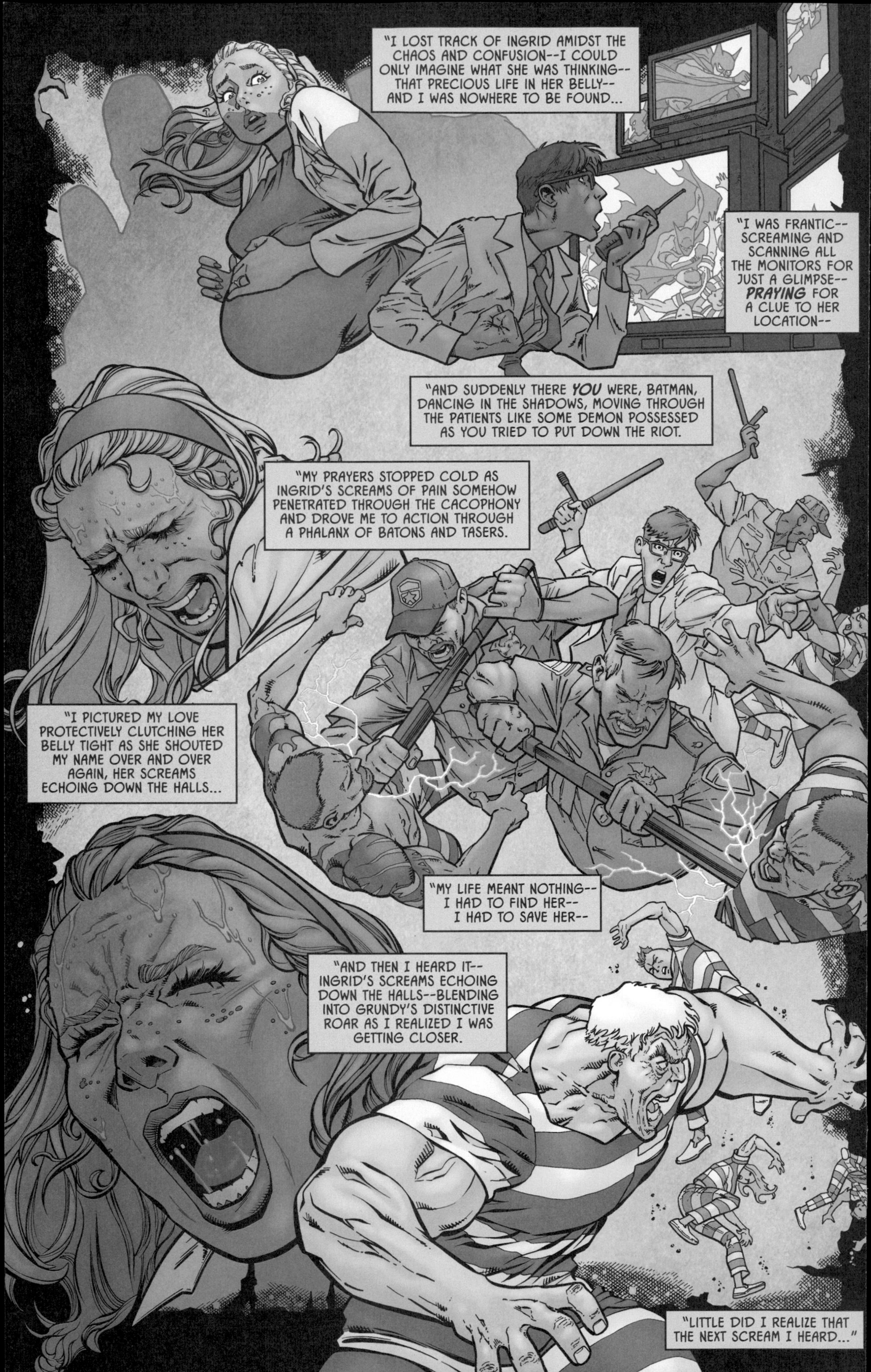
"I LOST TRACK OF INGRID AMIDST THE CHAOS AND CONFUSION--I COULD ONLY IMAGINE WHAT SHE WAS THINKING--THAT PRECIOUS LIFE IN HER BELLY--AND I WAS NOWHERE TO BE FOUND...
"I WAS FRANTIC--SCREAMING AND SCANNING ALL THE MONITORS FOR JUST A GLIMPSE--PRAYING FOR A CLUE TO HER LOCATION--
"AND SUDDENLY THERE YOU WERE, BATMAN, DANCING IN THE SHADOWS, MOVING THROUGH THE PATIENTS LIKE SOME DEMON POSSESSED AS YOU TRIED TO PUT DOWN THE RIOT.
"MY PRAYERS STOPPED COLD AS INGRID'S SCREAMS OF PAIN SOMEHOW PENETRATED THROUGH THE CACOPHONY AND DROVE ME TO ACTION THROUGH A PHALANX OF BATONS AND TASERS.
"I PICTURED MY LOVE PROTECTIVELY CLUTCHING HER BELLY TIGHT AS SHE SHOUTED MY NAME OVER AND OVER AGAIN, HER SCREAMS ECHOING DOWN THE HALLS...
"MY LIFE MEANT NOTHING--I HAD TO FIND HER--I HAD TO SAVE HER--
"AND THEN I HEARD IT--INGRID'S SCREAMS ECHOING DOWN THE HALLS--BLENDING INTO GRUNDY'S DISTINCTIVE ROAR AS I REALIZED I WAS GETTING CLOSER.
"LITTLE DID I REALIZE THAT THE NEXT SCREAM I HEARD..."

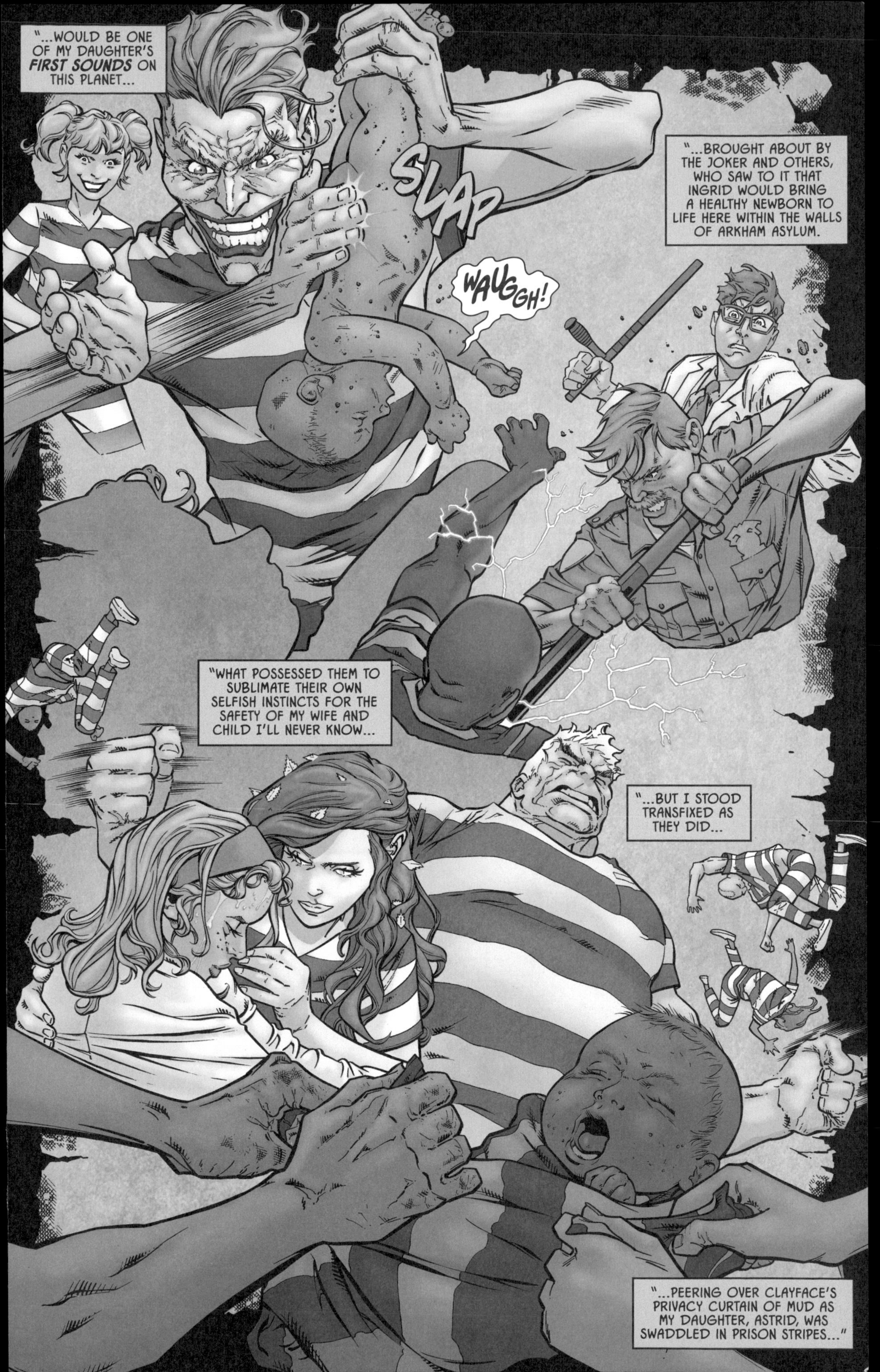
"...WOULD BE ONE OF MY DAUGHTER'S FIRST SOUNDS ON THIS PLANET...
SLAP
"...BROUGHT ABOUT BY THE JOKER AND OTHERS, WHO SAW TO IT THAT INGRID WOULD BRING A HEALTHY NEWBORN TO LIFE HERE WITHIN THE WALLS OF ARKHAM ASYLUM.
WAAUGGH!
"WHAT POSSESSED THEM TO SUBLIMATE THEIR OWN SELFISH INSTINCTS FOR THE SAFETY OF MY WIFE AND CHILD I'LL NEVER KNOW...
"...BUT I STOOD TRANSFIXED AS THEY DID...
"...PEERING OVER CLAYFACE'S PRIVACY CURTAIN OF MUD AS MY DAUGHTER, ASTRID, WAS SWADDLED IN PRISON STRIPES..."

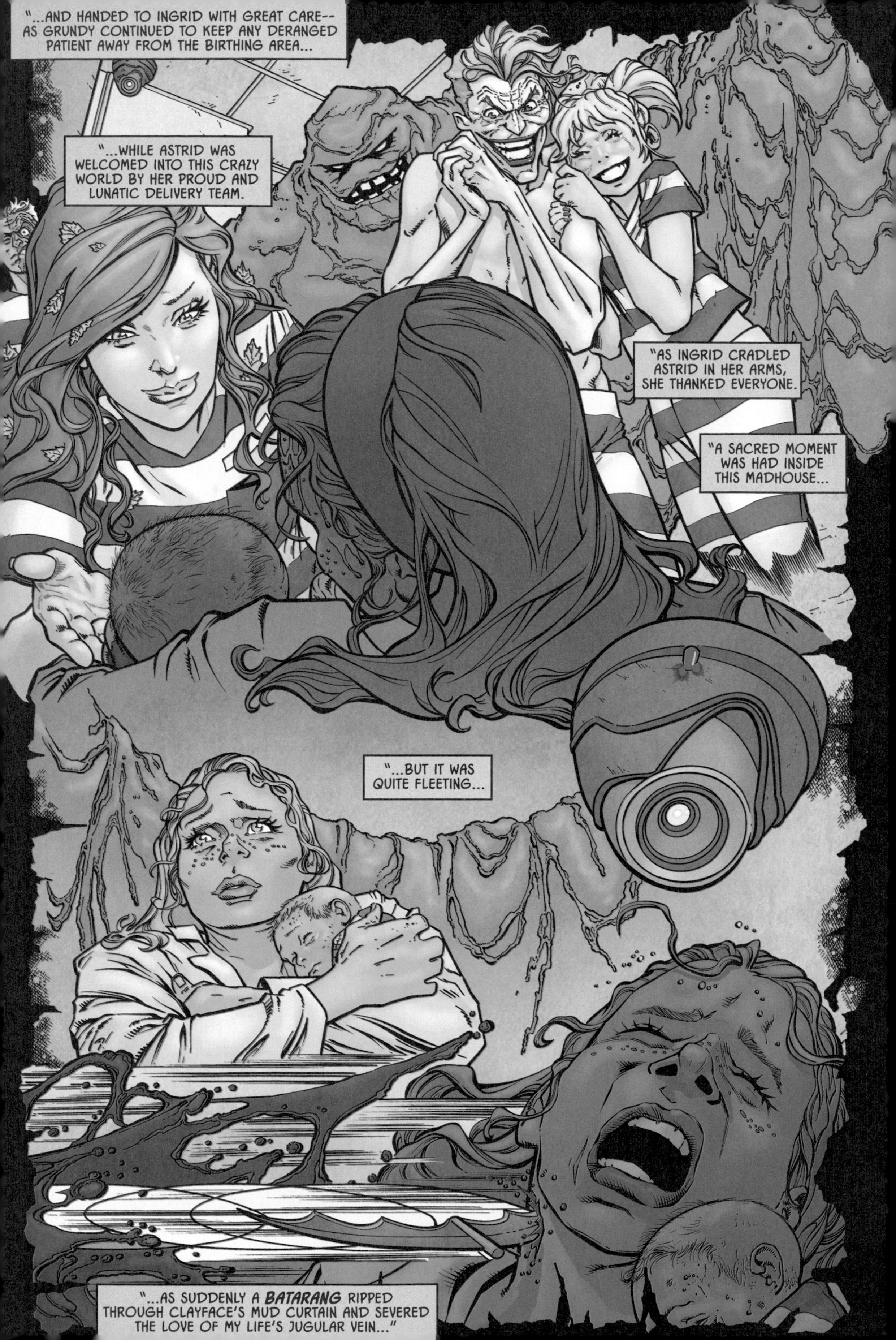
"...AND HANDED TO INGRID WITH GREAT CARE-- AS GRUNDY CONTINUED TO KEEP ANY DERANGED PATIENT AWAY FROM THE BIRTHING AREA...
"...WHILE ASTRID WAS WELCOMED INTO THIS CRAZY WORLD BY HER PROUD AND LUNATIC DELIVERY TEAM.
"AS INGRID CRADLED ASTRID IN HER ARMS, SHE THANKED EVERYONE.
"A SACRED MOMENT WAS HAD INSIDE THIS MADHOUSE...
"...BUT IT WAS QUITE FLEETING...
"...AS SUDDENLY A BATARANG RIPPED THROUGH CLAYFACE'S MUD CURTAIN AND SEVERED THE LOVE OF MY LIFE'S JUGULAR VEIN..."

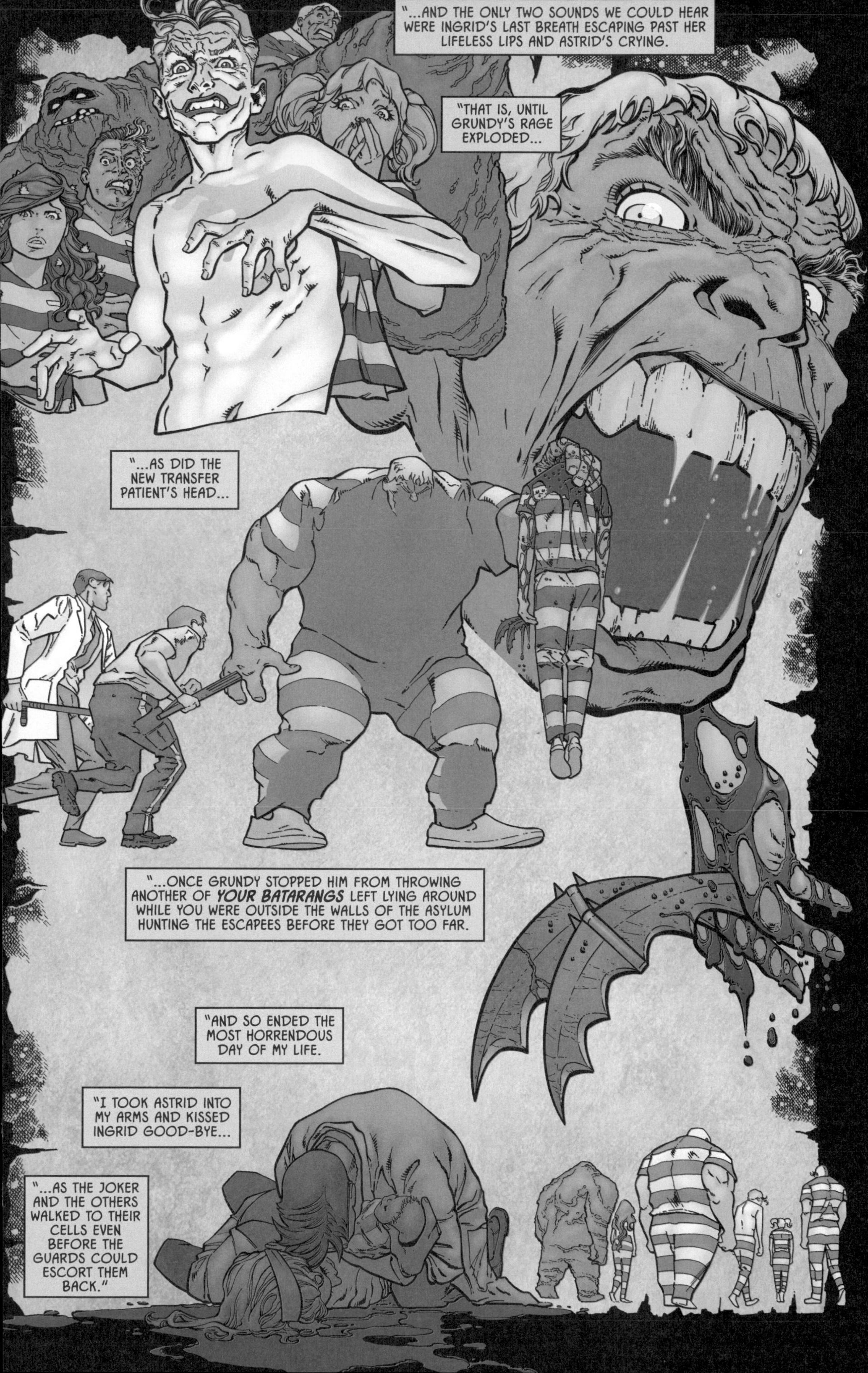
"...AND THE ONLY TWO SOUNDS WE COULD HEAR WERE INGRID'S LAST BREATH ESCAPING PAST HER LIFELESS LIPS AND ASTRID'S CRYING.
"THAT IS, UNTIL GRUNDY'S RAGE EXPLODED...
"...AS DID THE NEW TRANSFER PATIENT'S HEAD...
"...ONCE GRUNDY STOPPED HIM FROM THROWING ANOTHER OF YOUR BATARANGS LEFT LYING AROUND WHILE YOU WERE OUTSIDE THE WALLS OF THE ASYLUM HUNTING THE ESCAPEES BEFORE THEY GOT TOO FAR.
"AND SO ENDED THE MOST HORRENDOUS DAY OF MY LIFE.
"I TOOK ASTRID INTO MY ARMS AND KISSED INGRID GOOD-BYE...
"...AS THE JOKER AND THE OTHERS WALKED TO THEIR CELLS EVEN BEFORE THE GUARDS COULD ESCORT THEM BACK."

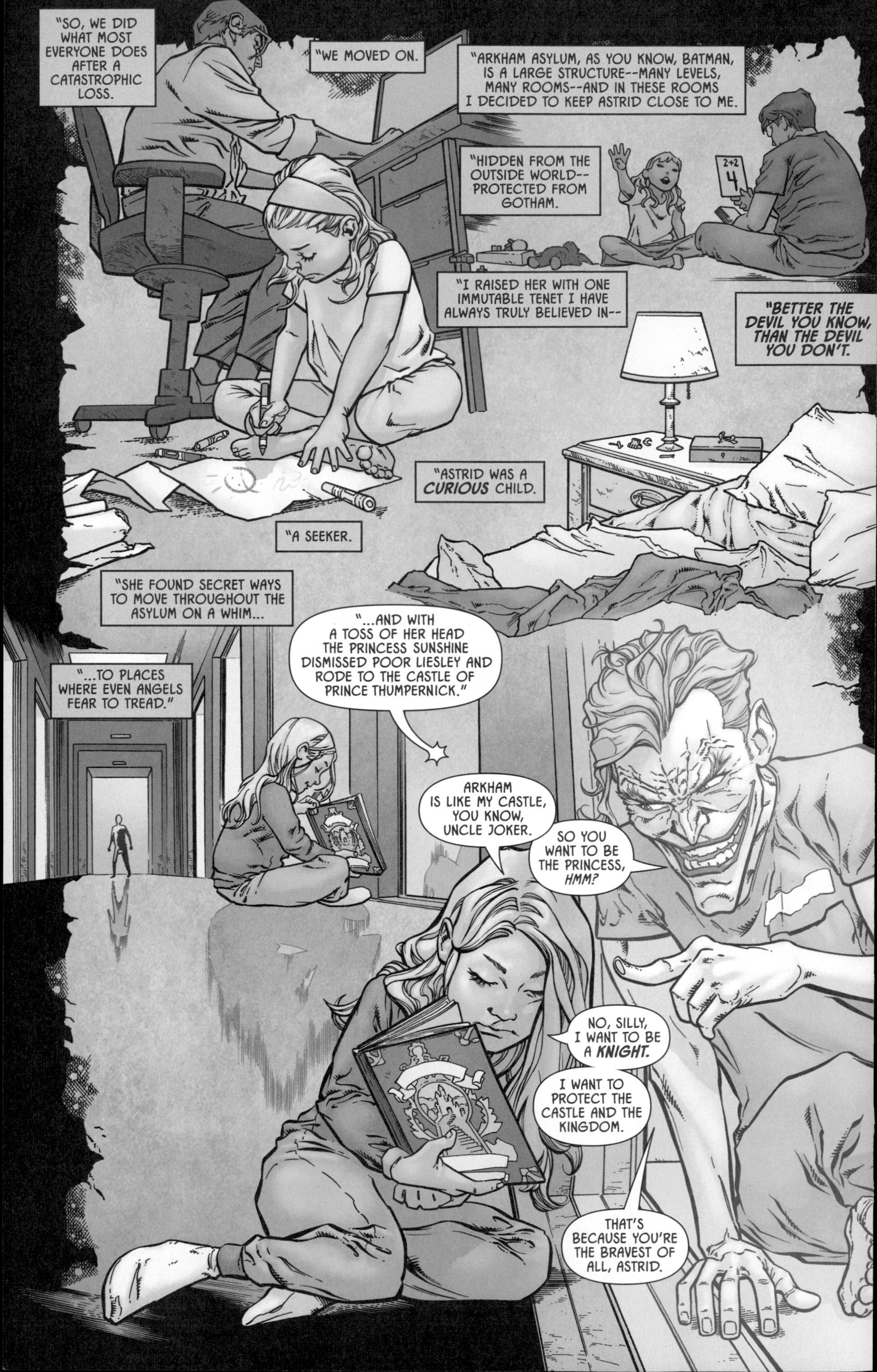
"SO, WE DID WHAT MOST EVERYONE DOES AFTER A CATASTROPHIC LOSS.
"WE MOVED ON.
"ARKHAM ASYLUM, AS YOU KNOW, BATMAN, IS A LARGE STRUCTURE--MANY LEVELS, MANY ROOMS--AND IN THESE ROOMS I DECIDED TO KEEP ASTRID CLOSE TO ME.
"HIDDEN FROM THE OUTSIDE WORLD--PROTECTED FROM GOTHAM.
2+2 4
"I RAISED HER WITH ONE IMMUTABLE TENET I HAVE ALWAYS TRULY BELIEVED IN--
"BETTER THE DEVIL YOU KNOW, THAN THE DEVIL YOU DON'T.
"ASTRID WAS A CURIOUS CHILD.
"A SEEKER.
"SHE FOUND SECRET WAYS TO MOVE THROUGHOUT THE ASYLUM ON A WHIM...
"...TO PLACES WHERE EVEN ANGELS FEAR TO TREAD."
"...AND WITH A TOSS OF HER HEAD THE PRINCESS SUNSHINE DISMISSED POOR LIESLEY AND RODE TO THE CASTLE OF PRINCE THUMPERNICK."
ARKHAM IS LIKE MY CASTLE, YOU KNOW, UNCLE JOKER.
SO YOU WANT TO BE THE PRINCESS, HMM?
NO, SILLY, I WANT TO BE A KNIGHT.
I WANT TO PROTECT THE CASTLE AND THE KINGDOM.
THAT'S BECAUSE YOU'RE THE BRAVEST OF ALL, ASTRID.

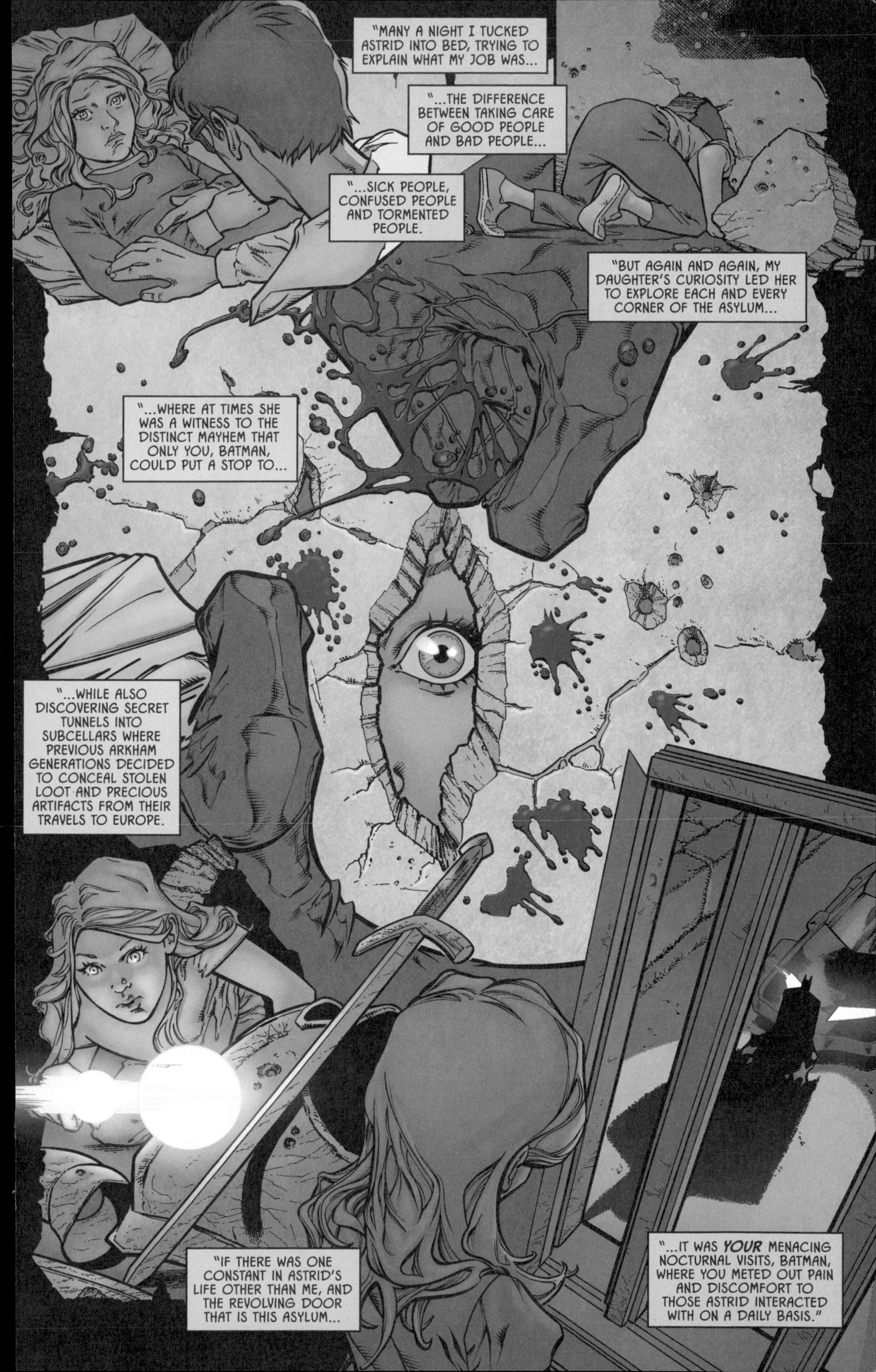
"MANY A NIGHT I TUCKED ASTRID INTO BED, TRYING TO EXPLAIN WHAT MY JOB WAS...
"...THE DIFFERENCE BETWEEN TAKING CARE OF GOOD PEOPLE AND BAD PEOPLE...
"...SICK PEOPLE, CONFUSED PEOPLE AND TORMENTED PEOPLE.
"BUT AGAIN AND AGAIN, MY DAUGHTER'S CURIOSITY LED HER TO EXPLORE EACH AND EVERY CORNER OF THE ASYLUM...
"...WHERE AT TIMES SHE WAS A WITNESS TO THE DISTINCT MAYHEM THAT ONLY YOU, BATMAN, COULD PUT A STOP TO...
"...WHILE ALSO DISCOVERING SECRET TUNNELS INTO SUBCELLARS WHERE PREVIOUS ARKHAM GENERATIONS DECIDED TO CONCEAL STOLEN LOOT AND PRECIOUS ARTIFACTS FROM THEIR TRAVELS TO EUROPE.
"IF THERE WAS ONE CONSTANT IN ASTRID'S LIFE OTHER THAN ME, AND THE REVOLVING DOOR THAT IS THIS ASYLUM...
"...IT WAS *YOUR* MENACING NOCTURNAL VISITS, BATMAN, WHERE YOU METED OUT PAIN AND DISCOMFORT TO THOSE ASTRID INTERACTED WITH ON A DAILY BASIS."

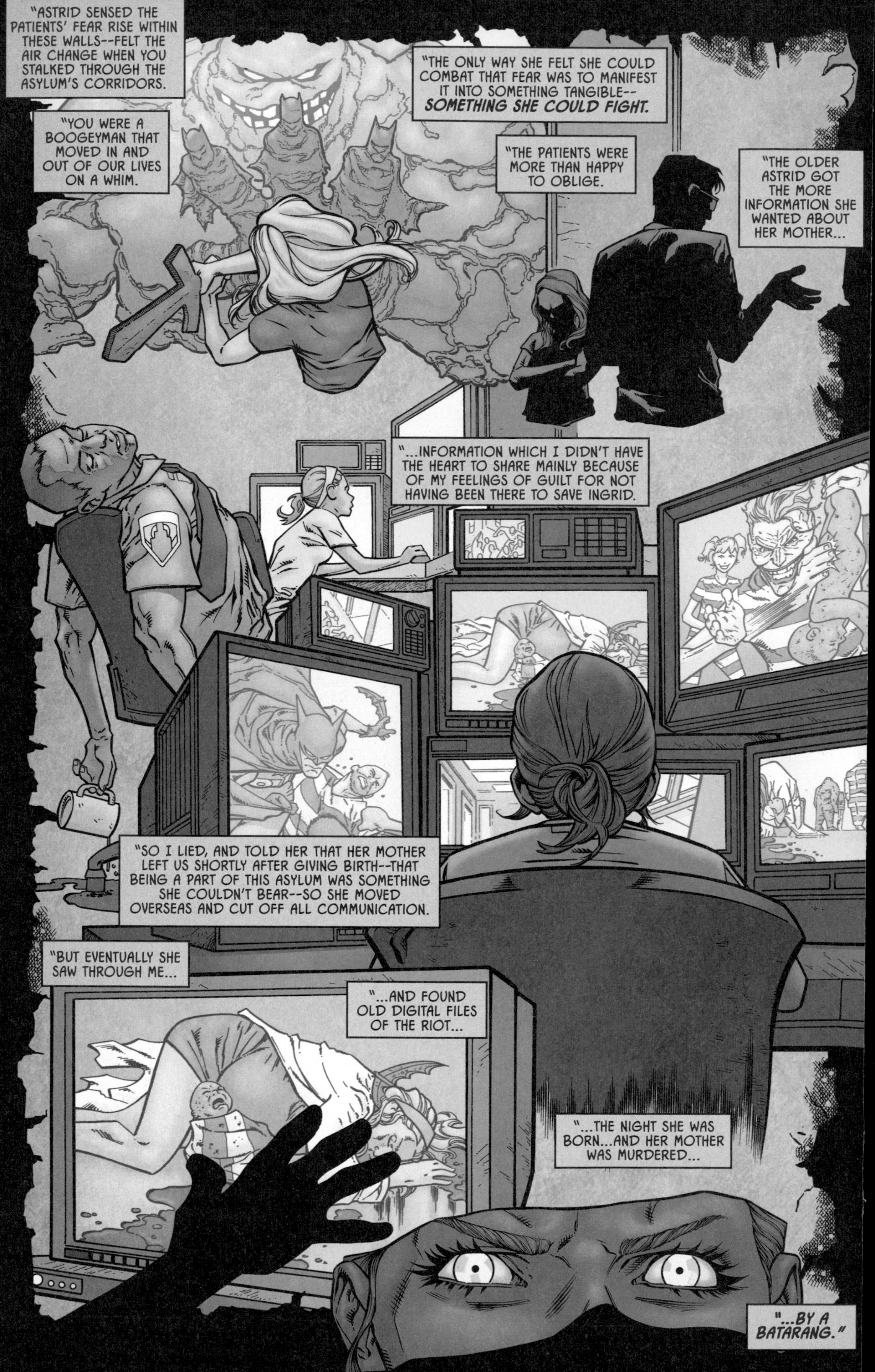
"ASTRID SENSED THE PATIENTS' FEAR RISE WITHIN THESE WALLS--FELT THE AIR CHANGE WHEN YOU STALKED THROUGH THE ASYLUM'S CORRIDORS.
"YOU WERE A BOOGEYMAN THAT MOVED IN AND OUT OF OUR LIVES ON A WHIM.
"THE ONLY WAY SHE FELT SHE COULD COMBAT THAT FEAR WAS TO MANIFEST IT INTO SOMETHING TANGIBLE-- SOMETHING SHE COULD FIGHT.
"THE PATIENTS WERE MORE THAN HAPPY TO OBLIGE.
"THE OLDER ASTRID GOT THE MORE INFORMATION SHE WANTED ABOUT HER MOTHER...
"...INFORMATION WHICH I DIDN'T HAVE THE HEART TO SHARE MAINLY BECAUSE OF MY FEELINGS OF GUILT FOR NOT HAVING BEEN THERE TO SAVE INGRID.
"SO I LIED, AND TOLD HER THAT HER MOTHER LEFT US SHORTLY AFTER GIVING BIRTH--THAT BEING A PART OF THIS ASYLUM WAS SOMETHING SHE COULDN'T BEAR--SO SHE MOVED OVERSEAS AND CUT OFF ALL COMMUNICATION.
"BUT EVENTUALLY SHE SAW THROUGH ME...
"...AND FOUND OLD DIGITAL FILES OF THE RIOT...
"...THE NIGHT SHE WAS BORN...AND HER MOTHER WAS MURDERED...
"...BY A BATARANG."

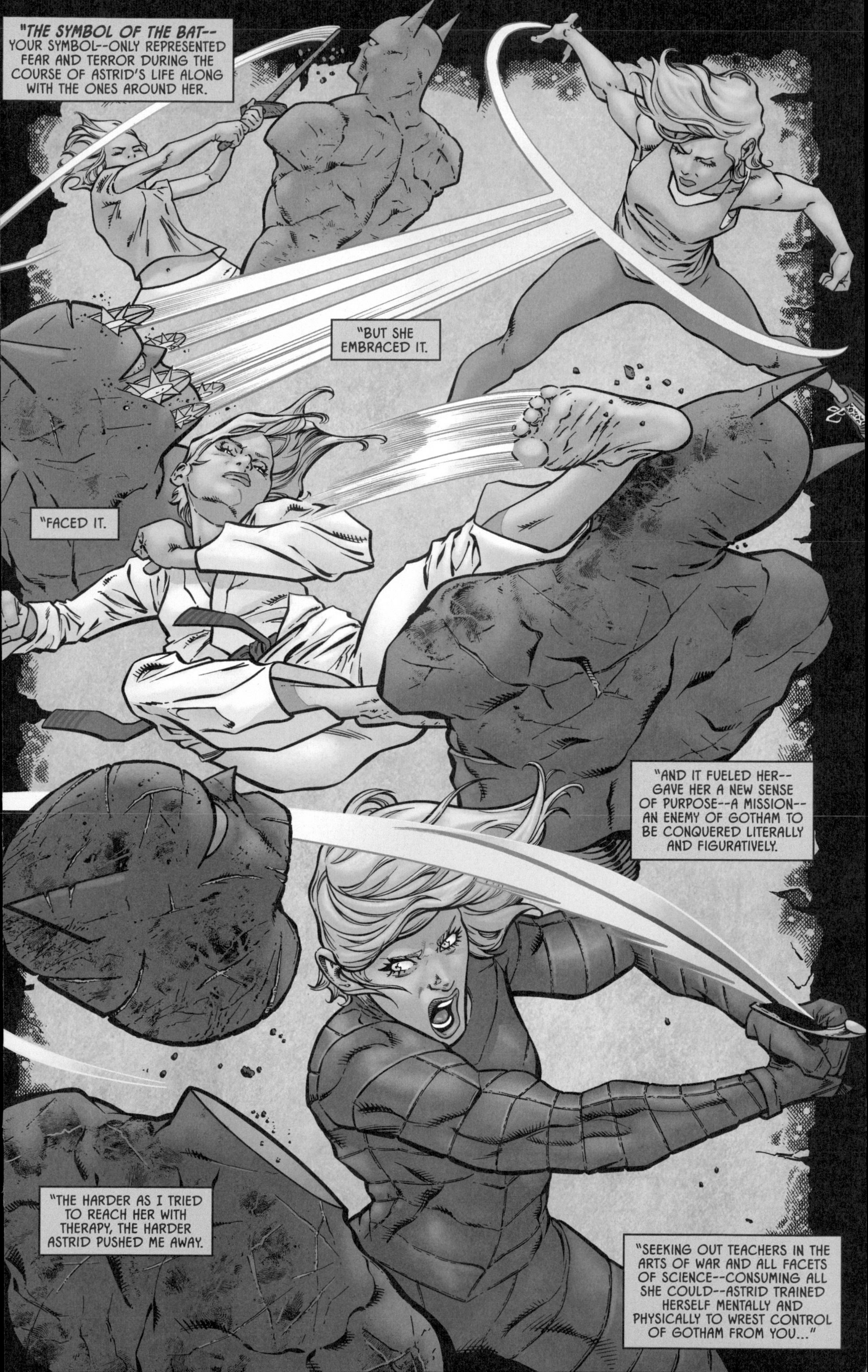
"THE SYMBOL OF THE BAT-- YOUR SYMBOL--ONLY REPRESENTED FEAR AND TERROR DURING THE COURSE OF ASTRID'S LIFE ALONG WITH THE ONES AROUND HER.
"BUT SHE EMBRACED IT.
"FACED IT.
"AND IT FUELED HER-- GAVE HER A NEW SENSE OF PURPOSE--A MISSION-- AN ENEMY OF GOTHAM TO BE CONQUERED LITERALLY AND FIGURATIVELY.
"THE HARDER AS I TRIED TO REACH HER WITH THERAPY, THE HARDER ASTRID PUSHED ME AWAY.
"SEEKING OUT TEACHERS IN THE ARTS OF WAR AND ALL FACETS OF SCIENCE--CONSUMING ALL SHE COULD--ASTRID TRAINED HERSELF MENTALLY AND PHYSICALLY TO WREST CONTROL OF GOTHAM FROM YOU..."

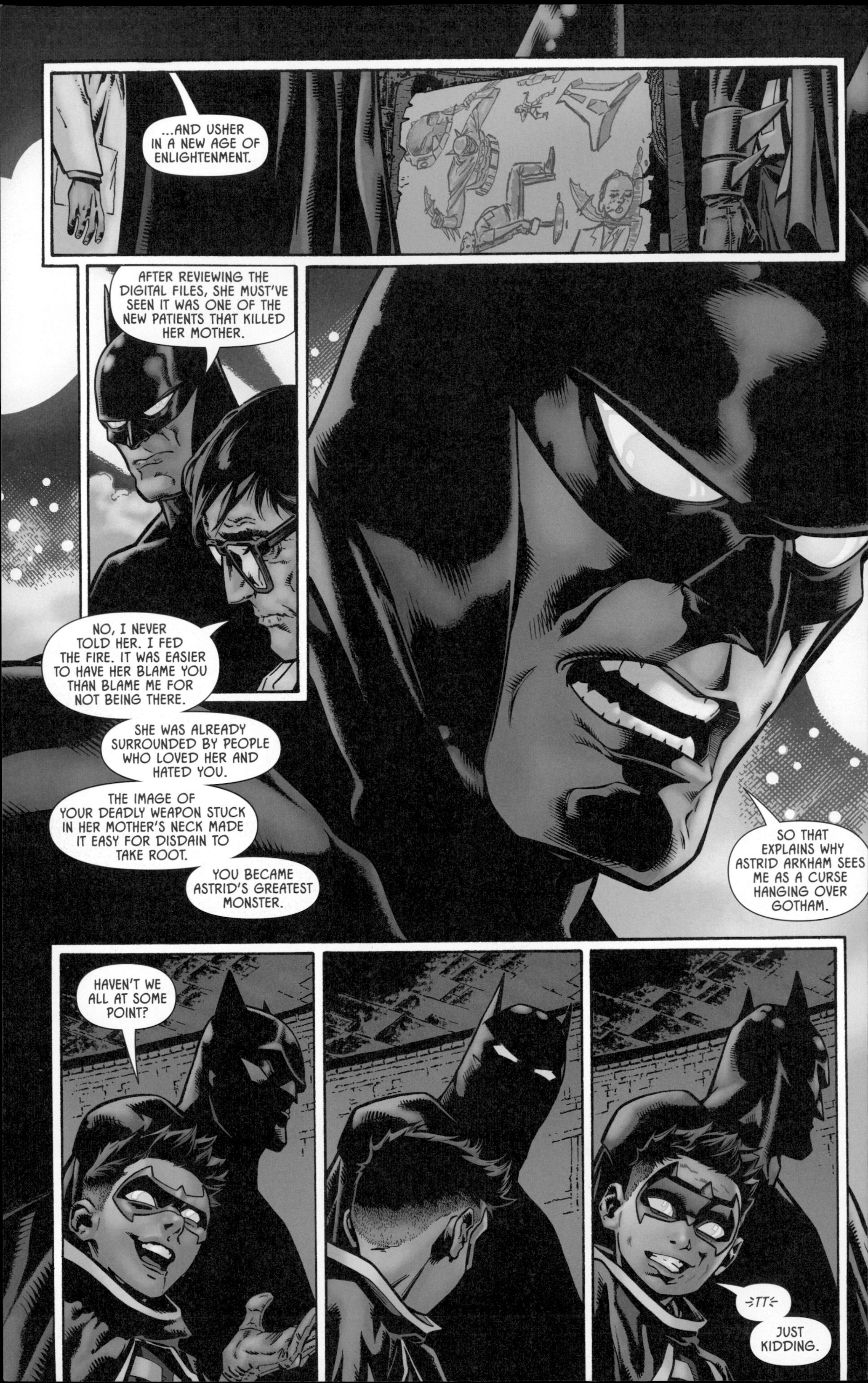
...AND USHER IN A NEW AGE OF ENLIGHTENMENT.
AFTER REVIEWING THE DIGITAL FILES, SHE MUST'VE SEEN IT WAS ONE OF THE NEW PATIENTS THAT KILLED HER MOTHER.
NO, I NEVER TOLD HER. I FED THE FIRE. IT WAS EASIER TO HAVE HER BLAME YOU THAN BLAME ME FOR NOT BEING THERE.
SHE WAS ALREADY SURROUNDED BY PEOPLE WHO LOVED HER AND HATED YOU.
THE IMAGE OF YOUR DEADLY WEAPON STUCK IN HER MOTHER'S NECK MADE IT EASY FOR DISDAIN TO TAKE ROOT.
YOU BECAME ASTRID'S GREATEST MONSTER.
SO THAT EXPLAINS WHY ASTRID ARKHAM SEES ME AS A CURSE HANGING OVER GOTHAM.
HAVEN'T WE ALL AT SOME POINT?
TT
JUST KIDDING.

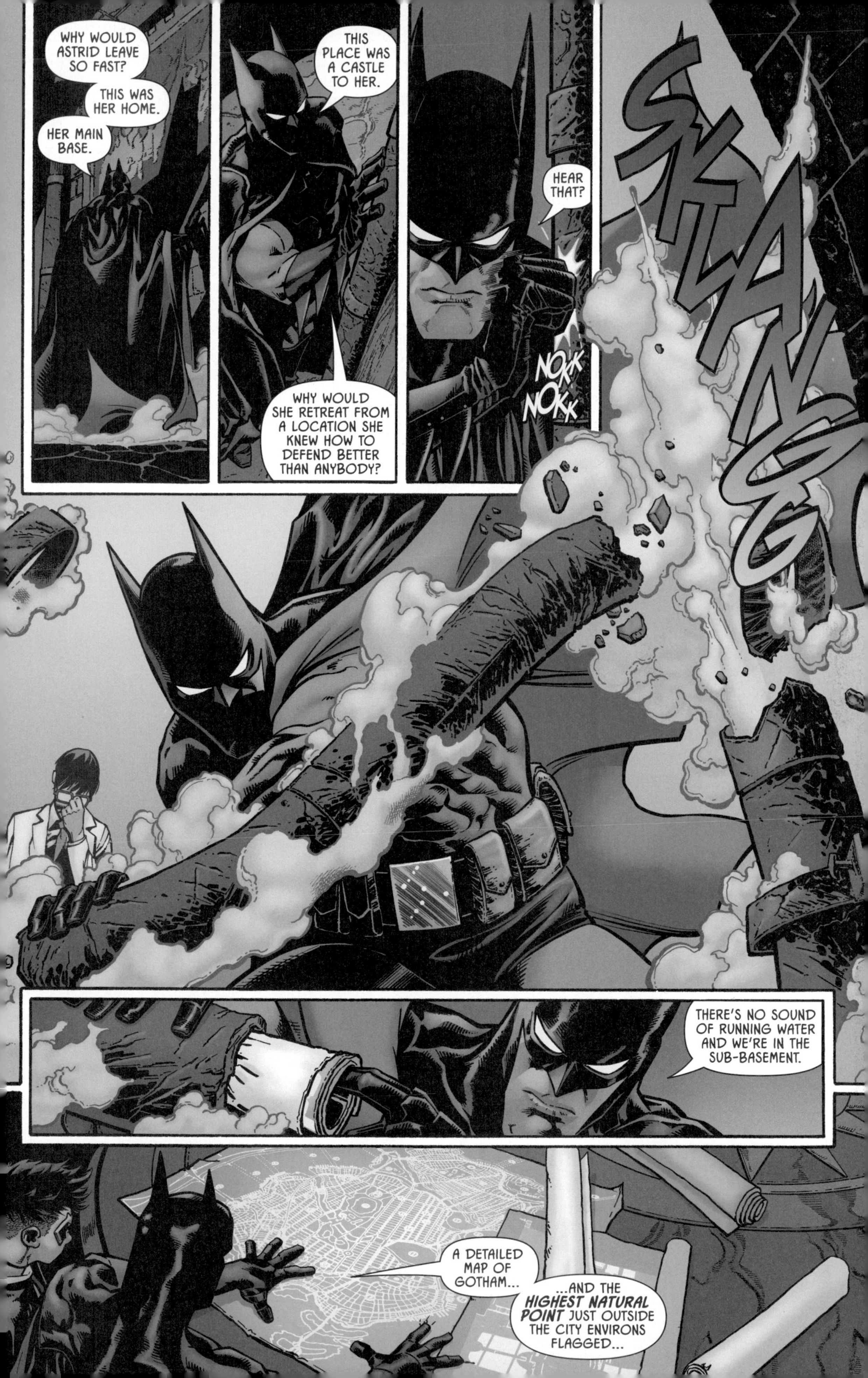
WHY WOULD ASTRID LEAVE SO FAST?
THIS WAS HER HOME.
HER MAIN BASE.
THIS PLACE WAS A CASTLE TO HER.
WHY WOULD SHE RETREAT FROM A LOCATION SHE KNEW HOW TO DEFEND BETTER THAN ANYBODY?
HEAR THAT?
NOKK NOKK
SKLANGG
THERE'S NO SOUND OF RUNNING WATER AND WE'RE IN THE SUB-BASEMENT.
A DETAILED MAP OF GOTHAM...
...AND THE HIGHEST NATURAL POINT JUST OUTSIDE THE CITY ENVIRONS FLAGGED...

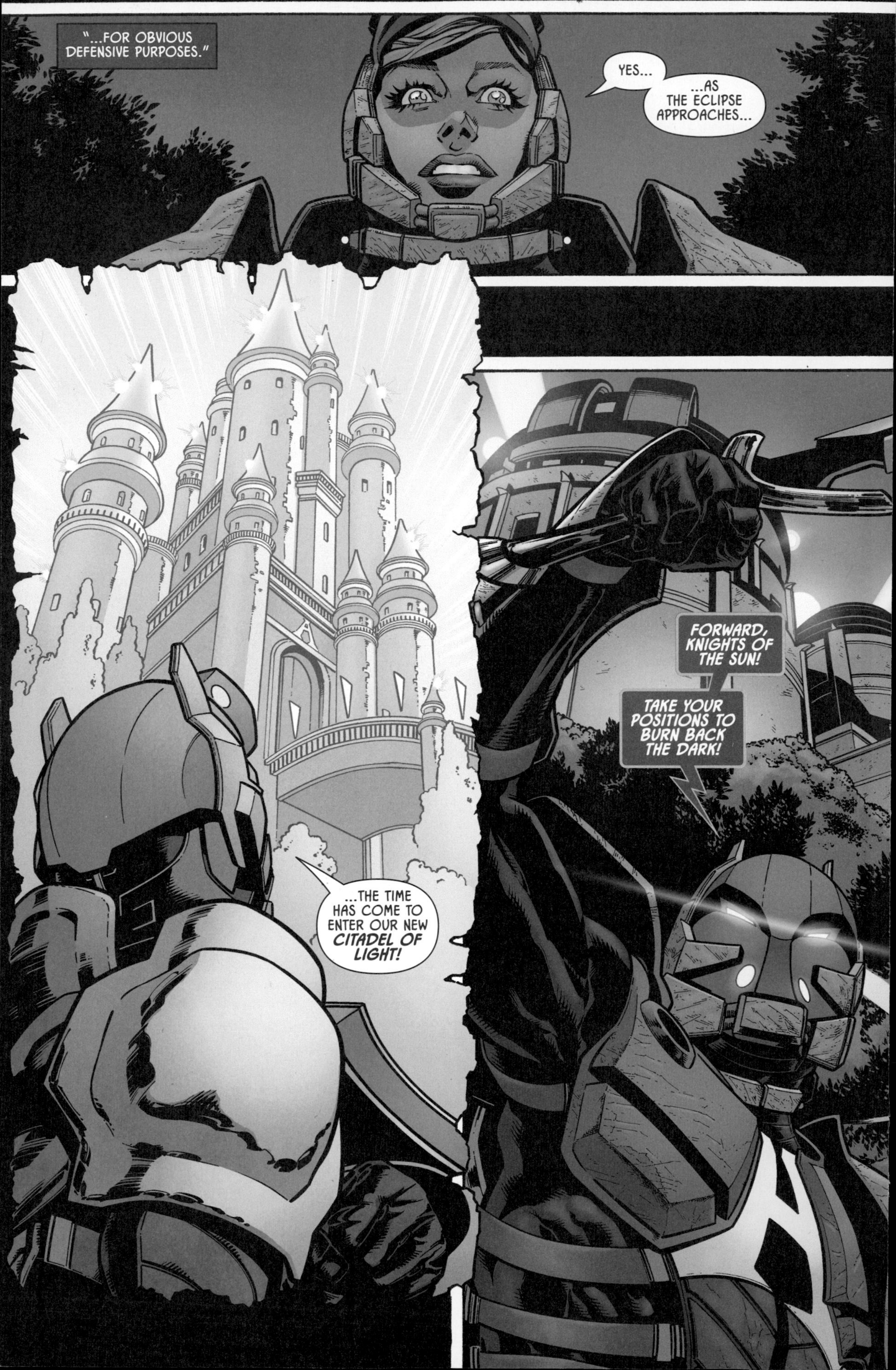
"...FOR OBVIOUS DEFENSIVE PURPOSES."
YES...
...AS THE ECLIPSE APPROACHES...
...THE TIME HAS COME TO ENTER OUR NEW *CITADEL OF LIGHT!*
FORWARD, KNIGHTS OF THE SUN!
TAKE YOUR POSITIONS TO BURN BACK THE DARK!

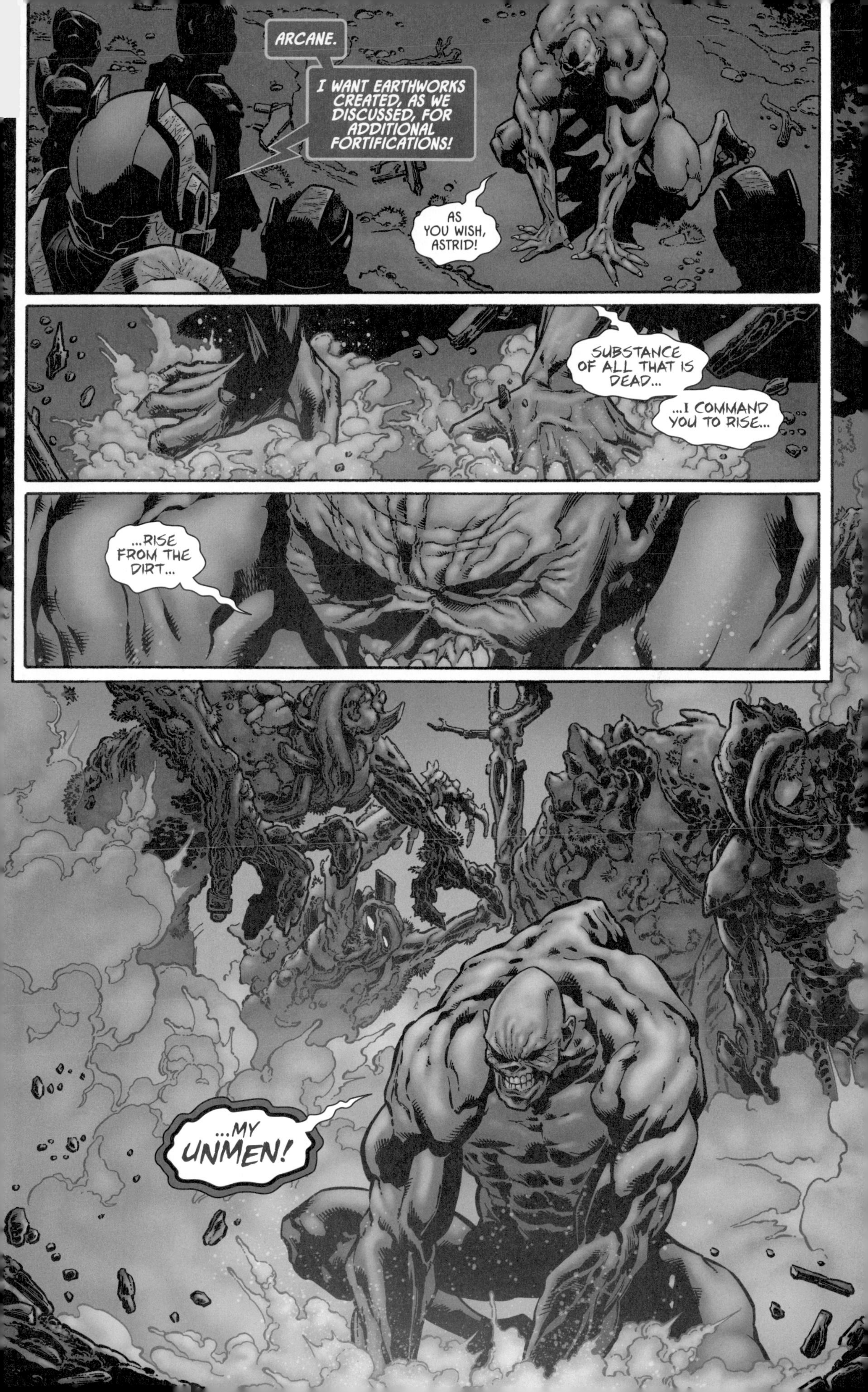
ARCANE.
I WANT EARTHWORKS CREATED, AS WE DISCUSSED, FOR ADDITIONAL FORTIFICATIONS!
AS YOU WISH, ASTRID!
SUBSTANCE OF ALL THAT IS DEAD...
...I COMMAND YOU TO RISE...
...RISE FROM THE DIRT...
...MY UNMEN!

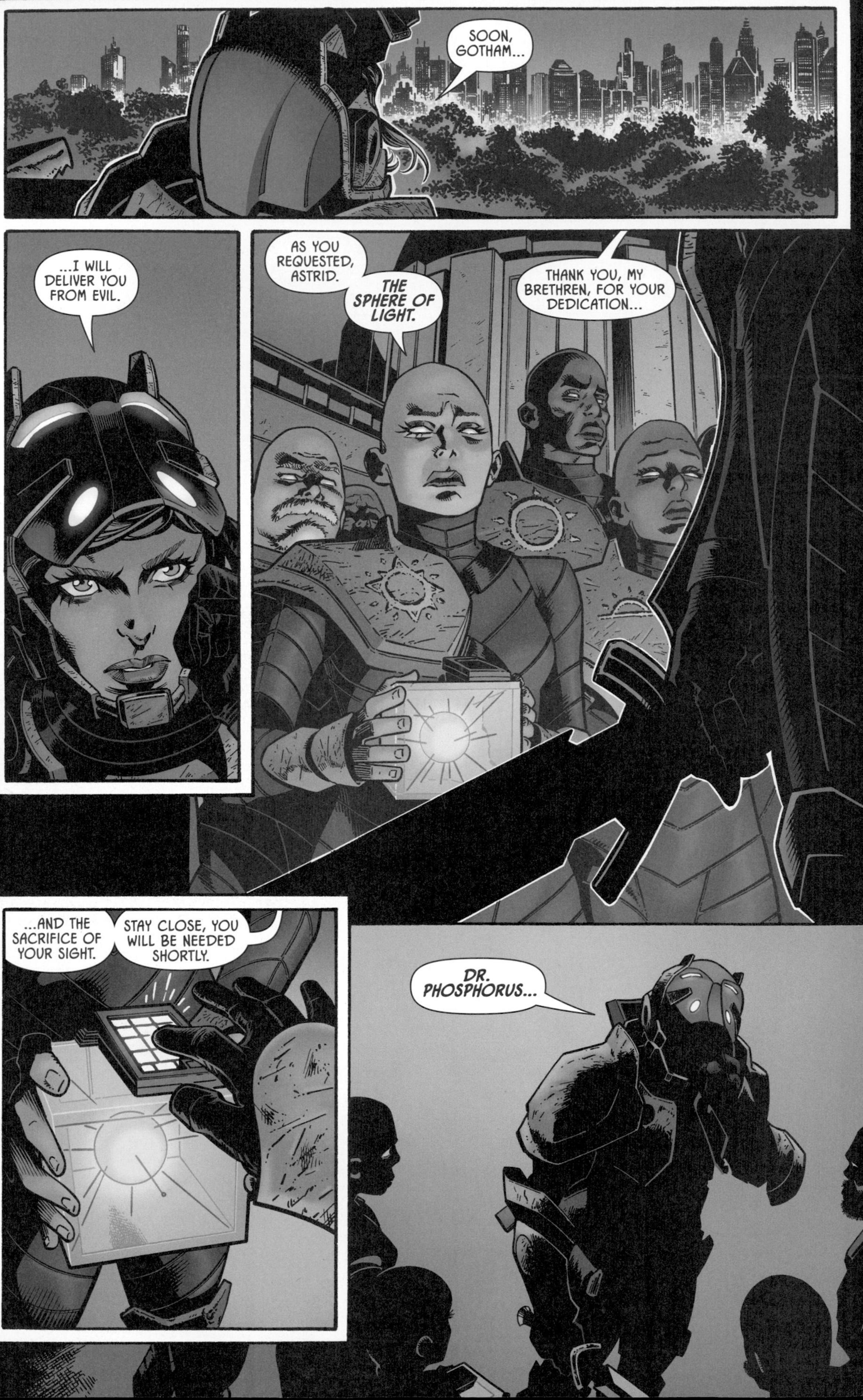
SOON, GOTHAM...
...I WILL DELIVER YOU FROM EVIL.
AS YOU REQUESTED, ASTRID.
THE SPHERE OF LIGHT.
THANK YOU, MY BRETHREN, FOR YOUR DEDICATION...
...AND THE SACRIFICE OF YOUR SIGHT.
STAY CLOSE, YOU WILL BE NEEDED SHORTLY.
DR. PHOSPHORUS...

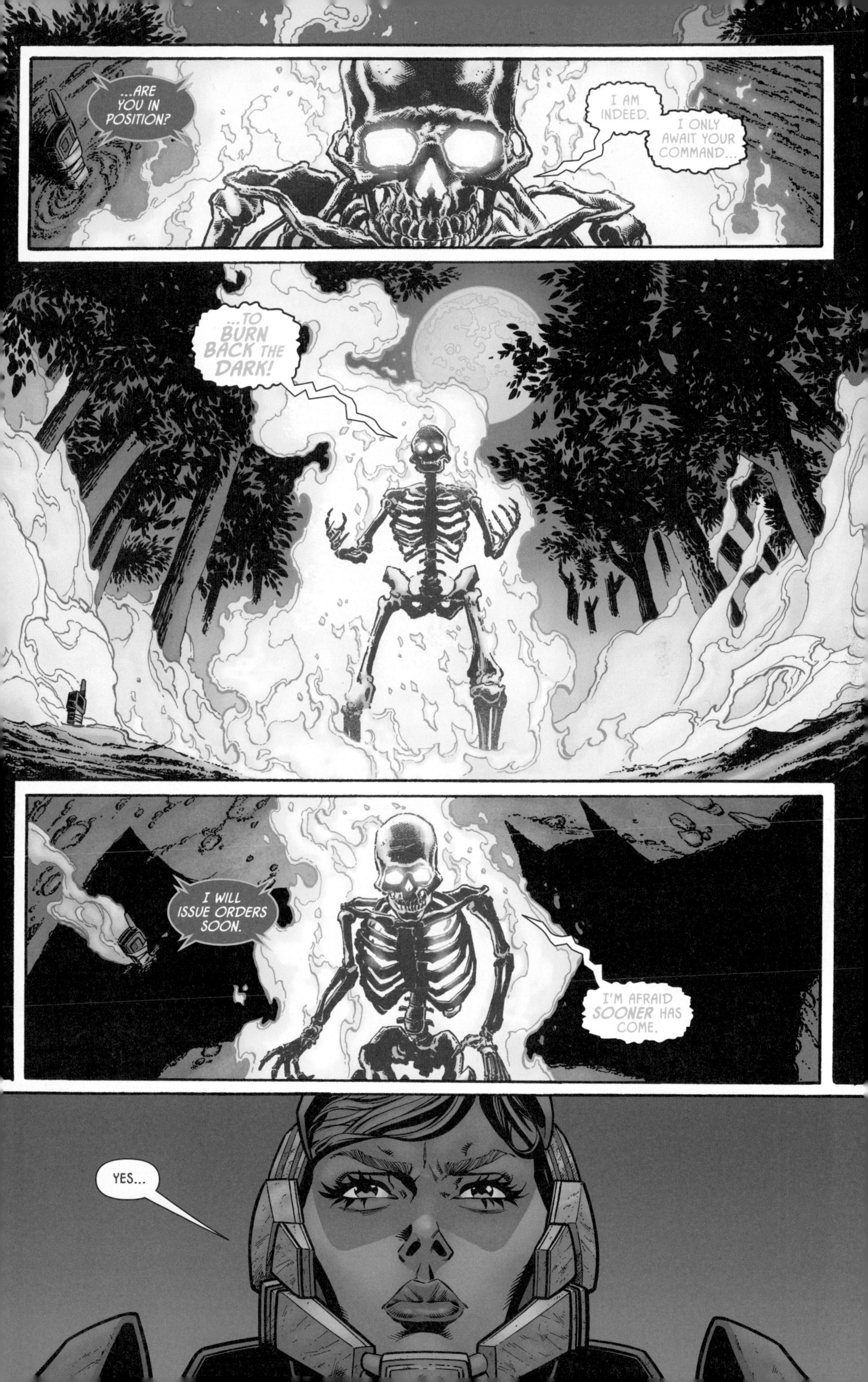
...ARE YOU IN POSITION?
I AM INDEED.
I ONLY AWAIT YOUR COMMAND...
...TO BURN BACK THE DARK!
I WILL ISSUE ORDERS SOON.
I'M AFRAID SOONER HAS COME.
YES...

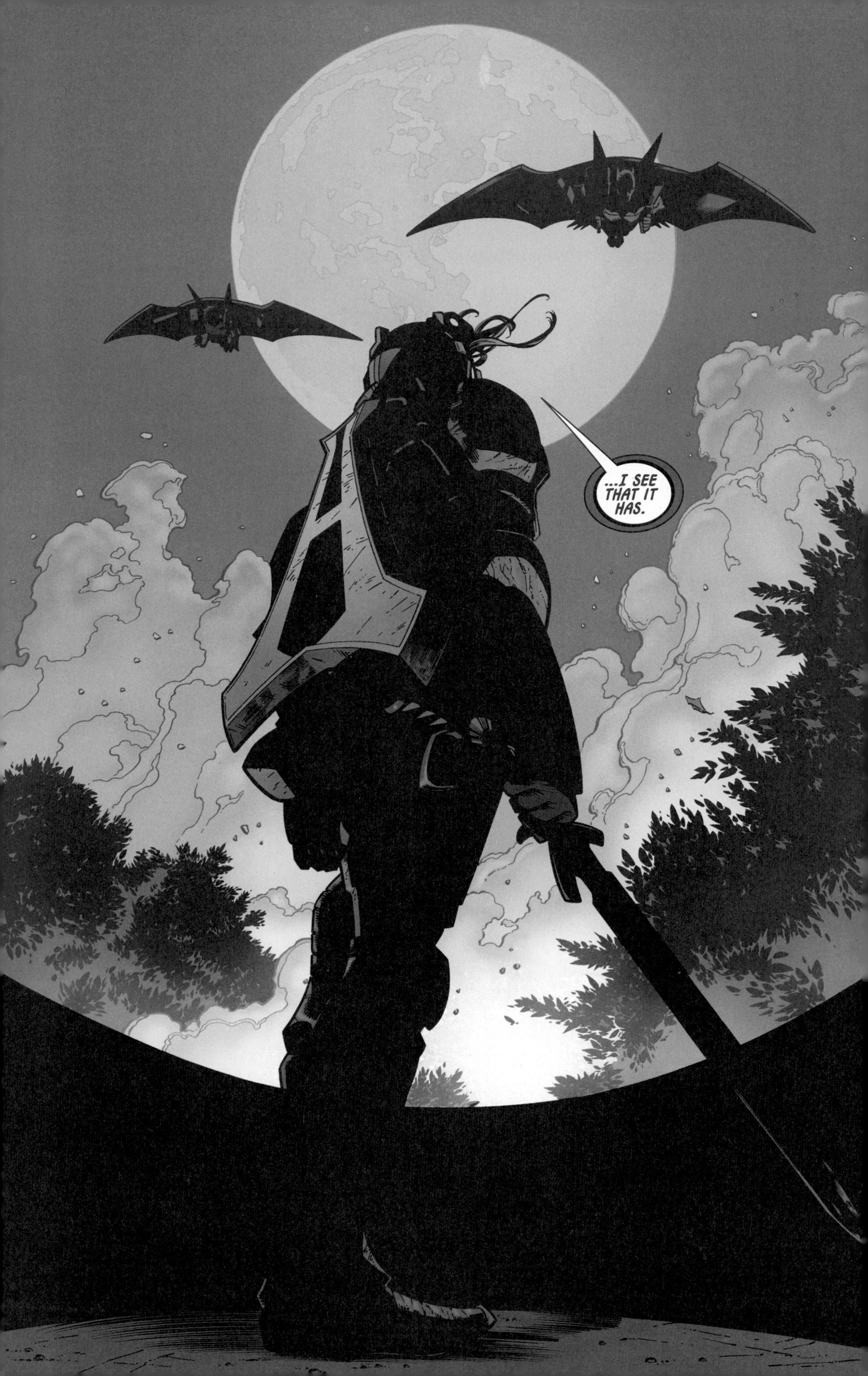
...I SEE THAT IT HAS.

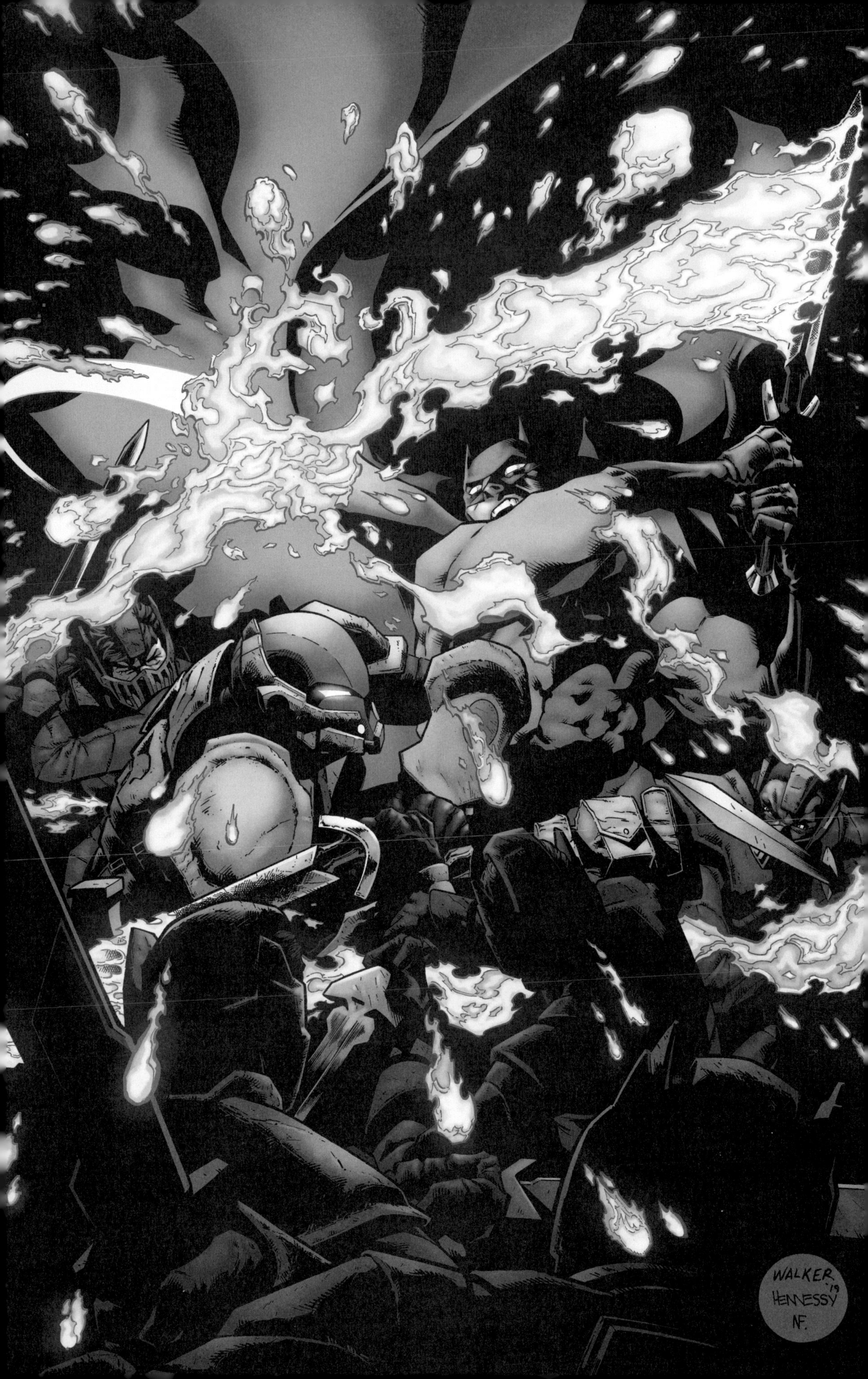
WALKER '19
HENNESSY
NF.

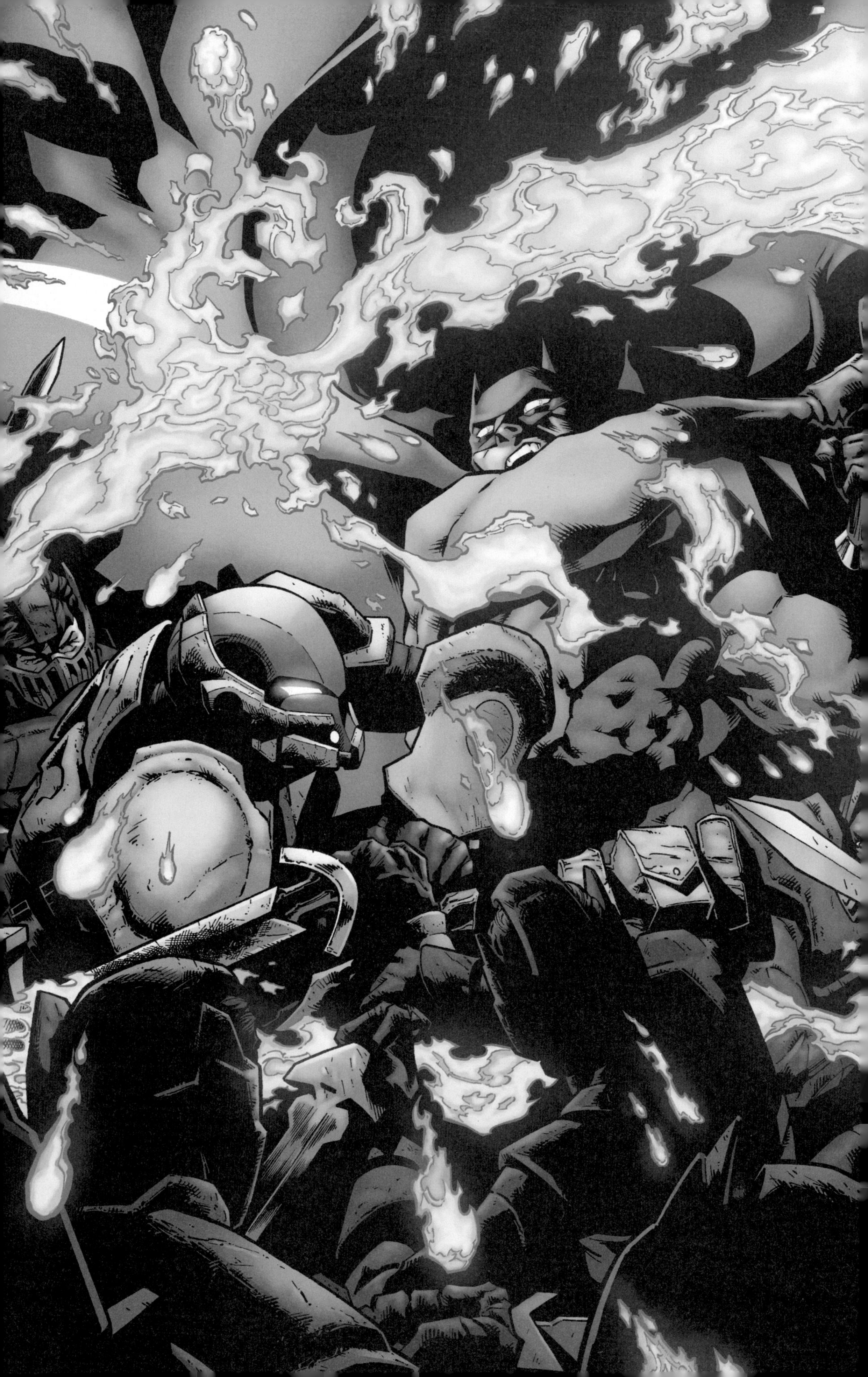

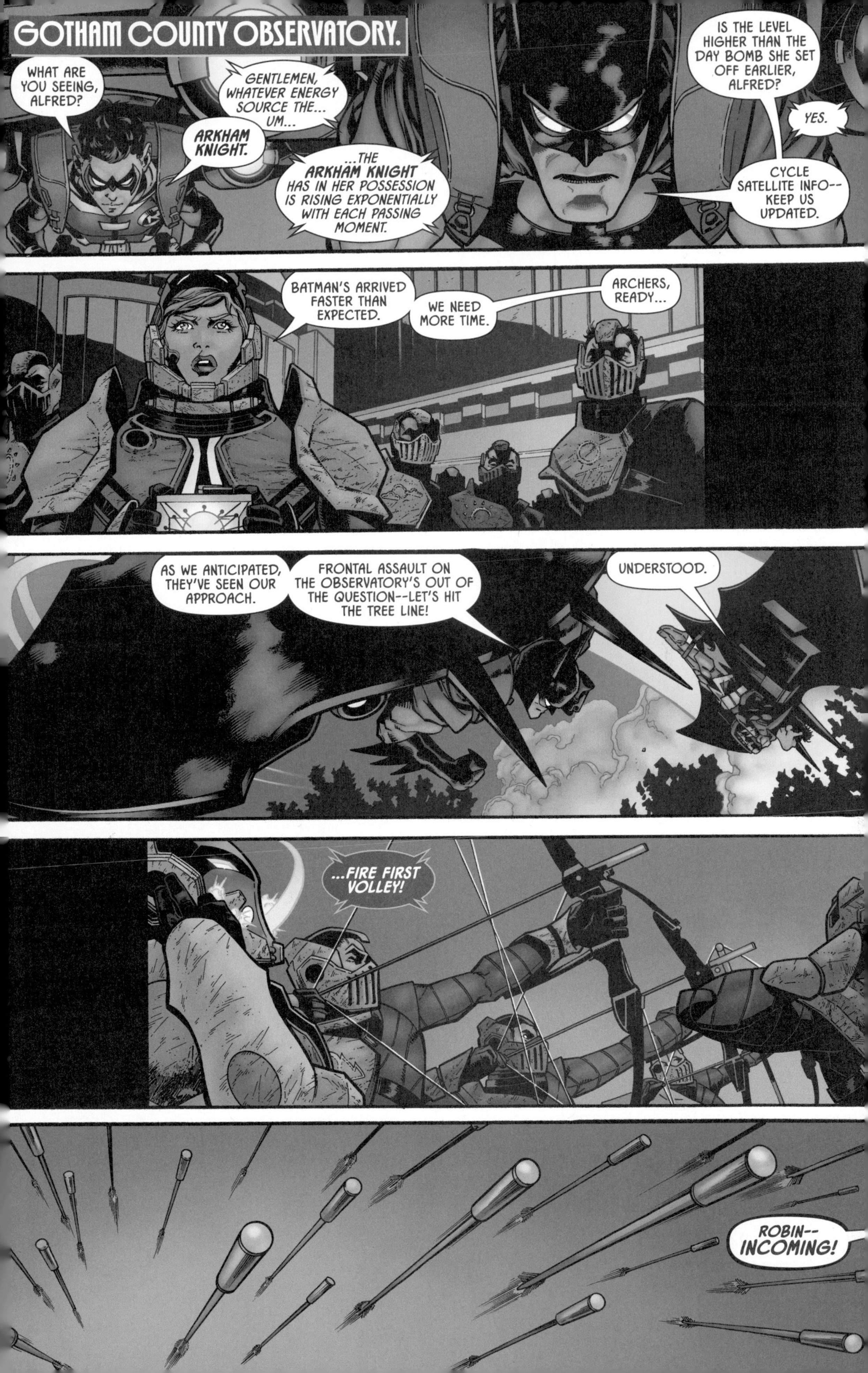
GOTHAM COUNTY OBSERVATORY.
WHAT ARE YOU SEEING, ALFRED?
GENTLEMEN, WHATEVER ENERGY SOURCE THE... UM...
ARKHAM KNIGHT.
...THE ARKHAM KNIGHT HAS IN HER POSSESSION IS RISING EXPONENTIALLY WITH EACH PASSING MOMENT.
IS THE LEVEL HIGHER THAN THE DAY BOMB SHE SET OFF EARLIER, ALFRED?
YES.
CYCLE SATELLITE INFO-- KEEP US UPDATED.
BATMAN'S ARRIVED FASTER THAN EXPECTED.
WE NEED MORE TIME.
ARCHERS, READY...
AS WE ANTICIPATED, THEY'VE SEEN OUR APPROACH.
FRONTAL ASSAULT ON THE OBSERVATORY'S OUT OF THE QUESTION--LET'S HIT THE TREE LINE!
UNDERSTOOD.
...FIRE FIRST VOLLEY!
ROBIN-- INCOMING!

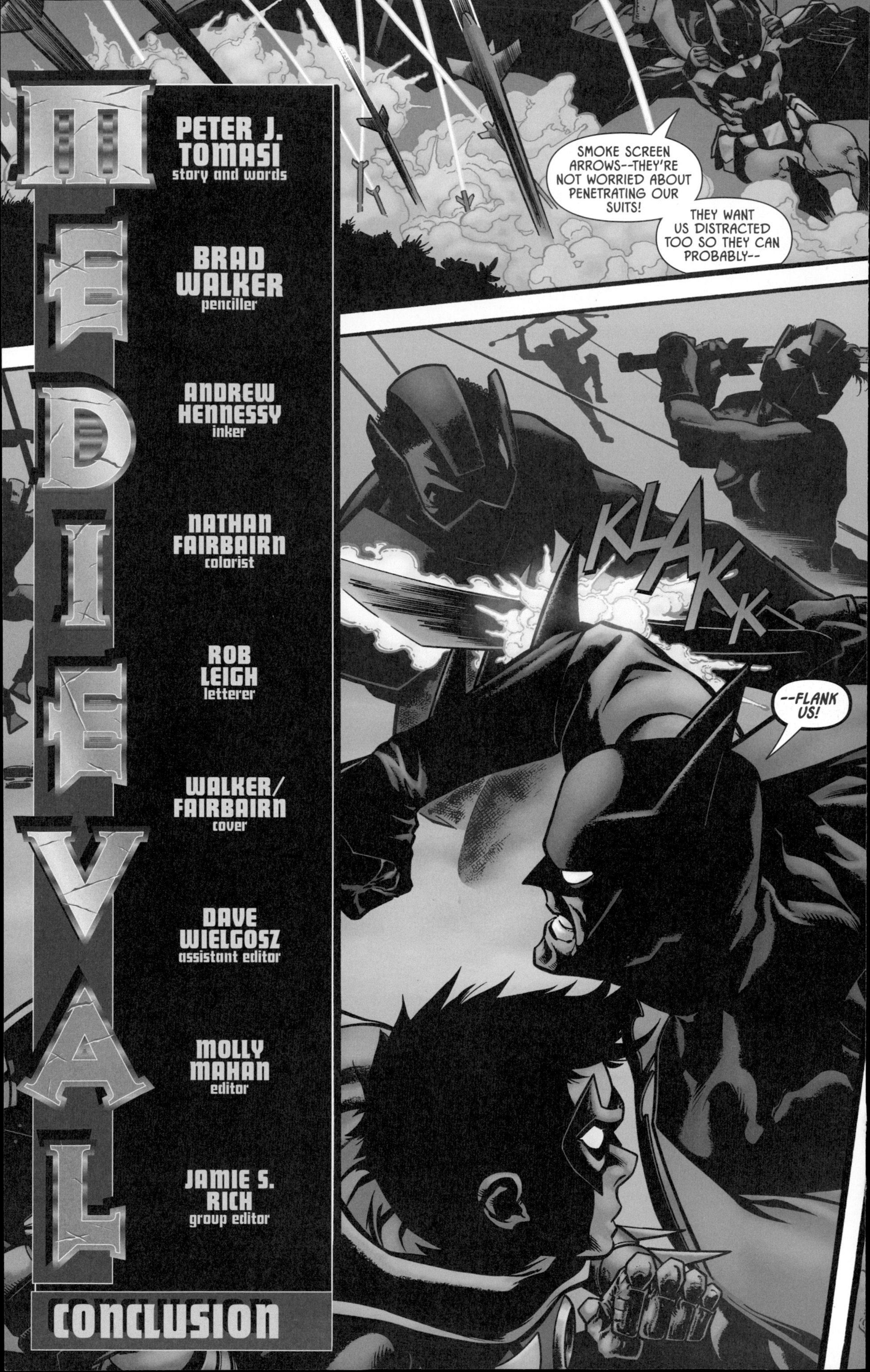
MEDIEVAL
PETER J. TOMASI
story and words
BRAD WALKER
penciller
ANDREW HENNESSY
inker
NATHAN FAIRBAIRN
colorist
ROB LEIGH
letterer
WALKER/FAIRBAIRN
cover
DAVE WIELGOSZ
assistant editor
MOLLY MAHAN
editor
JAMIE S. RICH
group editor
CONCLUSION
SMOKE SCREEN ARROWS--THEY'RE NOT WORRIED ABOUT PENETRATING OUR SUITS!
THEY WANT US DISTRACTED TOO SO THEY CAN PROBABLY--
KLAKK
--FLANK US!

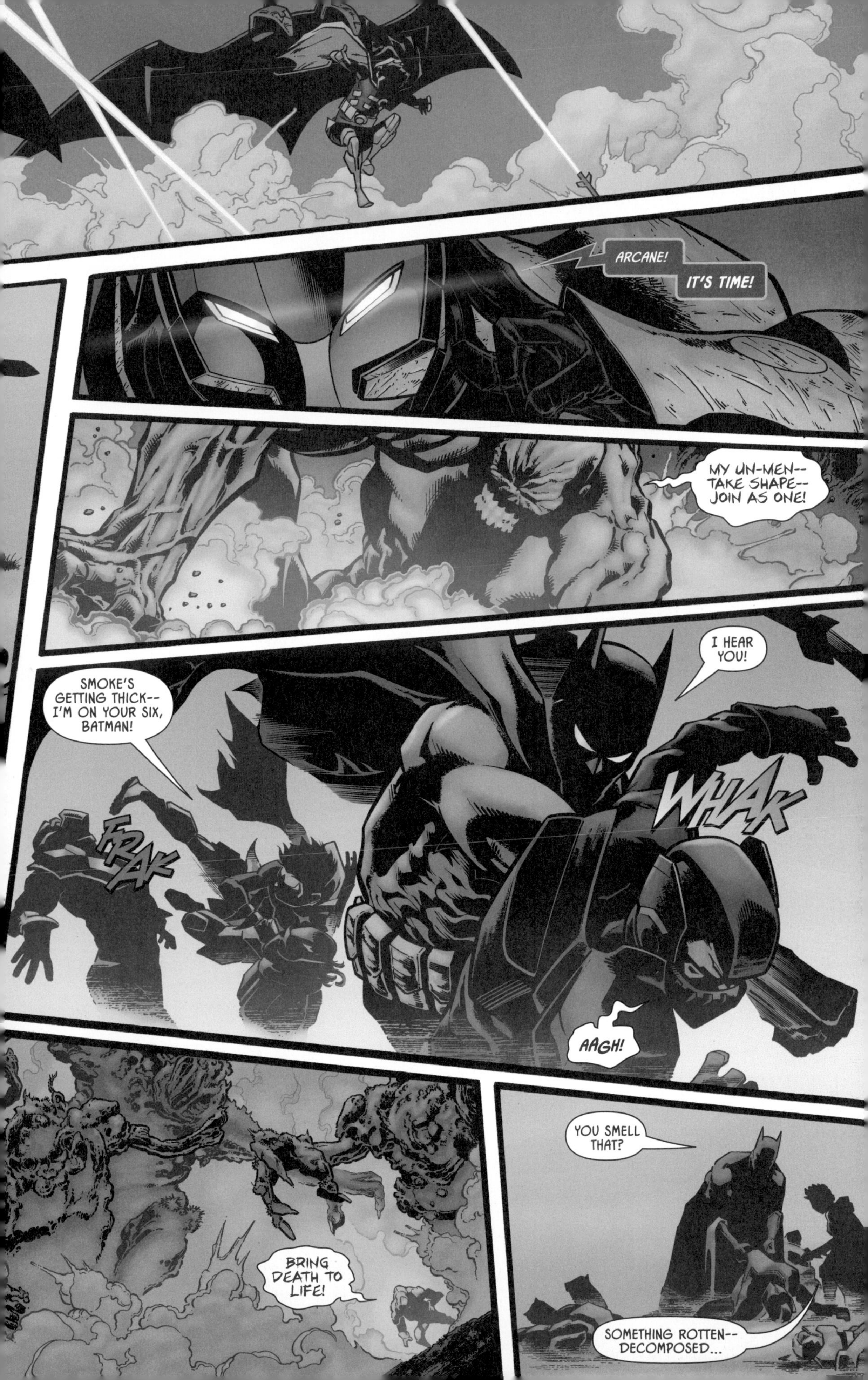
ARCANE!
IT'S TIME!
MY UN-MEN--TAKE SHAPE--JOIN AS ONE!
SMOKE'S GETTING THICK--I'M ON YOUR SIX, BATMAN!
I HEAR YOU!
FRAK
WHAK
AAGH!
BRING DEATH TO LIFE!
YOU SMELL THAT?
SOMETHING ROTTEN--DECOMPOSED...

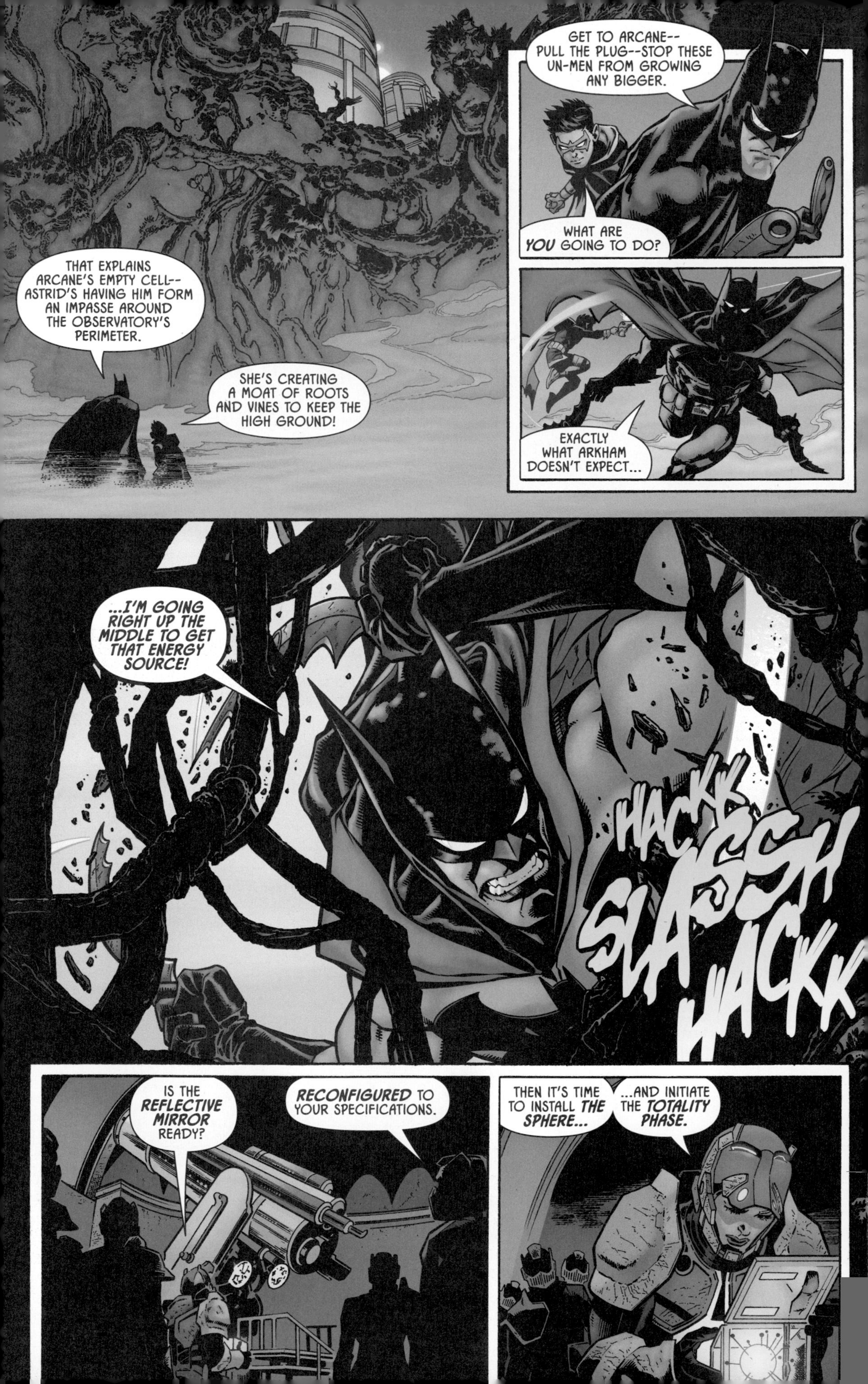
THAT EXPLAINS ARCANE'S EMPTY CELL--ASTRID'S HAVING HIM FORM AN IMPASSE AROUND THE OBSERVATORY'S PERIMETER.
SHE'S CREATING A MOAT OF ROOTS AND VINES TO KEEP THE HIGH GROUND!
GET TO ARCANE--PULL THE PLUG--STOP THESE UN-MEN FROM GROWING ANY BIGGER.
WHAT ARE *YOU* GOING TO DO?
EXACTLY WHAT ARKHAM DOESN'T EXPECT...
...I'M GOING RIGHT UP THE MIDDLE TO GET THAT ENERGY SOURCE!
HACKK
SLASSH
HACKK
IS THE *REFLECTIVE MIRROR* READY?
RECONFIGURED TO YOUR SPECIFICATIONS.
THEN IT'S TIME TO INSTALL *THE SPHERE...*
...AND INITIATE THE *TOTALITY PHASE.*

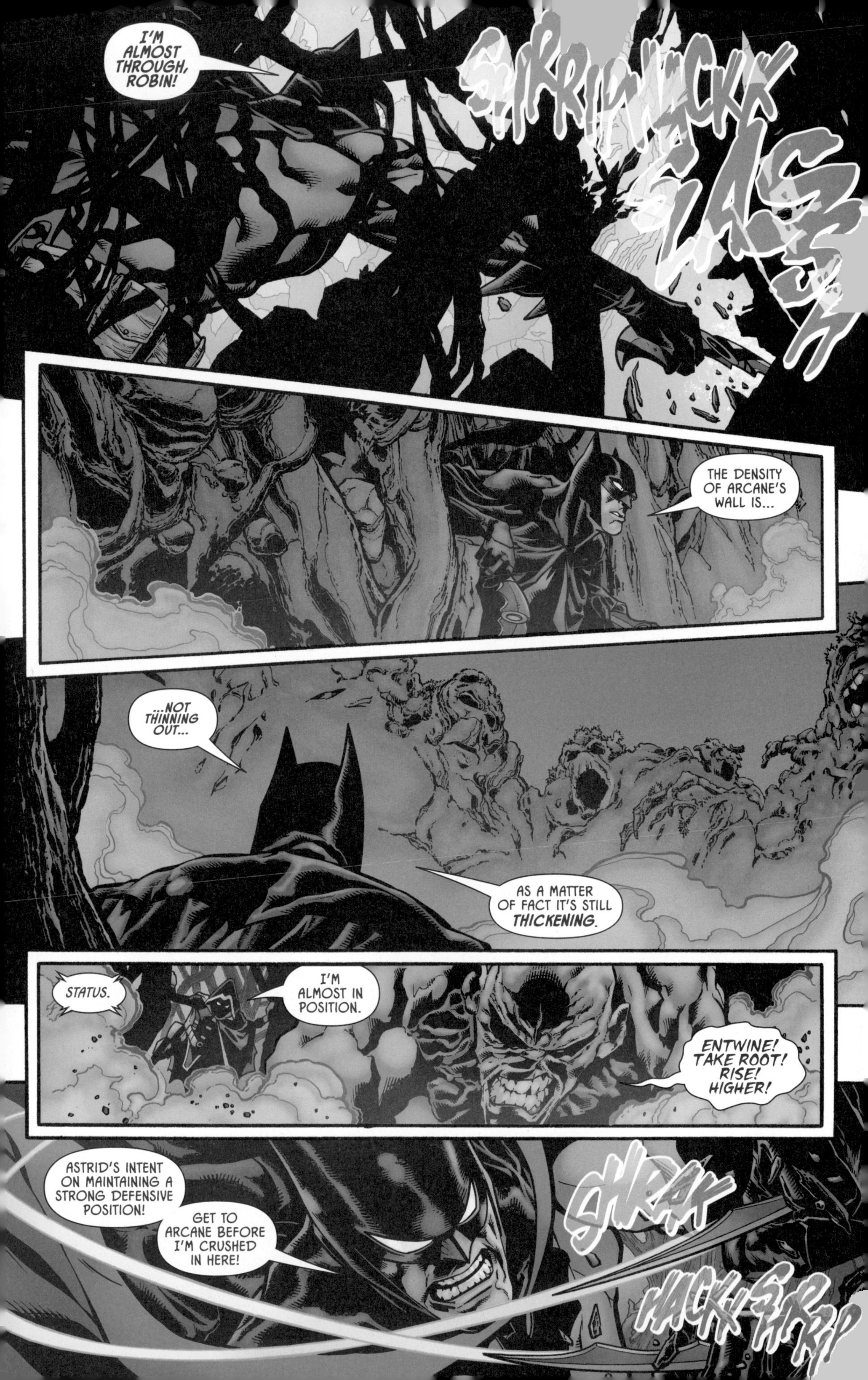

I'M ALMOST THROUGH, ROBIN!
SLASH
THE DENSITY OF ARCANE'S WALL IS...
...NOT THINNING OUT...
AS A MATTER OF FACT IT'S STILL THICKENING.
STATUS.
I'M ALMOST IN POSITION.
ENTWINE! TAKE ROOT! RISE! HIGHER!
ASTRID'S INTENT ON MAINTAINING A STRONG DEFENSIVE POSITION!
GET TO ARCANE BEFORE I'M CRUSHED IN HERE!
SHRAK

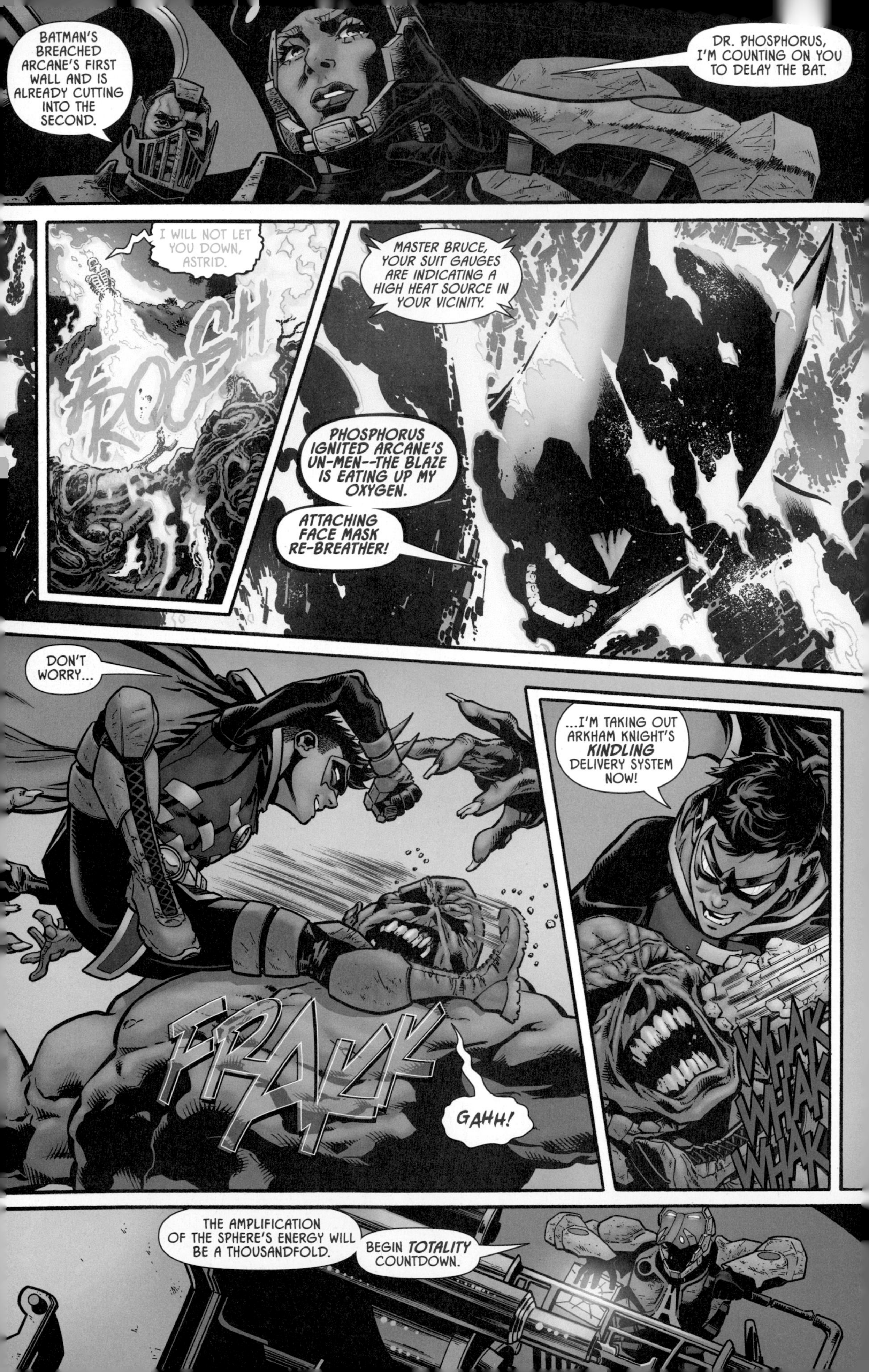
BATMAN'S BREACHED ARCANE'S FIRST WALL AND IS ALREADY CUTTING INTO THE SECOND.
DR. PHOSPHORUS, I'M COUNTING ON YOU TO DELAY THE BAT.
I WILL NOT LET YOU DOWN, ASTRID.
FROOSH
MASTER BRUCE, YOUR SUIT GAUGES ARE INDICATING A HIGH HEAT SOURCE IN YOUR VICINITY.
PHOSPHORUS IGNITED ARCANE'S UN-MEN--THE BLAZE IS EATING UP MY OXYGEN.
ATTACHING FACE MASK RE-BREATHER!
DON'T WORRY...
...I'M TAKING OUT ARKHAM KNIGHT'S KINDLING DELIVERY SYSTEM NOW!
FRAKK
GAHH!
WHAK WHAK WHAK WHAK
THE AMPLIFICATION OF THE SPHERE'S ENERGY WILL BE A THOUSANDFOLD.
BEGIN TOTALITY COUNTDOWN.

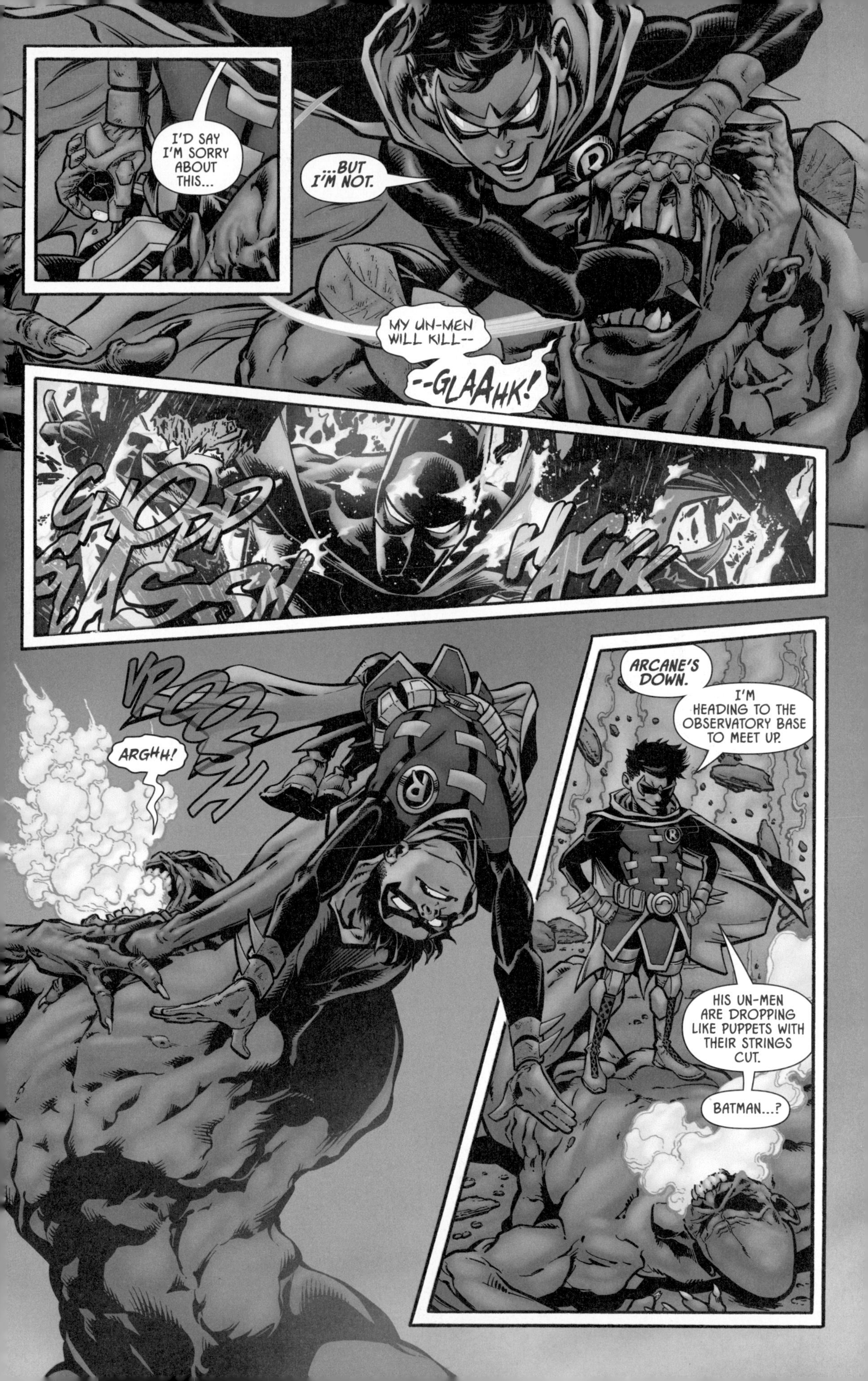
I'D SAY I'M SORRY ABOUT THIS...
...BUT I'M NOT.
MY UN-MEN WILL KILL--
--GLAAHK!
CHOP
SLASH
HACK
VROOOM
ARGHH!
ARCANE'S DOWN.
I'M HEADING TO THE OBSERVATORY BASE TO MEET UP.
HIS UN-MEN ARE DROPPING LIKE PUPPETS WITH THEIR STRINGS CUT.
BATMAN...?

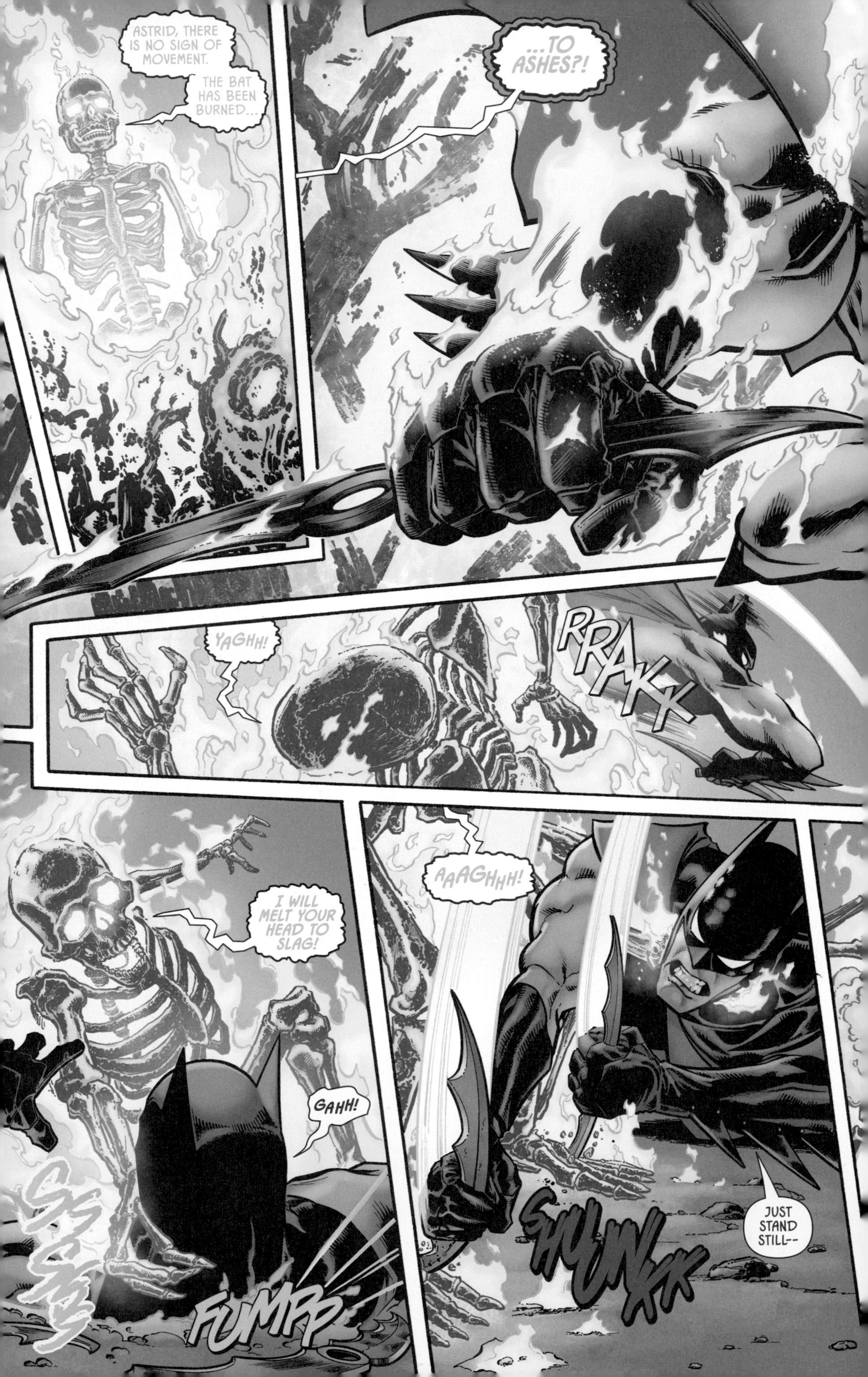
ASTRID, THERE IS NO SIGN OF MOVEMENT.
THE BAT HAS BEEN BURNED...
...TO ASHES?!
YAGHH!
RRAKKK
I WILL MELT YOUR HEAD TO SLAG!
GAHH!
FUMPP
AAAGHHH!
SHUNKK
JUST STAND STILL--

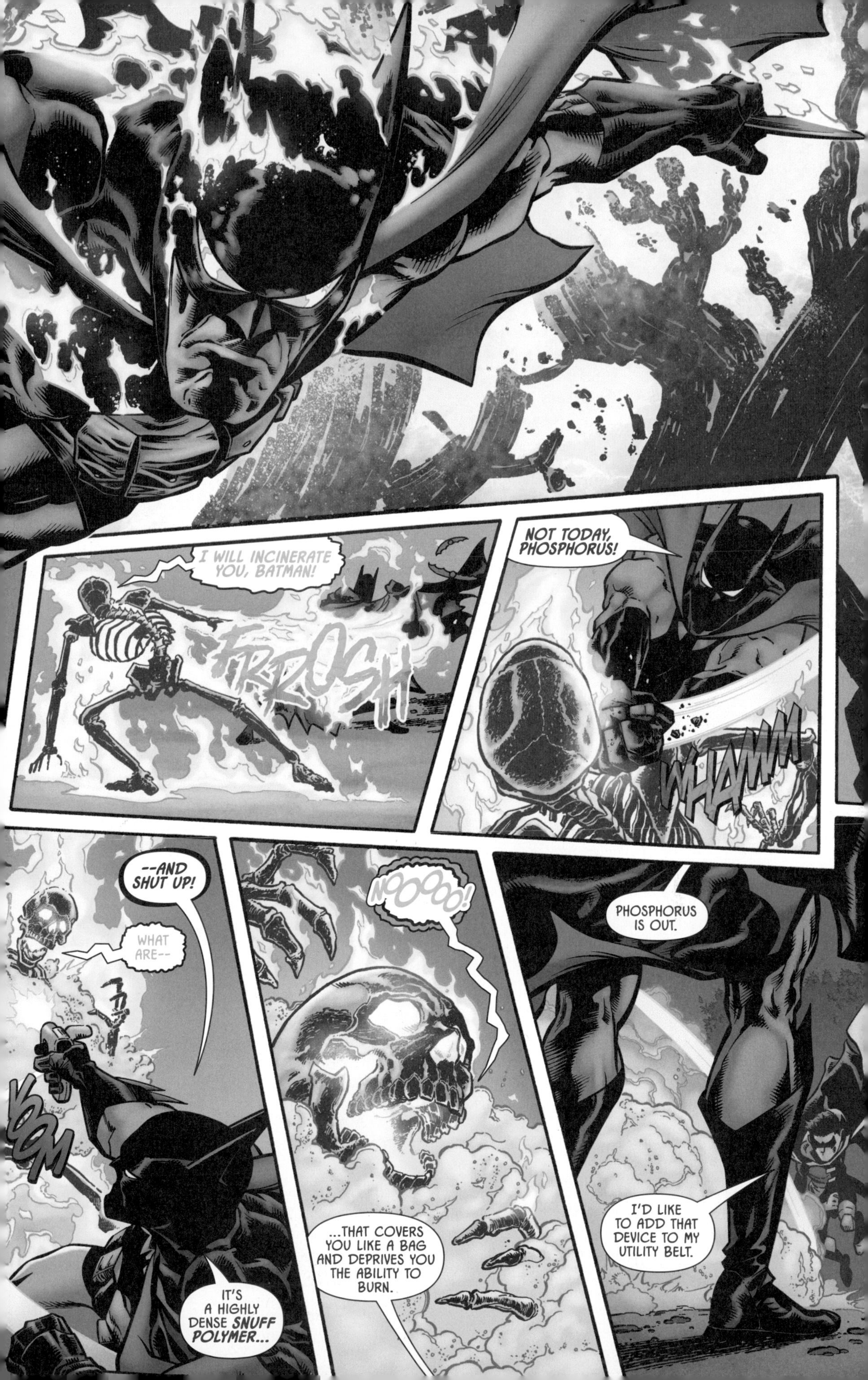

I WILL INCINERATE YOU, BATMAN!
FRROSH
NOT TODAY, PHOSPHORUS!
WHAMM
--AND SHUT UP!
WHAT ARE--
VOOM
IT'S A HIGHLY DENSE SNUFF POLYMER...
NOOOOO!
...THAT COVERS YOU LIKE A BAG AND DEPRIVES YOU THE ABILITY TO BURN.
PHOSPHORUS IS OUT.
I'D LIKE TO ADD THAT DEVICE TO MY UTILITY BELT.

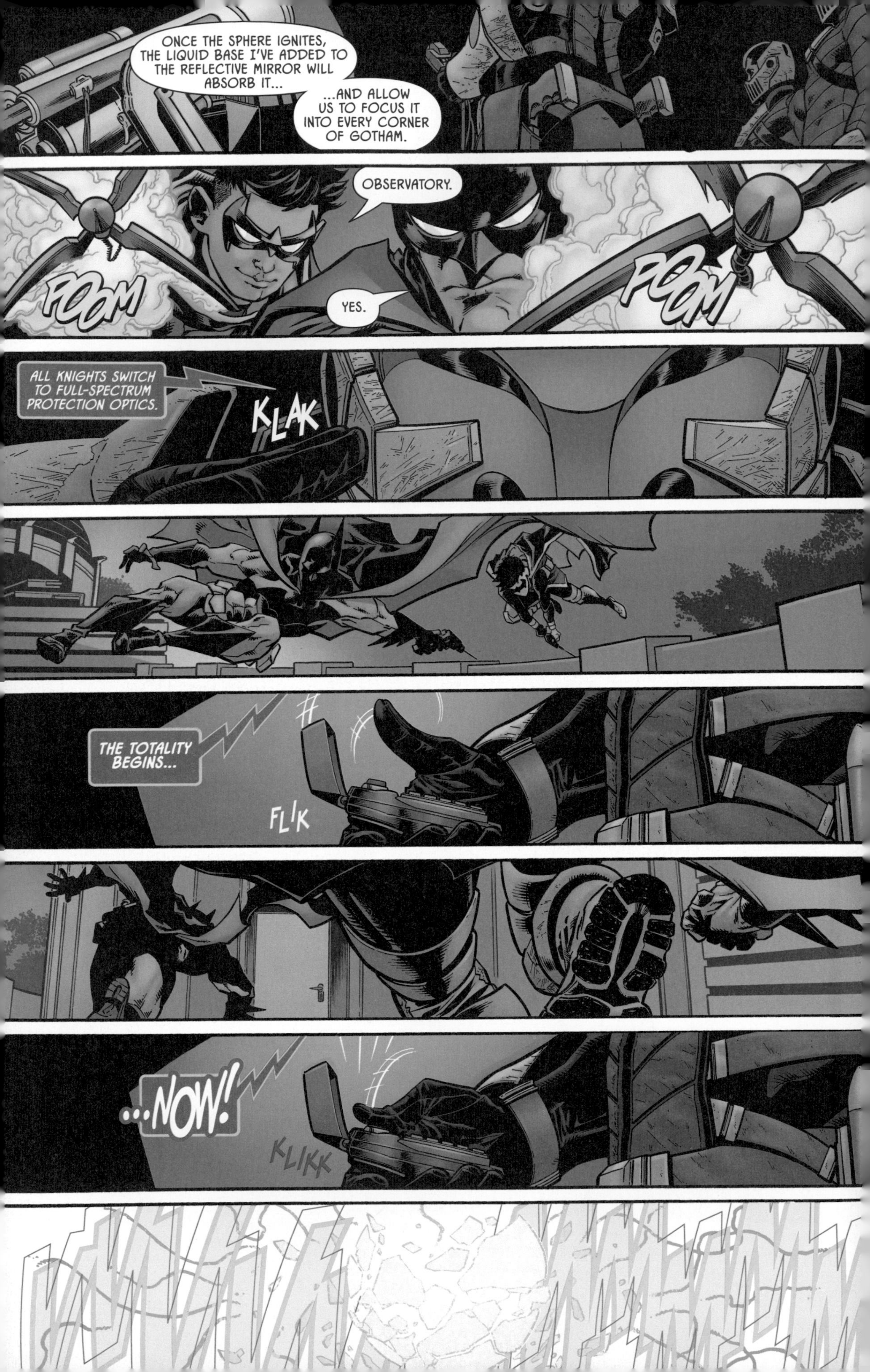
ONCE THE SPHERE IGNITES, THE LIQUID BASE I'VE ADDED TO THE REFLECTIVE MIRROR WILL ABSORB IT...
...AND ALLOW US TO FOCUS IT INTO EVERY CORNER OF GOTHAM.
POOM
OBSERVATORY.
YES.
POOM
ALL KNIGHTS SWITCH TO FULL-SPECTRUM PROTECTION OPTICS.
KLAK
THE TOTALITY BEGINS...
FLIK
...NOW!!
KLIKK

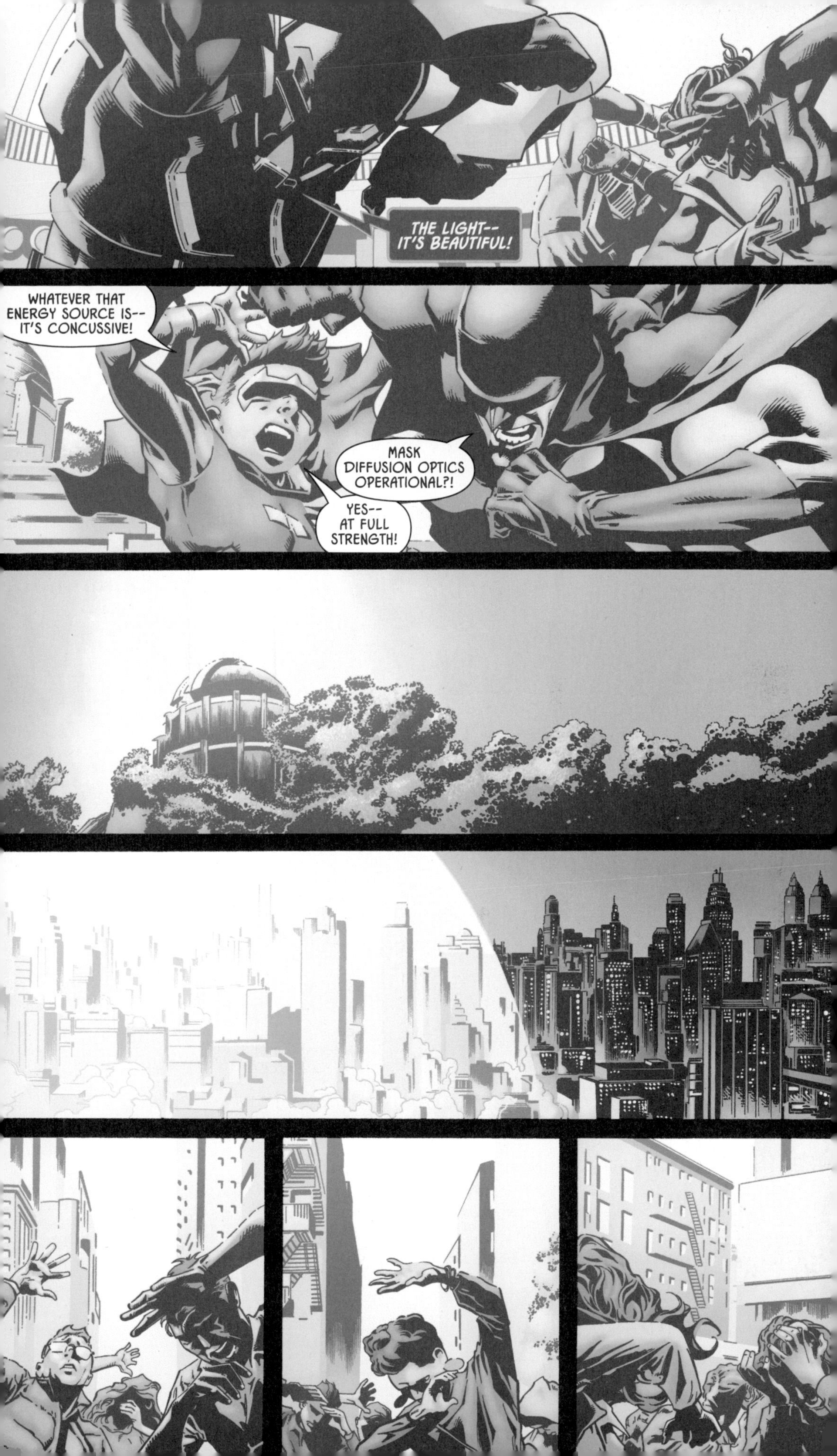
THE LIGHT-- IT'S BEAUTIFUL!
WHATEVER THAT ENERGY SOURCE IS-- IT'S CONCUSSIVE!
MASK DIFFUSION OPTICS OPERATIONAL?!
YES-- AT FULL STRENGTH!

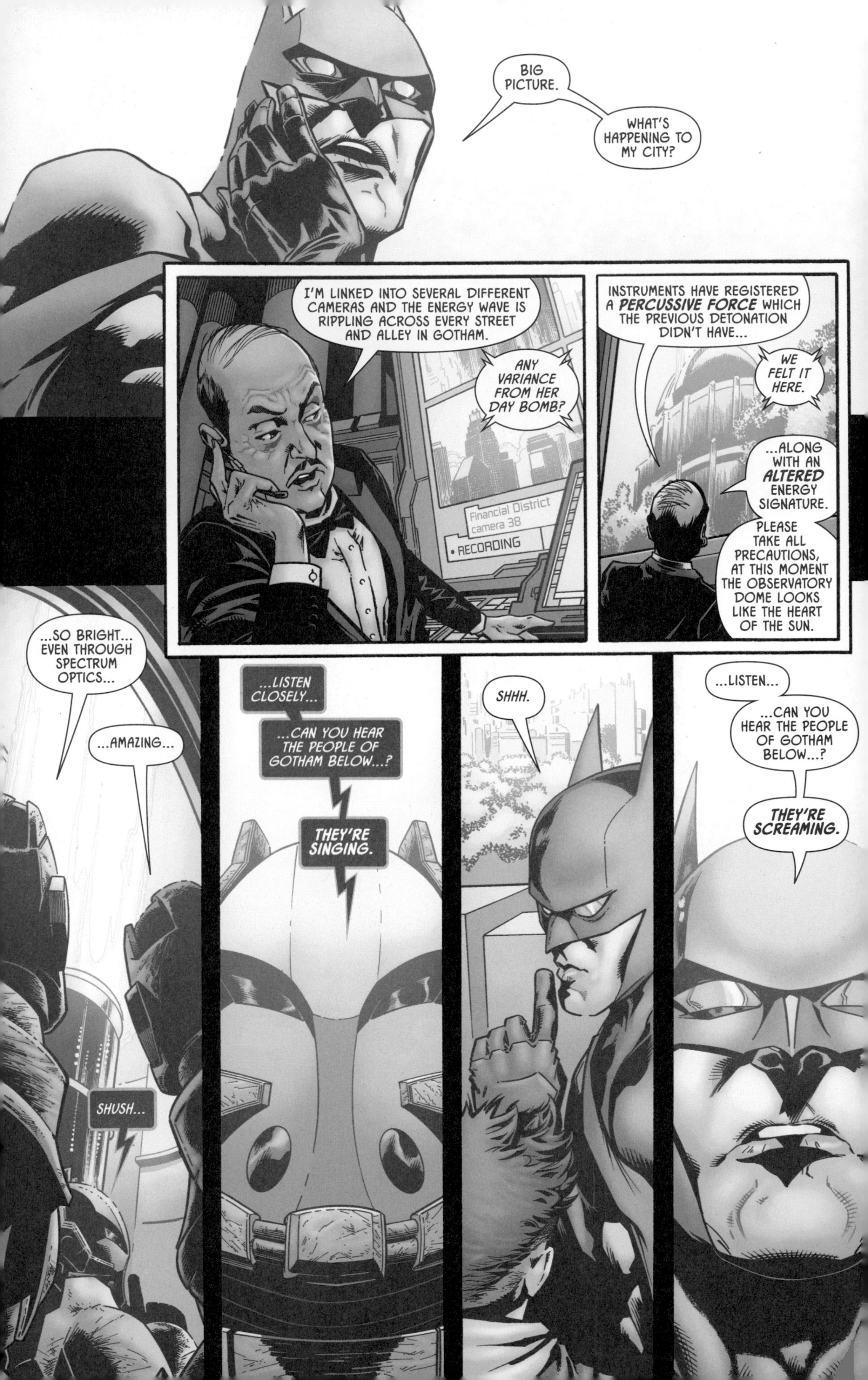
BIG PICTURE.
WHAT'S HAPPENING TO MY CITY?
I'M LINKED INTO SEVERAL DIFFERENT CAMERAS AND THE ENERGY WAVE IS RIPPLING ACROSS EVERY STREET AND ALLEY IN GOTHAM.
ANY VARIANCE FROM HER DAY BOMB?
Financial District camera 38
• RECORDING
INSTRUMENTS HAVE REGISTERED A PERCUSSIVE FORCE WHICH THE PREVIOUS DETONATION DIDN'T HAVE...
WE FELT IT HERE.
...ALONG WITH AN ALTERED ENERGY SIGNATURE.
PLEASE TAKE ALL PRECAUTIONS, AT THIS MOMENT THE OBSERVATORY DOME LOOKS LIKE THE HEART OF THE SUN.
...SO BRIGHT... EVEN THROUGH SPECTRUM OPTICS...
...AMAZING...
SHUSH...
...LISTEN CLOSELY...
...CAN YOU HEAR THE PEOPLE OF GOTHAM BELOW...?
THEY'RE SINGING.
SHHH.
...LISTEN...
...CAN YOU HEAR THE PEOPLE OF GOTHAM BELOW...?
THEY'RE SCREAMING.

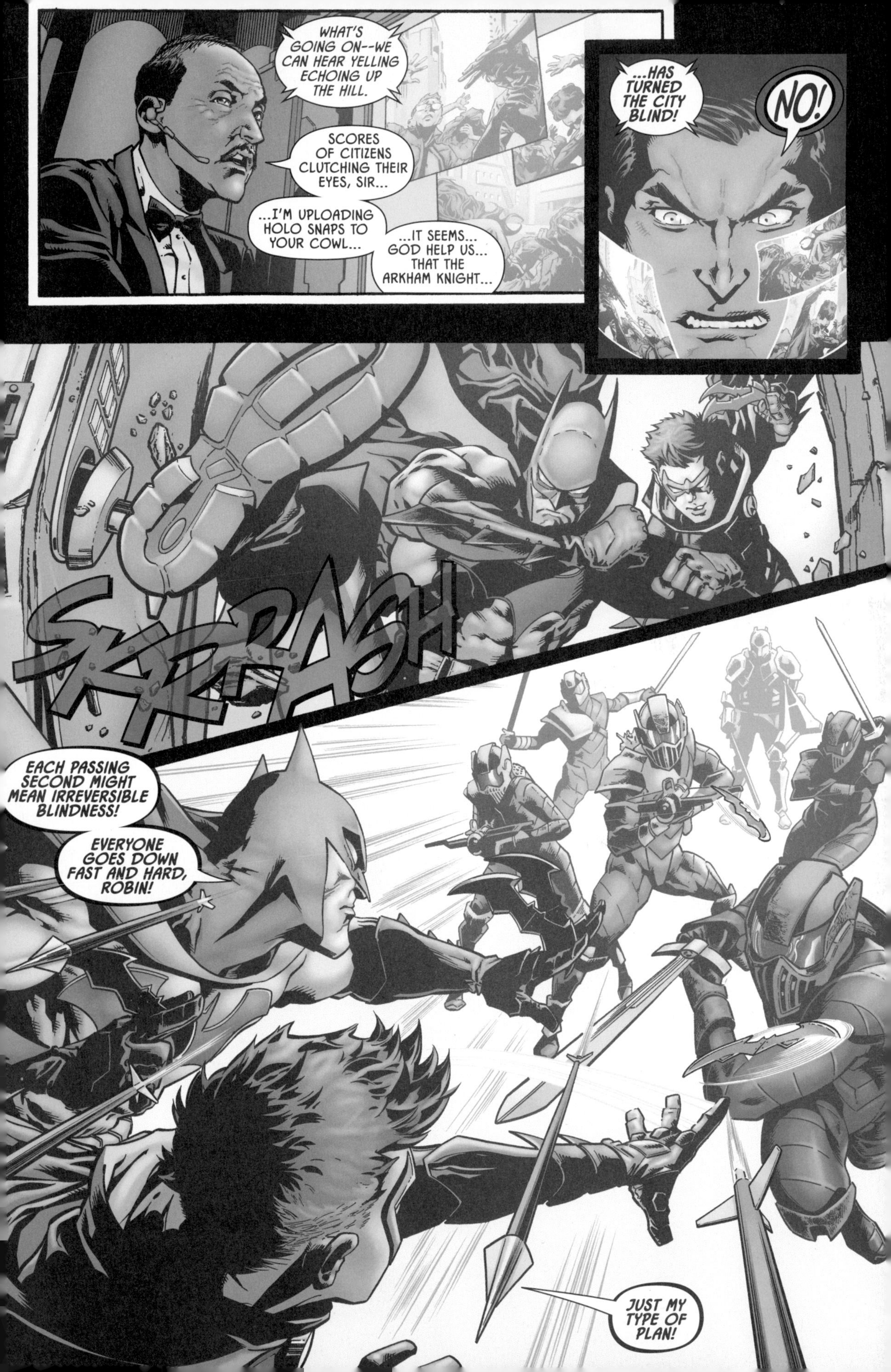
WHAT'S GOING ON--WE CAN HEAR YELLING ECHOING UP THE HILL.
SCORES OF CITIZENS CLUTCHING THEIR EYES, SIR...
...I'M UPLOADING HOLO SNAPS TO YOUR COWL...
...IT SEEMS... GOD HELP US... THAT THE ARKHAM KNIGHT...
...HAS TURNED THE CITY BLIND!
NO!
SKRRASH
EACH PASSING SECOND MIGHT MEAN IRREVERSIBLE BLINDNESS!
EVERYONE GOES DOWN FAST AND HARD, ROBIN!
JUST MY TYPE OF PLAN!

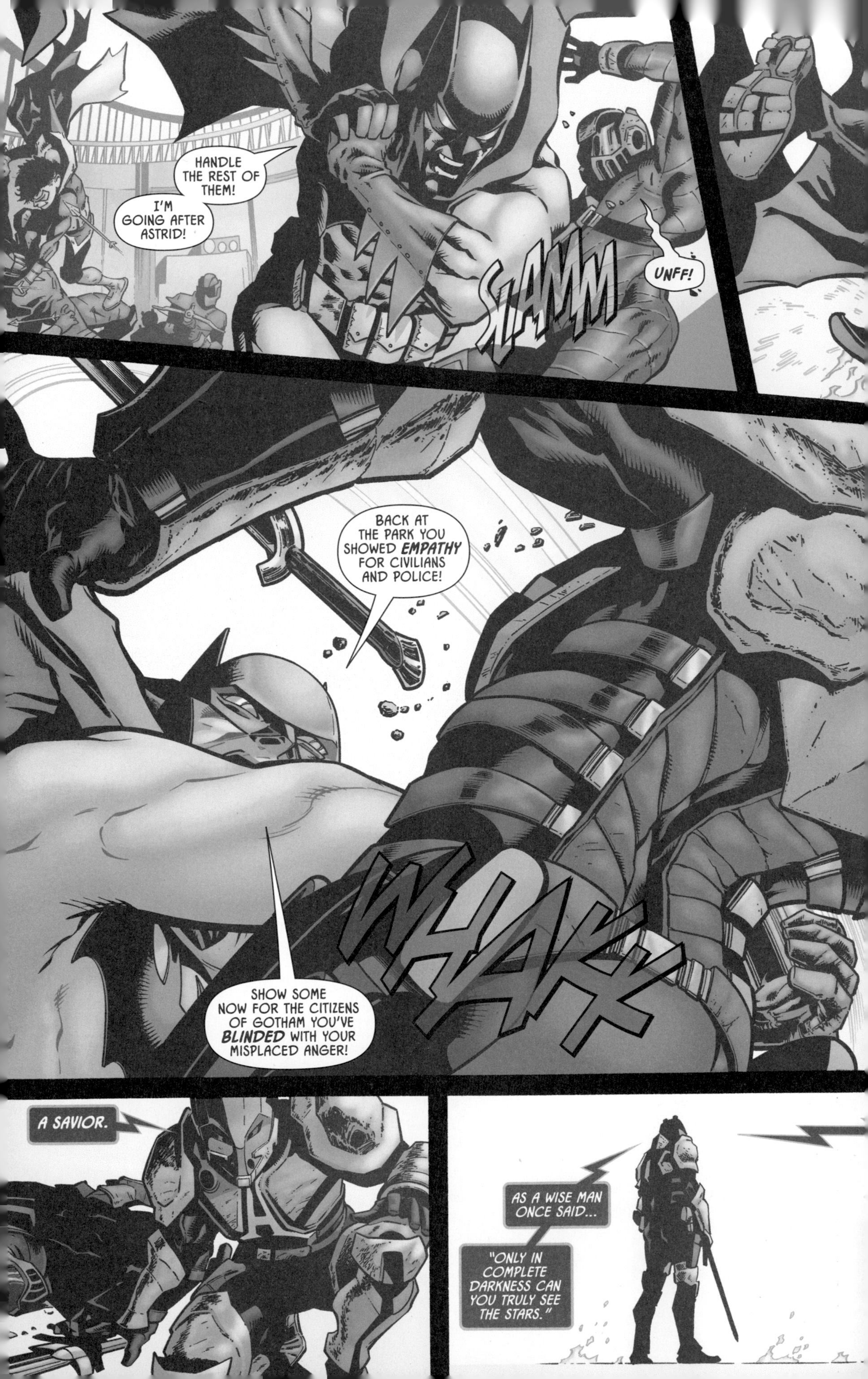
HANDLE THE REST OF THEM!
I'M GOING AFTER ASTRID!
SLAMM
UNFF!
BACK AT THE PARK YOU SHOWED EMPATHY FOR CIVILIANS AND POLICE!
WHAK
SHOW SOME NOW FOR THE CITIZENS OF GOTHAM YOU'VE BLINDED WITH YOUR MISPLACED ANGER!
A SAVIOR.
AS A WISE MAN ONCE SAID...
"ONLY IN COMPLETE DARKNESS CAN YOU TRULY SEE THE STARS."

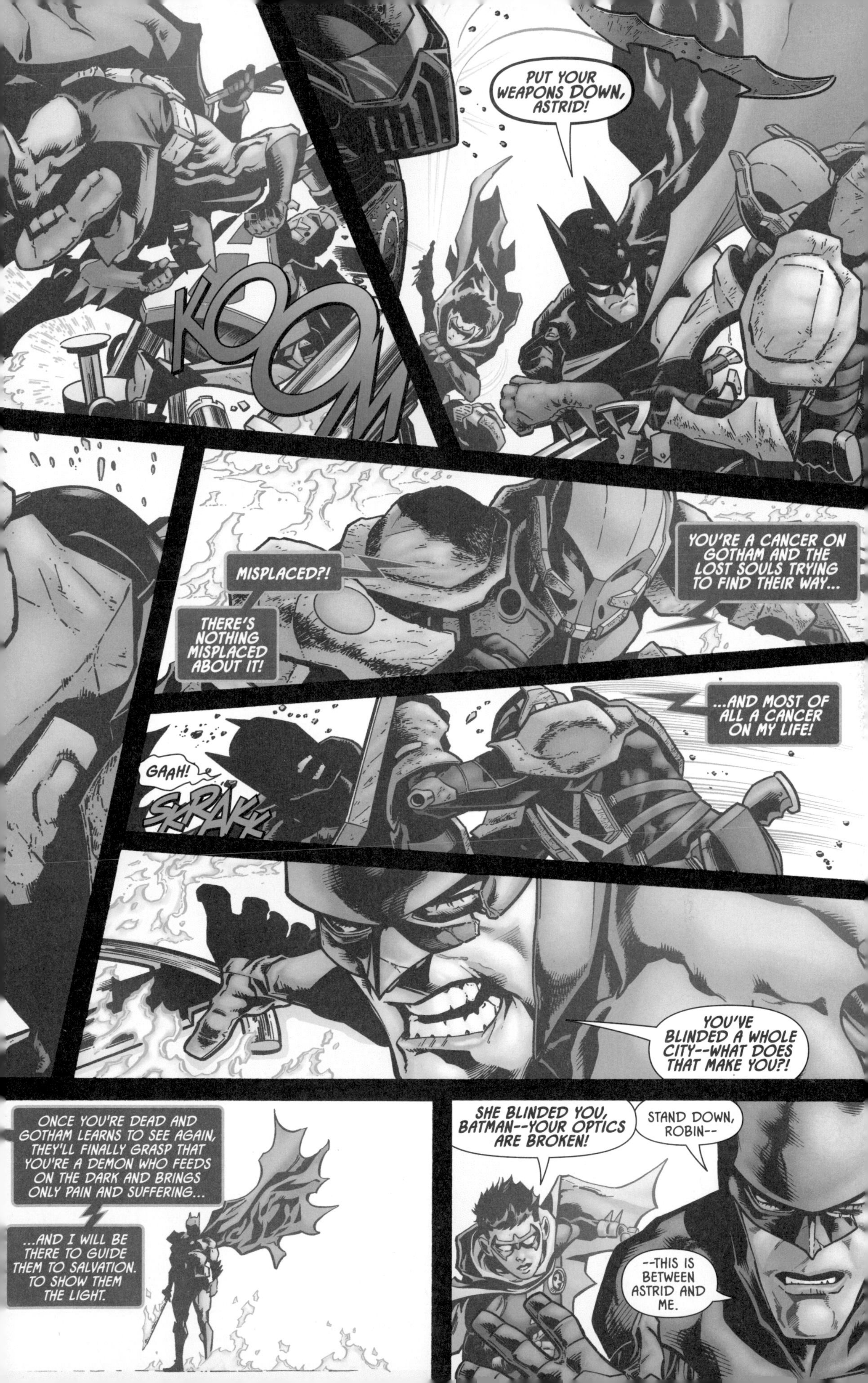
PUT YOUR WEAPONS DOWN, ASTRID!
KOOOM
MISPLACED?!
THERE'S NOTHING MISPLACED ABOUT IT!
YOU'RE A CANCER ON GOTHAM AND THE LOST SOULS TRYING TO FIND THEIR WAY...
...AND MOST OF ALL A CANCER ON MY LIFE!
GAAH!
SKRAKK
YOU'VE BLINDED A WHOLE CITY--WHAT DOES THAT MAKE YOU?!
ONCE YOU'RE DEAD AND GOTHAM LEARNS TO SEE AGAIN, THEY'LL FINALLY GRASP THAT YOU'RE A DEMON WHO FEEDS ON THE DARK AND BRINGS ONLY PAIN AND SUFFERING...
...AND I WILL BE THERE TO GUIDE THEM TO SALVATION. TO SHOW THEM THE LIGHT.
SHE BLINDED YOU, BATMAN--YOUR OPTICS ARE BROKEN!
STAND DOWN, ROBIN--
--THIS IS BETWEEN ASTRID AND ME.

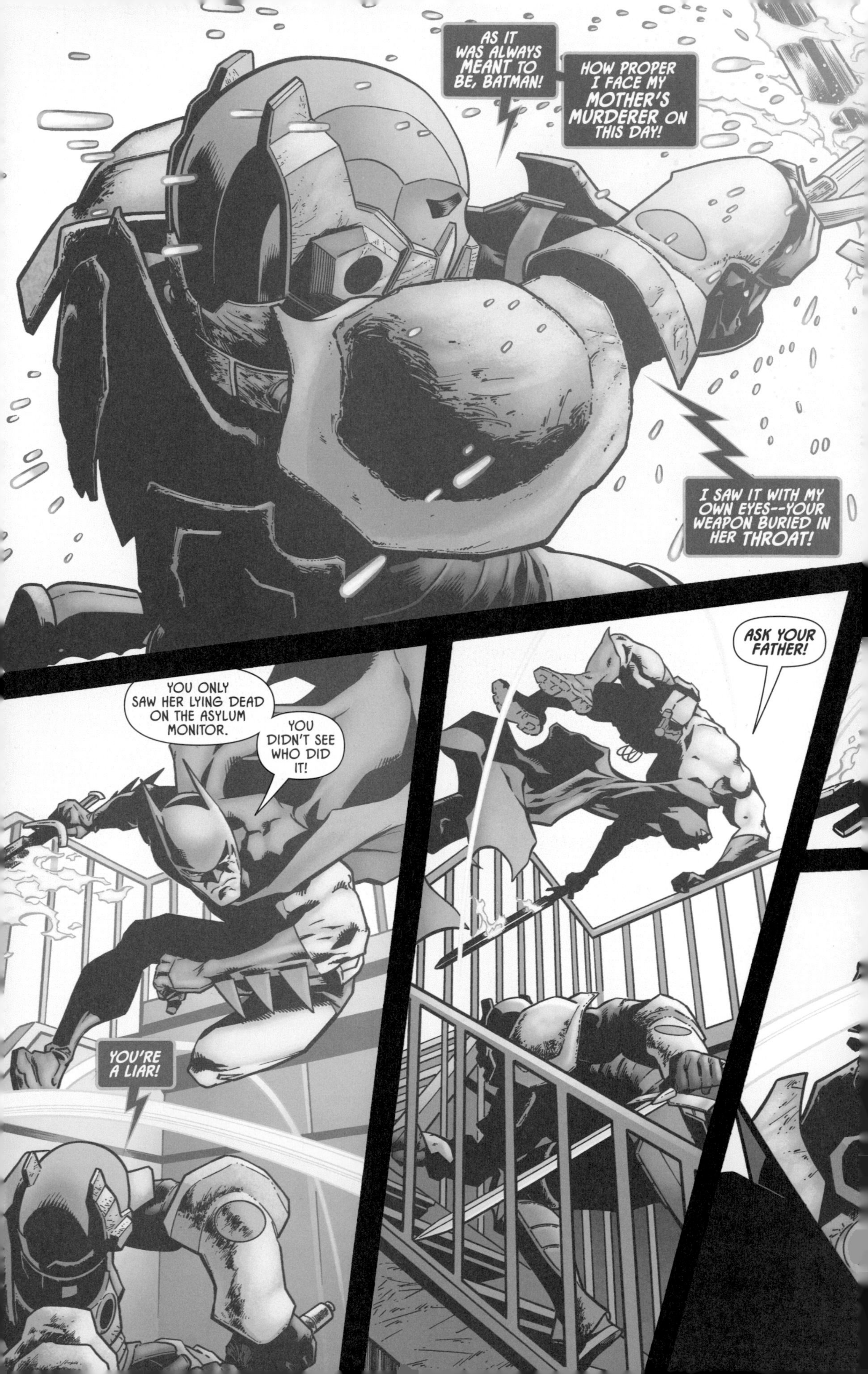
AS IT WAS ALWAYS MEANT TO BE, BATMAN!
HOW PROPER I FACE MY MOTHER'S MURDERER ON THIS DAY!
I SAW IT WITH MY OWN EYES--YOUR WEAPON BURIED IN HER THROAT!
YOU ONLY SAW HER LYING DEAD ON THE ASYLUM MONITOR.
YOU DIDN'T SEE WHO DID IT!
YOU'RE A LIAR!
ASK YOUR FATHER!

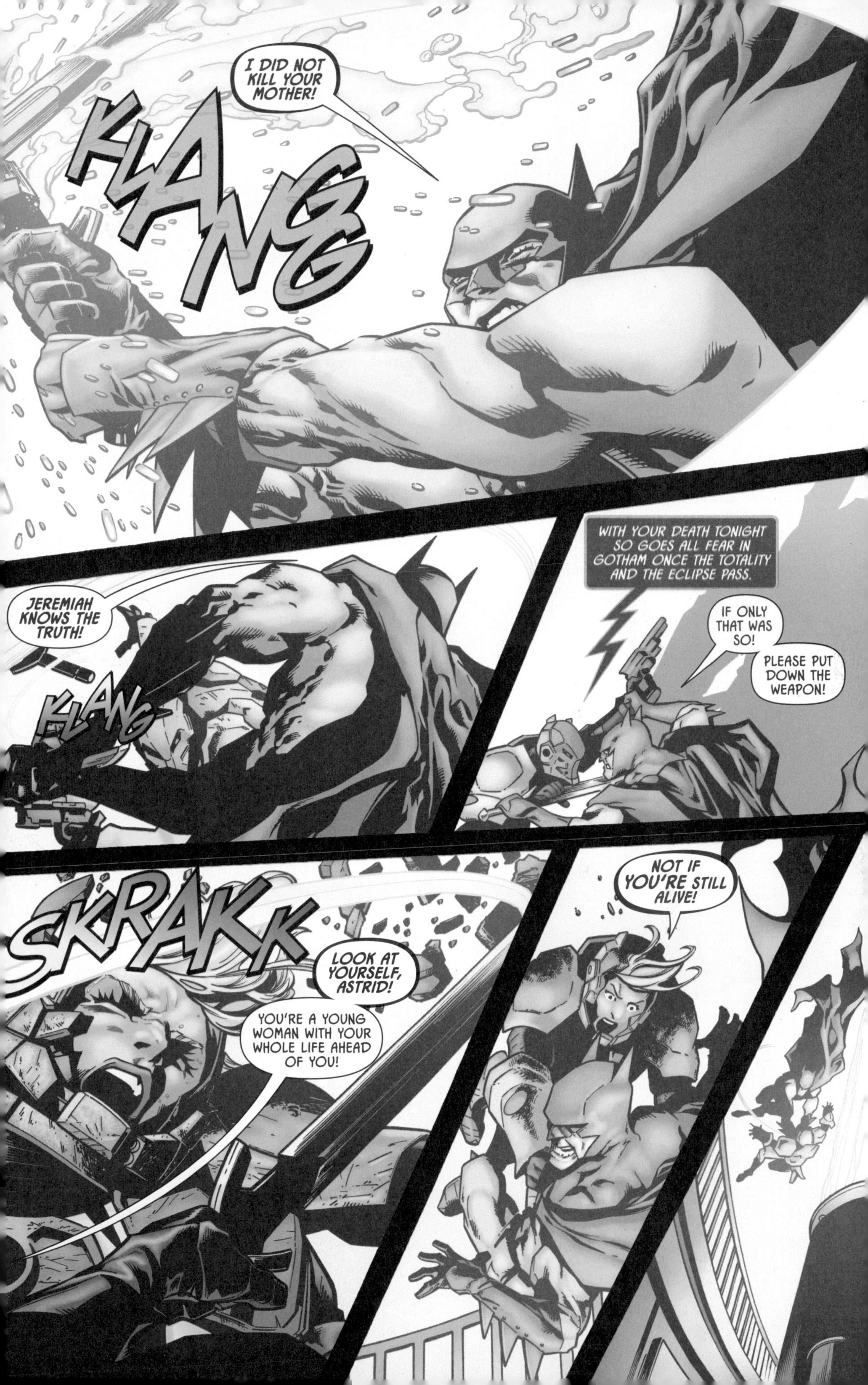
I DID NOT KILL YOUR MOTHER!
KLANNG
JEREMIAH KNOWS THE TRUTH!
KLANG
WITH YOUR DEATH TONIGHT SO GOES ALL FEAR IN GOTHAM ONCE THE TOTALITY AND THE ECLIPSE PASS.
IF ONLY THAT WAS SO!
PLEASE PUT DOWN THE WEAPON!
SKRAKK
LOOK AT YOURSELF, ASTRID!
YOU'RE A YOUNG WOMAN WITH YOUR WHOLE LIFE AHEAD OF YOU!
NOT IF YOU'RE STILL ALIVE!

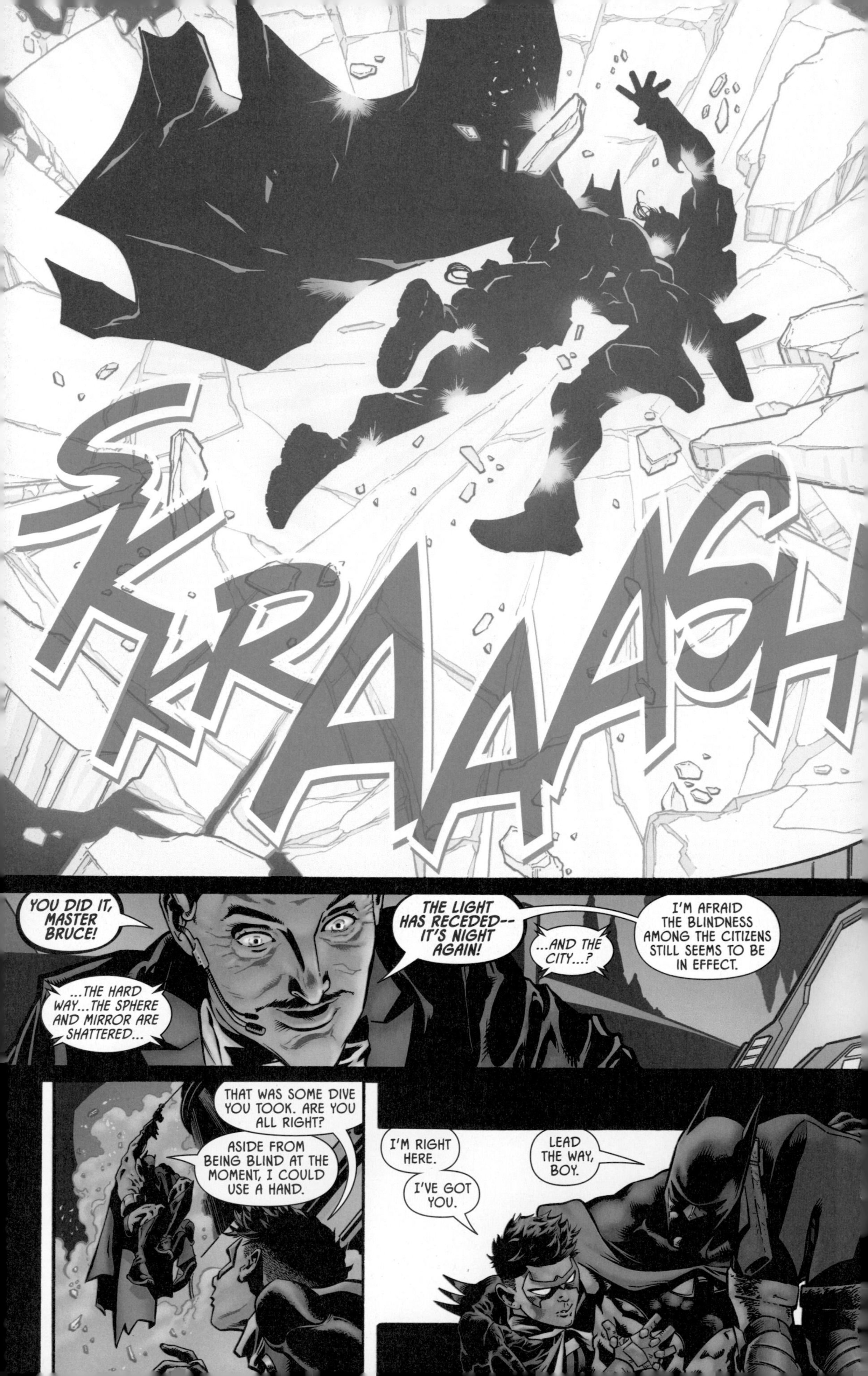
SKRAAASH
YOU DID IT, MASTER BRUCE!
...THE HARD WAY...THE SPHERE AND MIRROR ARE SHATTERED...
THE LIGHT HAS RECEDED-- IT'S NIGHT AGAIN!
...AND THE CITY...?
I'M AFRAID THE BLINDNESS AMONG THE CITIZENS STILL SEEMS TO BE IN EFFECT.
THAT WAS SOME DIVE YOU TOOK. ARE YOU ALL RIGHT?
ASIDE FROM BEING BLIND AT THE MOMENT, I COULD USE A HAND.
I'M RIGHT HERE.
I'VE GOT YOU.
LEAD THE WAY, BOY.

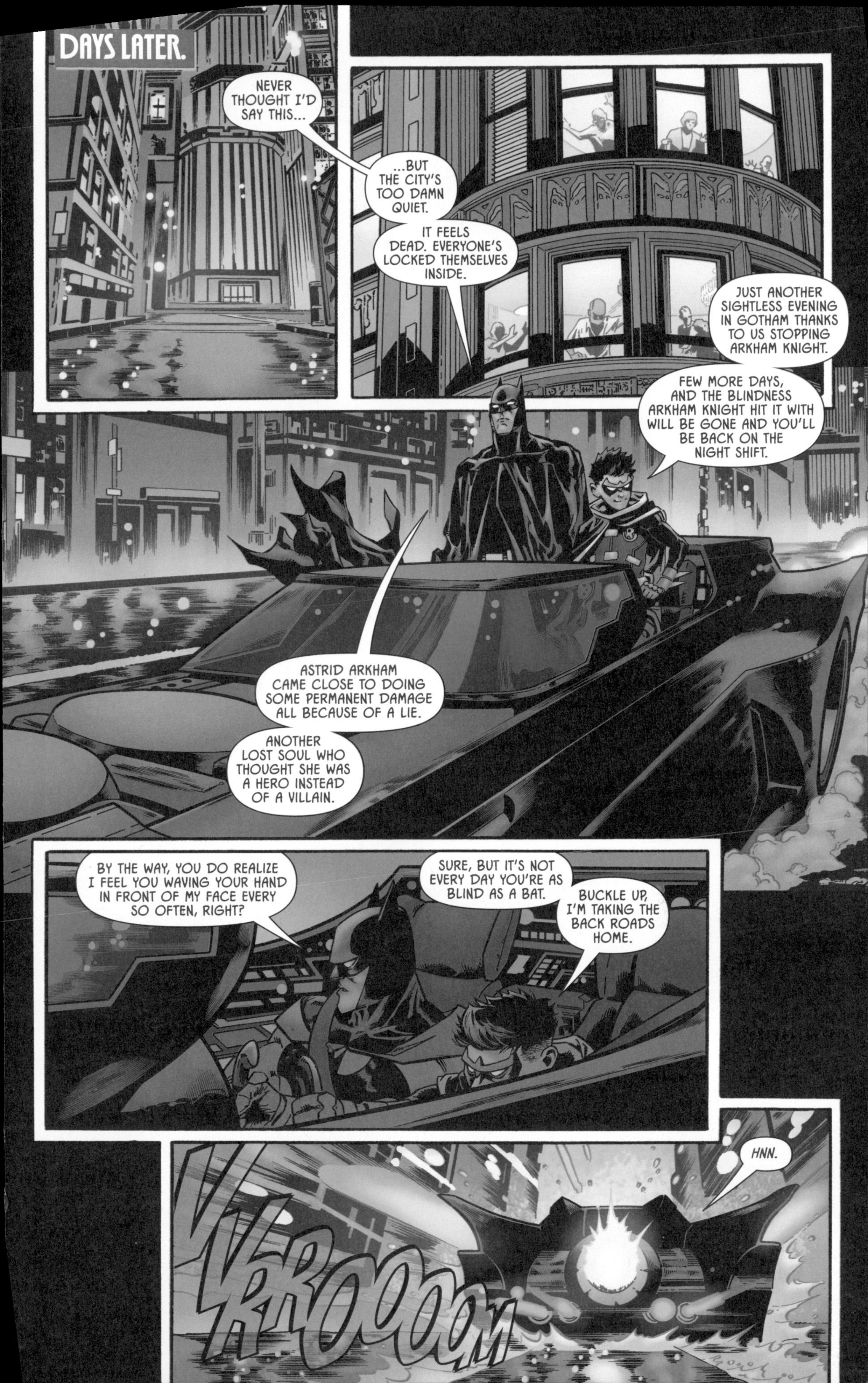
DAYS LATER.
NEVER THOUGHT I'D SAY THIS...
...BUT THE CITY'S TOO DAMN QUIET.
IT FEELS DEAD. EVERYONE'S LOCKED THEMSELVES INSIDE.
JUST ANOTHER SIGHTLESS EVENING IN GOTHAM THANKS TO US STOPPING ARKHAM KNIGHT.
FEW MORE DAYS, AND THE BLINDNESS ARKHAM KNIGHT HIT IT WITH WILL BE GONE AND YOU'LL BE BACK ON THE NIGHT SHIFT.
ASTRID ARKHAM CAME CLOSE TO DOING SOME PERMANENT DAMAGE ALL BECAUSE OF A LIE.
ANOTHER LOST SOUL WHO THOUGHT SHE WAS A HERO INSTEAD OF A VILLAIN.
BY THE WAY, YOU DO REALIZE I FEEL YOU WAVING YOUR HAND IN FRONT OF MY FACE EVERY SO OFTEN, RIGHT?
SURE, BUT IT'S NOT EVERY DAY YOU'RE AS BLIND AS A BAT.
BUCKLE UP, I'M TAKING THE BACK ROADS HOME.
HNN.
VRROOOOM

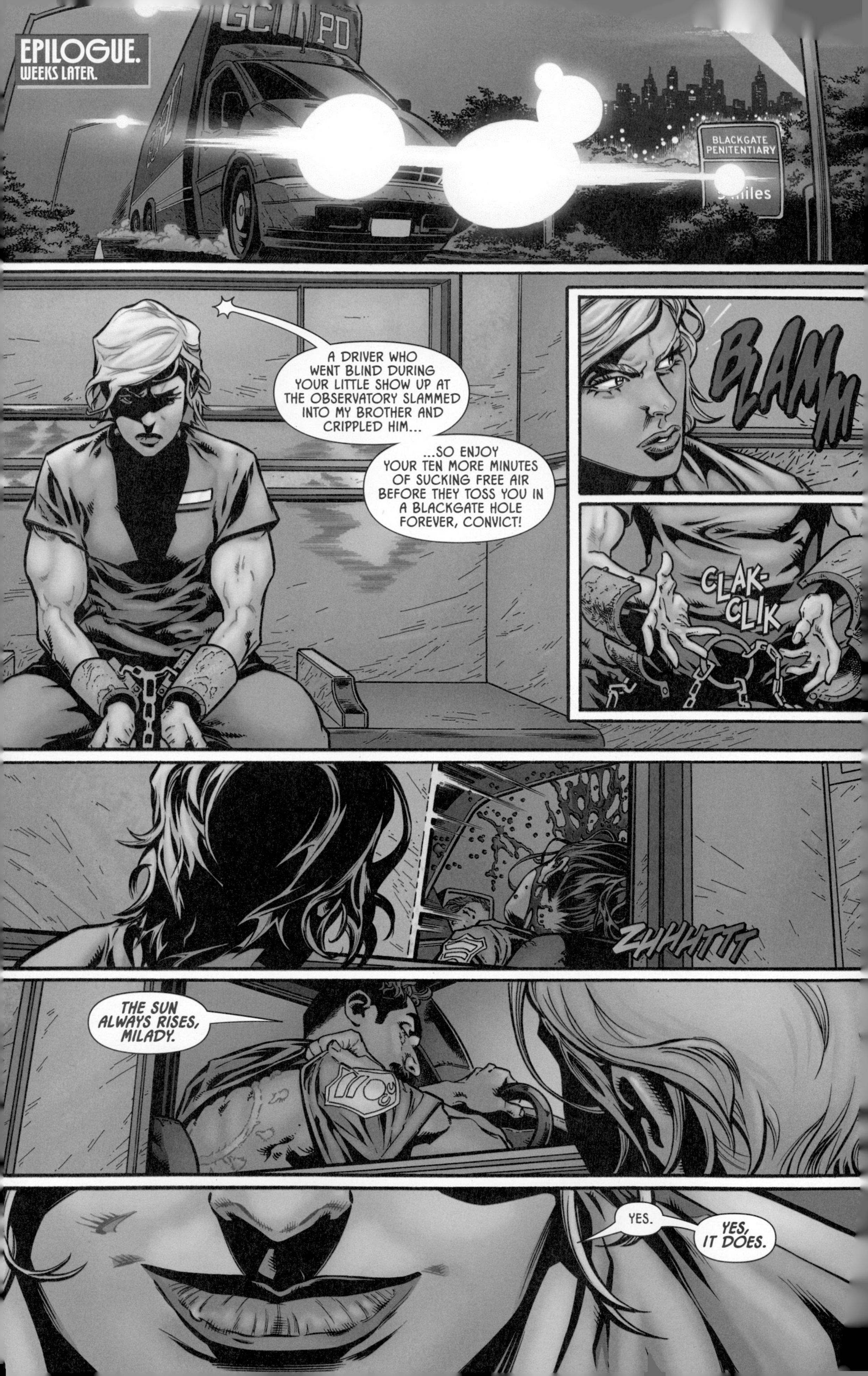

EPILOGUE.
WEEKS LATER.
GCPD
BLACKGATE PENITENTIARY
A DRIVER WHO WENT BLIND DURING YOUR LITTLE SHOW UP AT THE OBSERVATORY SLAMMED INTO MY BROTHER AND CRIPPLED HIM...
...SO ENJOY YOUR TEN MORE MINUTES OF SUCKING FREE AIR BEFORE THEY TOSS YOU IN A BLACKGATE HOLE FOREVER, CONVICT!
BLAMM
CLAK-CLIK
ZHHHTTT
THE SUN ALWAYS RISES, MILADY.
YES.
YES, IT DOES.

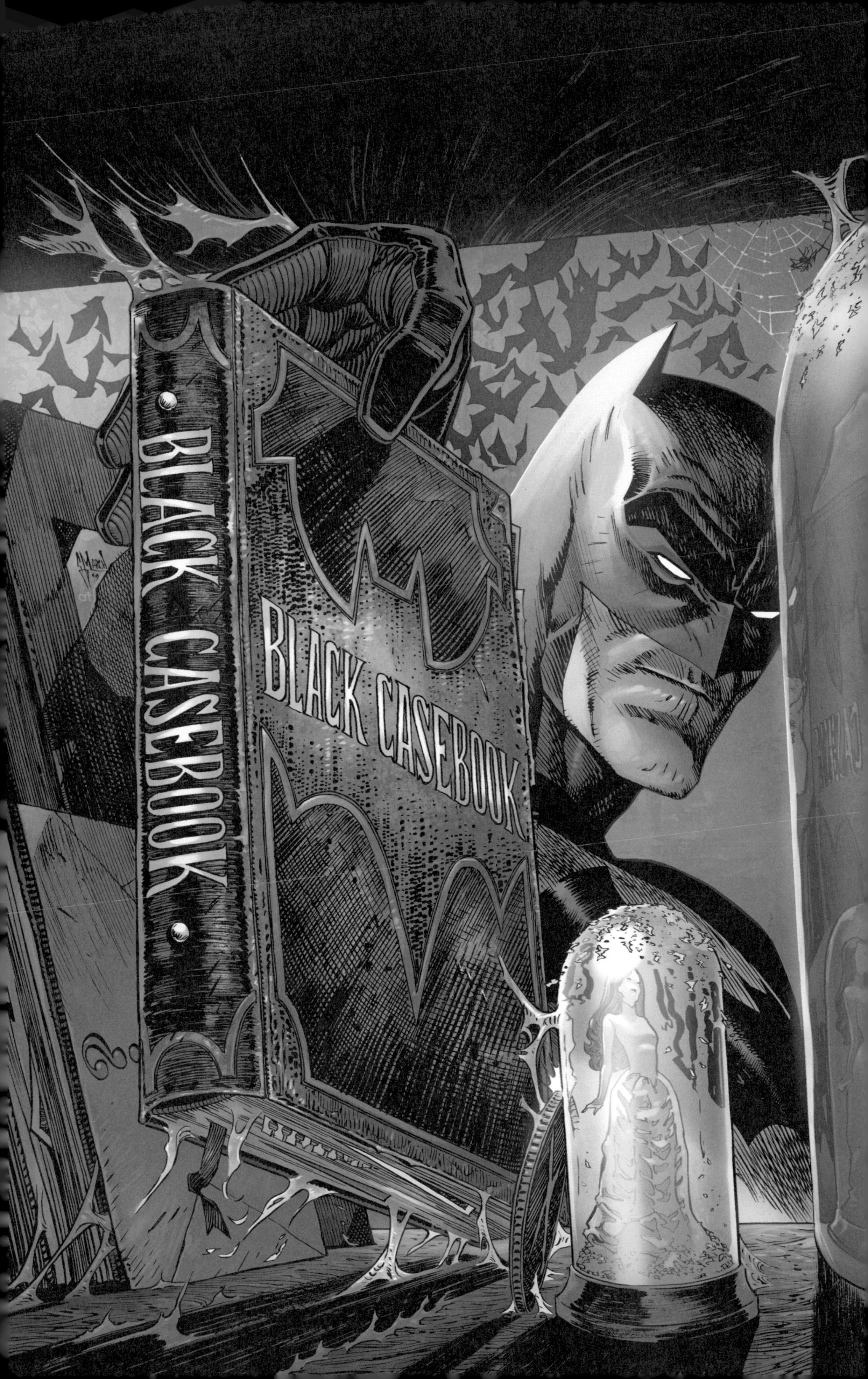
BLACK CASEBOOK
BLACK CASEBOOK

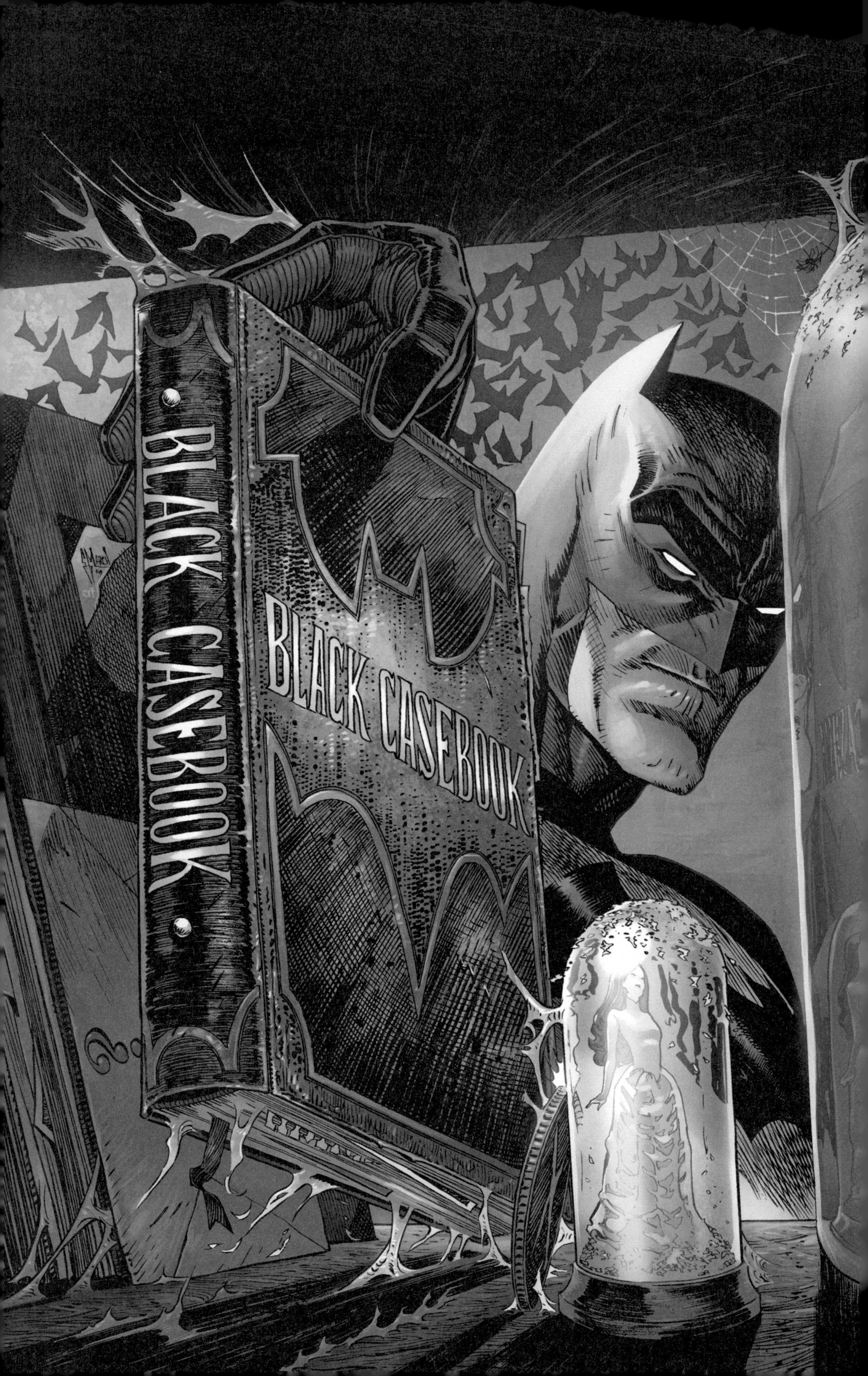
BLACK CASEBOOK
BLACK CASEBOOK

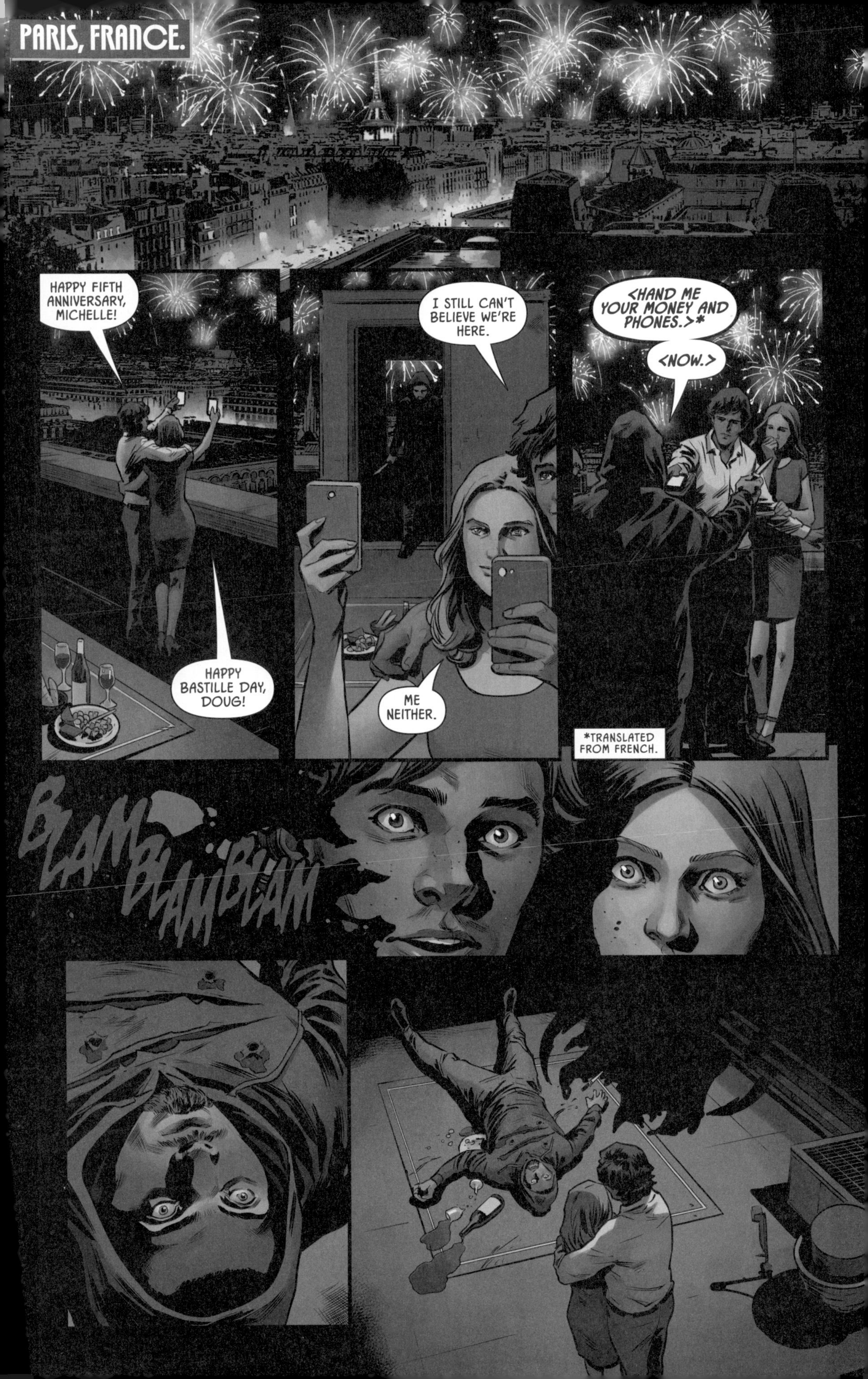
PARIS, FRANCE.
HAPPY FIFTH ANNIVERSARY, MICHELLE!
HAPPY BASTILLE DAY, DOUG!
I STILL CAN'T BELIEVE WE'RE HERE.
ME NEITHER.
<HAND ME YOUR MONEY AND PHONES.>*
<NOW.>
*TRANSLATED FROM FRENCH.
BLAM BLAM BLAM

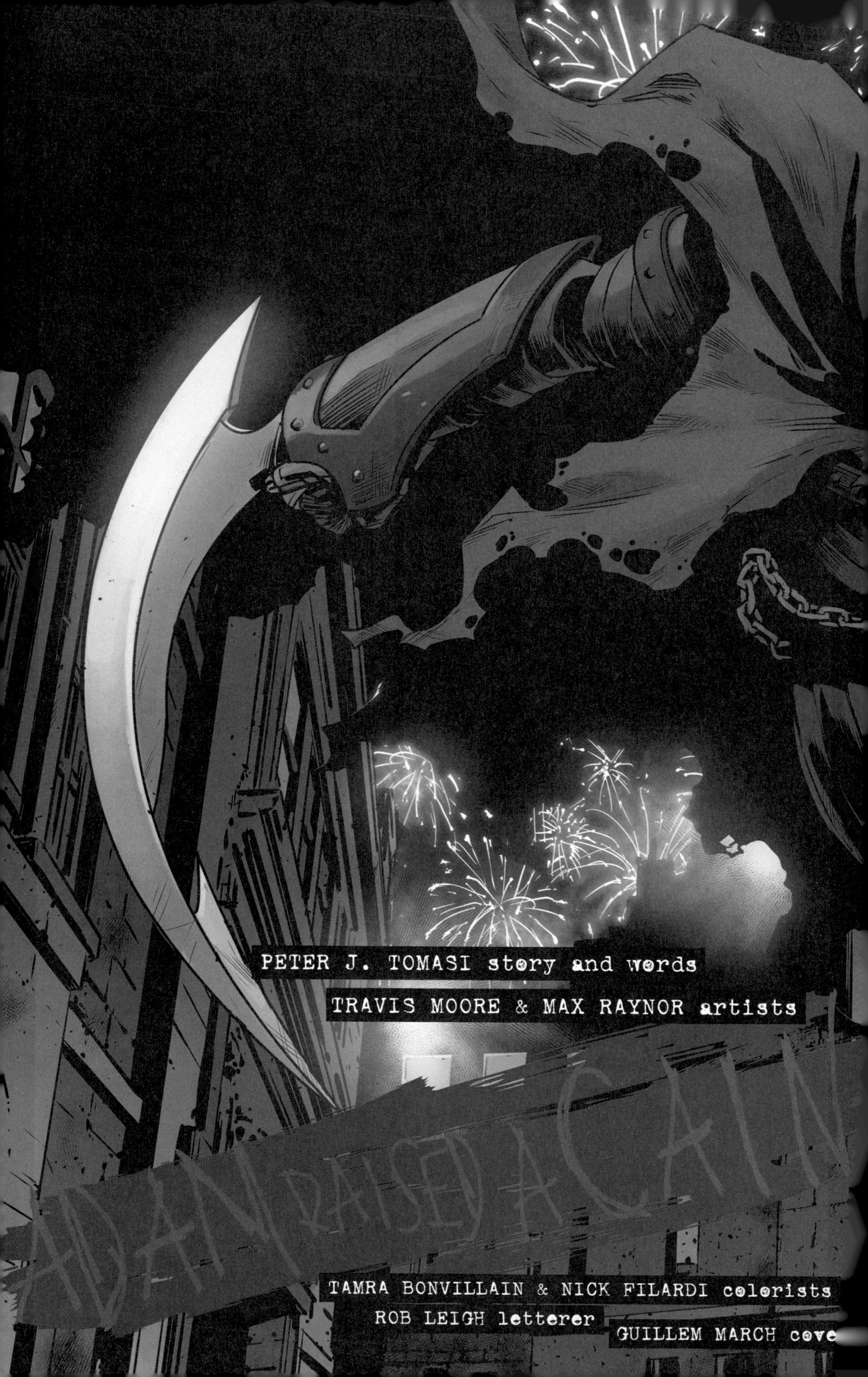
PETER J. TOMASI story and words
TRAVIS MOORE & MAX RAYNOR artists
ADAM RAISED A CAIN
TAMRA BONVILLAIN & NICK FILARDI colorists
ROB LEIGH letterer
GUILLEM MARCH cove

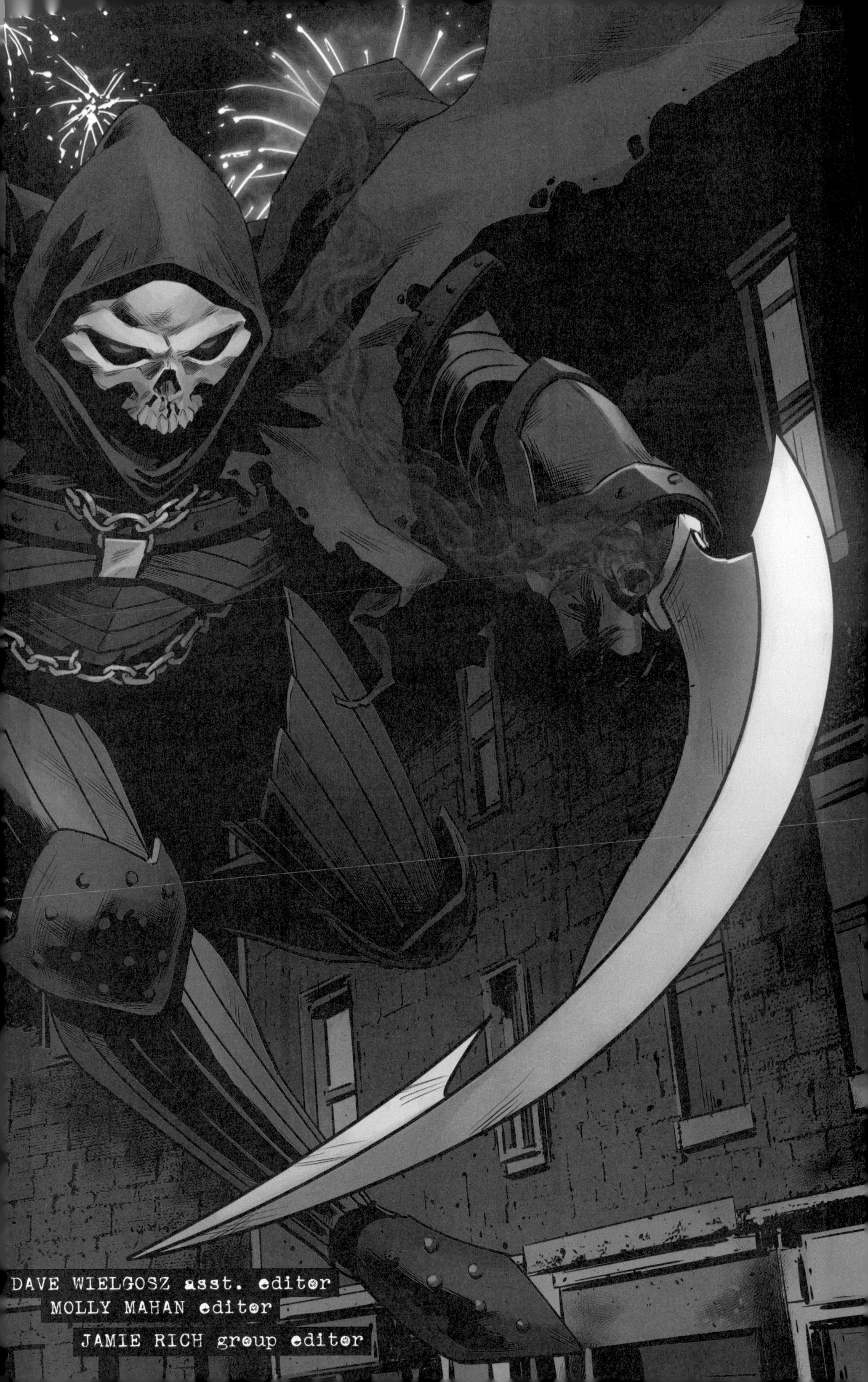
DAVE WIELGOSZ asst. editor
MOLLY MAHAN editor
JAMIE RICH group editor

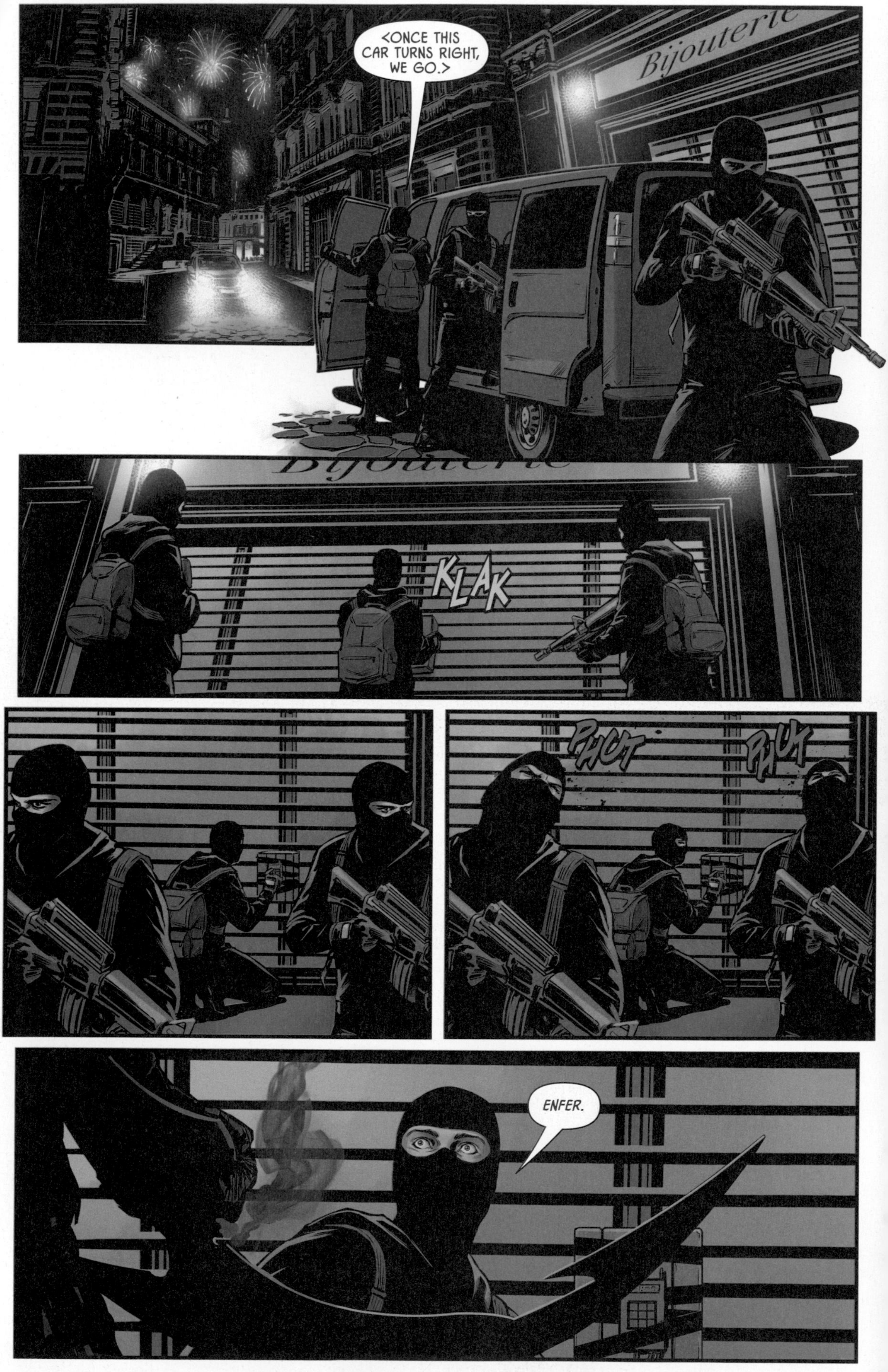
<ONCE THIS CAR TURNS RIGHT, WE GO.>
Bijouterie
KLAK
PHUT
PHUT
ENFER.

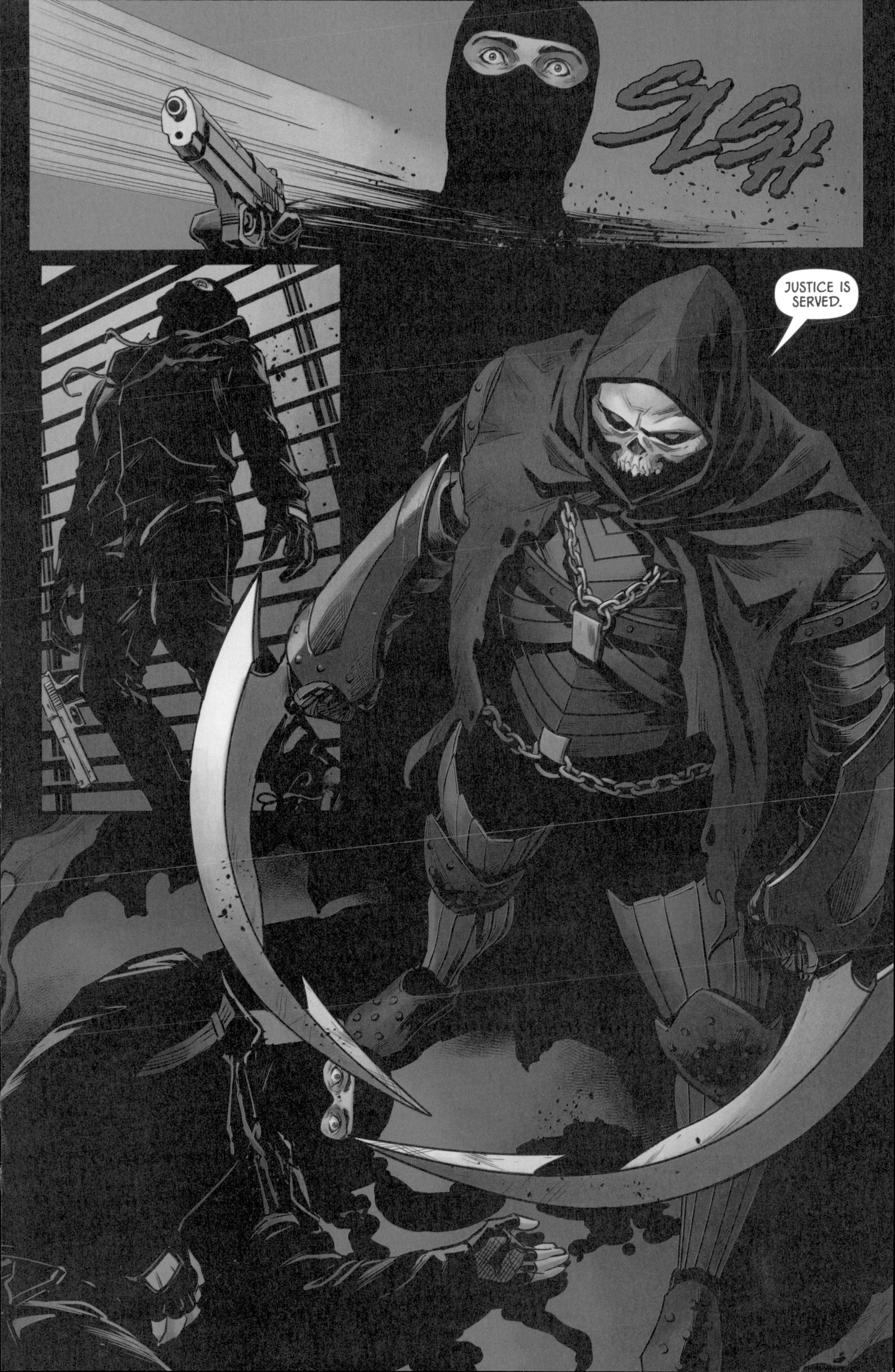
SLSH
JUSTICE IS SERVED.

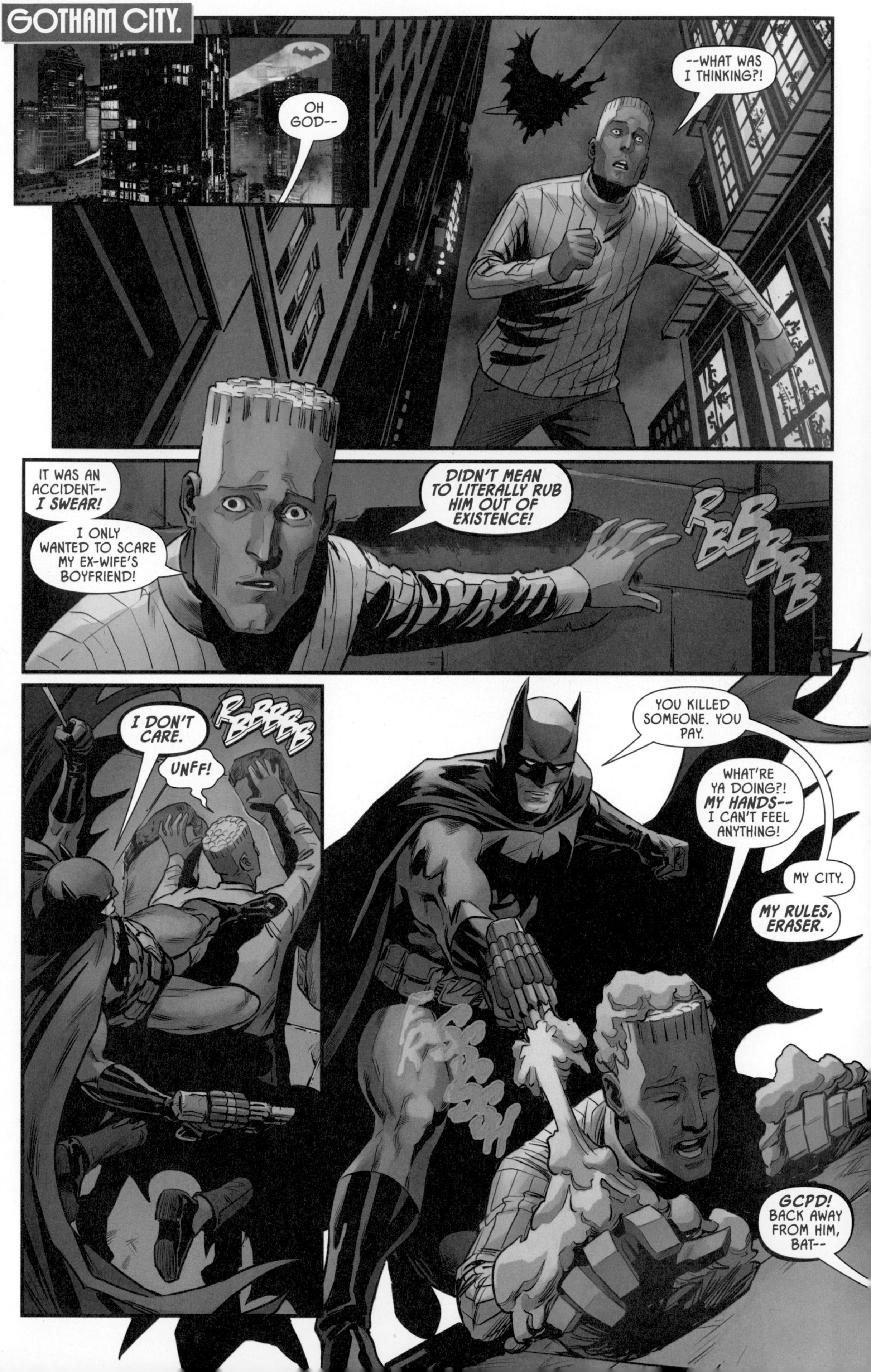
GOTHAM CITY.
OH GOD--
--WHAT WAS I THINKING?!
IT WAS AN ACCIDENT-- I SWEAR!
I ONLY WANTED TO SCARE MY EX-WIFE'S BOYFRIEND!
DIDN'T MEAN TO LITERALLY RUB HIM OUT OF EXISTENCE!
RBBBBBB
I DON'T CARE.
RBBBBB
UNFF!
YOU KILLED SOMEONE. YOU PAY.
WHAT'RE YA DOING?! MY HANDS-- I CAN'T FEEL ANYTHING!
MY CITY.
MY RULES, ERASER.
GCPD! BACK AWAY FROM HIM, BAT--

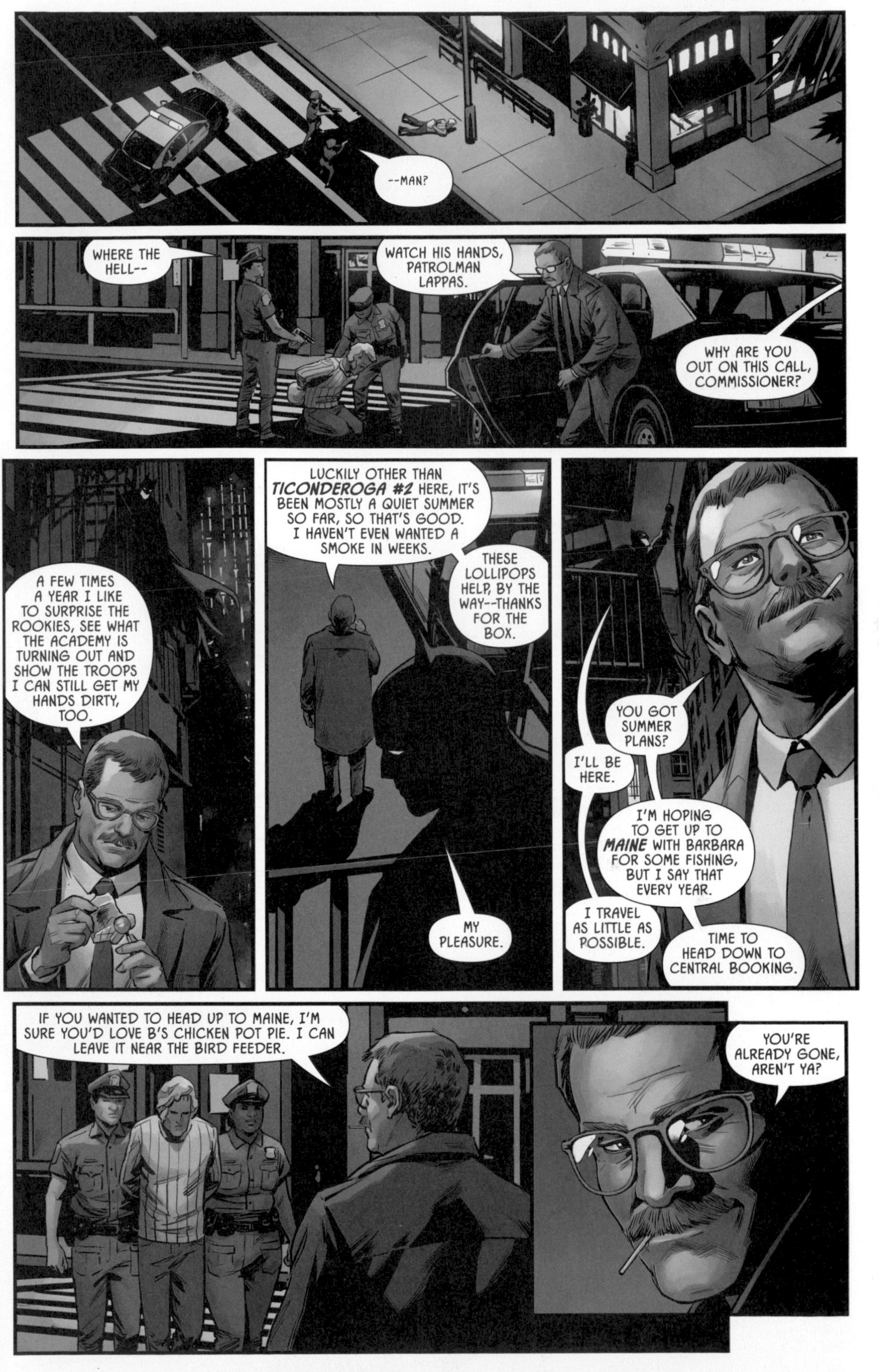
--MAN?
WHERE THE HELL--
WATCH HIS HANDS, PATROLMAN LAPPAS.
WHY ARE YOU OUT ON THIS CALL, COMMISSIONER?
A FEW TIMES A YEAR I LIKE TO SURPRISE THE ROOKIES, SEE WHAT THE ACADEMY IS TURNING OUT AND SHOW THE TROOPS I CAN STILL GET MY HANDS DIRTY, TOO.
LUCKILY OTHER THAN TICONDEROGA #2 HERE, IT'S BEEN MOSTLY A QUIET SUMMER SO FAR, SO THAT'S GOOD. I HAVEN'T EVEN WANTED A SMOKE IN WEEKS.
THESE LOLLIPOPS HELP, BY THE WAY--THANKS FOR THE BOX.
MY PLEASURE.
YOU GOT SUMMER PLANS?
I'LL BE HERE.
I'M HOPING TO GET UP TO MAINE WITH BARBARA FOR SOME FISHING, BUT I SAY THAT EVERY YEAR.
I TRAVEL AS LITTLE AS POSSIBLE.
TIME TO HEAD DOWN TO CENTRAL BOOKING.
IF YOU WANTED TO HEAD UP TO MAINE, I'M SURE YOU'D LOVE B'S CHICKEN POT PIE. I CAN LEAVE IT NEAR THE BIRD FEEDER.
YOU'RE ALREADY GONE, AREN'T YA?

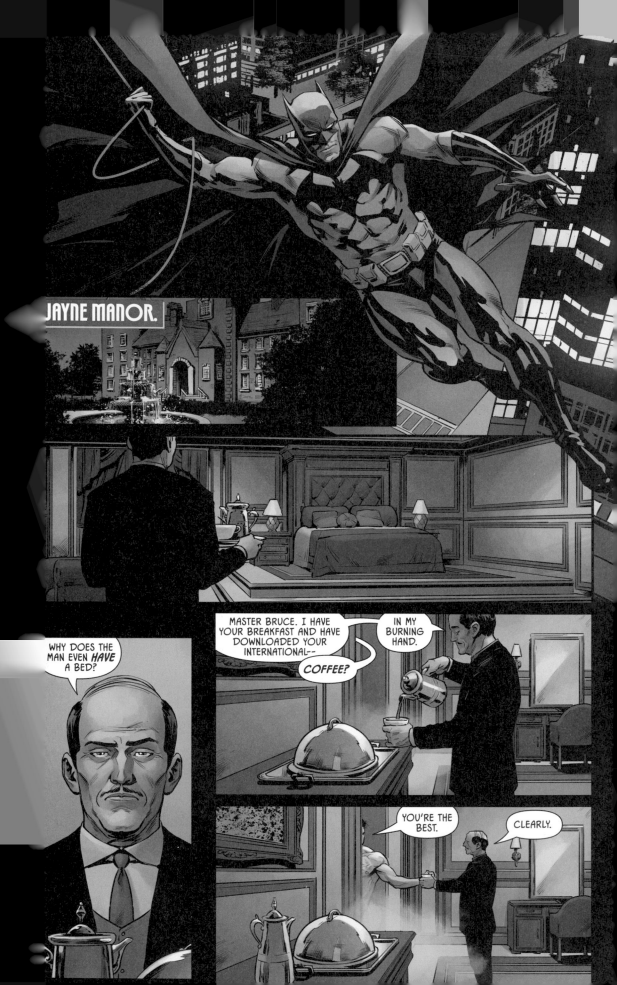

JAYNE MANOR.

WHY DOES THE MAN EVEN *HAVE* A BED?

MASTER BRUCE. I HAVE YOUR BREAKFAST AND HAVE DOWNLOADED YOUR INTERNATIONAL--

COFFEE?

IN MY BURNING HAND.

YOU'RE THE BEST.

CLEARLY.

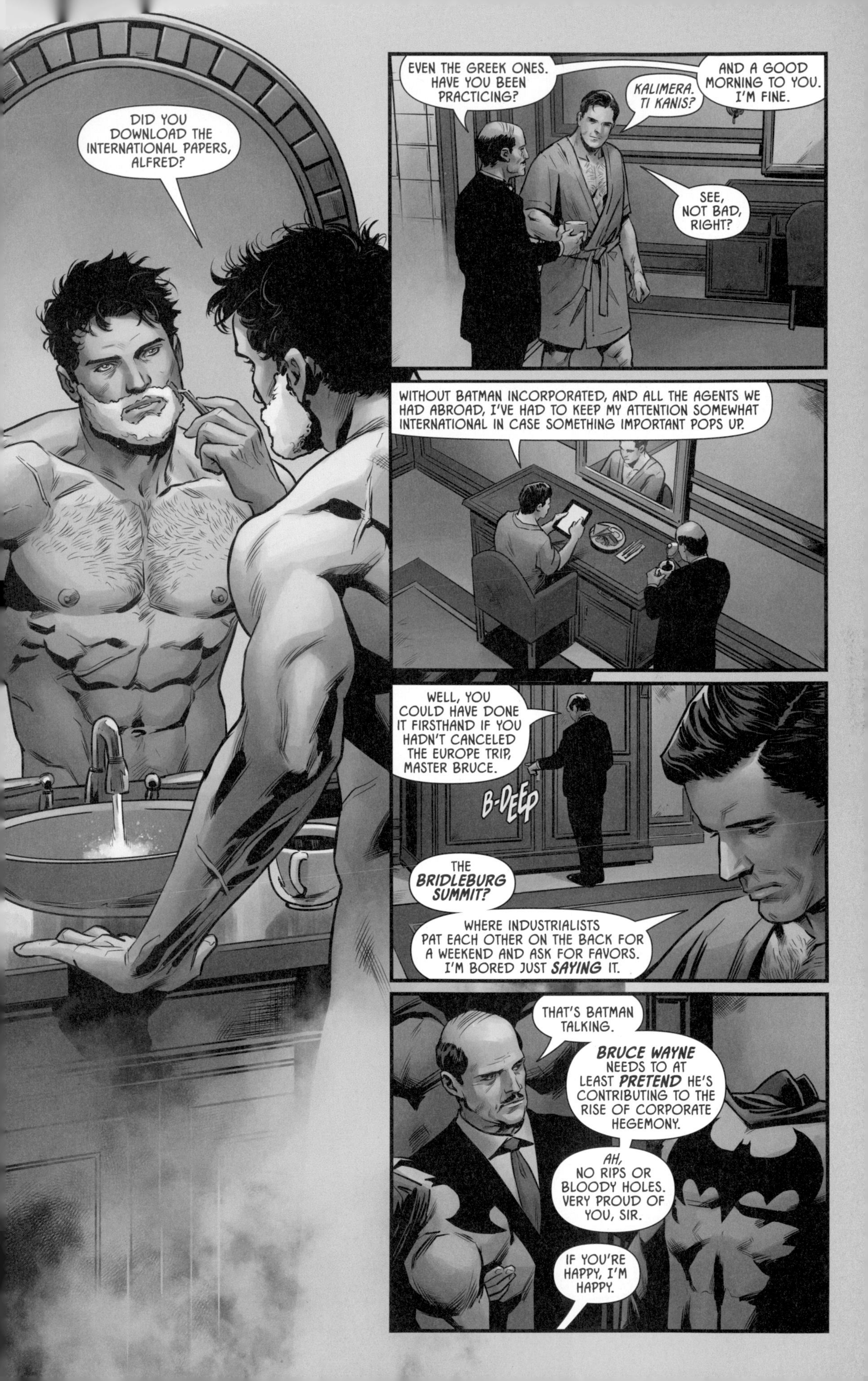
DID YOU DOWNLOAD THE INTERNATIONAL PAPERS, ALFRED?
EVEN THE GREEK ONES. HAVE YOU BEEN PRACTICING?
KALIMERA. TI KANIS?
AND A GOOD MORNING TO YOU. I'M FINE.
SEE, NOT BAD, RIGHT?
WITHOUT BATMAN INCORPORATED, AND ALL THE AGENTS WE HAD ABROAD, I'VE HAD TO KEEP MY ATTENTION SOMEWHAT INTERNATIONAL IN CASE SOMETHING IMPORTANT POPS UP.
WELL, YOU COULD HAVE DONE IT FIRSTHAND IF YOU HADN'T CANCELED THE EUROPE TRIP, MASTER BRUCE.
B-DEEP
THE BRIDLEBURG SUMMIT?
WHERE INDUSTRIALISTS PAT EACH OTHER ON THE BACK FOR A WEEKEND AND ASK FOR FAVORS. I'M BORED JUST SAYING IT.
THAT'S BATMAN TALKING.
BRUCE WAYNE NEEDS TO AT LEAST PRETEND HE'S CONTRIBUTING TO THE RISE OF CORPORATE HEGEMONY.
AH, NO RIPS OR BLOODY HOLES. VERY PROUD OF YOU, SIR.
IF YOU'RE HAPPY, I'M HAPPY.

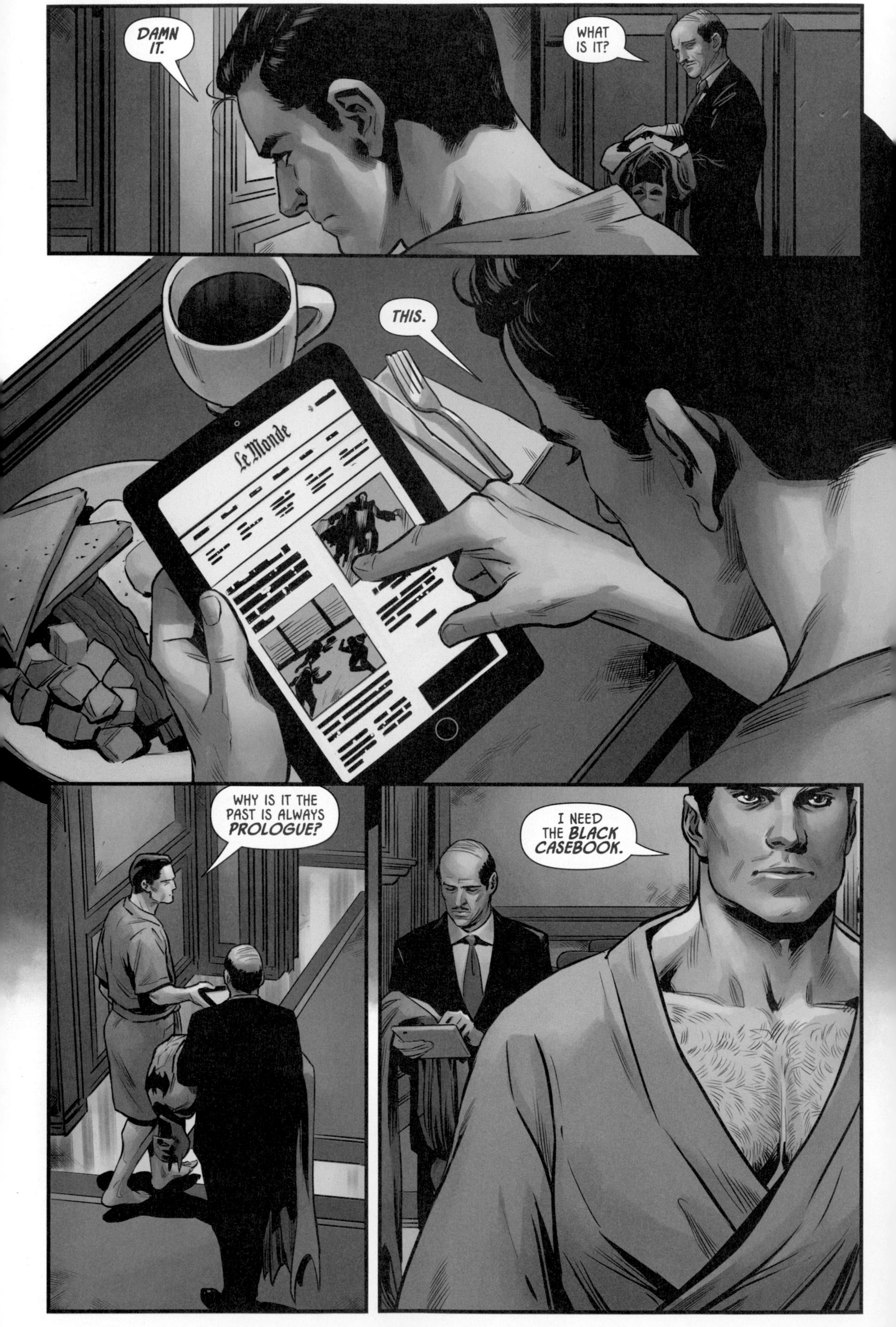
DAMN IT.
WHAT IS IT?
THIS.
Le Monde
WHY IS IT THE PAST IS ALWAYS PROLOGUE?
I NEED THE BLACK CASEBOOK.

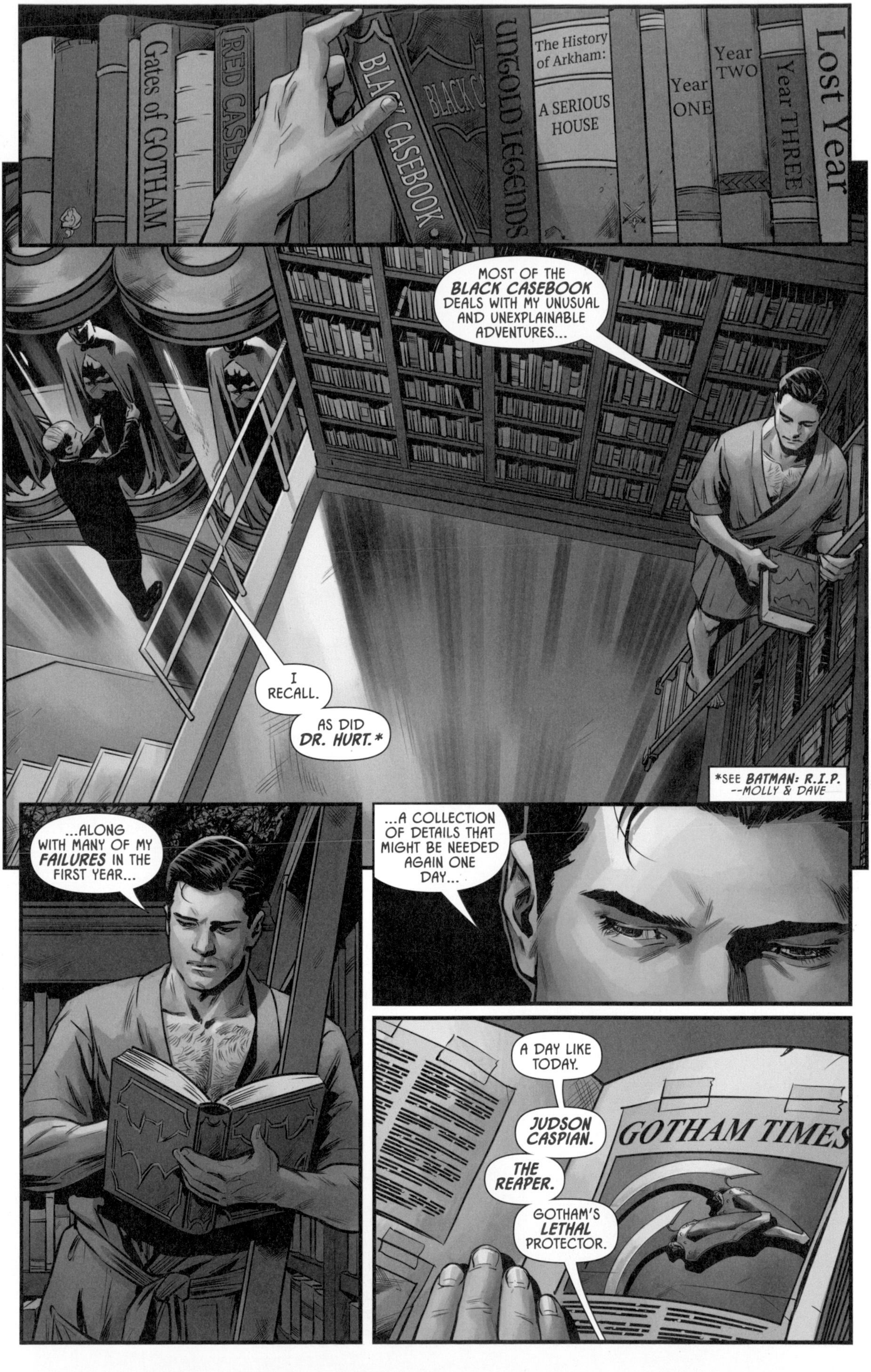
Gates of GOTHAM
RED CASEBOOK
BLACK CASEBOOK
UNGOLD LEGENDS
The History of Arkham: A SERIOUS HOUSE
Year ONE
Year TWO
Year THREE
Lost Year
MOST OF THE BLACK CASEBOOK DEALS WITH MY UNUSUAL AND UNEXPLAINABLE ADVENTURES...
I RECALL.
AS DID DR. HURT.*
*SEE BATMAN: R.I.P. --MOLLY & DAVE
...ALONG WITH MANY OF MY FAILURES IN THE FIRST YEAR...
...A COLLECTION OF DETAILS THAT MIGHT BE NEEDED AGAIN ONE DAY...
A DAY LIKE TODAY.
JUDSON CASPIAN.
THE REAPER.
GOTHAM'S LETHAL PROTECTOR.
GOTHAM TIMES

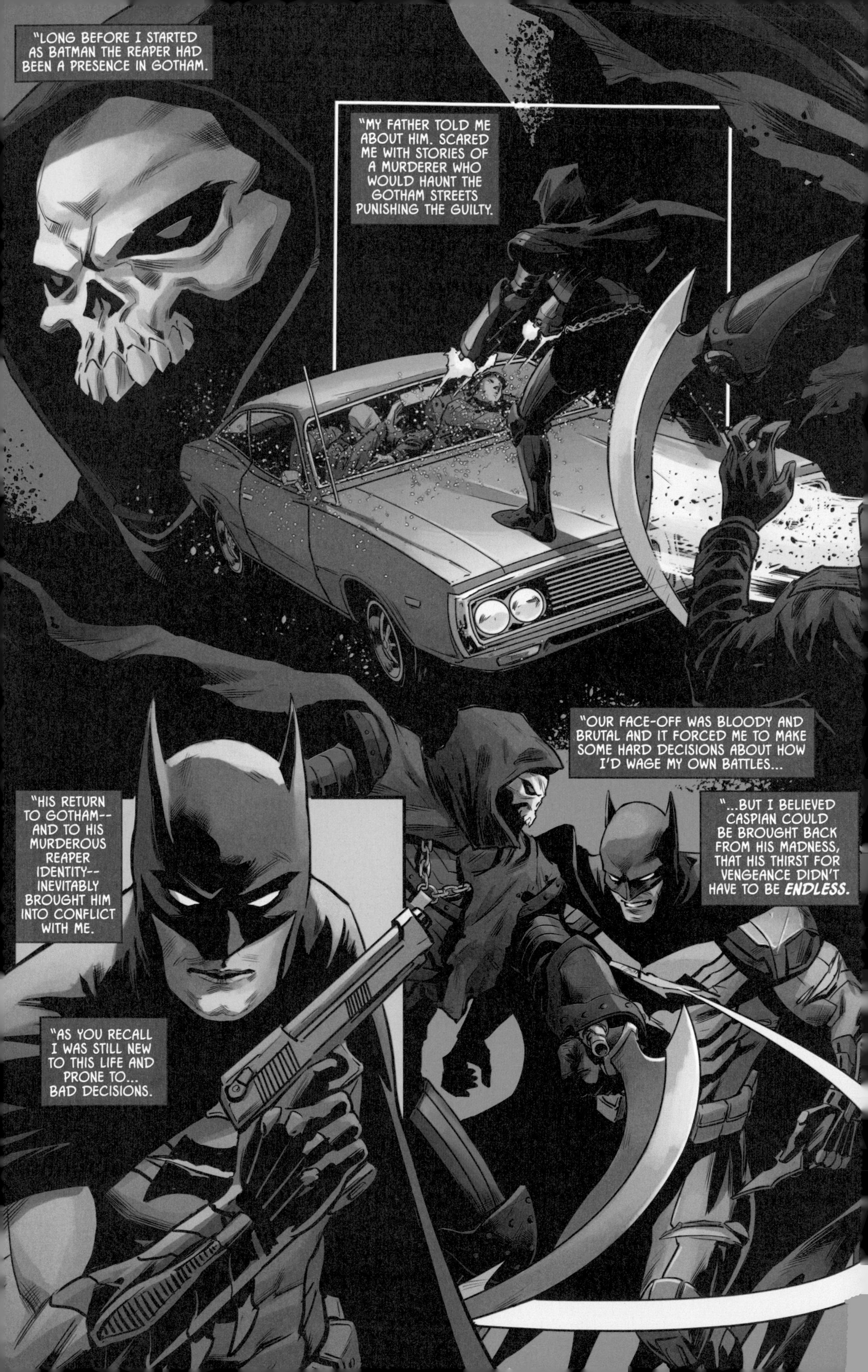
"LONG BEFORE I STARTED AS BATMAN THE REAPER HAD BEEN A PRESENCE IN GOTHAM.
"MY FATHER TOLD ME ABOUT HIM. SCARED ME WITH STORIES OF A MURDERER WHO WOULD HAUNT THE GOTHAM STREETS PUNISHING THE GUILTY.
"HIS RETURN TO GOTHAM-- AND TO HIS MURDEROUS REAPER IDENTITY-- INEVITABLY BROUGHT HIM INTO CONFLICT WITH ME.
"AS YOU RECALL I WAS STILL NEW TO THIS LIFE AND PRONE TO... BAD DECISIONS.
"OUR FACE-OFF WAS BLOODY AND BRUTAL AND IT FORCED ME TO MAKE SOME HARD DECISIONS ABOUT HOW I'D WAGE MY OWN BATTLES...
"...BUT I BELIEVED CASPIAN COULD BE BROUGHT BACK FROM HIS MADNESS, THAT HIS THIRST FOR VENGEANCE DIDN'T HAVE TO BE ***ENDLESS.***

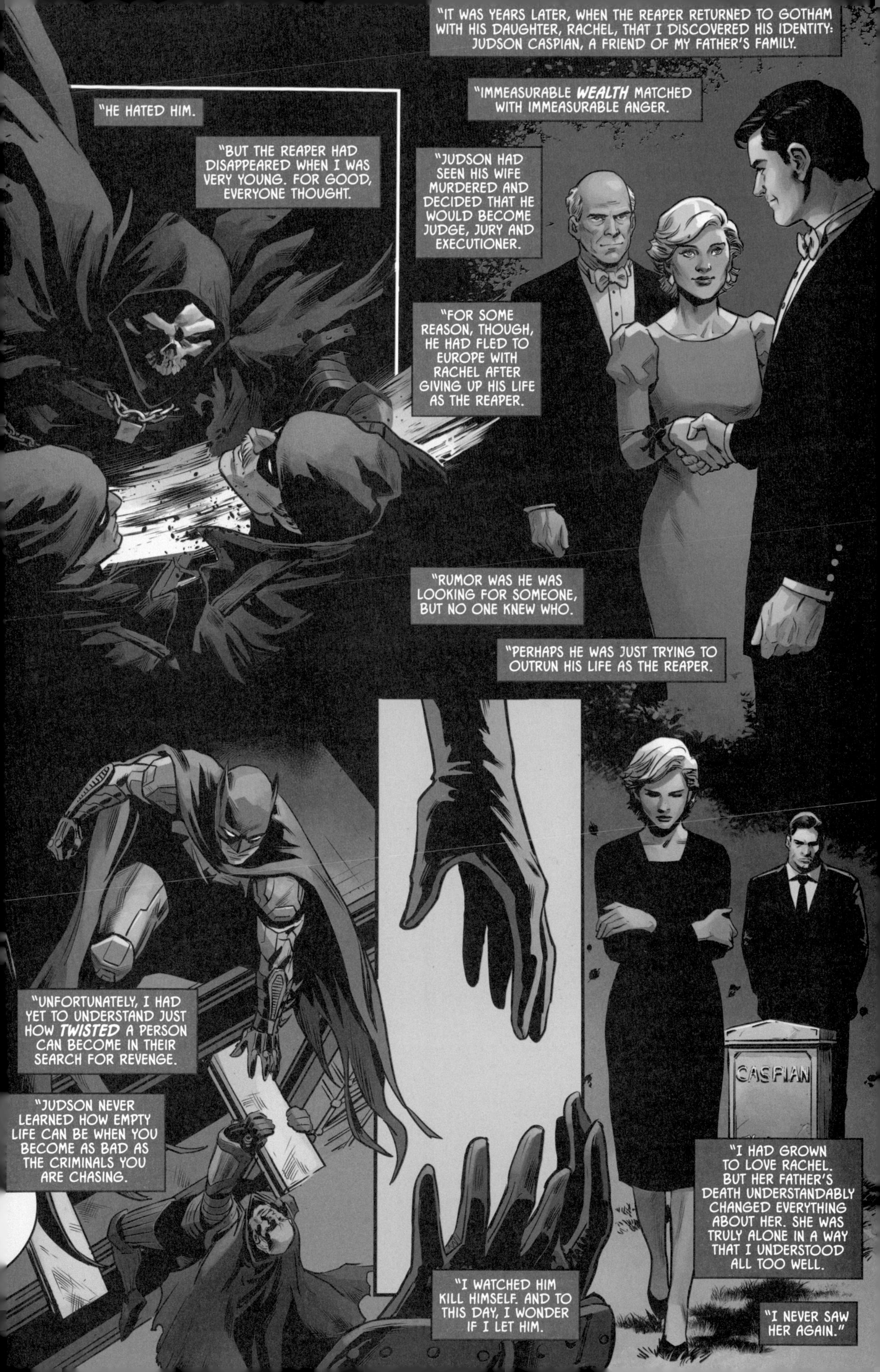
"HE HATED HIM.
"BUT THE REAPER HAD DISAPPEARED WHEN I WAS VERY YOUNG. FOR GOOD, EVERYONE THOUGHT.
"IT WAS YEARS LATER, WHEN THE REAPER RETURNED TO GOTHAM WITH HIS DAUGHTER, RACHEL, THAT I DISCOVERED HIS IDENTITY: JUDSON CASPIAN, A FRIEND OF MY FATHER'S FAMILY.
"IMMEASURABLE WEALTH MATCHED WITH IMMEASURABLE ANGER.
"JUDSON HAD SEEN HIS WIFE MURDERED AND DECIDED THAT HE WOULD BECOME JUDGE, JURY AND EXECUTIONER.
"FOR SOME REASON, THOUGH, HE HAD FLED TO EUROPE WITH RACHEL AFTER GIVING UP HIS LIFE AS THE REAPER.
"RUMOR WAS HE WAS LOOKING FOR SOMEONE, BUT NO ONE KNEW WHO.
"PERHAPS HE WAS JUST TRYING TO OUTRUN HIS LIFE AS THE REAPER.
"UNFORTUNATELY, I HAD YET TO UNDERSTAND JUST HOW TWISTED A PERSON CAN BECOME IN THEIR SEARCH FOR REVENGE.
"JUDSON NEVER LEARNED HOW EMPTY LIFE CAN BE WHEN YOU BECOME AS BAD AS THE CRIMINALS YOU ARE CHASING.
"I WATCHED HIM KILL HIMSELF. AND TO THIS DAY, I WONDER IF I LET HIM.
CASPIAN
"I HAD GROWN TO LOVE RACHEL. BUT HER FATHER'S DEATH UNDERSTANDABLY CHANGED EVERYTHING ABOUT HER. SHE WAS TRULY ALONE IN A WAY THAT I UNDERSTOOD ALL TOO WELL.
"I NEVER SAW HER AGAIN."

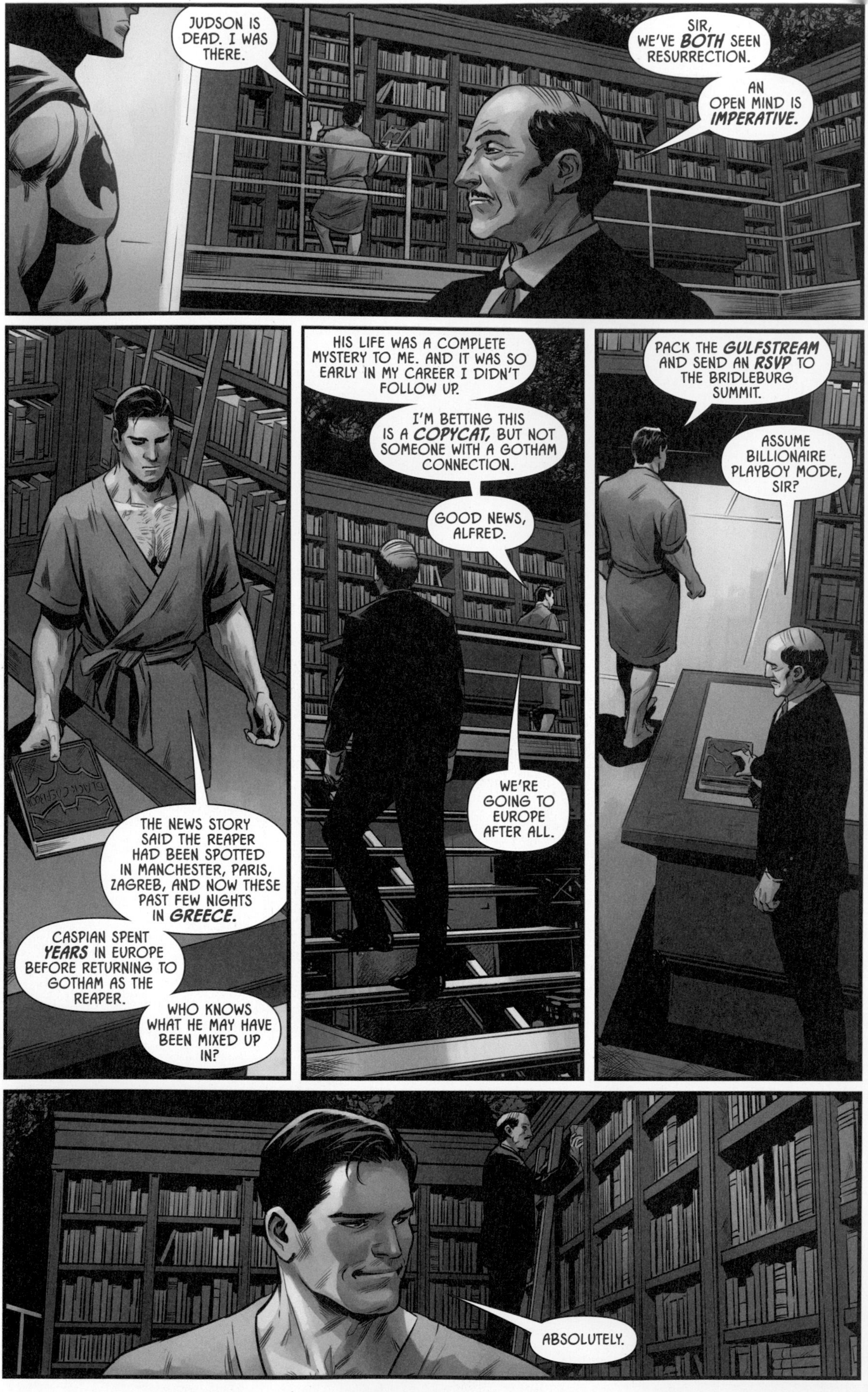
JUDSON IS DEAD. I WAS THERE.
SIR, WE'VE BOTH SEEN RESURRECTION.
AN OPEN MIND IS IMPERATIVE.
THE NEWS STORY SAID THE REAPER HAD BEEN SPOTTED IN MANCHESTER, PARIS, ZAGREB, AND NOW THESE PAST FEW NIGHTS IN GREECE.
CASPIAN SPENT YEARS IN EUROPE BEFORE RETURNING TO GOTHAM AS THE REAPER.
WHO KNOWS WHAT HE MAY HAVE BEEN MIXED UP IN?
HIS LIFE WAS A COMPLETE MYSTERY TO ME. AND IT WAS SO EARLY IN MY CAREER I DIDN'T FOLLOW UP.
I'M BETTING THIS IS A COPYCAT, BUT NOT SOMEONE WITH A GOTHAM CONNECTION.
GOOD NEWS, ALFRED.
WE'RE GOING TO EUROPE AFTER ALL.
PACK THE GULFSTREAM AND SEND AN RSVP TO THE BRIDLEBURG SUMMIT.
ASSUME BILLIONAIRE PLAYBOY MODE, SIR?
ABSOLUTELY.

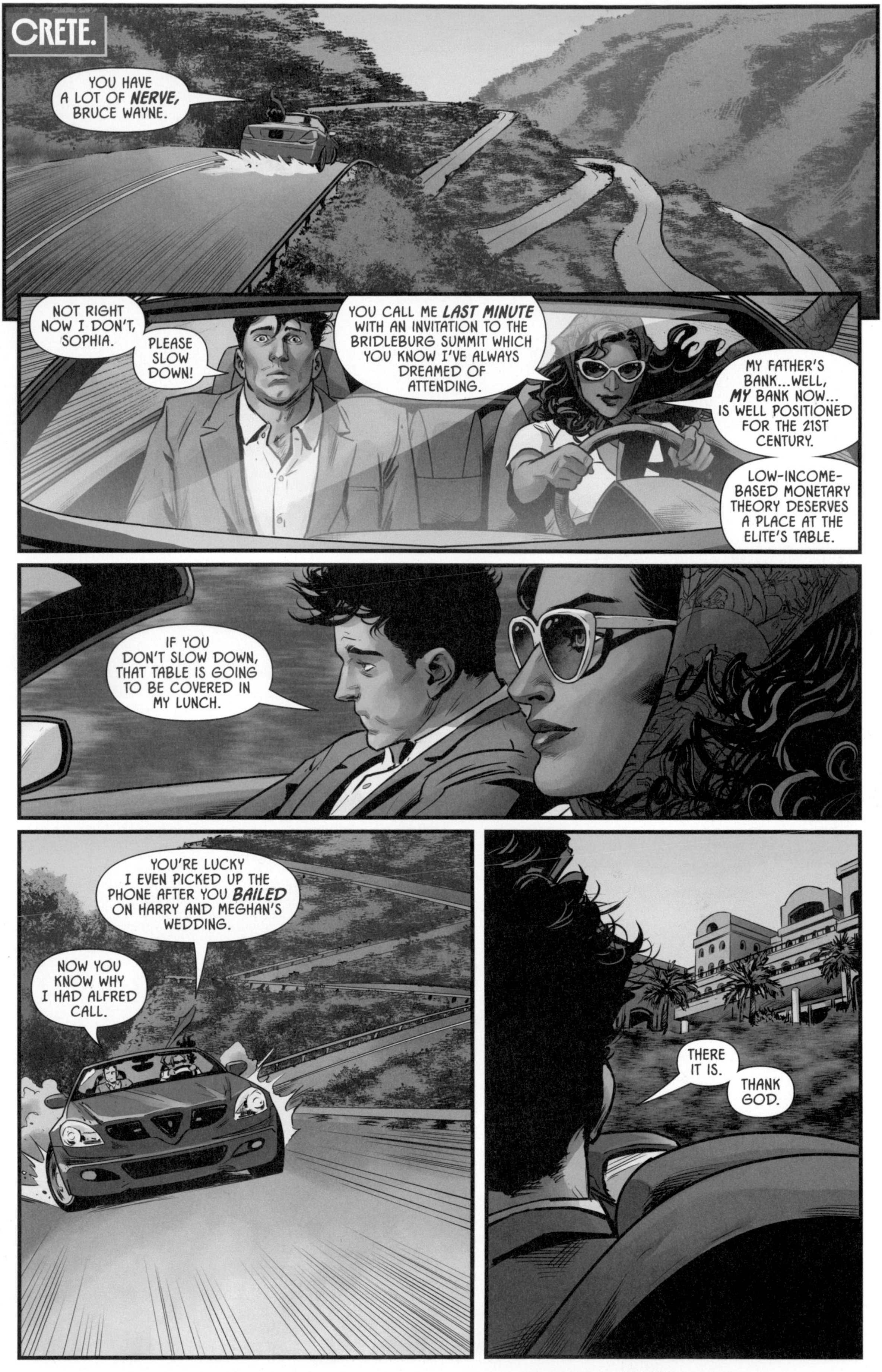
CRETE.
YOU HAVE A LOT OF NERVE, BRUCE WAYNE.
NOT RIGHT NOW I DON'T, SOPHIA.
PLEASE SLOW DOWN!
YOU CALL ME LAST MINUTE WITH AN INVITATION TO THE BRIDLEBURG SUMMIT WHICH YOU KNOW I'VE ALWAYS DREAMED OF ATTENDING.
MY FATHER'S BANK...WELL, MY BANK NOW... IS WELL POSITIONED FOR THE 21ST CENTURY.
LOW-INCOME-BASED MONETARY THEORY DESERVES A PLACE AT THE ELITE'S TABLE.
IF YOU DON'T SLOW DOWN, THAT TABLE IS GOING TO BE COVERED IN MY LUNCH.
YOU'RE LUCKY I EVEN PICKED UP THE PHONE AFTER YOU BAILED ON HARRY AND MEGHAN'S WEDDING.
NOW YOU KNOW WHY I HAD ALFRED CALL.
THERE IT IS.
THANK GOD.

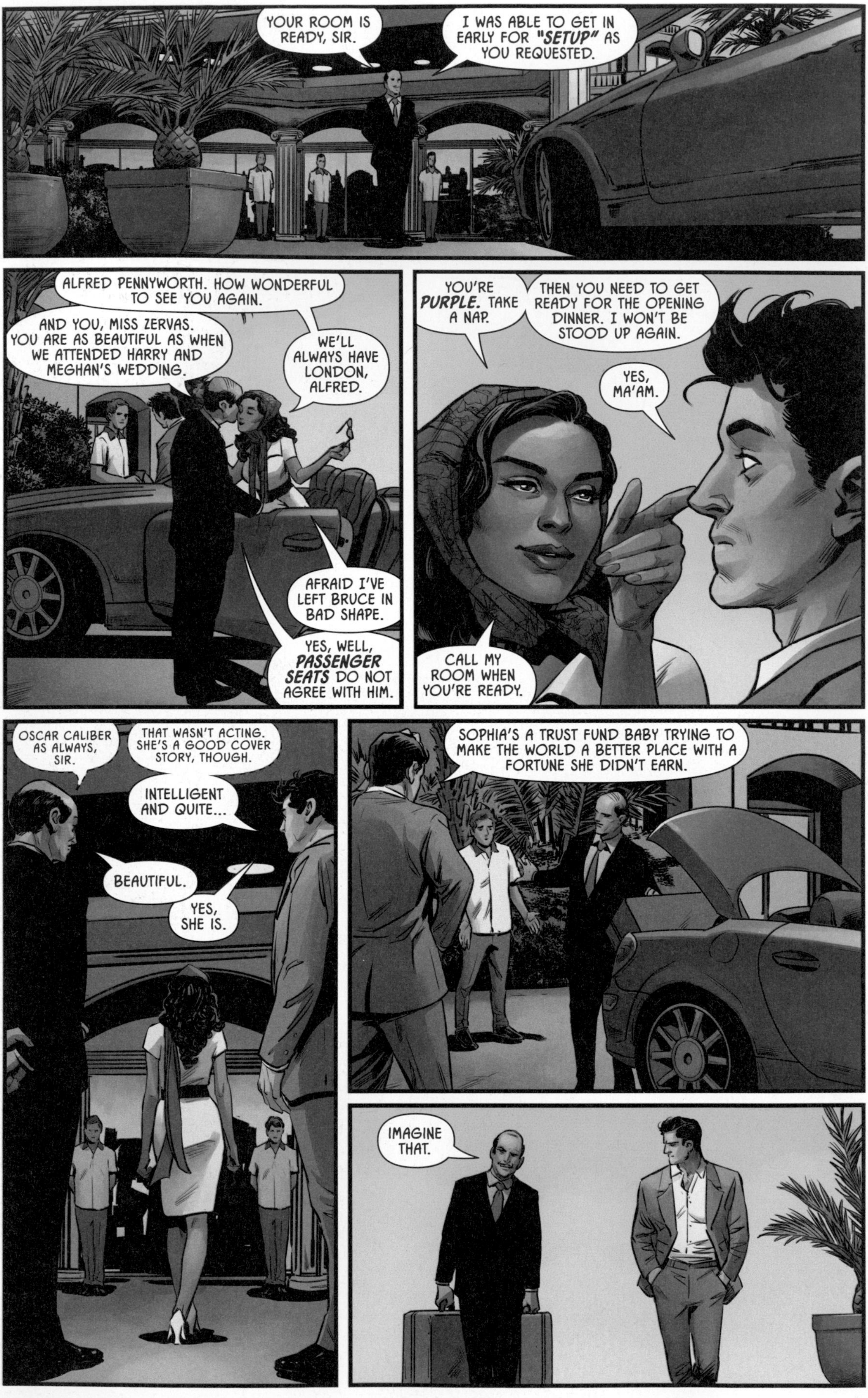
YOUR ROOM IS READY, SIR.
I WAS ABLE TO GET IN EARLY FOR "SETUP" AS YOU REQUESTED.
ALFRED PENNYWORTH. HOW WONDERFUL TO SEE YOU AGAIN.
AND YOU, MISS ZERVAS. YOU ARE AS BEAUTIFUL AS WHEN WE ATTENDED HARRY AND MEGHAN'S WEDDING.
WE'LL ALWAYS HAVE LONDON, ALFRED.
AFRAID I'VE LEFT BRUCE IN BAD SHAPE.
YES, WELL, PASSENGER SEATS DO NOT AGREE WITH HIM.
YOU'RE PURPLE. TAKE A NAP.
THEN YOU NEED TO GET READY FOR THE OPENING DINNER. I WON'T BE STOOD UP AGAIN.
YES, MA'AM.
CALL MY ROOM WHEN YOU'RE READY.
OSCAR CALIBER AS ALWAYS, SIR.
THAT WASN'T ACTING. SHE'S A GOOD COVER STORY, THOUGH.
INTELLIGENT AND QUITE...
BEAUTIFUL.
YES, SHE IS.
SOPHIA'S A TRUST FUND BABY TRYING TO MAKE THE WORLD A BETTER PLACE WITH A FORTUNE SHE DIDN'T EARN.
IMAGINE THAT.

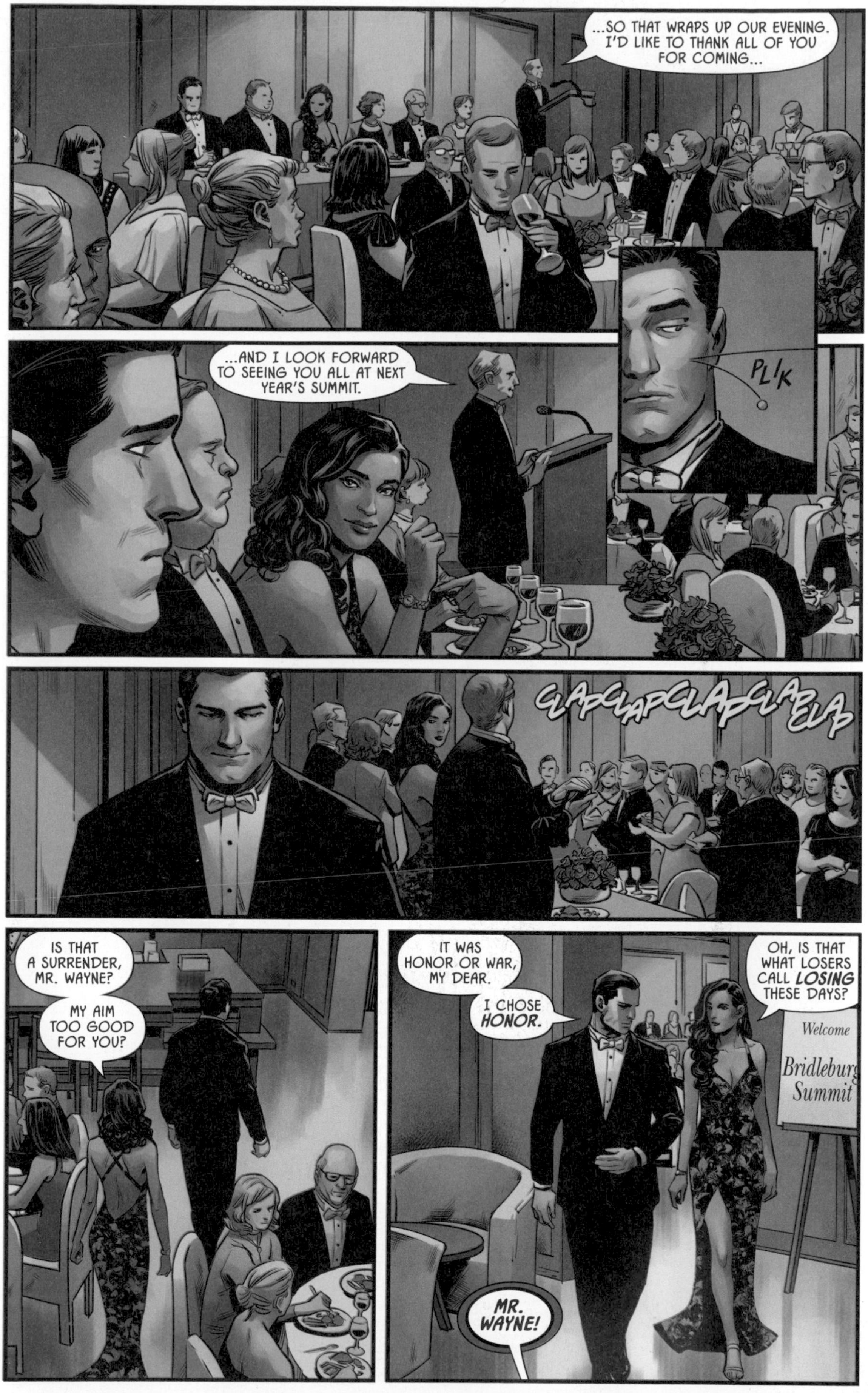
...SO THAT WRAPS UP OUR EVENING. I'D LIKE TO THANK ALL OF YOU FOR COMING...
PLIK
...AND I LOOK FORWARD TO SEEING YOU ALL AT NEXT YEAR'S SUMMIT.
CLAPCLAPCLAPCLAPCLAP
IS THAT A SURRENDER, MR. WAYNE?
MY AIM TOO GOOD FOR YOU?
IT WAS HONOR OR WAR, MY DEAR.
I CHOSE HONOR.
OH, IS THAT WHAT LOSERS CALL LOSING THESE DAYS?
Welcome
Bridleburg
Summit
MR. WAYNE!

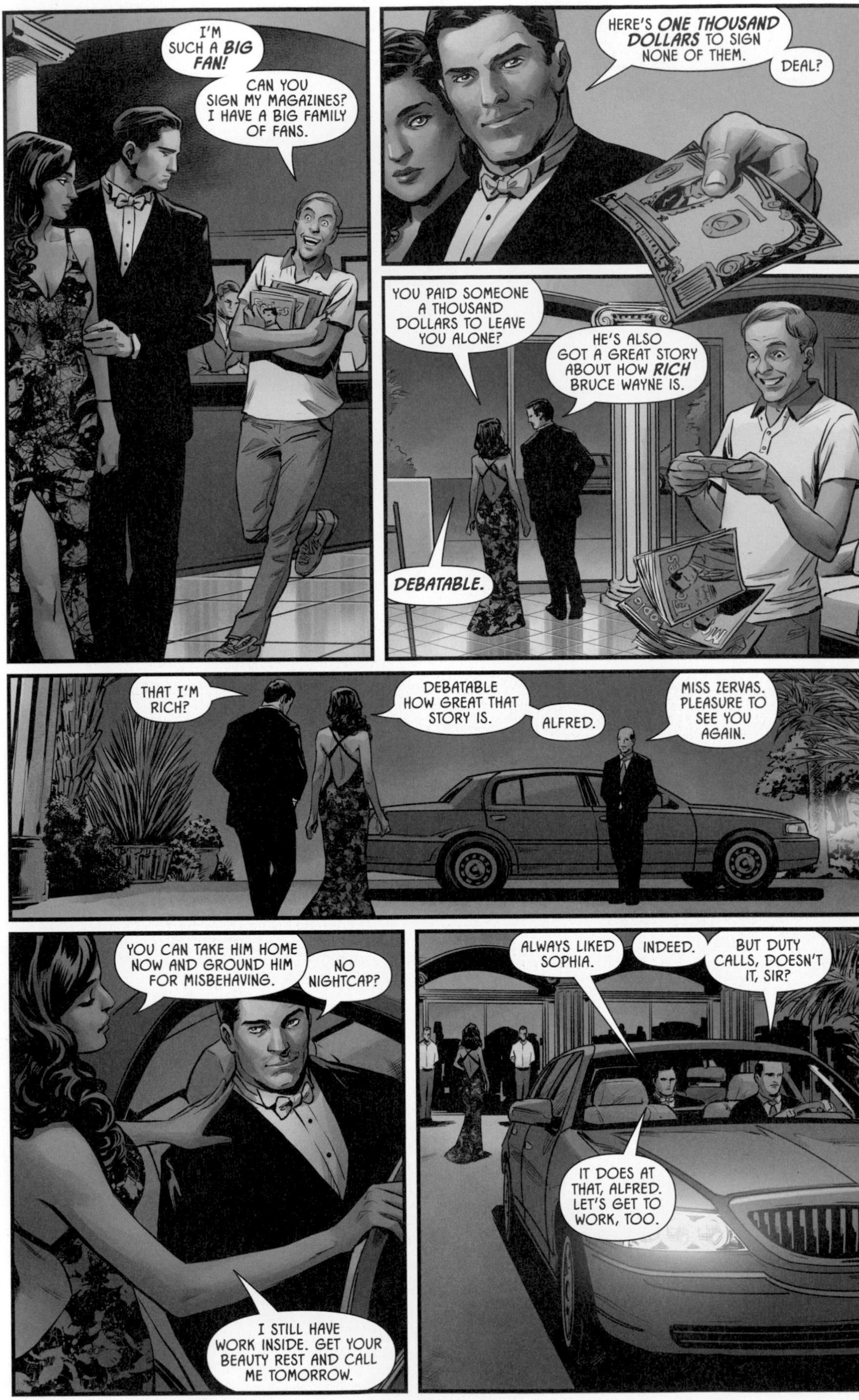
I'M SUCH A BIG FAN!
CAN YOU SIGN MY MAGAZINES? I HAVE A BIG FAMILY OF FANS.
HERE'S ONE THOUSAND DOLLARS TO SIGN NONE OF THEM.
DEAL?
YOU PAID SOMEONE A THOUSAND DOLLARS TO LEAVE YOU ALONE?
HE'S ALSO GOT A GREAT STORY ABOUT HOW RICH BRUCE WAYNE IS.
DEBATABLE.
THAT I'M RICH?
DEBATABLE HOW GREAT THAT STORY IS.
ALFRED.
MISS ZERVAS. PLEASURE TO SEE YOU AGAIN.
YOU CAN TAKE HIM HOME NOW AND GROUND HIM FOR MISBEHAVING.
NO NIGHTCAP?
I STILL HAVE WORK INSIDE. GET YOUR BEAUTY REST AND CALL ME TOMORROW.
ALWAYS LIKED SOPHIA.
INDEED.
BUT DUTY CALLS, DOESN'T IT, SIR?
IT DOES AT THAT, ALFRED. LET'S GET TO WORK, TOO.

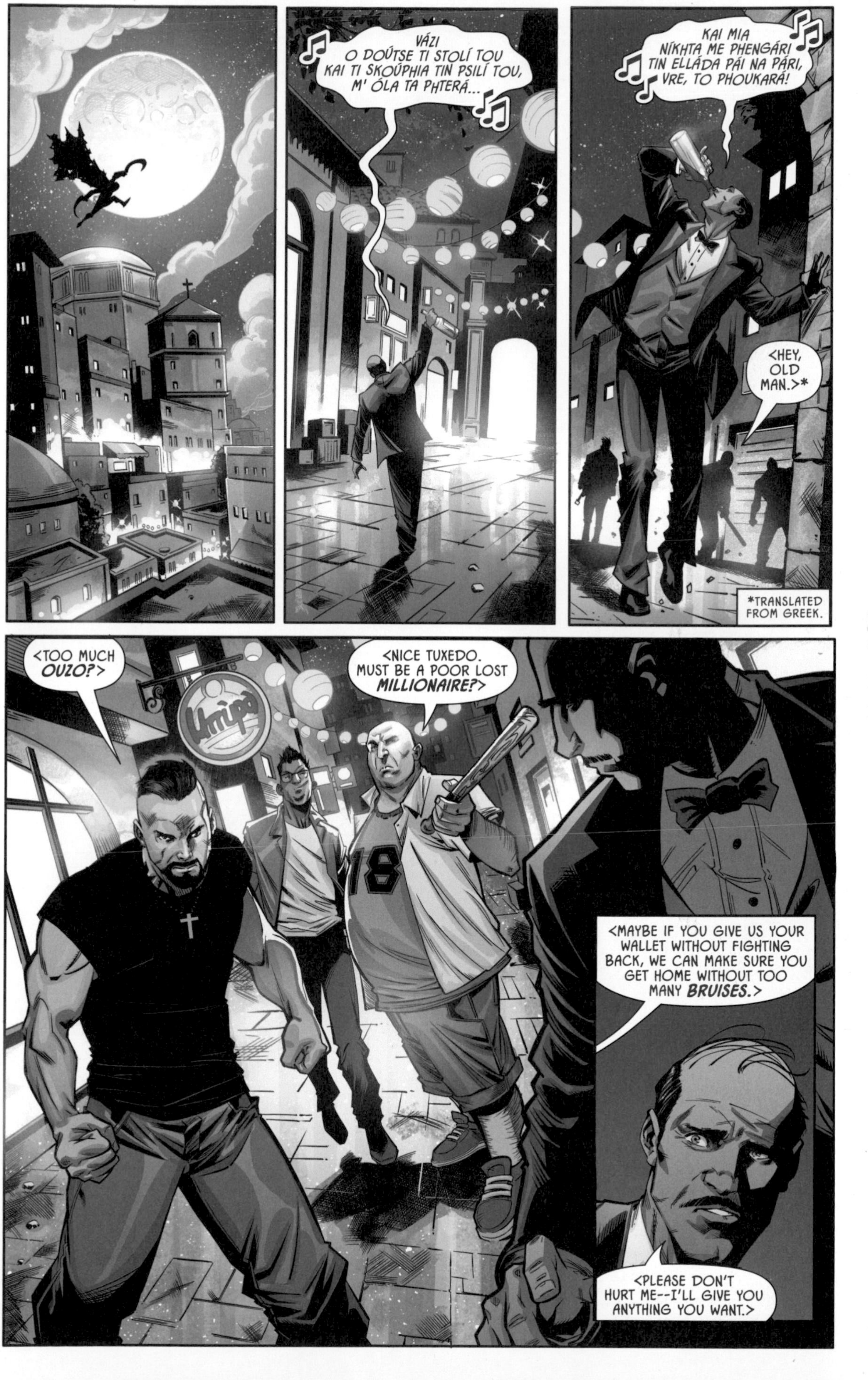
VÁZI O DOÚTSE TI STOLÍ TOU KAI TI SKOÚPHIA TIN PSILÍ TOU, M' ÓLA TA PHTERÁ...
KAI MIA NÍKHTA ME PHENGÁRI TIN ELLÁDA PÁI NA PÁRI, VRE, TO PHOUKARÁ!
<HEY, OLD MAN.>*
*TRANSLATED FROM GREEK.
<TOO MUCH OUZO?>
<NICE TUXEDO. MUST BE A POOR LOST MILLIONAIRE?>
<MAYBE IF YOU GIVE US YOUR WALLET WITHOUT FIGHTING BACK, WE CAN MAKE SURE YOU GET HOME WITHOUT TOO MANY BRUISES.>
<PLEASE DON'T HURT ME--I'LL GIVE YOU ANYTHING YOU WANT.>

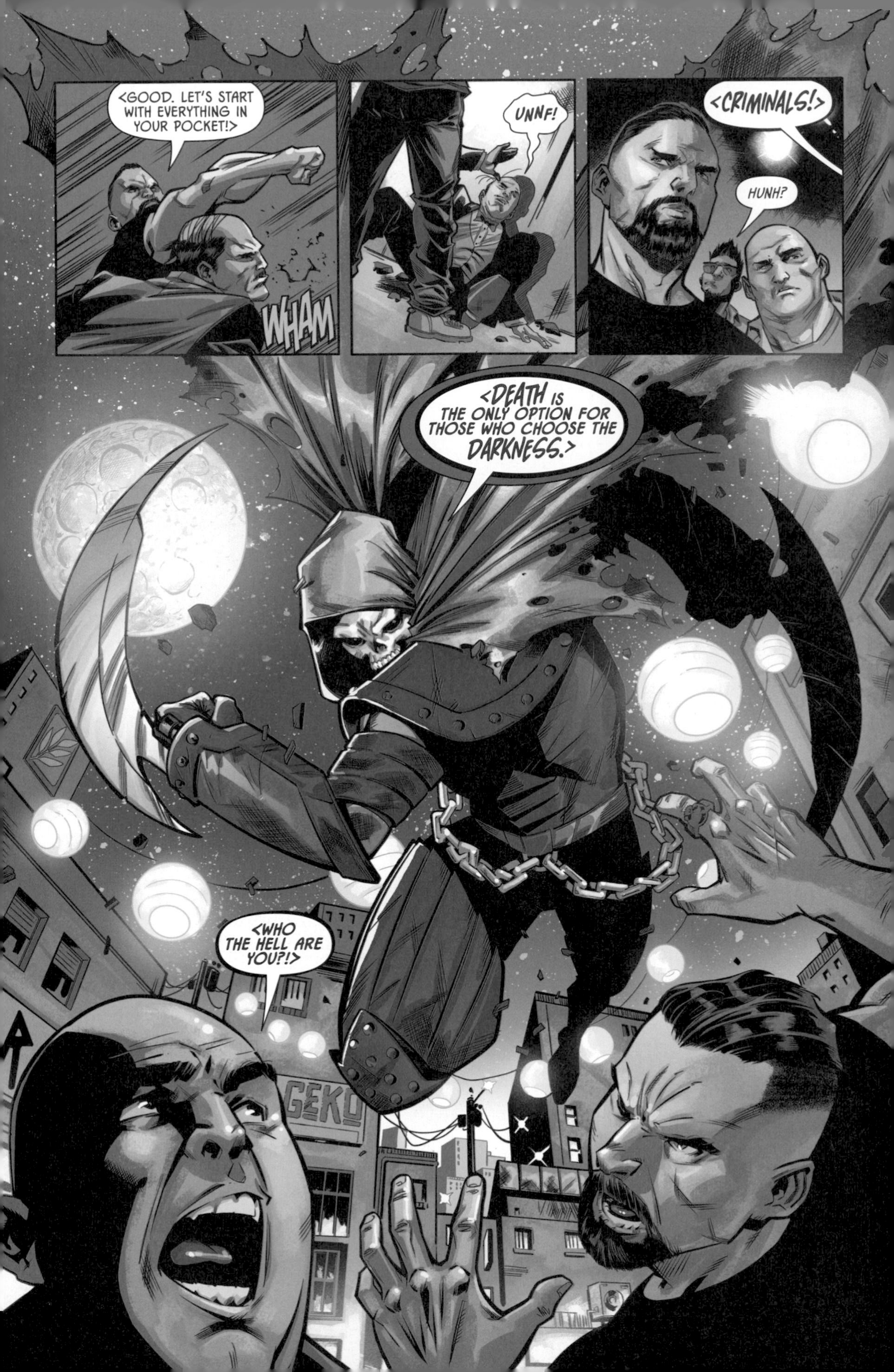
<GOOD. LET'S START WITH EVERYTHING IN YOUR POCKET!>
WHAM
UNNF!
<CRIMINALS!>
HUNH?
<DEATH IS THE ONLY OPTION FOR THOSE WHO CHOOSE THE DARKNESS.>
<WHO THE HELL ARE YOU?!>
GEKO

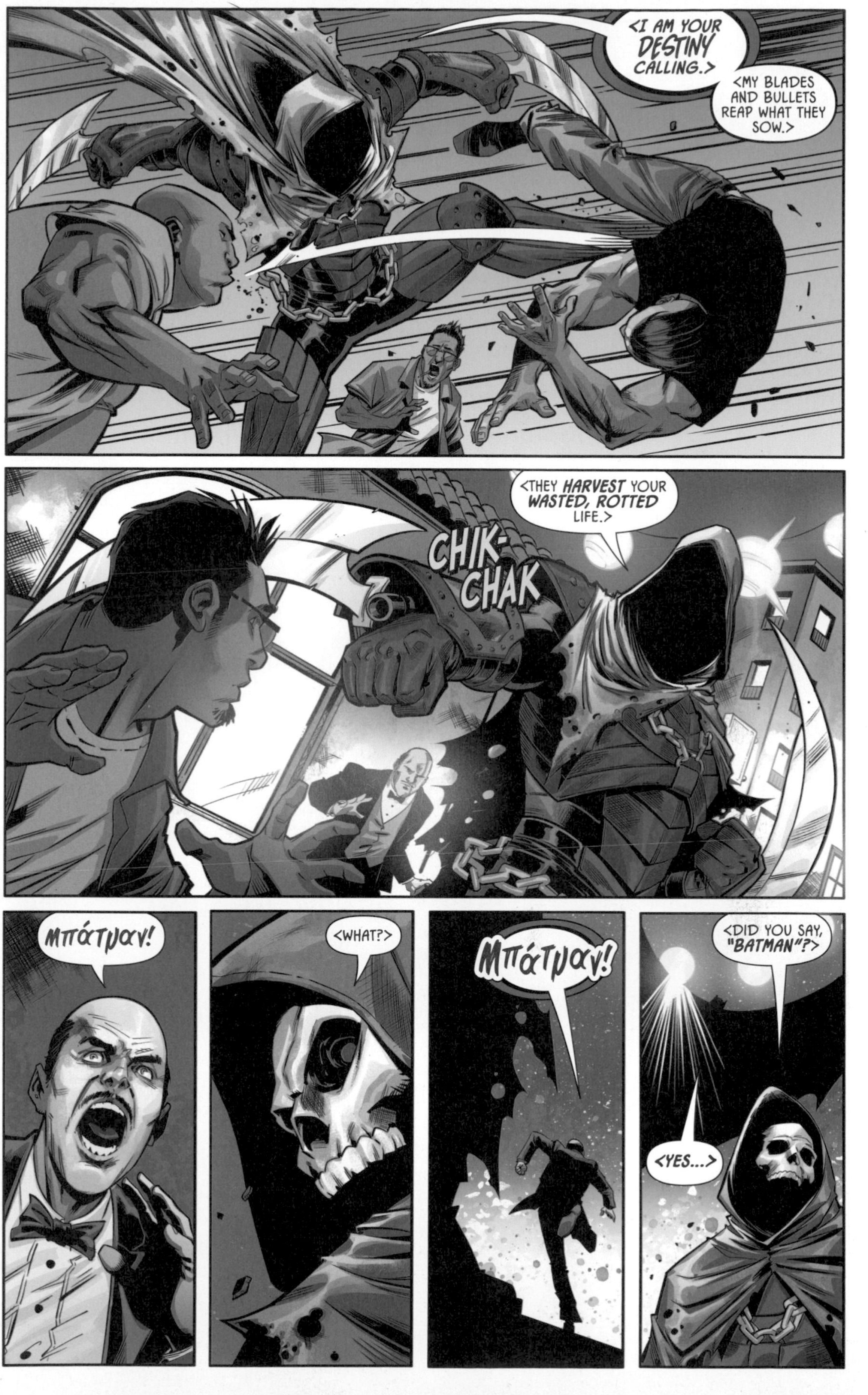

<I AM YOUR DESTINY CALLING.>
<MY BLADES AND BULLETS REAP WHAT THEY SOW.>
<THEY HARVEST YOUR WASTED, ROTTED LIFE.>
CHIK-CHAK
Μπάτμαν!
<WHAT?>
Μπάτμαν!
<DID YOU SAY, "BATMAN"?>
<YES...>

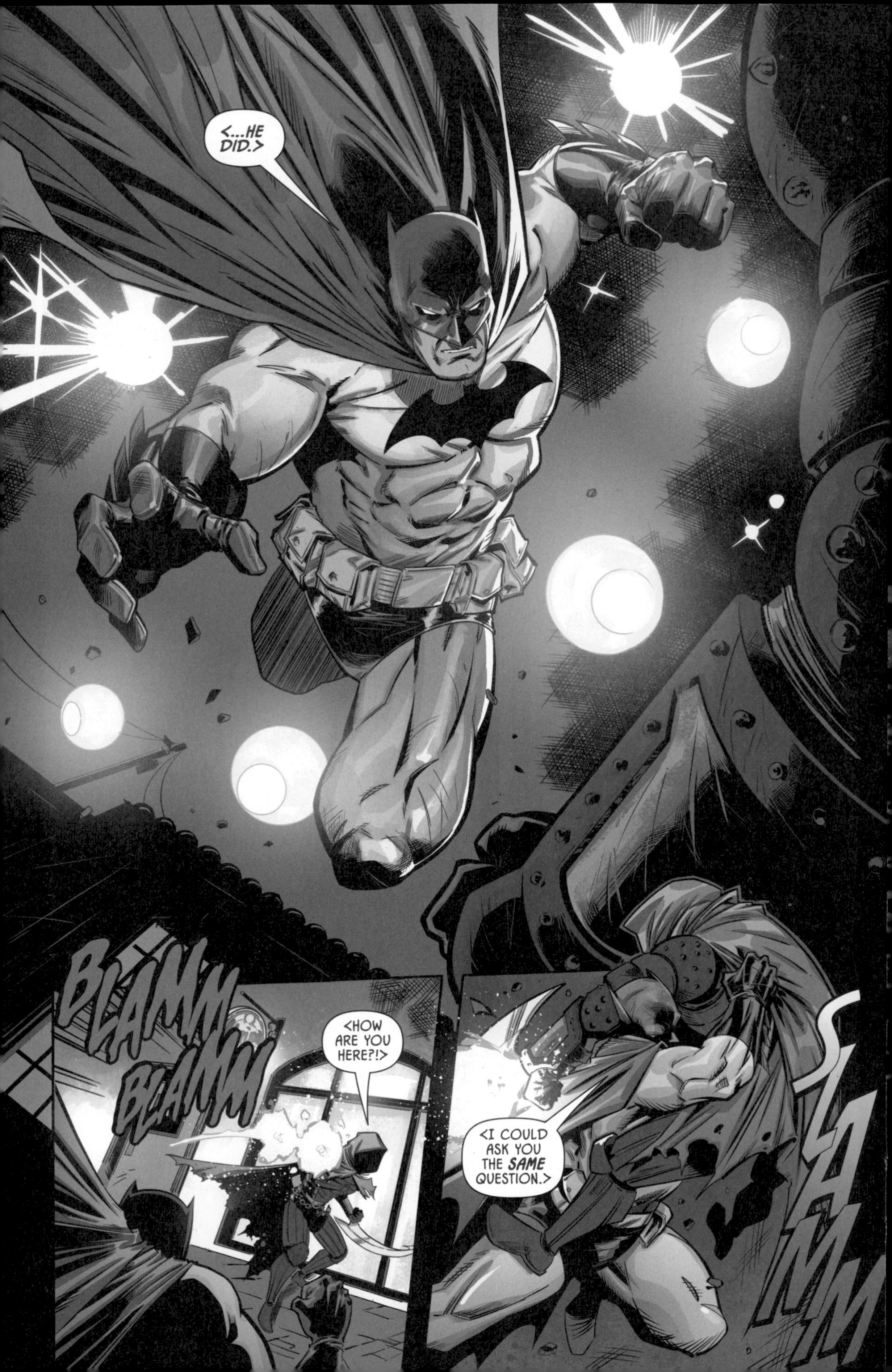

<...HE DID.>
BLAMM
BLAMM
<HOW ARE YOU HERE?!>
<I COULD ASK YOU THE **SAME** QUESTION.>
SLAMM

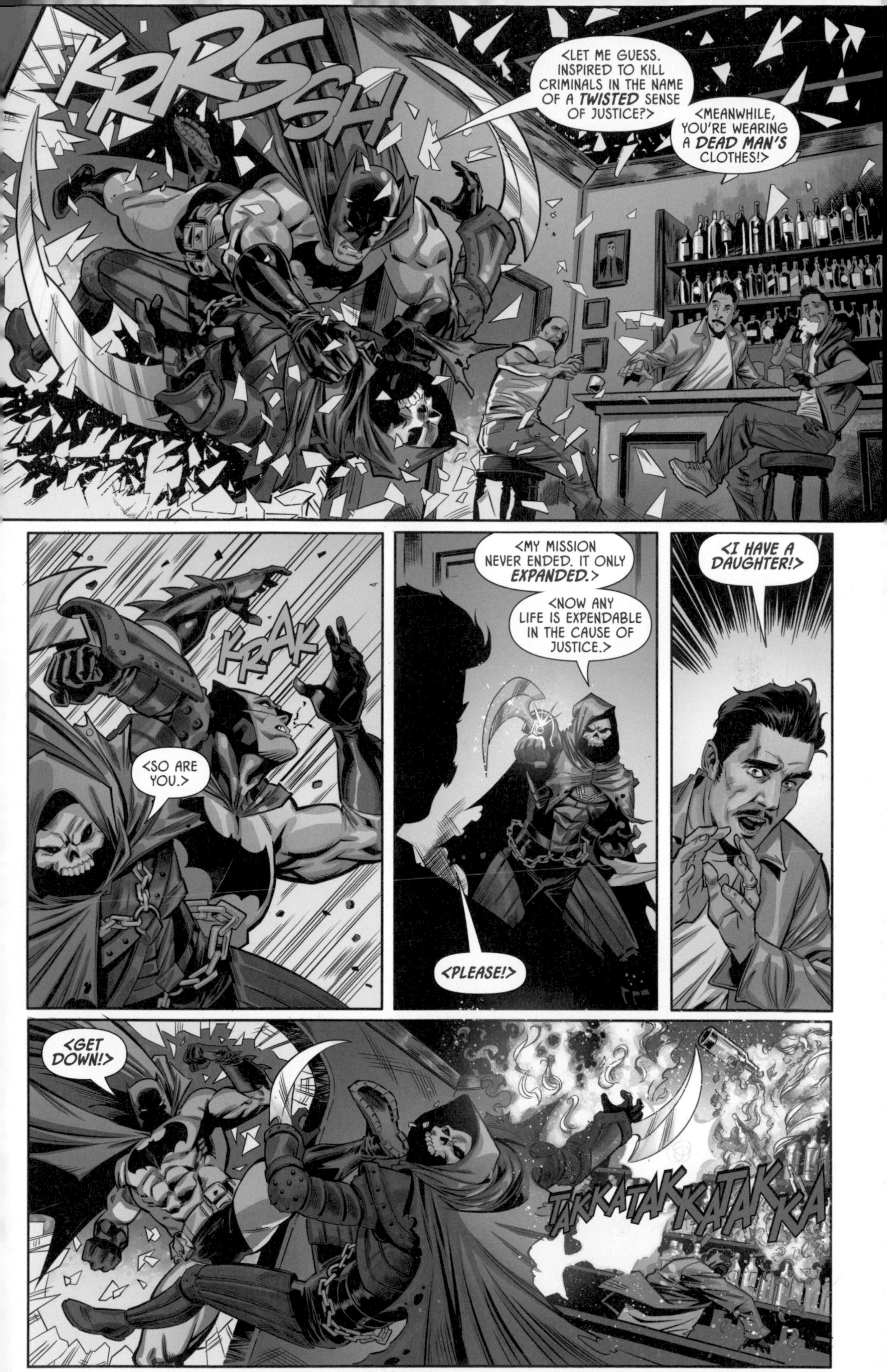
KRRSSH
<LET ME GUESS. INSPIRED TO KILL CRIMINALS IN THE NAME OF A TWISTED SENSE OF JUSTICE?>
<MEANWHILE, YOU'RE WEARING A DEAD MAN'S CLOTHES!>
KRAK
<SO ARE YOU.>
<MY MISSION NEVER ENDED. IT ONLY EXPANDED.>
<NOW ANY LIFE IS EXPENDABLE IN THE CAUSE OF JUSTICE.>
<PLEASE!>
<I HAVE A DAUGHTER!>
<GET DOWN!>
TAKKATAKKATAKKA

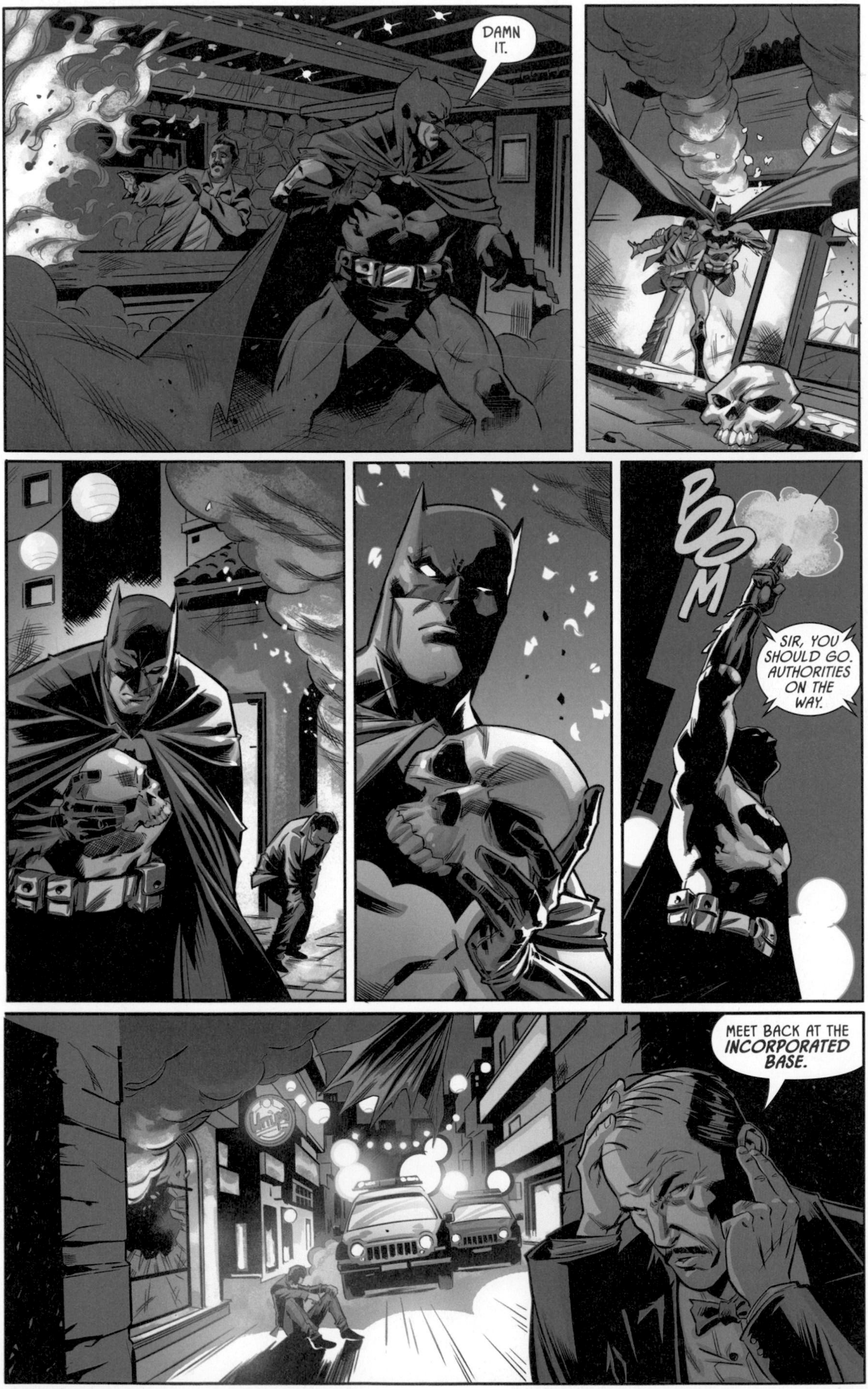
DAMN IT.
BOOM
SIR, YOU SHOULD GO. AUTHORITIES ON THE WAY.
MEET BACK AT THE INCORPORATED BASE.

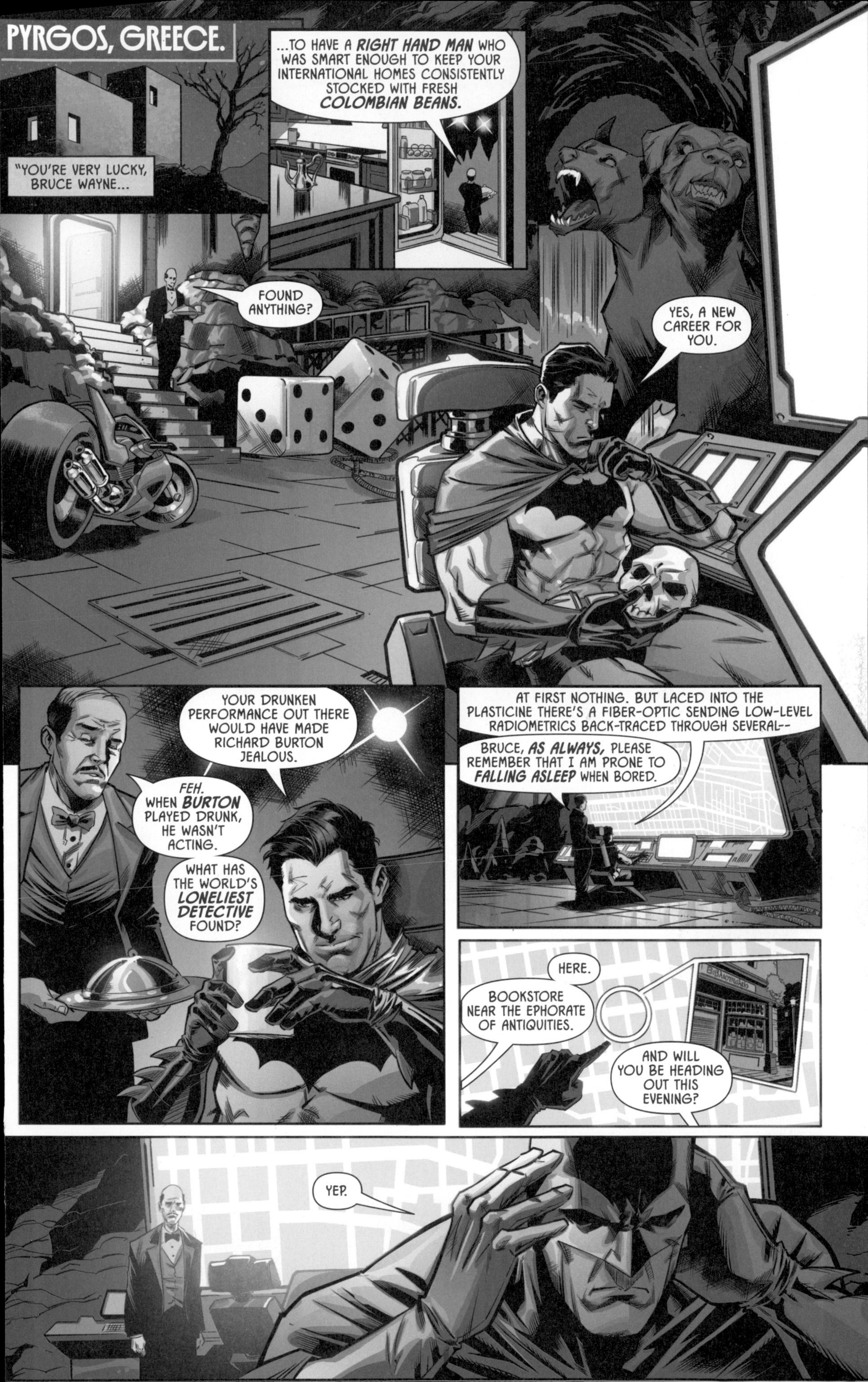
PYRGOS, GREECE.
"YOU'RE VERY LUCKY, BRUCE WAYNE...
...TO HAVE A RIGHT HAND MAN WHO WAS SMART ENOUGH TO KEEP YOUR INTERNATIONAL HOMES CONSISTENTLY STOCKED WITH FRESH COLOMBIAN BEANS.
FOUND ANYTHING?
YES, A NEW CAREER FOR YOU.
YOUR DRUNKEN PERFORMANCE OUT THERE WOULD HAVE MADE RICHARD BURTON JEALOUS.
FEH. WHEN BURTON PLAYED DRUNK, HE WASN'T ACTING.
WHAT HAS THE WORLD'S LONELIEST DETECTIVE FOUND?
AT FIRST NOTHING. BUT LACED INTO THE PLASTICINE THERE'S A FIBER-OPTIC SENDING LOW-LEVEL RADIOMETRICS BACK-TRACED THROUGH SEVERAL--
BRUCE, AS ALWAYS, PLEASE REMEMBER THAT I AM PRONE TO FALLING ASLEEP WHEN BORED.
HERE.
BOOKSTORE NEAR THE EPHORATE OF ANTIQUITIES.
AND WILL YOU BE HEADING OUT THIS EVENING?
YEP.

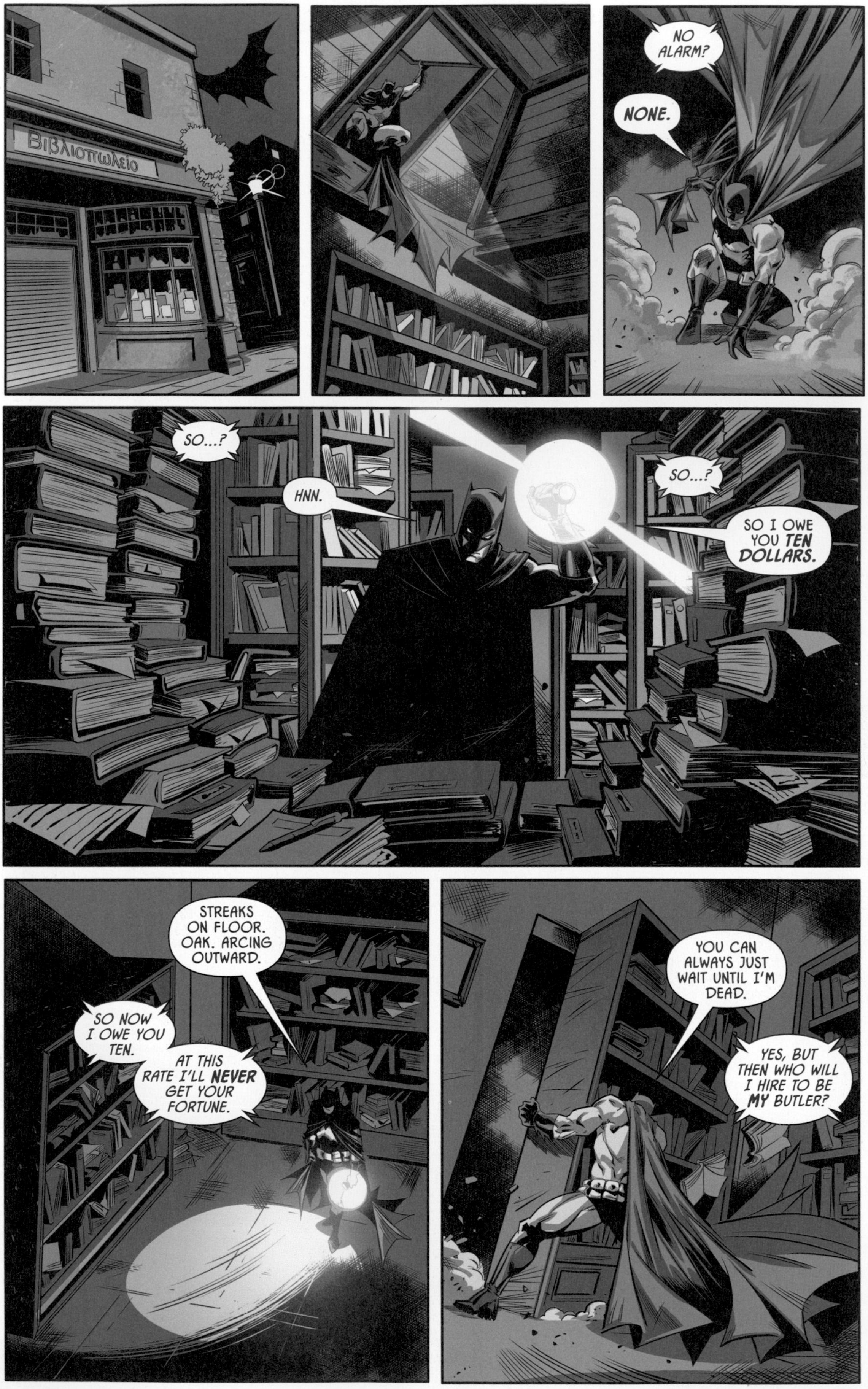
Βιβλιοπωλείο
NO ALARM?
NONE.
SO...?
HNN.
SO...?
SO I OWE YOU **TEN DOLLARS.**
STREAKS ON FLOOR. OAK. ARCING OUTWARD.
SO NOW I OWE YOU TEN.
AT THIS RATE I'LL **NEVER** GET YOUR FORTUNE.
YOU CAN ALWAYS JUST WAIT UNTIL I'M DEAD.
YES, BUT THEN WHO WILL I HIRE TO BE **MY** BUTLER?

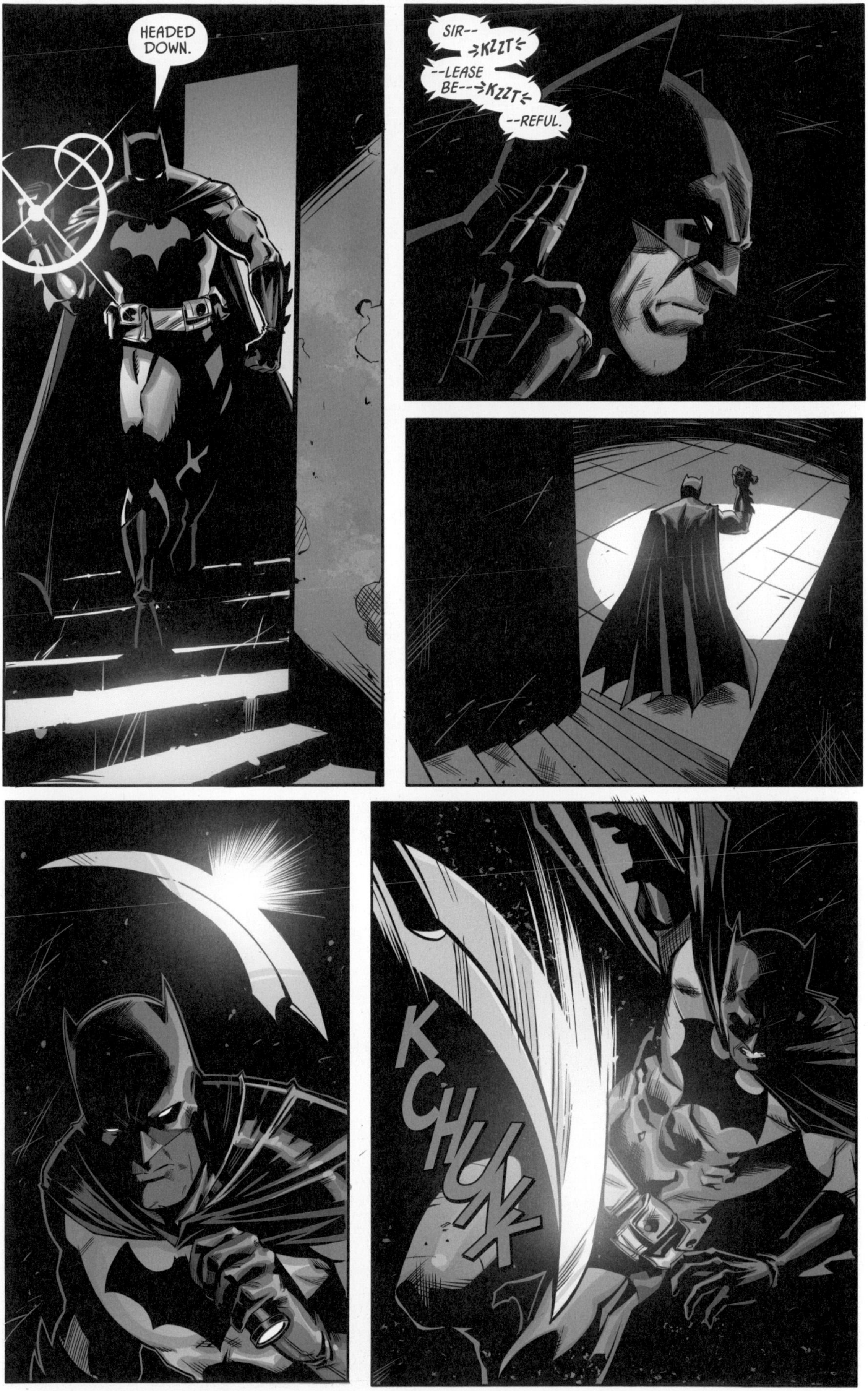
HEADED DOWN.
SIR--
KZZT
--LEASE BE--
KZZT
--REFUL.
KCHUNK

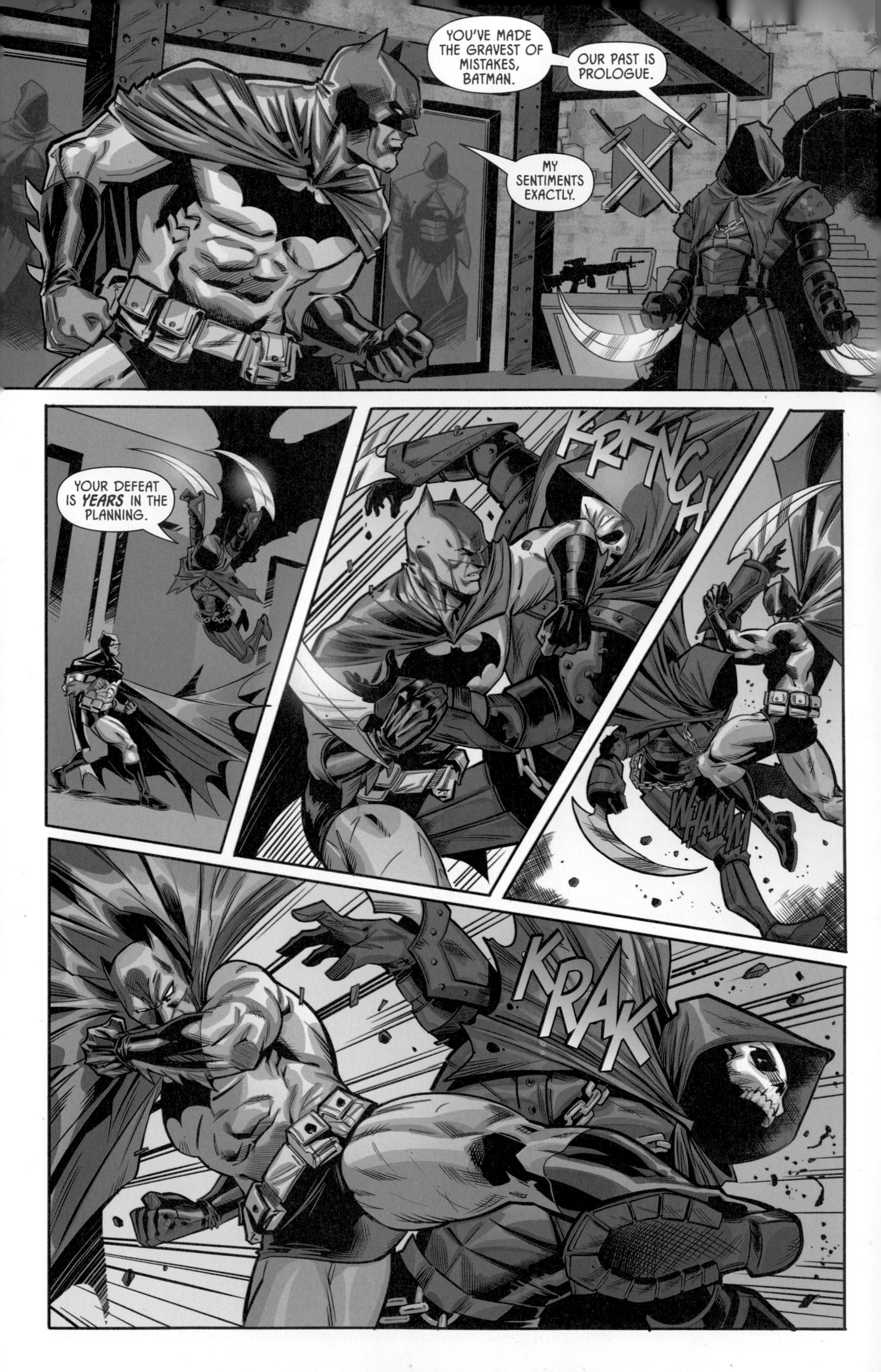

YOU'VE MADE THE GRAVEST OF MISTAKES, BATMAN.
OUR PAST IS PROLOGUE.
MY SENTIMENTS EXACTLY.
YOUR DEFEAT IS **YEARS** IN THE PLANNING.
KRKNCH
WHAM
KRAK

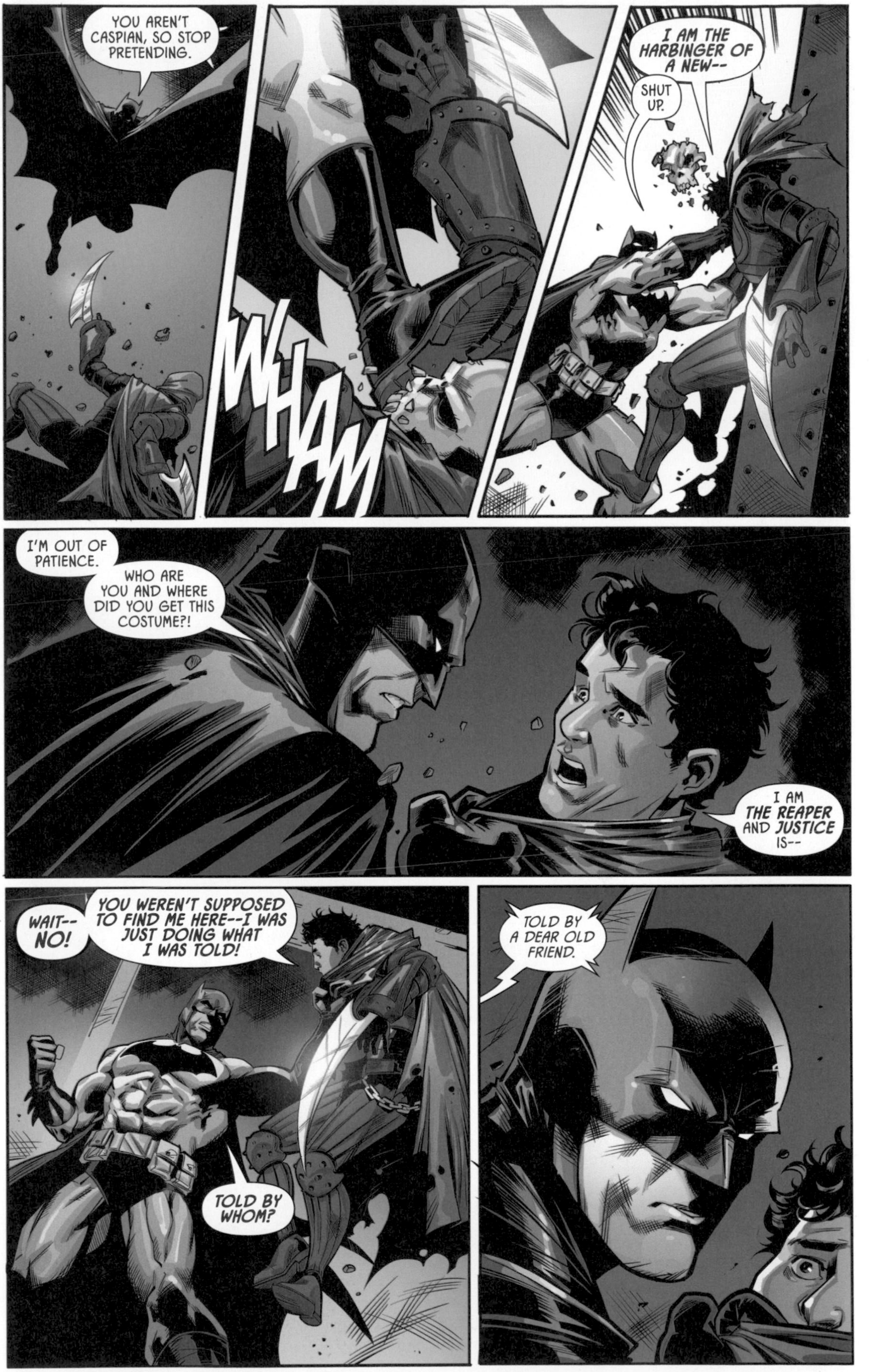
YOU AREN'T CASPIAN, SO STOP PRETENDING.
WHAM
I AM THE HARBINGER OF A NEW--
SHUT UP.
I'M OUT OF PATIENCE.
WHO ARE YOU AND WHERE DID YOU GET THIS COSTUME?!
I AM THE REAPER AND JUSTICE IS--
WAIT-- NO!
YOU WEREN'T SUPPOSED TO FIND ME HERE--I WAS JUST DOING WHAT I WAS TOLD!
TOLD BY WHOM?
TOLD BY A DEAR OLD FRIEND.

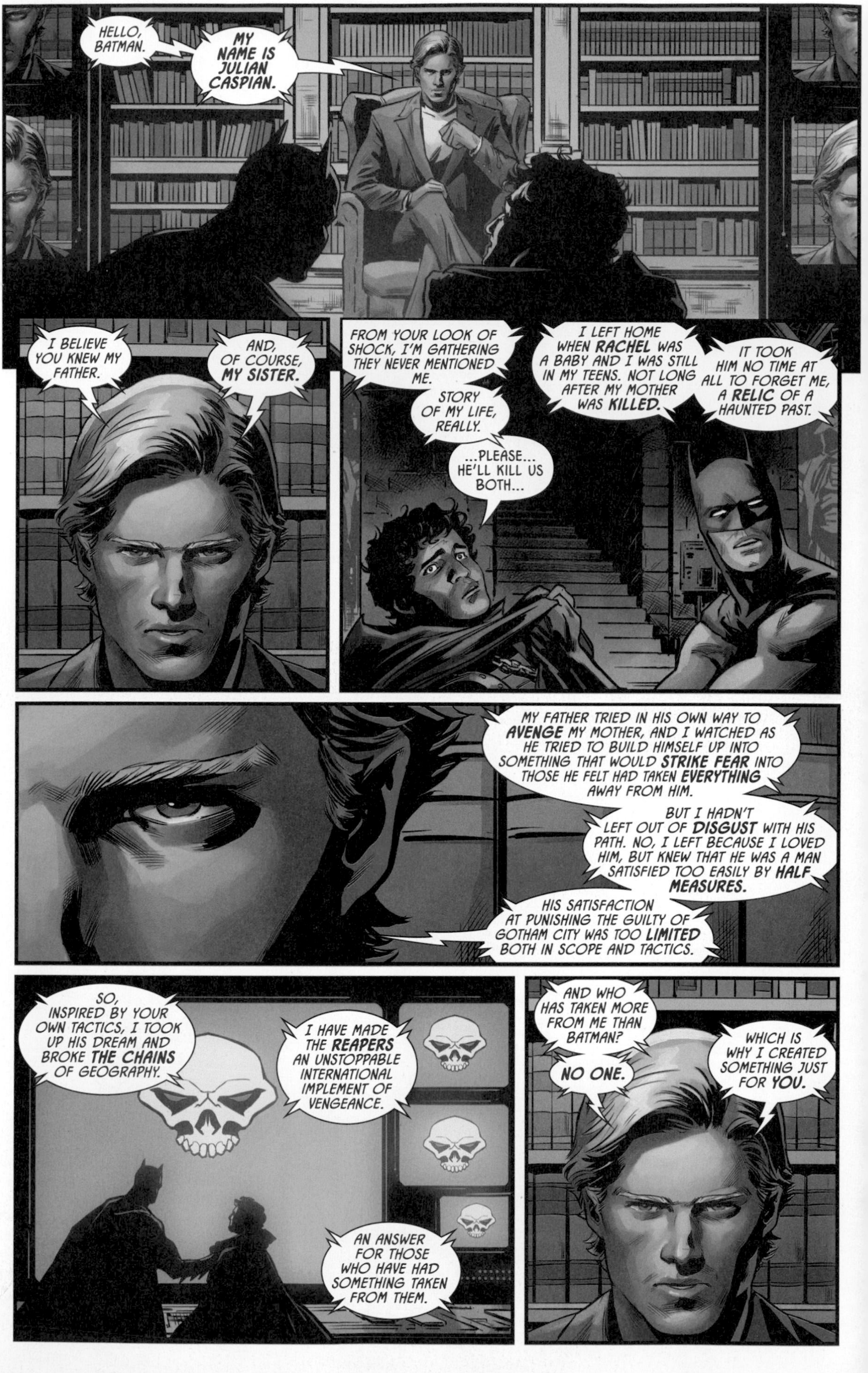
HELLO, BATMAN.
MY NAME IS JULIAN CASPIAN.
I BELIEVE YOU KNEW MY FATHER.
AND, OF COURSE, MY SISTER.
FROM YOUR LOOK OF SHOCK, I'M GATHERING THEY NEVER MENTIONED ME.
STORY OF MY LIFE, REALLY.
...PLEASE... HE'LL KILL US BOTH...
I LEFT HOME WHEN RACHEL WAS A BABY AND I WAS STILL IN MY TEENS. NOT LONG AFTER MY MOTHER WAS KILLED.
IT TOOK HIM NO TIME AT ALL TO FORGET ME, A RELIC OF A HAUNTED PAST.
MY FATHER TRIED IN HIS OWN WAY TO AVENGE MY MOTHER, AND I WATCHED AS HE TRIED TO BUILD HIMSELF UP INTO SOMETHING THAT WOULD STRIKE FEAR INTO THOSE HE FELT HAD TAKEN EVERYTHING AWAY FROM HIM.
BUT I HADN'T LEFT OUT OF DISGUST WITH HIS PATH. NO, I LEFT BECAUSE I LOVED HIM, BUT KNEW THAT HE WAS A MAN SATISFIED TOO EASILY BY HALF MEASURES.
HIS SATISFACTION AT PUNISHING THE GUILTY OF GOTHAM CITY WAS TOO LIMITED BOTH IN SCOPE AND TACTICS.
SO, INSPIRED BY YOUR OWN TACTICS, I TOOK UP HIS DREAM AND BROKE THE CHAINS OF GEOGRAPHY.
I HAVE MADE THE REAPERS AN UNSTOPPABLE INTERNATIONAL IMPLEMENT OF VENGEANCE.
AN ANSWER FOR THOSE WHO HAVE HAD SOMETHING TAKEN FROM THEM.
AND WHO HAS TAKEN MORE FROM ME THAN BATMAN?
NO ONE.
WHICH IS WHY I CREATED SOMETHING JUST FOR YOU.

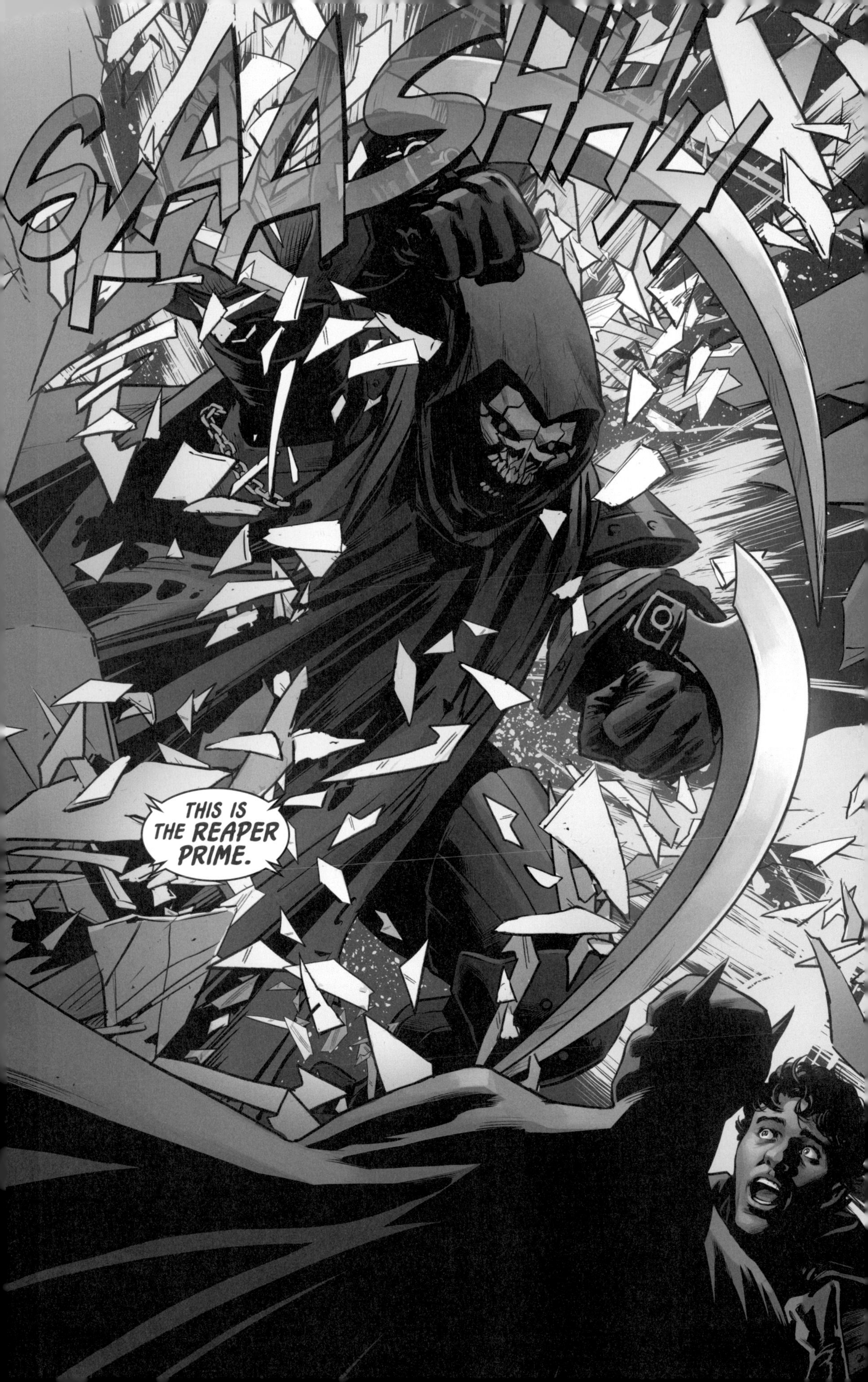
SHHH
THIS IS THE REAPER PRIME.

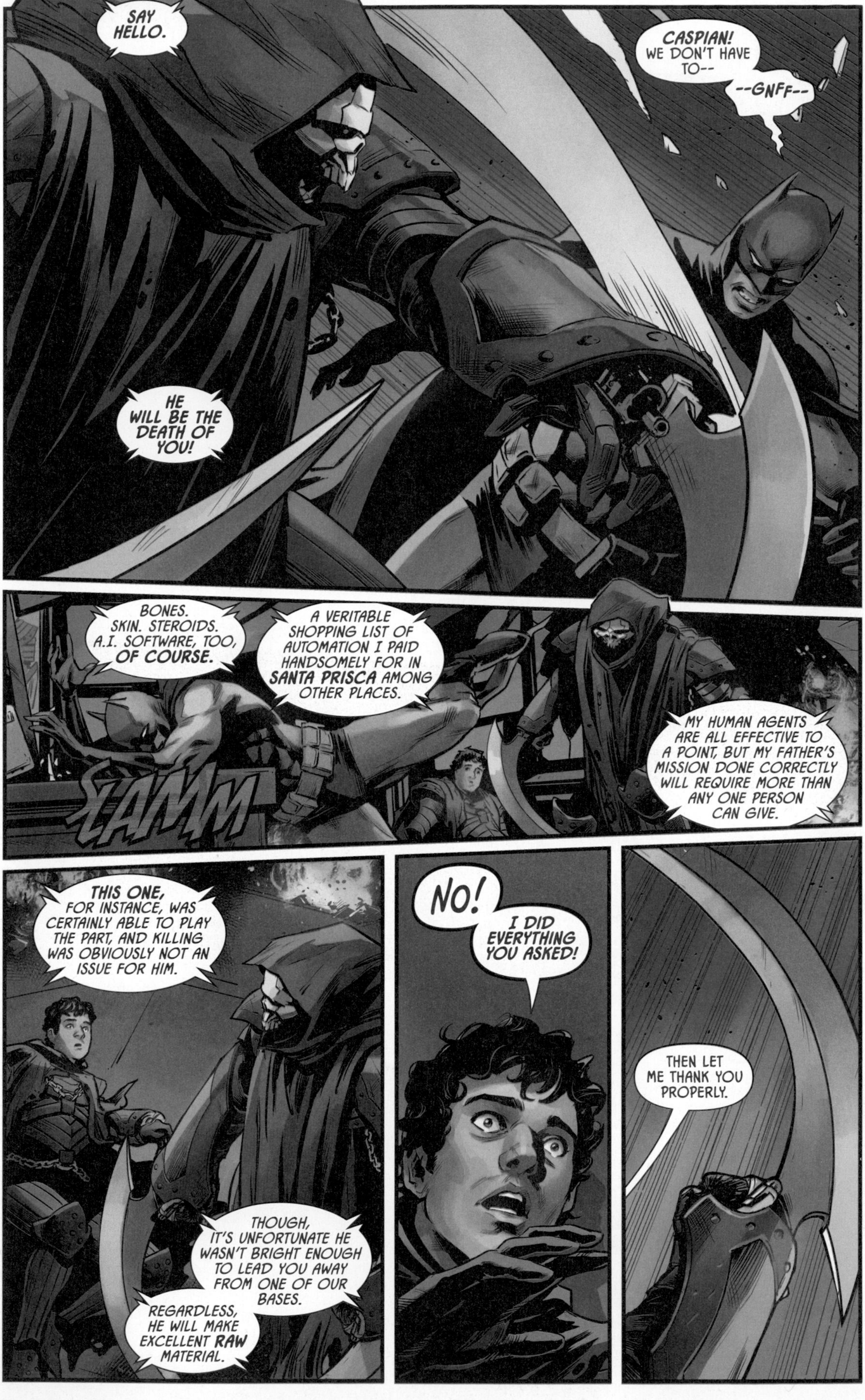
SAY HELLO.
CASPIAN! WE DON'T HAVE TO--
--GNFF--
HE WILL BE THE DEATH OF YOU!
BONES. SKIN. STEROIDS. A.I. SOFTWARE, TOO, OF COURSE.
A VERITABLE SHOPPING LIST OF AUTOMATION I PAID HANDSOMELY FOR IN SANTA PRISCA AMONG OTHER PLACES.
SLAMM
MY HUMAN AGENTS ARE ALL EFFECTIVE TO A POINT, BUT MY FATHER'S MISSION DONE CORRECTLY WILL REQUIRE MORE THAN ANY ONE PERSON CAN GIVE.
THIS ONE, FOR INSTANCE, WAS CERTAINLY ABLE TO PLAY THE PART, AND KILLING WAS OBVIOUSLY NOT AN ISSUE FOR HIM.
THOUGH, IT'S UNFORTUNATE HE WASN'T BRIGHT ENOUGH TO LEAD YOU AWAY FROM ONE OF OUR BASES.
REGARDLESS, HE WILL MAKE EXCELLENT RAW MATERIAL.
NO!
I DID EVERYTHING YOU ASKED!
THEN LET ME THANK YOU PROPERLY.

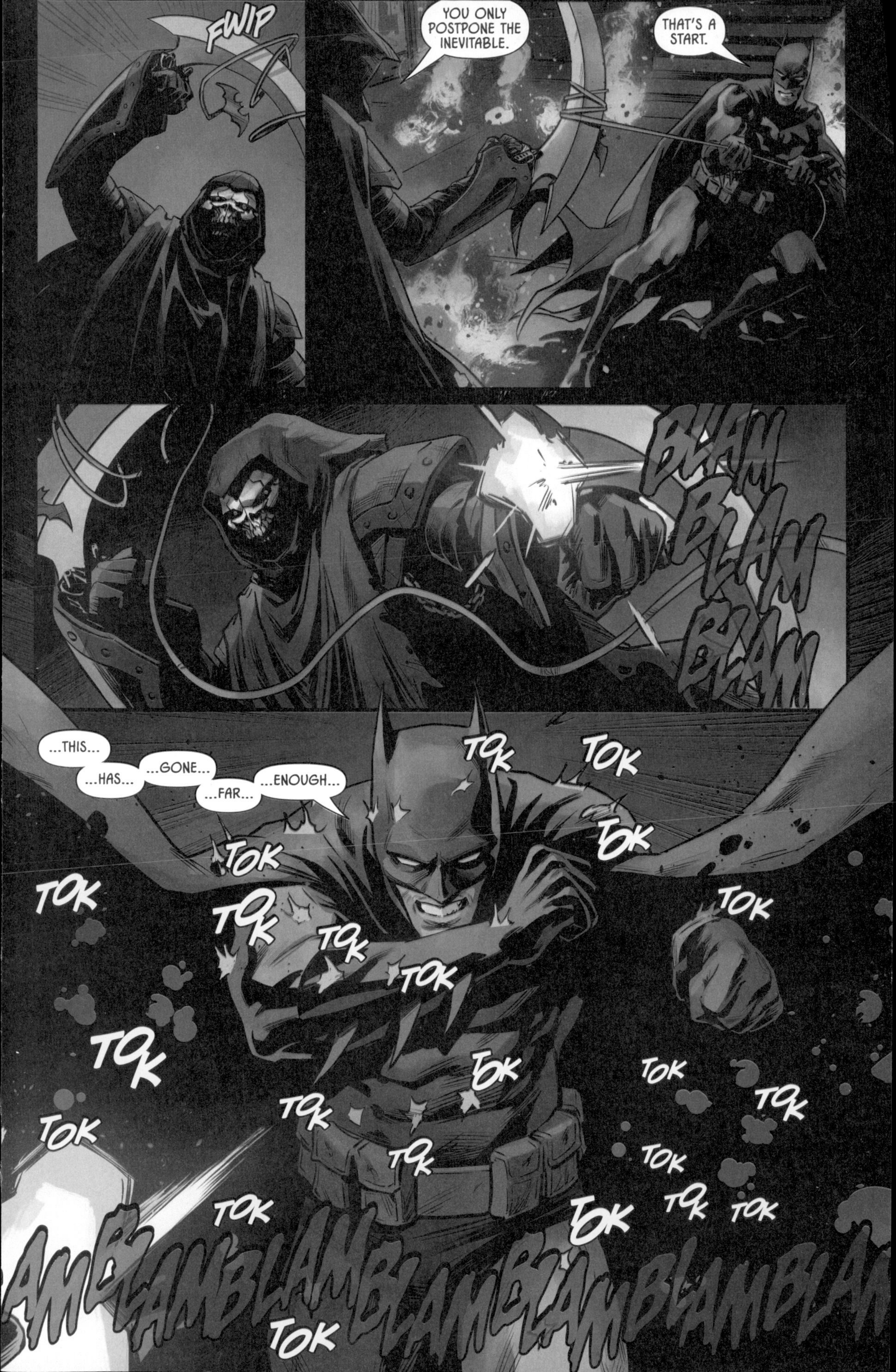
FWIP
YOU ONLY POSTPONE THE INEVITABLE.
THAT'S A START.
BLAM BLAM BLAM BLAM
...THIS...
...HAS...
...GONE...
...FAR...
...ENOUGH...
TOK TOK TOK TOK TOK TOK TOK TOK TOK TOK TOK TOK TOK TOK TOK TOK TOK TOK TOK TOK TOK TOK TOK
BLAMBLAMBLAMBLAMBLAMBLAMBLAM

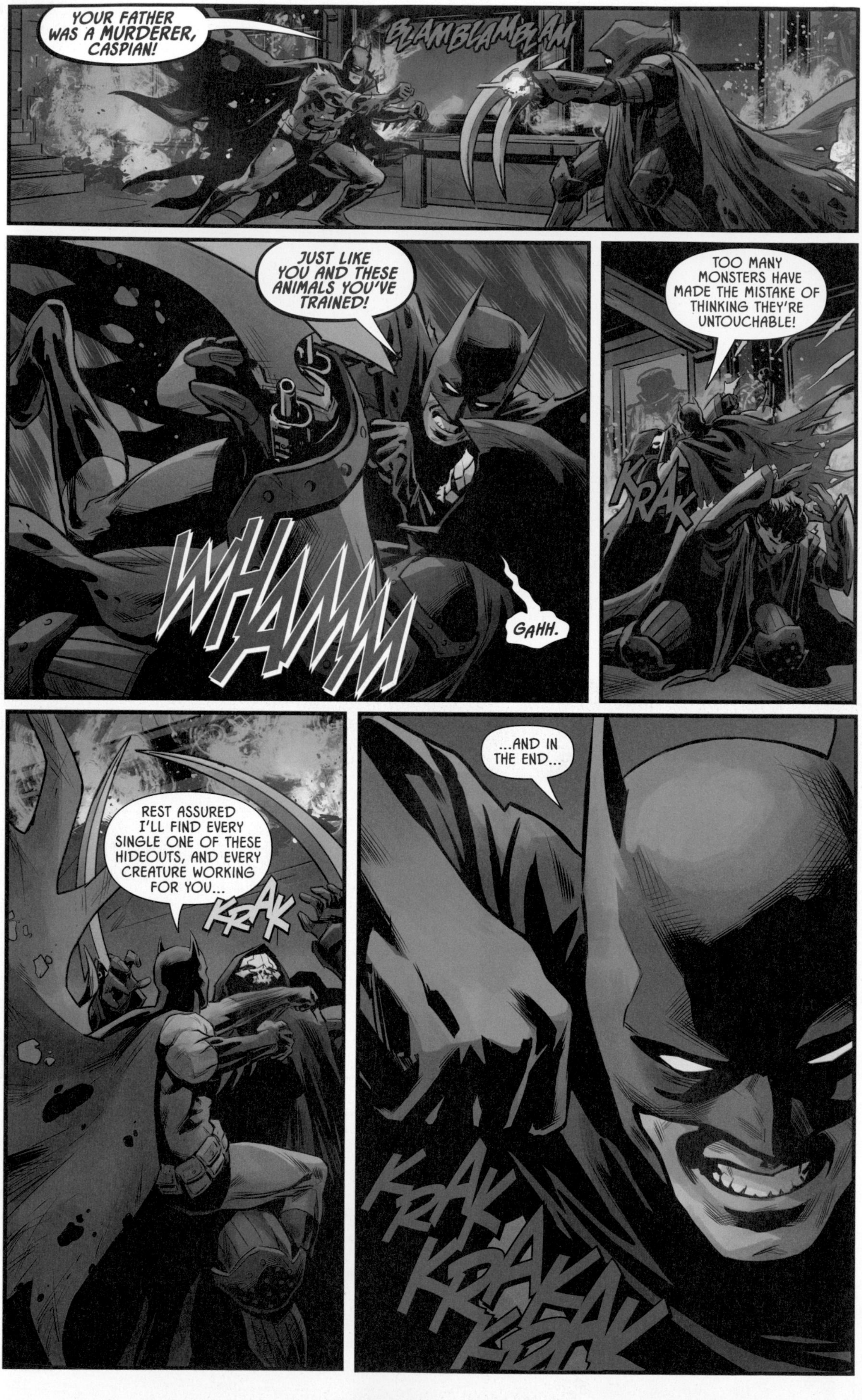
YOUR FATHER WAS A MURDERER, CASPIAN!
BLAMBLAMBLAM
JUST LIKE YOU AND THESE ANIMALS YOU'VE TRAINED!
WHAMM
GAHH.
TOO MANY MONSTERS HAVE MADE THE MISTAKE OF THINKING THEY'RE UNTOUCHABLE!
KRAK
REST ASSURED I'LL FIND EVERY SINGLE ONE OF THESE HIDEOUTS, AND EVERY CREATURE WORKING FOR YOU...
KRAK
...AND IN THE END...
KRAK KRAK KRAK

KRAKK
...I WILL FIND YOU AND I WILL BEAT YOU.
JUST LIKE I BEAT YOUR FATHER.
UGNN.
STAY WITH ME, WE'RE LEAVING.
...UNN... HIT...STOMACH ...BLEEDING...
...LOOK OUT... BEHIND YOU...
THE REAPER ALWAYS BRINGS FINALITY, BATMAN.
TKTKTKTKTKTKTKTKTKTKTKTKTKTKTK

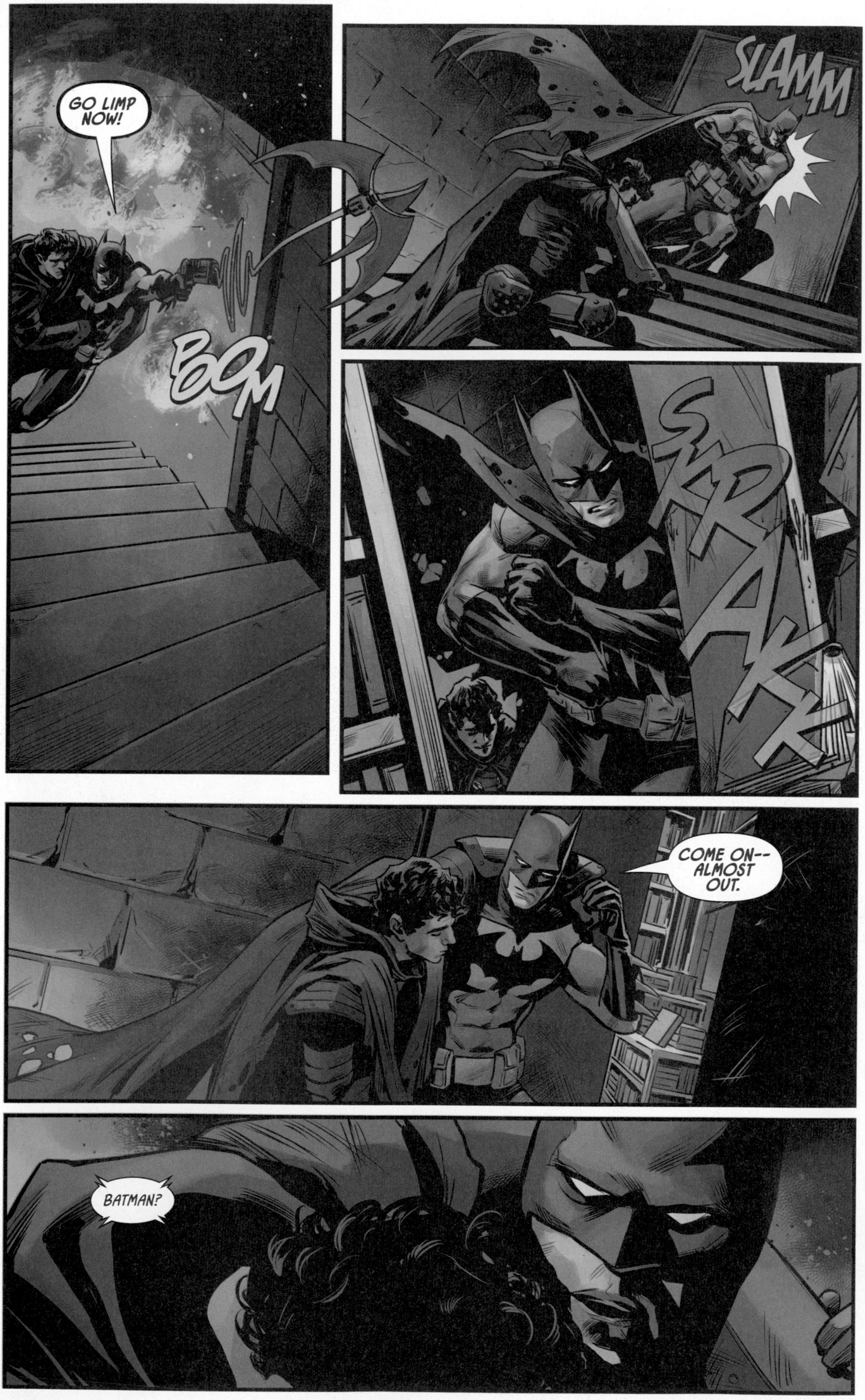
GO LIMP NOW!
BOOM
SLAMM
SKRAKK
COME ON-- ALMOST OUT.
BATMAN?

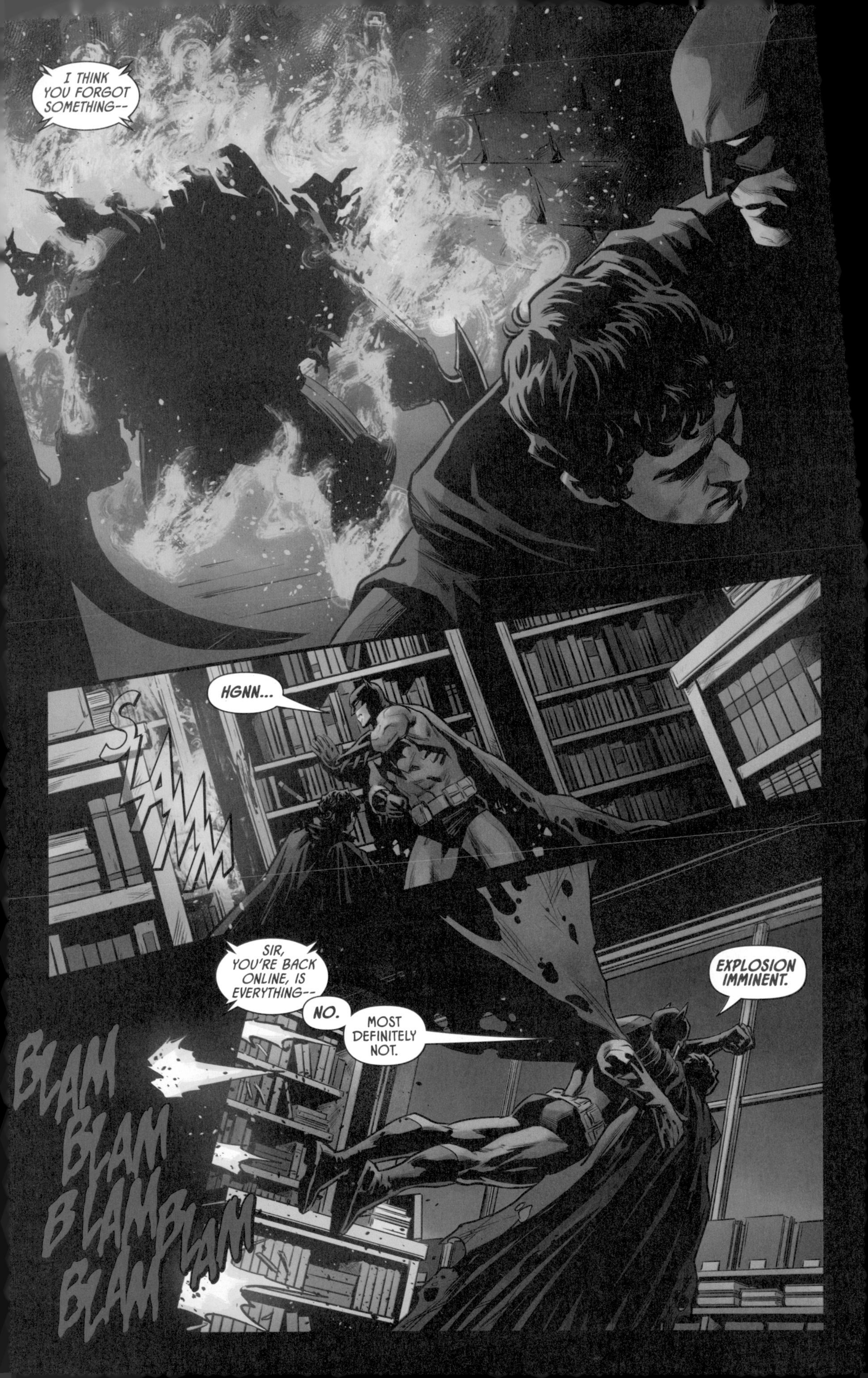
I THINK YOU FORGOT SOMETHING--
HGNN...
SLAMM
SIR, YOU'RE BACK ONLINE, IS EVERYTHING--
NO.
MOST DEFINITELY NOT.
EXPLOSION IMMINENT.
BLAM BLAM BLAM BLAM BLAM BLAM

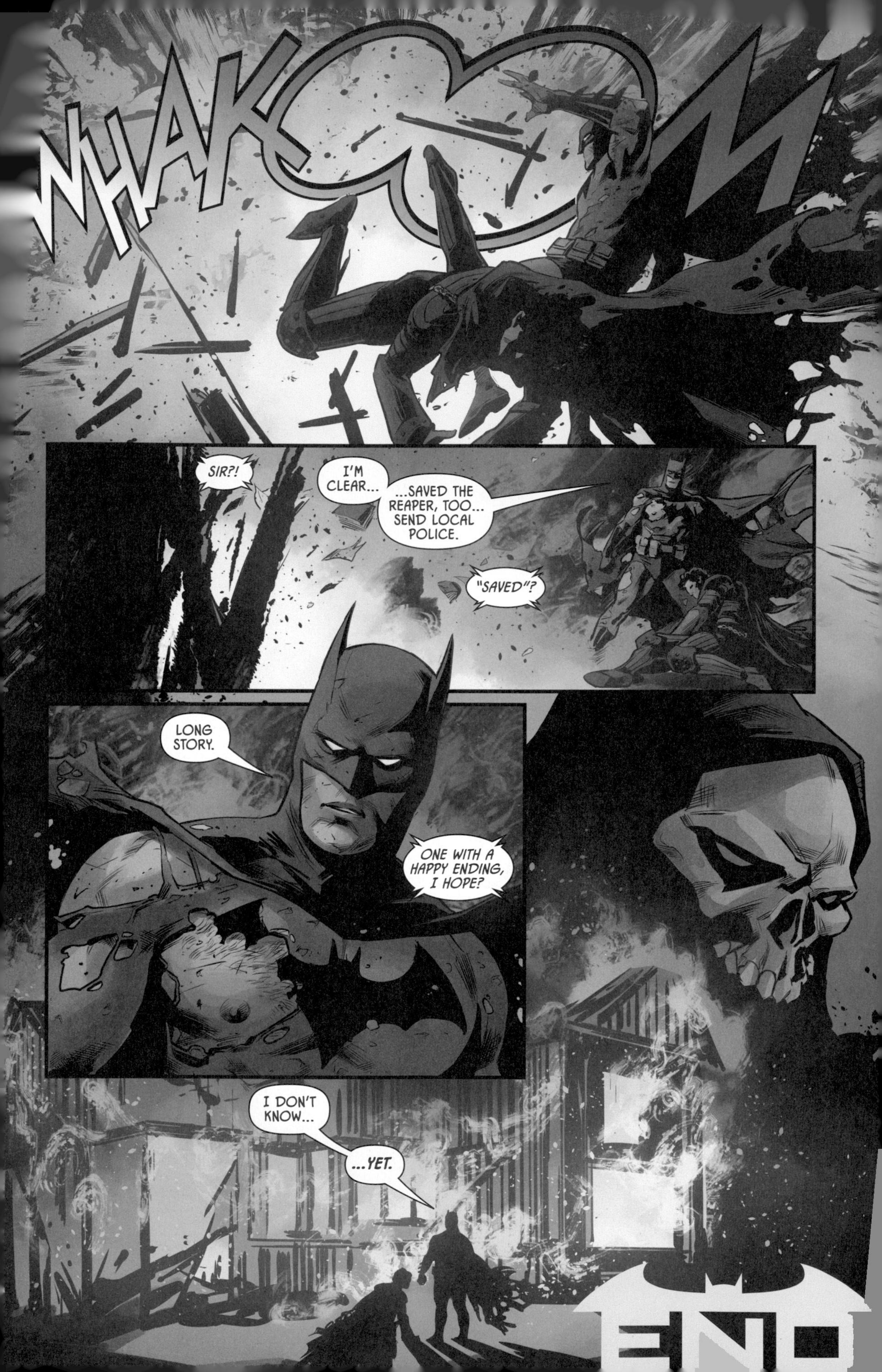
WHAKOOM
SIR?!
I'M CLEAR...
...SAVED THE REAPER, TOO... SEND LOCAL POLICE.
"SAVED"?
LONG STORY.
ONE WITH A HAPPY ENDING, I HOPE?
I DON'T KNOW...
...YET.
END

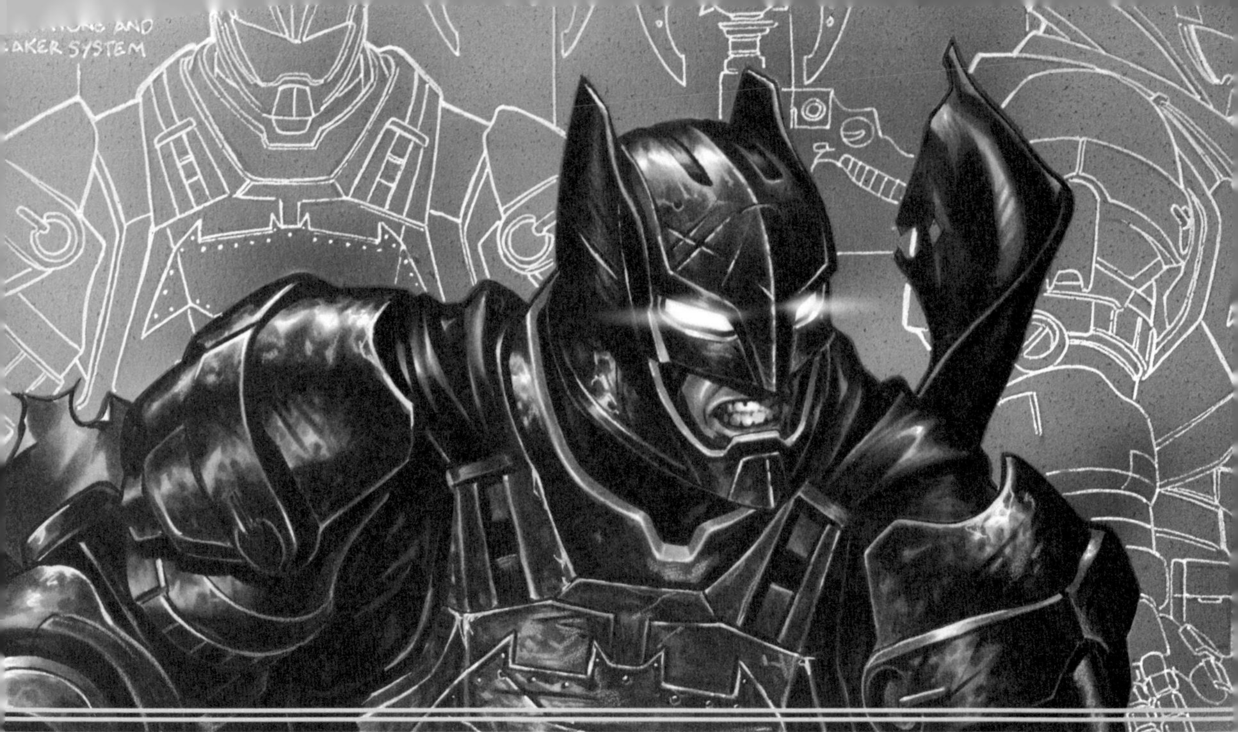

VARIANT COVER GALLERY

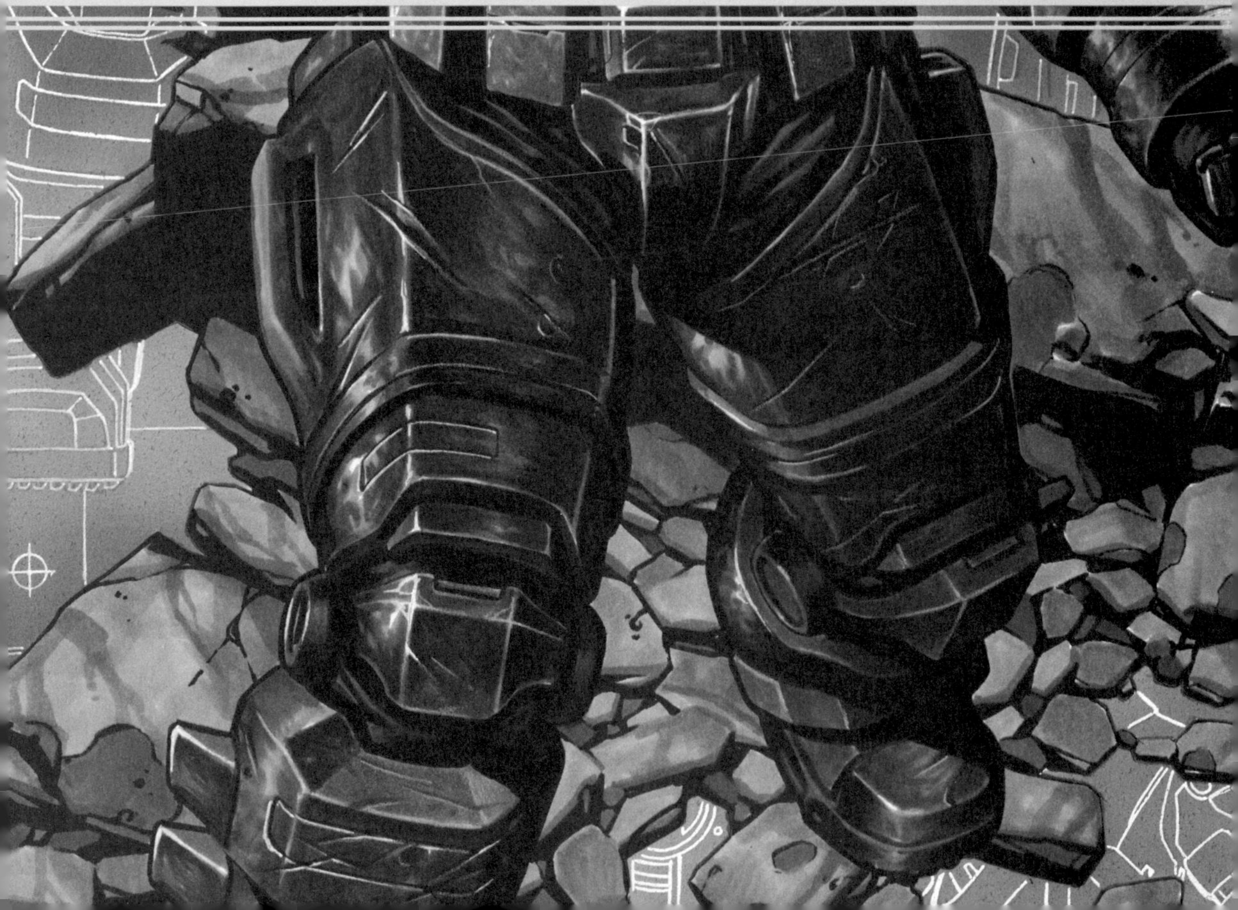

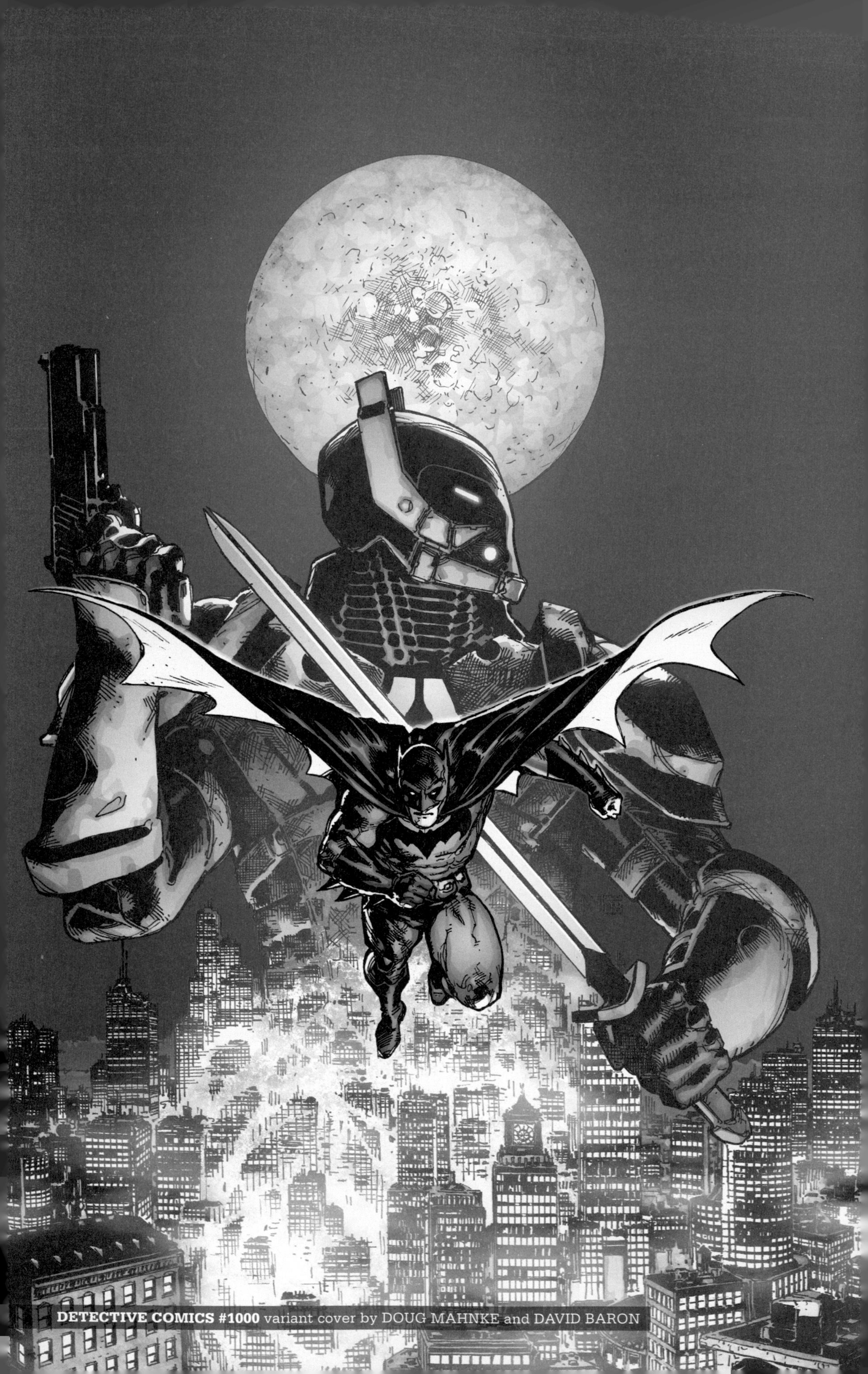

DETECTIVE COMICS #1000 variant cover by DOUG MAHNKE and DAVID BARON

DETECTIVE COMICS #1001 variant cover by DAVID FINCH and TOMEU MOREY

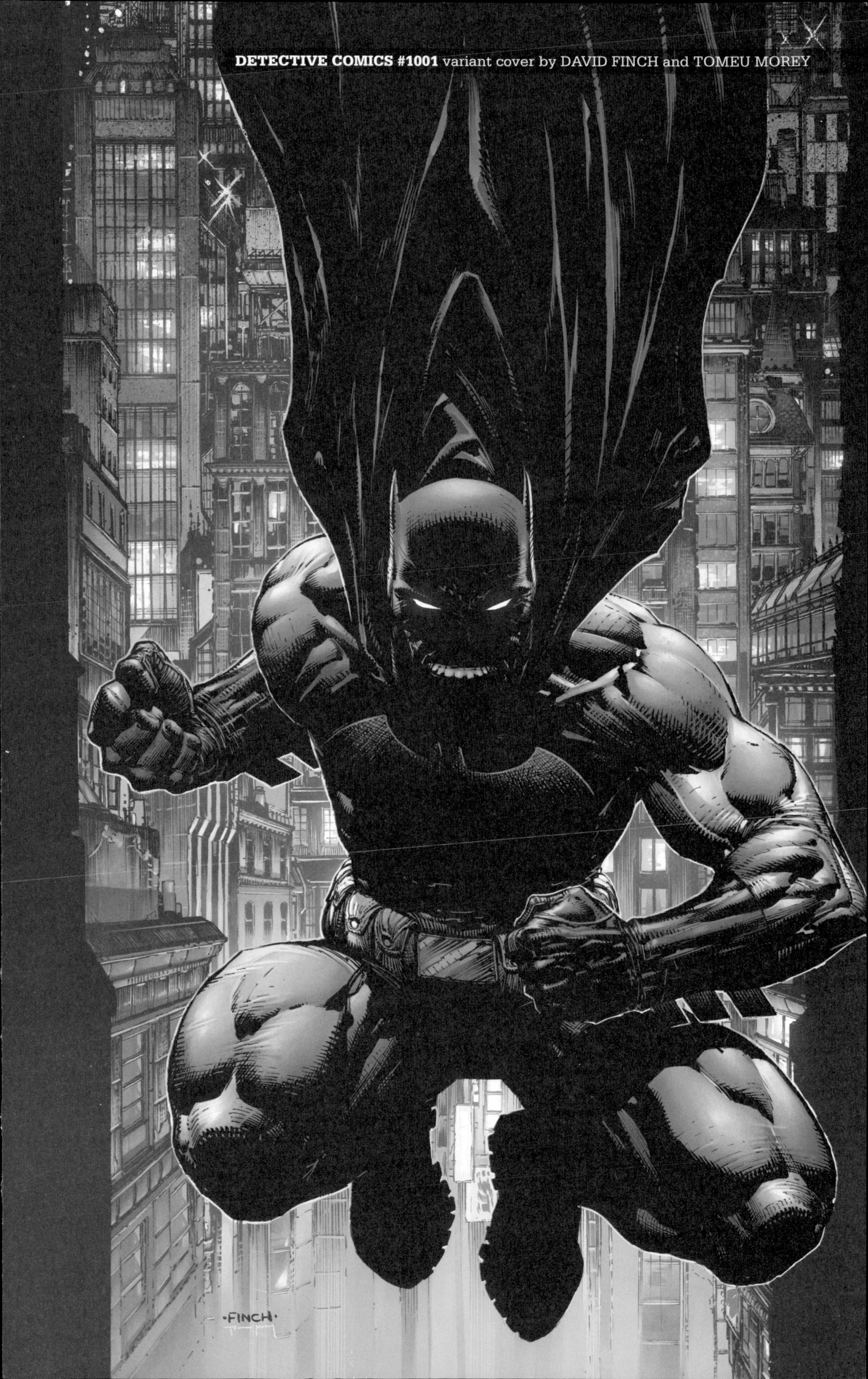
FINCH

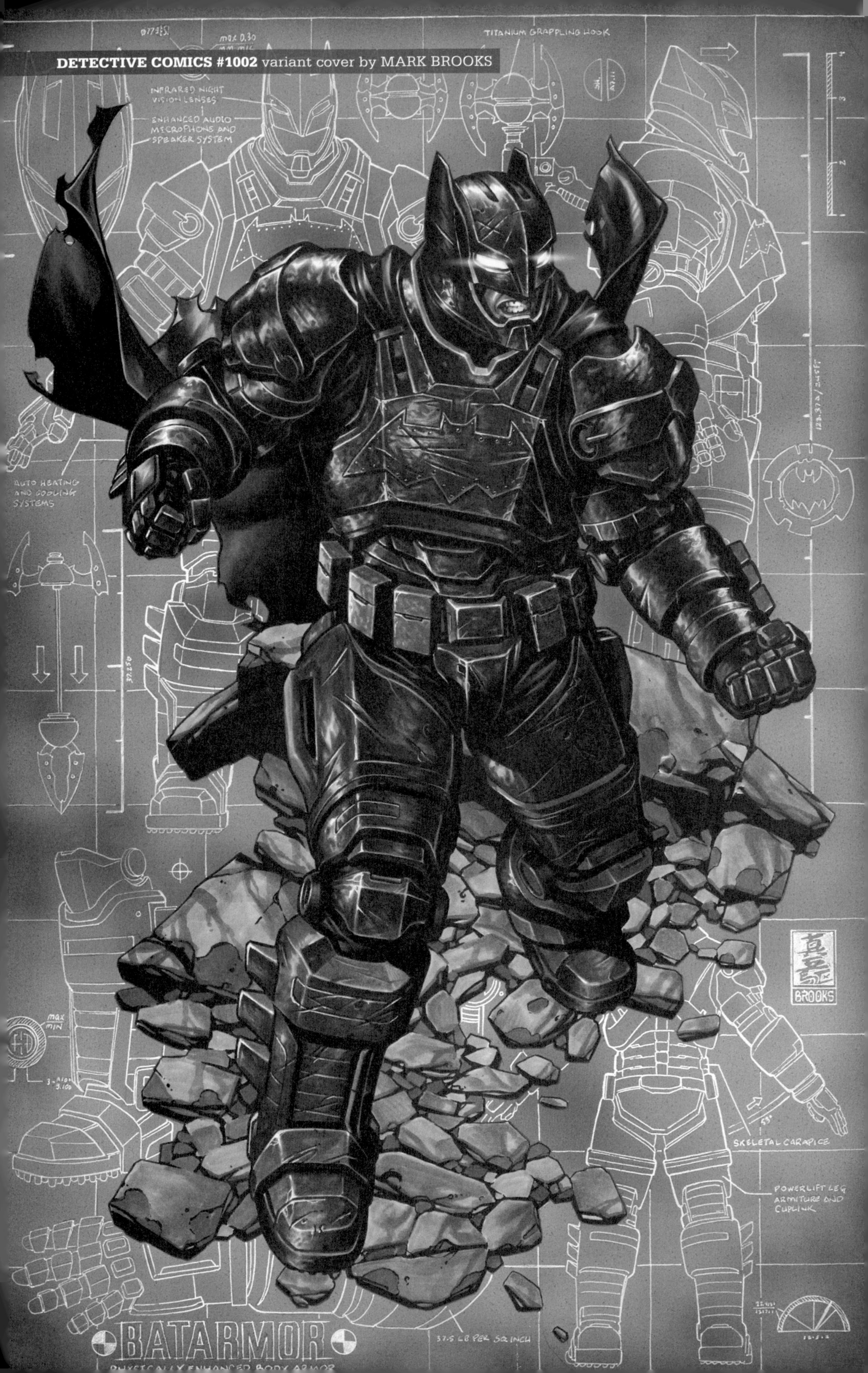
TITANIUM GRAPPLING HOOK
INFRARED NIGHT VISION LENSES
ENHANCED AUDIO MICROPHONE AND SPEAKER SYSTEM
AUTO HEATING AND COOLING SYSTEMS
SKELETAL CARAPICE
POWERLIFT LEG ARMITURE AND CUPLINK
BROOKS
BATARMOR
37.5 LB PER SQ INCH

DETECTIVE COMICS #1002 variant cover by MARK BROOKS

DETECTIVE COMICS #1005 variant cover by STJEPAN SEJIC

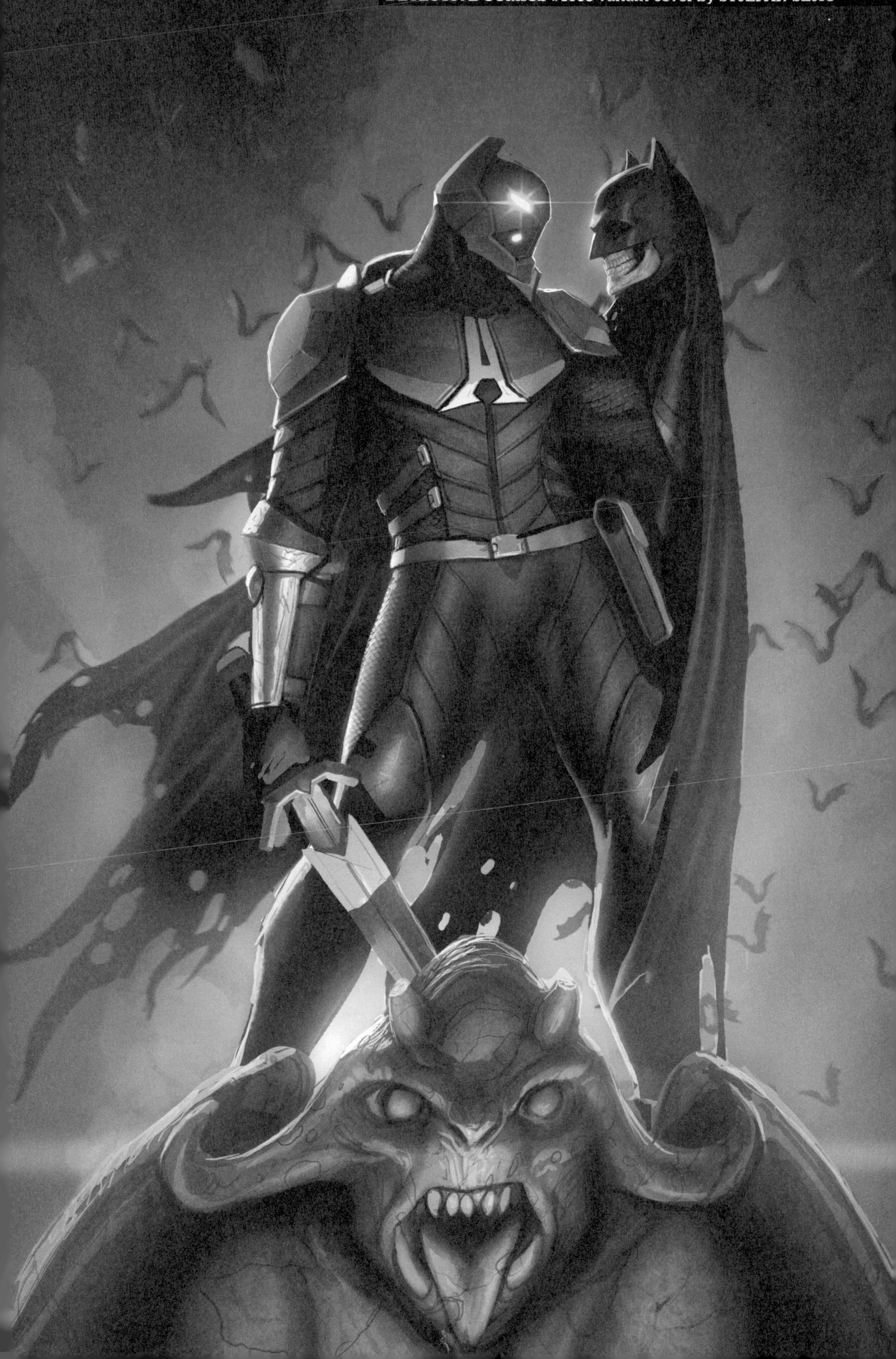

DETECTIVE COMICS #1003 variant cover by MARK BROOKS

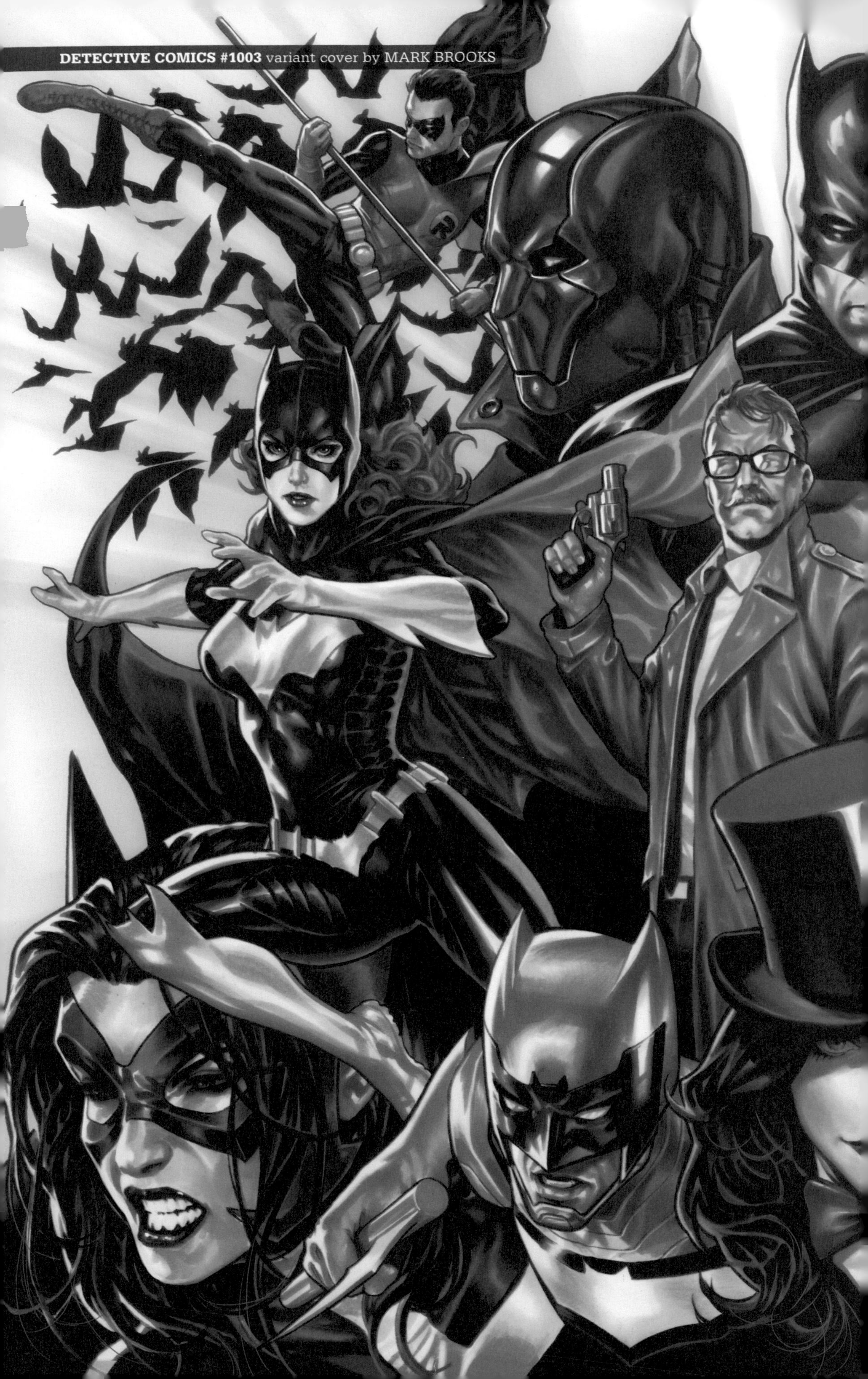

DETECTIVE COMICS #1004 variant cover by MARK BROOKS

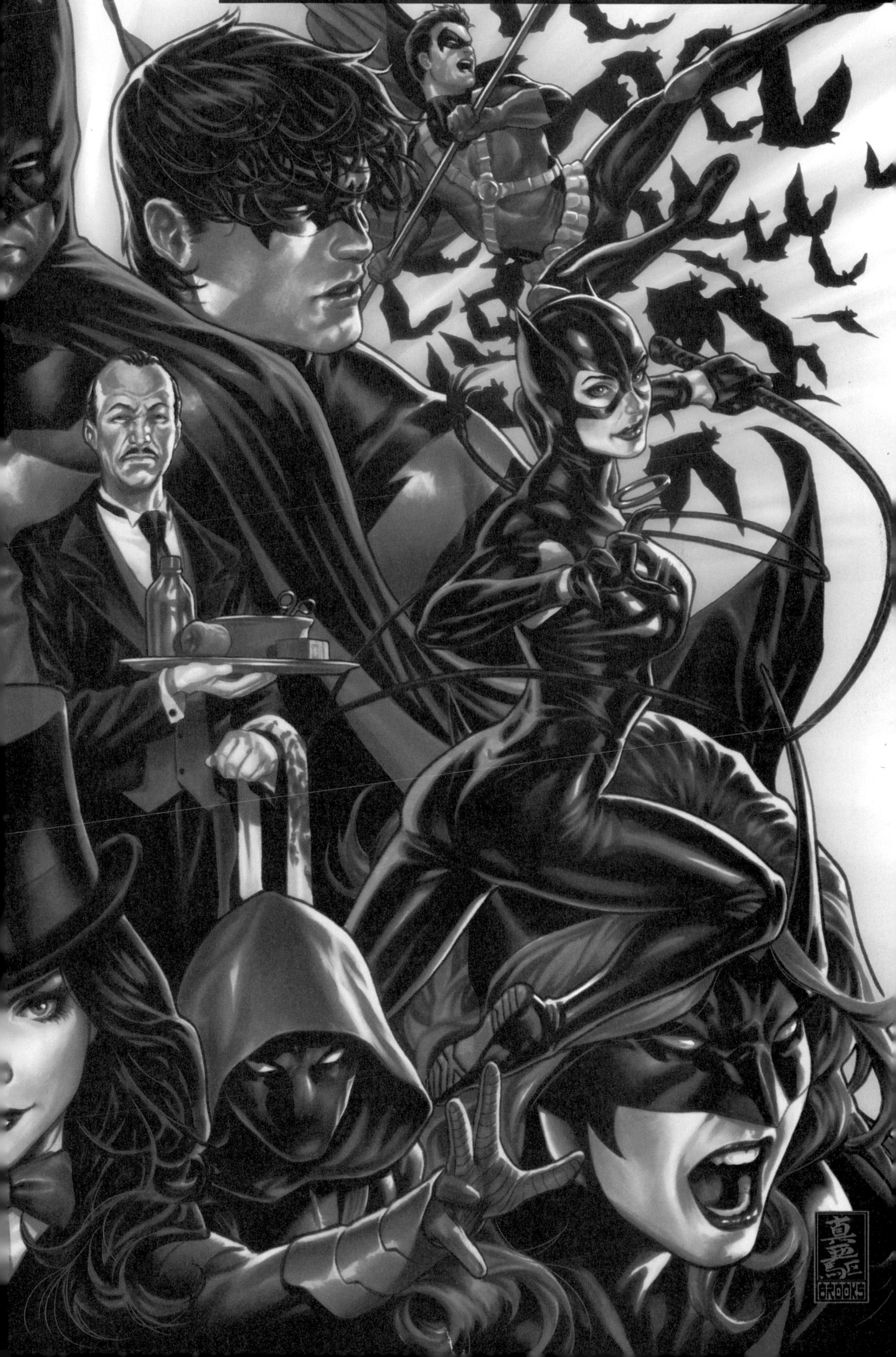
BROOKS

VOL.1 I AM GOTHAM
TOM KING • DAVID FINCH

"Batman is getting a brand-new voice."
– USA TODAY

"A great showcase for the new team as well as offering a taste of the new flavor they'll be bringing to Gotham City." **– IGN**

DC UNIVERSE REBIRTH

BATMAN

VOL. 1: I AM GOTHAM
TOM KING
with DAVID FINCH

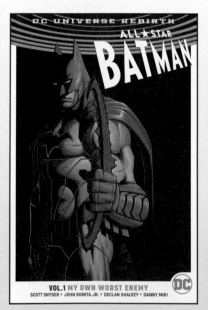

VOL.1 MY OWN WORST ENEMY
SCOTT SNYDER • JOHN ROMITA JR. • DECLAN SHALVEY • DANNY MIKI

**ALL-STAR BATMAN VOL. 1:
MY OWN WORST ENEMY**

VOL.1 BETTER THAN BATMAN
TIM SEELEY • JAVIER FERNÁNDEZ • CHRIS SOTOMAYOR

**NIGHTWING VOL. 1:
BETTER THAN BATMAN**

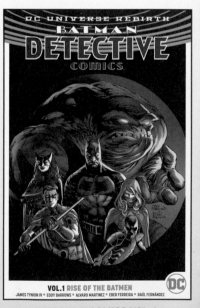

VOL.1 RISE OF THE BATMEN
JAMES TYNION IV • EDDY BARROWS • ALVARO MARTINEZ • EBER FERREIRA • RAÚL FERNÁNDEZ

**DETECTIVE COMICS VOL. 1:
RISE OF THE BATMEN**

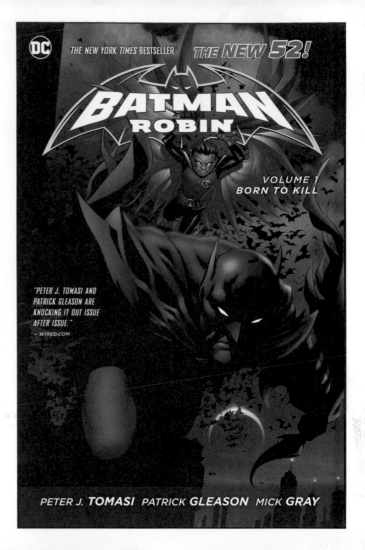
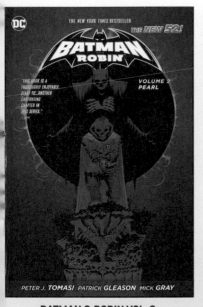

BATMAN: THE DARK KNIGHT: MASTER RACE

FRANK MILLER with BRIAN AZZARELLO, ANDY KUBERT and KLAUS JANSON

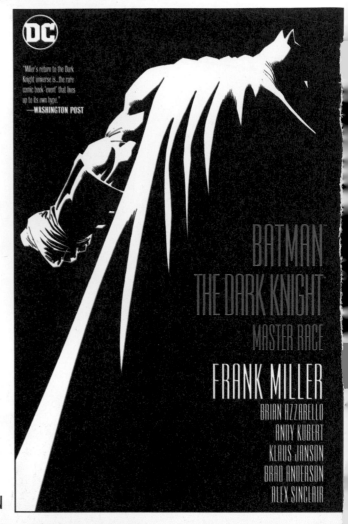

BATMAN: THE DARK KNIGHT RETURNS

BATMAN: THE DARK KNIGHT STRIKES AGAIN

BATMAN: THE DARK KNIGHT: MASTER RACE : THE COVERS